In the Kingdom of Ice

ALSO BY HAMPTON SIDES

Hellhound on His Trail
Blood and Thunder
Americana
Ghost Soldiers
Stomping Grounds

In the Kin

HAMPTON SIDES

The Grand and Terrible Polar Voyage
of the USS *Jeannette*

GDOM OF ICE

 DOUBLEDAY New York London Toronto Sydney Auckland

All rights reserved. Published in the United States by Doubleday,
a division of Random House LLC, New York, and in Canada
by Random House of Canada Limited, Toronto, Penguin Random House companies.

www.doubleday.com

DOUBLEDAY and the portrayal of an anchor with a dolphin are registered
trademarks of Random House LLC.

Book design by Maria Carella
Maps designed by Jeffrey L. Ward
Endpaper illustration: William Bradford, *Icebergs in the Arctic* (1882)
Jacket design by John Fontana
Jacket photograph © Emmanuel Berthier/Hemis/Corbis

Library of Congress Cataloging-in-Publication Data
Sides, Hampton.
   In the kingdom of ice : the grand and terrible polar voyage of the USS *Jeannette* /
Hampton Sides. — First edition.
      pages cm
   Includes bibliographical references.
   ISBN 978-0-385-53537-3 — ISBN 978-0-385-53538-0 (ebook) 1. *Jeannette*
(Steamer)—History. 2. Shipwrecks—Arctic Ocean—History—19th century.
3. Shipwreck survival—Arctic Ocean—History—19th century. 4. Shipwreck
survival—Siberia—History—19th century. 5. Bennett, James Gordon, [date].
6. De Long, George W. (George Washington), [date]. I. Title.
   G530.J37S53 2014
   910.4'52—dc23   2014004367

MANUFACTURED IN THE UNITED STATES OF AMERICA

10 9 8 7 6 5 4 3 2 1

First Edition

To My Brother

LINK SIDES

1957–2013

In the kingdom of ice, far from the world,
      lamentations rise from the ship,
As she battles the slabs and the growling swirls,
      and writhes in their throttling grip.
The crusted floes crack in fits and in sprees,
      and in fury flog her planked hide,
Spent sailors fall upon supplicant knees,
      yearning for kith and hearthside.
The hungry ice clutches more tightly,
      to check the flight of its prey,
The captain's command rings forthrightly,
      "All hands quit while ye may!"
See how the rough men pine and weep,
      as she falters and slips,
High in the masts, the haunted winds whine,
      a dirge to the truest of ships
That bore them so long, yet now in the murk,
      the proud boat twists to her bed,
And when the day hath ended its work,
      Northern Lights paint her grave purple-red.

—"The Sinking of the *Jeannette*," by Joachim Ringelnatz

The privilege isn't given to everyone. . . . You must have suffered first, have suffered greatly, have gained some miserable knowledge. In that way your eyes are opened to it.

—Henry James, 1881

CONTENTS

The Company of the USS *Jeannette*

NAVAL OFFICERS
Lieutenant George De Long, commanding
Lieutenant Charles Chipp, executive officer
Master John Danenhower, navigation officer
George Melville, engineer
Dr. James Ambler, surgeon

CIVILIAN SCIENTISTS
Jerome Collins, meteorologist, correspondent to the *New York Herald*
Raymond Newcomb, naturalist

SPECIAL DUTY
William Dunbar, ice pilot
John Cole, boatswain
Walter Lee, machinist
James Bartlett, first-class fireman
George Boyd, second-class fireman
Alfred Sweetman, carpenter

SEAMEN

William Nindemann	Louis Noros
Herbert Leach	Henry Wilson
Carl Görtz	Peter Johnson
Edward Starr	Henry Warren
Heinrich Kaack	Albert Kuehne
Frank Mansen	Hans Erichsen
Adolph Dressler	Nelse Iverson
Walter Sharvell	George Lauterbach

COOK AND STEWARD

Ah Sam
Charles Tong Sing

INUIT HUNTERS AND DOG DRIVERS

Alexey
Aneguin

In the Kingdom of Ice

PROLOGUE: BAPTISM BY ICE

On a misty morning in late April 1873, the *Tigress,* a steam barkentine out of Conception Bay, Newfoundland, was pushing through the loose floes and bergs off the coast of Labrador, heading for the seasonal seal-hunting grounds. Late in the morning, the *Tigress* encountered something strange: A lone Inuit in a kayak was hailing the ship, waving his arms and screaming at the top of his lungs. The native man was clearly in some kind of trouble. He had ventured much farther out into the perilous open waters of the North Atlantic than any Eskimo ordinarily would. When the *Tigress* pulled closer to him, he yelled, in accented English, "American steamer! American steamer!"

The crew of the *Tigress* leaned over the railings and tried to decipher what the Inuit was talking about. Just then, the fog parted enough to reveal, in the middle distance, a jagged floe piece, on which more than a dozen men and women, plus several children, appeared to be trapped. Seeing the ship, the marooned party erupted in cheers and fired guns into the air.

The *Tigress*'s captain, Isaac Bartlett, ordered rescue boats put in the water. When the stranded people—nineteen in all—were brought aboard, it was immediately apparent that they had suffered a horrific ordeal. Emaciated, filthy, and frostbitten, they had haunted looks in their eyes. Their lips and teeth were greasy from a just-finished breakfast of seal intestine.

"How long have you been on the ice?" Captain Bartlett asked them.

The senior member of the group, an American named George Tyson, stepped forward. "Since the fifteenth of October," he replied.

Bartlett tried to understand what Tyson was saying. October 15 was 196 days earlier. These people, whoever they were, had been stranded on this ice slab for nearly seven months. Their precarious floe had been, Tyson said, a "God-made raft."

Bartlett questioned Tyson further and learned, to his astonishment, that these pitiful castaways had been aboard the *Polaris,* a ship famous around the world. (This was the "American steamer!" the Inuit had been screaming about.) The *Polaris,* an unprepossessing steam tug that had been reinforced for the ice, was the exploring vessel of an American polar expedition, partly funded by Congress and supported by the U.S. Navy, that had left New London, Connecticut, two years earlier and, after a few stops along the way to Greenland, had not been heard from since.

AFTER PENETRATING JUST beyond the 82nd parallel, a nautical latitude record at the time, the *Polaris* had become trapped in the ice high along the west coast of Greenland. Then, in November 1871, the expedition commander, a brooding, eccentric visionary from Cincinnati named Charles Francis Hall, had died under mysterious circumstances after drinking a cup of coffee that, he suspected, had been laced with poison. Following Hall's death, the leaderless expedition had completely unraveled.

On the night of October 15, 1872, a large piece of ice on which Tyson and eighteen other expedition members were temporarily encamped had suddenly broken away from the vicinity of the ship and started drifting into Baffin Bay. The party of castaways, which included several Inuit families and a newborn infant, was never able to rejoin the *Polaris,* and they resigned themselves to their slab of ice. They helplessly floated toward the south, through the winter and spring, sleeping in igloos and living on seals, narwhals, seabirds, and the occasional polar bear. Not having any fuel with which to cook, they ate only raw meat, organs, and blood, when they were lucky enough to have it, for the duration of their drift.

Tyson said they had been "fools of fortune." Huddled miserably on their ever-shrinking slab, they were batted around "like a shuttlecock," he said, by heaving seas, crashing icebergs, and powerful gales. Amazingly, though, no one in the stranded party had died. In all, they had drifted eighteen hundred miles.

Dumbfounded by Tyson's story, Captain Bartlett welcomed the unfortunates to his ship, fed them a warm meal of codfish, potatoes, and coffee, and in due course delivered them to St. John's, Newfoundland, where they were met by a U.S. Navy vessel and taken straight to Washington. A hasty interrogation of Tyson and other survivors revealed, among other things, that the *Polaris,* though damaged, was likely still intact and that the balance of the expedition—fourteen members—might yet be alive, trapped on their leaky ship somewhere high in the Greenland ice. Naval authorities, after cross-examining the survivors, learned that the *Polaris* had suffered a crisis of leadership nearly from the start, that mutiny had been discussed, and that Charles Hall may indeed have been poisoned. (Nearly a century later, forensic experts exhumed his corpse and detected toxic quantities of arsenic in tissue samples.) Tyson, though refusing to name names, cried foul. "Those who have baffled and spoiled this expedition," he roared, "cannot escape their God!"

The American public, stunned by this woeful tale of a national voyage gone spectacularly wrong, clamored for a relief expedition to return to the Arctic to hunt for survivors. And so, with President Ulysses S. Grant's approval, the Navy promptly dispatched a ship, the USS *Juniata,* to Greenland to commence a search for the hobbled *Polaris.*

The *Juniata,* under the command of Daniel L. Braine, was a battle-scabbed sloop of war that had seen much action in the Atlantic blockade during the Civil War. Newspapers across America celebrated her departure from New York on June 23. The *Juniata*'s mission to Greenland had all the elements: Here was a thrilling rescue story of national import—and also a detective story, with a whiff of intrigue and possible murder. A correspondent from the *New York Herald* would be joining the *Juniata* at St. John's to report on the search. In large part because of the *Herald*'s presence, the hunt for the *Polaris* would become the sensation of the late summer of 1873.

THE SECOND-IN-COMMAND ABOARD the *Juniata* was a young lieutenant from New York City named George De Long. Twenty-eight years old, his keen blue-gray eyes framed by pince-nez glasses,

De Long was a man in a hurry to do great things. He was large and broad-shouldered and weighed 195 pounds. A graduate of the U.S. Naval Academy, ginger-haired and fair-skinned, he had a shaggy mustache that drooped prodigiously over the corner creases of his mouth. Whenever he had a moment to sit, he could usually be found smoking a meerschaum pipe, his head buried in a book. The warmth of his smile and the softness of his fleshy face were offset by a certain truculence in his jawline, a feature observers often remarked upon. De Long was a determined, straight-ahead sort of man, efficient and thorough, and he burned with ambition. One of his expressions, a motto of sorts, was "Do it now."

De Long had sailed over much of the world—Europe, the Caribbean, South America, and all along the Eastern Seaboard—but he had never been to the Arctic before, and he was not especially looking forward to the journey. De Long was far more accustomed to the tropics. He had never paid attention to the great quest for the North Pole, which had so ferociously preoccupied explorers like Hall and thrilled the public. To De Long, the *Juniata*'s cruise to Greenland was just another assignment.

He did not seem to think much of St. John's, where the *Juniata* stopped to take on stores and where shipbuilders sheathed her bow in iron for the coming encounters with the ice. When the *Juniata* reached the half-frozen hamlet of Sukkertoppen, on Greenland's southwestern coast, De Long wrote to his wife, "I never in my life saw such a dreary land of desolation and I hope I may never find myself cast away in such a perfectly God-forsaken place . . . The 'town,' such as it is, consists of two houses and about a dozen huts made of mud and wood. I went into one and have been scratching ever since."

De Long was positively smitten with his wife, Emma, a young French-American woman from Le Havre. He hated being so far away from her. He and Emma had been married for more than two years but had scarcely seen each other, for De Long's Navy assignments had kept him almost constantly at sea. Sylvie, their baby girl, was nearly a stranger to him. The De Longs had a little apartment on Twenty-second Street in Manhattan, yet he was never there. Emma said her husband was a man "destined always to be separated from the ones he loved." There was not much he could do about his prolonged absences—this was the life of a career naval officer.

At times, though, De Long dreamed of taking a leave and living another kind of existence with Emma and Sylvie, somewhere in the American West, or in the countryside in the south of France. From Greenland, he wrote to Emma about his fantasy. "I cannot help thinking how much happier we should be if we were together," he said. "When we are apart I devise so many schemes ... How nice it would be to go to some quiet place in Europe and pass a year by ourselves, where the Navy Department would not bother me with its orders, or any troubles come to make us uneasy. I think, darling, when I finish this cruise I might be able to get a year's absence and we might spend it together where it would not be expensive and have a little home of our own. Don't you think we could do that?"

De Long's disdain for the polar landscape soon wore off. As the *Juniata* crossed the Arctic Circle and pressed ever farther up the ragged west coast of the world's largest island, something began to take hold of him. He became more and more intrigued by the Arctic, by its lonely grandeur, by its mirages and strange tricks of light, its mock moons and blood-red halos, its thick, misty atmospheres, which altered and magnified sounds, leaving the impression that one was living under a dome. He felt as though he were breathing rarefied air. He became intrigued by the phenomenon of the "ice blink," the spectral glow in the low sky that indicated the presence of a large frozen pack ahead. The scenery grew more impressive: ice-gouged fjords, towering bergs calved fresh from glaciers, the crisp sound of cold surf lapping against the pack, ringed seals peeking through gaps in the ice, bowhead whales spouting in the deep gray channel. This was the purest wilderness De Long had ever seen, and he began to fall in love with it.

BY LATE JULY, when the *Juniata* arrived at Disko Island, a windswept place of bubbling hot springs and Viking legends far up the coast of Greenland, De Long's baptism by ice was nearly complete. Dressed head to toe in furs and wearing sealskin boots, he had gotten into the swing of things. "We have taken on board twelve dogs for sleds," he wrote, "and we are now really worth looking at. The ship is black with dirt and coal dust, dogs packed away among the coal, sheep tied up forward and beef hanging around right and left with fish here and there. We are really in a good state to go anywhere."

As he continued northward, De Long found himself absorbed by the question of what had happened to Charles Francis Hall and his expedition. Where had it gone wrong? What decisions had led to its demise? Where was the *Polaris* now, and were there any survivors? As a Navy officer, he was intrigued by matters of hierarchy, discipline, and motivation—how an operation was organized, and how that organization might fall apart. De Long felt himself being pulled deeper into a mystery infinitely more interesting than the dreary duties of his ordinary life at sea.

On July 31, the *Juniata* arrived at the tiny ice-clogged village of Upernavik, four hundred miles above the Arctic Circle, and here the plot of this polar detective story began to thicken. De Long and Captain Braine went ashore to meet with a Danish official named Krarup Smith, the inspector royal of North Greenland. Inspector Smith had some interesting things to say about Charles Hall, who had stopped here with his entire expedition two years earlier, before disappearing in the High Arctic. Smith did not know where the *Polaris* was now, or whether there were any survivors, but he did offer one intriguing detail: Hall, he said, had had a presentiment of his own death.

When he arrived in Upernavik, Hall hinted that there was dissension in the ranks, that some of the men were plotting to remove him from command. He sensed that he would never make it home, that he would die in the Arctic. Hall felt so sure of this that, for safekeeping, he left a bundle of valuable papers and other artifacts with Inspector Smith.

The reporter for the *New York Herald*, Martin Maher, noted that Smith "narrated with considerable minuteness the details of a quarrel" in which certain members of the expedition "endeavored to prejudice the crew of the ship against" Hall.

To hear Smith tell it now, the Hall expedition had been doomed before it even ventured into the ice. "The officers and crew of the *Polaris* were utterly demoralized," Maher reported, and "Captain Hall evidently had some kind of misgiving or premonition of death."

UPERNAVIK WAS AS far north as Captain Braine felt comfortable taking the *Juniata*. Despite her iron sheathing, she was not really designed or equipped to handle significant quantities of ice. The ship did, however, have a smaller boat, dubbed the *Little Juniata,* that was more agile, capable of navigating through the confusion of bergs and floes. Rigged as a sloop, the twenty-eight-foot launch carried a small steam engine, which powered a three-bladed screw propeller. Braine wanted a half dozen of his men to take the *Little Juniata* and continue the search for another four hundred miles along the fjord-riddled coast, up to a place called Cape York.

This secondary probe, which Braine estimated would take several weeks, was a dubious undertaking at best. The *Little Juniata* seemed a frightfully vulnerable craft, not much more than an open boat. Ice fields like these had crushed entire whaling fleets. Braine knew he could not order anyone to undertake this risky assignment; he had to rely on volunteers.

De Long was the first to raise his hand, and it was soon decided that he would captain the little vessel. De Long's second-in-command would be a quiet, reliable fellow Naval Academy graduate from upstate New York named Charles Winans Chipp. Seven others cast their lot with De Long, including an Eskimo interpreter, an ice pilot, and Martin Maher from the *Herald*. Braine bid them farewell, noting in his written instructions to De Long, "I shall await with great interest your return to this ship from the hazardous duty for which you have volunteered."

They nosed away from the *Juniata* on August 2, carrying provisions for sixty days and towing a dinghy loaded with twelve hundred pounds of coal. The little steam engine clanked away as De Long threaded through a series of fog-shrouded islands and thousands of small icebergs called growlers. They stopped at a few remote Inuit settlements—Kingitok, Tessi-Ussak—and then headed into a void, dodging massive bergs that dwarfed the boat.

Maher said he had "never witnessed a more glorious scene . . . Looking abroad on the immense fields of ice, glittering in the rays of the sun, and the thousands of huge, craggy icebergs as they sulkily floated out into Baffin's Bay, one became awed by the dreadful majesty of the elements, and wondered how it would be possible to avoid being crushed to atoms."

Eventually the *Little Juniata* was brought to a standstill in fields of unbroken pack, and De Long was forced repeatedly to ram the ice in order to break free, splintering the greenheart planks that reinforced the hull. They were enveloped in a dense freezing fog, and all the rigging became rimed in ice. "Absolutely hemmed in, we were now in a most perilous position, and sudden destruction threatened us," wrote Maher. "We forced a passage westward at length, and after a terrific struggle of twelve hours, found open water again."

De Long could not have been happier. He and Lieutenant Chipp were enjoying the cruise—and rising to its challenges. "Our boat is a beauty, doing everything but talking," he wrote in a letter later mailed to Emma. "Now do not be alarmed if you do not hear from me for some time. If by any accident we should be frozen up all winter you will not hear from me again till spring. But be of good cheer. I expect to be back to the ship in fifteen days."

Forty miles south of Cape York, De Long anchored to a large berg in order to hack away chunks of ice for the *Little Juniata*'s freshwater stores. A large fracture suddenly developed in an overhanging arm of the berg. Sensing danger, De Long pulled away only moments before a huge block of ice fell, smashing into the sea. This, in turn, caused the entire berg to wobble, then to upend. If De Long had been only a few feet closer, the *Little Juniata* would have been destroyed.

So far, De Long had not seen any sign of the *Polaris,* or any evidence of survivors; it was perhaps quixotic to think they would, given the scale of this fogbound wilderness. But as the commander inched into higher latitudes, approaching the 75th parallel, he found himself pulled into an ever-larger mystery. The complexity of the High Arctic spread before him like a riddle. He had never felt so alive, so engaged in the moment. He realized that he was becoming what the Arctic scientists liked to call a "pagophile"—a creature that is happiest in the ice.

ON AUGUST 8, the *Little Juniata* became enveloped in thick fog. The seas grew restive, and within a few hours she was in a full-on gale, the tiny vessel pitching in ice-chunked swells. "At every one of the fearful plunges," De Long later wrote, "solid seas came aboard and showers of spray were thrown over, deluging everything in the boat. Our bailing made little impression."

The storm had turned the existing ice fields into a dangerous roil, while also breaking off new slabs from surrounding icebergs and hurling them into the heaving sea. The *Little Juniata* was in constant peril of being ground to pieces. "Looking back at it now makes me tremble," De Long wrote, "and I can only say that it was a miracle of Divine Providence that we were saved." Said Martin Maher in the *Herald*: "The waves, lashed to a fury, burst against these mountains of ice, breaking off ponderous-looking, solid masses, which fell into the sea with a deafening sound. The destruction of the boat and all on board now seemed imminent. We were bound up in this terrible place, the appalling precipices of ice casting off their missiles of death."

The gale raged for thirty-six hours. Somehow the *Little Juniata* held together, and when the storm abated, De Long was determined to resume his dash for Cape York despite the ominous fields of ice spread before him. "I was not disposed to quit without a fight," he wrote. But he was running dangerously low on coal, and his men were miserable—freezing, hungry, soaked to the bone. He couldn't get the boiler lit, as the kindling and tinder were thoroughly saturated. One of his men, after holding a friction match against his body for several hours, finally succeeded in lighting a candle, and soon the spluttery steam engine was coaxed back to life.

De Long smashed through the ice for a day, but he could see that continuing the journey would be beyond foolhardy. He had to consider "how far the lives of our little party were to be jeopardized," he wrote, noting that he felt a responsibility that "I do not desire to have again." De Long conferred with Lieutenant Chipp, whom he had come to admire for his calm sense of judgment. On August 10, Lieutenant George De Long did something he rarely ever did: He gave up. "Prosecuting the search for the *Polaris* people any longer was out of the question," he said. They had ventured more than four hundred miles and had crossed the 75th parallel. But now, only eight miles from Cape York, the *Little Juniata* was turning around.

(Unbeknownst to De Long, all the remaining survivors of the *Polaris*—fourteen in total—had been picked up in June by a Scottish whaling vessel. They would eventually be taken to Dundee, Scotland, and would not return home to the United States until the fall.)

De Long steered the *Little Juniata* through intermittent ice fields toward the south. Running out of coal to fuel the steam engine, he was forced to improvise, burning slabs of pork in the furnace.

After a round-trip journey of more than eight hundred miles, the *Little Juniata* reunited with her mother ship in mid-August. Captain Braine had all but given up on the little steam launch, but now De Long was welcomed aboard the *Juniata* as a lost hero. "The ship was wild with excitement," De Long wrote, "the men manning the rigging and cheering us. When I stepped over the side, so buried in furs as to be almost invisible, they made as much fuss over me as if I had risen from the dead, and when the Captain shook hands with me he was trembling from head to foot."

———

THE *JUNIATA* RETURNED to St. John's, then made its way for New York, where it arrived with much fanfare in mid-September. At the docks, De Long dodged reporters and slipped quietly away to his wife and baby daughter.

When he reunited with Emma, however, she instantly noticed a change. George had turned twenty-nine while in Greenland, but that was not it. Something was fundamentally different about him, something new in his eyes, in his demeanor. It was as though he had contracted a fever. He was already talking about returning to the Arctic. He became absorbed in Arctic literature and Arctic maps. He submitted his name for the next Navy expedition that might head for the High North.

"The adventure had affected him deeply and would not let him rest," Emma wrote. She began to suspect that their sabbatical in the French countryside, the one he had dreamed about while in Greenland, would never come to pass. "The polar virus was in George's blood to stay."

The essential question, the one that had animated Charles Hall and other explorers before him, had begun to pull at De Long: How would man reach the North Pole? And once there, what would it be like? Were there open sea routes? Unknown species of fish and animals? Monsters that lived on the ice? Lost civilizations, even? Were there whirlpools, as many people believed, that led to the bowels of the earth? Were woolly mammoths and other prehistoric creatures still wandering the Arctic solitudes? What other natural wonders might be found along the way? Or was the pole something else altogether—a verdant land warmed by vast ocean currents?

The more he pondered the problem of the North Pole, said Emma, "the greater became his desire to give that answer which alone would satisfy the world. The Arctic had cast its spell over him and from the moment of his return to New York its great mystery fascinated him."

PART ONE

———◆◆◆———

A Great Blank Space

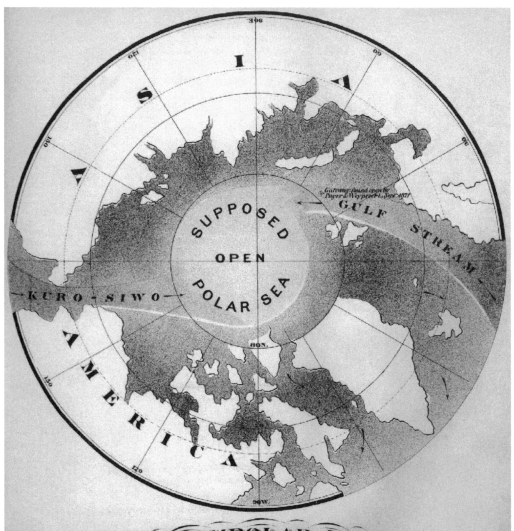

ASIA

AMERICA

Gateway found open by Payer & Weyprecht, Sept 1871

SUPPOSED OPEN POLAR SEA

GULF STREAM

KURO-SIWO

80N.

90W.

CIRCUMPOLAR MAP

EXHIBITING THE

INTER-OCEANIC CIRCULATION, as suggested in his report on the KURO-SIWO in 1855-6,

(See U.S. Japan Expedition Vol. II. Pag. 369 & 370)

and to illustrate Addresses upon the

THERMOMETRIC GATEWAYS to the POLE" in 1868, and the "THERMAL PATHS to the POLE" in 1872

BY

SILAS BENT.

EXPLANATIONS:

The Red Coloring indicates Warm Water.
" Blue " " Ice & cold Water.
" Arrows show the direction of Currents.

I · A Shocking Sabbath Carnival of Death

Close to midnight on the evening of Sunday, November 8, 1874, as the early edition of the next day's *New York Herald* was being born, the gaslit building at the corner of Broadway and Ann Street bustled. The telegraph machines hammered away, the press platens churned, the setting room clinked with the frenetic rearranging of movable metal type, the copy editors clamored for last-minute changes—and outside, in the cool autumn air, the crews of deliverymen pulled up to the freight docks with their dray horses and wagons, waiting to load the hemp-tied bundles and carry them to every precinct of the slumbering city.

Following routine, the night editor had the draft edition of the paper brought up to the publisher for his approval. This was no mean feat: The proprietor of the *New York Herald* could be a tyrannical micromanager, and he wielded his blue pencil like a bowie knife, often scribbling barely legible comments that trailed along the margins and then off the page. After his usual wine-drenched dinner at Delmonico's, he would return to his office to drink pots of coffee and torment his staff until the paper was finally put to bed. The editors dreaded his tirades and expected him to demand, well into the wee hours, that they rip up the entire layout and start over again.

JAMES GORDON BENNETT JR. was a tall, thin, regal man of thirty-two years with a trim mustache and fine tapering hands. His blue-gray eyes seemed cold and imperious, yet they also carried glints of mischief. He wore impeccable French suits and dress shoes of supple Italian leather. To facilitate his long, if erratic, work hours, he kept a bed in his penthouse office, where he liked to snatch an early-morning nap.

By most reckonings, Bennett was the third-richest man in New York City, with an assured annual income just behind those of William B. Astor and Cornelius Vanderbilt. Bennett was not only the publisher but also the editor in chief and sole owner of the *Herald,* probably the largest and most influential newspaper in the world. He had inherited the paper from his father, James Gordon Bennett Sr. The *Herald* had a reputation for being as entertaining as it was informative, its pages suffused with its owner's sly sense of humor. But its pages were also packed with news; Bennett outspent all other papers to get the latest reports via telegraph and the transatlantic cable. For the newspaper's longer feature stories, Bennett did whatever was necessary to acquire the talents of the biggest names in American letters—writers like Mark Twain, Stephen Crane, and Walt Whitman.

Bennett was also one of New York's more flamboyant bachelors, known for affairs with burlesque stars and drunken sprees in Newport. He was a member of the Union Club and an avid sportsman. Eight years earlier, he had won the first transatlantic yacht race. He would play an instrumental role in bringing the sport of polo to the United States, as well as competitive bicycling and competitive ballooning. In 1871, at the age of twenty-nine, Bennett had become the youngest commodore in the history of the New York Yacht Club—a post he still held.

The Commodore, as everyone called Bennett, was known for racing fleet horses as well as sleek boats. Late at night, sometimes fueled with brandy, he would take out his four-in-hand carriage and careen wild-eyed down the moonlit turnpikes around Manhattan. Alert bystanders tended to be both puzzled and shocked by these nocturnal escapades, for Bennett nearly always raced in the nude.

JAMES GORDON BENNETT'S most original contribution to modern journalism could be found in his notion that a newspaper should not merely report stories; it should *create* them. Editors should not only cover the news, he felt; they should orchestrate large-scale public dramas that stir emotions and get people talking. As one historian of American journalism later put it, Bennett had the "ability to seize upon dormant situations and bring them to life." It was Bennett who, in 1870, had sent Henry Stanley to find the missionary-explorer David Livingstone in remote Africa. Never mind that Livingstone had not exactly *needed* finding. The dispatches Stanley had sent back to the *Herald* in 1872 had caused an international sensation—one that Bennett was forever seeking to re-create.

Critics scoffed that these exclusives were merely "stunts," and perhaps they were. But Bennett had a conviction that a first-rate reporter, if turned loose on the world to pursue some human mystery or solve some geographical puzzle, would invariably come back with interesting stories that would sell papers and extend knowledge at the same time. Bennett was willing to spend profligately to get these kinds of articles into his paper on a routine basis. His paper was many things, but it was rarely dull.

Now, on this early November morning, the *Herald's* night editor must have been cringing as he had the still-warm draft of the first edition sent to his mercurial boss. The *Herald* contained a lead story that, if executed properly, was guaranteed to cause the kind of stir Gordon Bennett delighted in. It was one of the most incredible and tragic news exclusives that had ever run in the *Herald's* pages. The story was headlined "A Shocking Sabbath Carnival of Death."

The Commodore scanned the paper and began to take in the horrifying details: Late that Sunday afternoon, right around closing time at the zoo in the middle of Central Park, a rhinoceros had managed to escape from its cage. It had then rampaged through the grounds, killing one of its keepers—goring him almost beyond recognition. Other zookeepers, who had been in the midst of feeding the animals, had rushed to the scene, and somehow in the confusion, a succession of carnivorous beasts—including a polar bear, a panther, a Numidian lion, several hyenas, and a Bengal tiger—had slipped from their pens. What happened next made for difficult reading. The animals, some of which had first attacked each other, had then turned on nearby pedestrians who happened to be strolling through Central Park. People had been trampled, mauled, dismembered—and worse.

The *Herald* reporters had diligently captured every detail: How the panther was seen crouching over a man's body, "gnawing horribly at his head." How the African lioness, after "saturating herself in the blood" of several victims, had been shot by a party of Swedish immigrants. How the rhino had killed a seamstress named Annie Thomas and had then run north, only to stumble to its death in the bowels of a deep sewer excavation. How the polar bear had maimed and killed two men before tramping off toward Central Park's upper reservoir. How, at Bellevue Hospital, the doctors were "kept busy dressing the fearful wounds" and found it "necessary to perform a number of amputations . . . One young girl is said to have died under the knife."

At press time, many of the escaped animals were still at large, prompting Mayor William Havemeyer to issue a proclamation that called for a rigid curfew until "the peril" had subsided. "The hospitals are full of the wounded," the *Herald* reported. "The park, from end to end, is marked with injury, and in its artificial forests the wild beasts lurk, to pounce at any moment on the unwary pedestrians."

Bennett did not break out his blue pencil. For once, he had no changes to suggest. He is said to have leaned back among his pillows and "groaned" at this remarkable story.

THE *HERALD* REPORT was written in an even tone. Its authors had peppered it with intimate details and filled the roster of victims with the names of real, in some cases quite prominent, New Yorkers. But the story was entirely a hoax. With Bennett's enthusiastic encouragement, the editors had concocted the tale to demonstrate that the city had no evacuation plan in the event of a large-scale emergency—and also to point out that many of the cages at the Central Park Zoo were flimsy and in bad need of repair. The outmoded Central Park menagerie, the editors later noted, was a far cry from the state-of-the-art zoo at the Jardin des Plantes in Paris. It was time for New York City to rise to the level of a world-class city, and for the nation, whose one hundredth birthday was approaching in just over a year and a half, to have at least one world-class park to display the planet's wildest creatures.

Lest anyone say that the *Herald* had deceived its readers, the editors had covered their bases. Anyone who'd read "A Shocking Sabbath Carnival of Death" to its end (buried discreetly in the back pages) would have found the following disclaimer: "Of course, the entire story given above is a pure fabrication. Not one word of it is true." Still, the paper contended, the city fathers had devoted no thought to what might happen in an authentic emergency. "How is New York prepared to meet such a catastrophe?" the *Herald* asked. "From causes quite as insignificant the greatest calamities of history have sprung."

Bennett knew from experience that very few New Yorkers would bother to read the article all the way to its conclusion, and he was right. That morning, as the usual clouds of anthracite coal fumes began to rise over the stirring city, people turned to their morning papers—and were plunged in chaos and confusion. Alarmed citizens made for the city's piers in hopes of escaping by small boat or ferry. Many thousands of people, heeding the mayor's "proclamation," stayed inside all day, awaiting word that the crisis had passed. Still others loaded their rifles and marched into the park to hunt for rogue animals.

It should have been immediately apparent to even the most naïve reader that the piece was a spoof. But this was a more credulous era, a time before radio and telephones and rapid transit, when city dwellers got their information mainly from the papers and often found it hard to tease rumor from truth.

Later editions took the story even further. Now the *Herald* reported that the governor of New York himself, a Civil War hero named John Adams Dix, had marched into the streets and shot the Bengal tiger as a personal trophy. A much-expanded list detailed other animals that had escaped from the zoo, including a tapir, an anaconda, a wallaby, a gazelle, two capuchin monkeys, a white-haired porcupine, and four Syrian sheep. A grizzly bear had entered the St. Thomas Church on Fifth Avenue, and there, in the center aisle, it "sprang upon the shoulders of an aged lady, and buried his fangs in her neck."

The editors of rival newspapers were thoroughly perplexed. It was not the first time the *Herald* had scooped them, but why had their reporters failed to glean even an inkling of this obviously momentous event? The city editor of the *New York Times* stormed over to police headquarters on Mulberry Street to scold the department for feeding the story to the *Herald* while ignoring his esteemed paper. Even some staffers of the *Herald* fell for the prank: One of Bennett's most celebrated war correspondents, who apparently had not gotten the memo, showed up at the office that morning armed with two big revolvers, ready to prowl the streets.

Predictably, Bennett's rivals excoriated the *Herald* for its irresponsible conduct—and for spreading widespread panic that could have resulted in loss of life. A *Times* editorial observed, "No such carefully prepared story could appear without the consent of the proprietor or editor—supposing that this strange newspaper *has* an editor, which seems rather a violent stretch of the imagination."

Such expressions of righteous indignation fell on deaf ears. The Wild Animal Hoax, as it came to be affectionately known, only brought more readers to the *Herald*. It seemed to solidify the notion that Bennett had his finger on the pulse of his city—and that his daily journal had a sense of fun. "The incident helped rather than hurt the paper," one historian of New York journalism later noted. "It had given the town something to talk about and jarred it as it had never been jarred before. The public seemed to like the joke."

Bennett was enormously pleased with the whole affair—it still ranks as one of the great newspaper hoaxes of all time. The story even managed to accomplish its ostensible goal: The zoo's cages were, in fact, repaired.

True, it was not nearly as sensational a success as Stanley's finding Livingstone. Bennett would have to keep looking for an encore to that lucrative saga. His reporters were out in the field, in every corner of the globe, hunting down the next blockbuster story. He had correspondents in Australia, in Africa, in China. They were covering the debauchery of faded European royals, the high jinks of Wall Street, and the gunslinging of the Wild West. They were wandering throughout the Reconstruction South, too, reporting on all its colorful frauds.

The direction that most interested Gordon Bennett, though, was north. He sensed that the greatest mysteries lay in that direction, under the midnight sun. The fur-cloaked men who ventured into the Arctic had become national idols—the aviators, the astronauts, the knights-errant of their day. People couldn't get enough of them. They were a special breed of scientist-adventurer, Bennett felt, their quest informed by a kind of dark romance and a desperate chivalry. Bennett, who took reckless risks in his own sporting life, expected his reporters to do the same while pursuing their assignments. In this heroic age of exploration, the Commodore was adamant that his best correspondents should head for the ice zones to follow the gallant and obsessive characters who now were aiming for the ultimate grail.

2 · Ne Plus Ultra

The North Pole. The top of the world. The acme, the apogee, the apex. It was a magnetic region but also a magnetic idea. It loomed as a public fixation and a planetary enigma—as alluring and unknown as the surface of Venus or Mars. The North Pole was both a physical place and a geographer's abstraction, a pinpointable location where curved lines met on the map. It was a spot on the globe where, if you could stand there, any direction you headed in would be, by definition, *south*. It was a place of perpetual darkness for one half of the year and perpetual sunlight for the other. There, in a sense, chronology stood still, for at the pole all the time zones of the world converged.

These things the experts understood, or at least believed they understood. But nearly everything else about the pole—whether it was ice or land or sea, whether it was warm or cold, whether it was humid or desert, whether it was desolate or inhabited, whether there were mountains or labyrinthine tunnels that fed into the earth, whether the laws of gravity or geomagnetism even obtained there—remained a terrific puzzle.

This puzzle had driven Charles Hall nearly insane with wonder. Before venturing on the *Polaris* expedition, he had written, "There is a great, sad blot upon the present age & this is the blank on our maps & artificial globes from about the parallel 80° North up to the North Pole. I, for one, hang my head in shame when I think how many thousands of years ago it was that God gave to man this beautiful world—*the whole of it*—to subdue, & yet that part of it that must be most interesting and glorious remains as unknown to us as though it had never been created."

The "polar problem," as it was sometimes called in the press, had taken on a quality of nagging, gnawing obsession. People *had* to know what was Up There—not only scientists and explorers but the general public. The North Pole was, said the London *Athenaeum,* the "unattainable object of our dreams." An eminent German geographer named Ernst Behm compared humanity's ignorance of what lay at the poles to the insatiable curiosity felt by a home owner who doesn't know what his own attic looks like. "As a family will, of course, know all the rooms of its own house," Behm wrote, "so man, from the very beginning, has been inspired with a desire to become acquainted with all the lands, oceans, and zones of the planet assigned to him for a dwelling-place."

A *New York Times* editorial at the time echoed Behm's sentiment: "Man will not be content with a mystery unexplored, will not rest with a perpetual interrogation point at the end of the earth's axis, whose query he cannot answer."

By the 1870s, no greater mystery existed on the face of the earth. (Antarctica was, of course, equally mysterious, but the South Pole was considered a less obtainable goal for the leading exploring nations, all of which happened to be located in the Northern Hemisphere.) It was hard to comprehend how profoundly the world needed to scratch the Arctic itch. Speculation about what lay at the North Pole permeated popular culture and world literature, from the books of Jules Verne to Mary Shelley's *Frankenstein* (whose scientist-protagonist pursues his monster across the floes all the way to the North Pole). Many practical considerations were floated as justifications for pursuing the polar grail—landmasses that might be claimed, minerals seized, shipping routes discovered, colonies founded, new species described. There was a riddle of geography to solve, and personal glory to be won. But the quest was ultimately about something even more elemental and atavistic: to reach the farthest place, the ne plus ultra, where no human had been before.

"Within the charmed circle of the Arctic," argued the *Atlantic Monthly,* "lay the goal of geographical ambition . . . the final solution of the polar problem. And it may be said that long years of fruitless effort and frightful suffering seem only to have whetted the appetite for discovery; and the more we know of our planet the more ardent

becomes the desire of geographers to view the mysterious extremity."
An 1871 article in the journal *Nature* characterized the search for
the pole as *the* paramount scientific and geographical riddle of the
age: "The immense tract of hitherto unvisited land or sea which sur-
rounds the northern end of the axis of our earth, is the largest, as it is
the most important field of discovery that remains for this or a future
generation to work out."

To be sure, nationalism also drove the obsession. Americans,
slowly emerging from the devastation of the Civil War, yearned to
prove themselves on the international stage. Polar exploration, some
suggested, could help unify the divided country—it was an endeavor
that everyone, North and South, could agree on. An ambitious expedition of discovery provided a way for the still-mending republic to
flex her power in a quasi-military, but ultimately peaceful, way.

It was a British naval officer, William Parry, who in 1827 led what
is widely regarded as the first serious expedition specifically aiming to
reach the North Pole. Ever since then, the British Admiralty had led
most of the cutting-edge polar explorations. This was largely due to
the nearly evangelical zeal of Second Secretary of the Admiralty John
Barrow for all things Arctic, and to the fact that after the defeat of
Napoleon, the Royal Navy had had few major wars to fight throughout much of the 1800s. The great ships of the world's mightiest navy
were rotting away largely unused, and many officers had been rel-
egated to half wages with little to do, yet with ambitions still burning
in their breasts. The British primarily focused their efforts on finding
a navigable sea route across the top of Canada—and on searching for
previous English expeditions that had disappeared while looking for
this elusive Northwest Passage.

But now, in the 1870s, attention was shifting away from finding the Northwest Passage and more toward the goal of reaching the
North Pole itself, as an object of pure, abstract exploration. Not only
England but France, Russia, Sweden, Germany, Italy, and the Austro-
Hungarian Empire had mounted, or were now proposing, expeditions to reach the pole first. The United States considered herself a
viable contender in this grand chase, and many Americans fervently
wished to see the Stars and Stripes planted at the top of the world.

America's desire to push north could be considered, in some ways,
an extension of Manifest Destiny, the country's pioneering surge
toward the west. With the completion of the transcontinental railroad in 1869, the western frontier was closing—or at least its conquest

was reaching a different phase, one that consisted less of adventurous exploration and more of the messy backfill work of occupation and settlement. But in 1867, the United States had purchased Alaska from the czar for the paltry sum of $7.2 million, and this enormous new frontier lay untapped and largely unknown. Thus the national movement west, having reached California, had taken a right turn and become a movement north.

In 1873, the country was still digesting this acquisition, was still trying to learn about the immensity of what America owned in her Far North and why she owned it. The money spent on Russian America remained controversial—Alaska was still widely referred to as "Seward's Icebox" and "Seward's Folly" and "Seward's Polar Bear Garden," in derision of former secretary of state William Seward, who had championed and then negotiated the purchase. Yet the American people also wanted to know what might lie beyond the country's new northern borders—and they were hungry for a hero to personify the country's northern tilt.

George De Long was beginning to think he might be that person. Ever since he'd experienced the Arctic firsthand, the worm of his imagination had started to turn on the polar problem. He sought to add his name to the pantheon—though some might call it a rogues' gallery—of explorers of the Far North. His goal became nothing less than solving the supreme mystery: reaching the North Pole itself. "If I do not succeed," he wrote, "it will be a grand thing to add my name to the list of those who have tried."

The quest first engaged his intellect, and then, little by little, his emotions. He would not relax his grip on the question for the rest of his life.

EVEN BEFORE HE arrived in New York, De Long had become a celebrity for his exploits aboard the *Little Juniata*. Martin Maher, the correspondent for the *New York Herald,* had transmitted lengthy dispatches via telegraph from St. John's, and the paper's editors had run them prominently in serialized form. Maher cast the *Little Juniata*'s eight-hundred-mile round-trip journey along the Greenland coast as a heroic voyage of nearly historic proportions. De Long's volunteering for a dangerous mission to save people he did not even know resonated with the public—as did his willingness to keep pushing northward even as the ice began to entomb his tiny steam launch.

De Long and his *Little Juniata* were the toast of the nation. "Her famous trip to Cape York," proclaimed Maher,

> was by far the most daring and brilliant feat of the whole expedition. Bold in conception and masterly in its execution, the plan was such as few would have attempted to carry out. But the case was urgent and the call for volunteers was answered with a will. It is unnecessary to reiterate the unprecedented struggle of the little craft through the fast-gathering ice; how, even when the fuel was more than half expended, the gallant commander determined to push ahead, in the very teeth of a furious tempest; how, beaten back again and again, his cry was still "Onward!"; how entering what is known in Arctic parlance as a false lead, the launch was held as if in an iron vise, and not until she had butted against the solid ice with might and main was she at length set free, only to encounter the steadfast and impassable barrier that finally foiled all further efforts to progress. Call the experiment foolhardy if you will, [but] the heroism of Lieutenant De Long and his brave associates must ever remain a sterling tribute of self-sacrifice and devotion in the noble cause so cheerfully undertaken.

De Long was embarrassed by all this attention. He "abhorred public acclaim," Emma said, "and avoided it diligently. He had done his duty and did not see any reason for enlarging upon it." At the same time, he perceived publicity's power and recognized that his celebrity could be useful as he began to plan for a return to the Arctic.

One of the reasons the newspapers lavished so much praise on De Long was that all the other *Polaris* news that trickled in that autumn was so uniformly dark and depressing. Here was an expedition that had fallen into disarray even before it left the United States. The voyage lacked discipline and a clear sense of mission. Cliques had formed, feeding intrigue and distrust—for example, a large contingent of Germans on board the *Polaris* scarcely even spoke with the Americans. The expedition leader, Charles Hall, had been belittled, then challenged, then apparently murdered.

When he died, the others breathed a sigh of relief, only to plunge into demoralization and anarchy. The expedition's logbooks, records, and scientific instruments had all been lost. The men who had stayed on board the *Polaris* apparently made no effort to find their comrades when the ice floe on which they were encamped broke away and began to drift from the ship. The castaways, meanwhile, had lived in perpetual fear and suspicion of one another, often contemplating cannibalism. A naval inquiry later dredged up all sorts of unsavory behavior. The entire expedition was a grim and gothic story all around—a story with few heroes that emphatically cast America in a negative light. Noted the *Times* of London: "Death, in a hundred ghastly shades, dogs the shadow of this phantom ship."

For a sensible person, the voyage of the *Polaris* would have served as a cautionary tale about the perils of *ever* going into the Arctic. But not for George De Long. De Long was already analyzing the Hall expedition and determining how he would have done it differently, more efficiently, more scientifically. If he were captain of a polar expedition, De Long vowed, he would make better use of cutting-edge technology. His vessel would be staffed with Navy officers who would enforce a rigid code of discipline, so that mutiny would never rear its head. He would pick his crew more carefully—there would be no cliques, no imbalances of rank or nationality. He would more staunchly reinforce his ship for the ice, and equip it with more plentiful stores of food, medicine, and scientific instruments.

De Long felt a need to redeem Hall's mistakes and claim a prize for the Navy—and for the United States.

AS A RESULT of his new fame, De Long found himself moving in new social circles. On the night of November 1, 1873, he was invited to a dinner party at the home of Henry Grinnell, a well-known New York philanthropist and a wealthy shipping magnate. Grinnell was an Arctic enthusiast who, over the previous few decades, had funded numerous expeditions—both British and American—to the High North. He was a dignified, white-bearded man of seventy-four years, an elegant dresser with bulging glassy eyes and a probing mind. One of the founders of the American Geographical Society, Grinnell had the most extensive collection of Arctic books, maps, and charts in America. His name was indelibly imprinted on the Arctic—a large section of Ellesmere Island had been called Grinnell Land in his honor. No one in the United States had devoted more thought or monetary might toward solving the polar problem.

On this evening, a Saturday, Grinnell had summoned a collection of scientists, geographers, explorers, and mariners to his fine home at 17 Bond Street in Manhattan to discuss the latest ideas in Arctic exploration. In Grinnell's drawing room, with maps ranged all around the table, the assembled gentlemen treated De Long as a hero and the presumptive commander of America's next foray into the Arctic. The session was meant to be a postmortem of the Hall expedition—which Grinnell himself had largely funded. What could be learned from the debacle? How would a future expedition be organized differently? And perhaps most important, what route would it take?

The growing consensus seemed to be that Greenland was not the best portal for reaching the pole. Hall's disastrous expedition offered only the latest evidence of that region's treacheries. De Long, seeking a better polar route, had already done some research. Shortly after returning from Greenland, he had paid a visit to New Bedford, Massachusetts, the de facto whaling capital of the United States. There he had consulted with a number of whaling captains, a weather-wizened class of men who understood Arctic currents and winds better than anyone else. These old salts told him that by aiming for the pole via Greenland, De Long would make unnecessarily hard work for himself—it was "going uphill," one of them said. They believed that the prevailing currents and winds around Greenland tended to push the ice pack toward the *south,* so that sailing that way would require constant battling against the floes.

But, they said, if De Long were to make for the pole via the North Pacific and the Bering Strait, he would find much smoother sailing; effectively, he would be traveling "downhill." De Long took these insights for what they were: not scientifically proven facts, merely empirical observations from practical professionals who every year ventured to the edges of the ice pack in pursuit of valuable animal oil. Still, the point the captains were making was simple: Why work against nature when you can work *with* it?

In 1869, in fact, a French expedition, to be commanded by a scientist named Gustave Lambert, had planned to try for the pole via the Bering Strait, but that expedition had been called off because of the outbreak of the Franco-Prussian War. Two years later, during the siege of Paris, Lambert was killed in battle, and the expedition was never undertaken.

Now the men at Grinnell's house nursed their brandies and stroked their beards in thought. They seemed intrigued by the notion of a polar expedition through the Bering Strait. It was a route that had never been tried before—and one that would use America's new territory of Alaska as a launching pad. On that cold night in November, in the smoky salon on Bond Street, the idea hung brilliantly in the air. Grinnell raised a glass to it: By all means, *downhill to the pole!*

De Long was grateful for Grinnell's invitation, and for Grinnell's support of his candidacy as the next polar avatar. And he was not too shy to approach Grinnell directly: Will you underwrite the expedition? he asked.

Grinnell surprised everyone by saying no. He was done with funding polar explorations. The polar problem still intrigued him, but he was an old, tired man with many health concerns. He'd spent enough on these expeditions. His days as a patron of the High North were over. The Hall expedition, perhaps, had scared him.

But who would take up where he was leaving off? De Long wanted to know. Where should he turn? The Navy, he recognized, would foot only so many bills. Arctic exploration, if it was to continue, needed a new sponsor.

When De Long trolled the room for ideas, only one answer presented itself: *Bennett.*

3 · The Lord of Creation

few months later, on the early morning of May 5, 1874, a crowd gathered at the corner of Thirty-eighth Street and Fifth Avenue in New York. Some of the city's most fashionable gentlemen milled about, making bets with one another as they stood beside their polished coaches and hansom cabs. Waiting teams of manicured horses stamped their hooves on the muddy avenue, and a northerly wind stirred the elms that lined the misty rows of brown-stone mansions. The side streets were thronged with carriages of all kinds—victorias, barouches, hackney cabs, omnibuses. It was a Tuesday morning, and a fine drizzle fell over the city. Fat beads of moisture dripped from the telegraph wires that hummed overhead. Yet the mood on Fifth Avenue was festive, and even at this early hour, some men could be seen passing around whiskey flasks and sniffing spoonfuls of snuff.

Standing in the center of the crowd, stretching and performing light calisthenics, was a short, muscular man named John Whipple. A young patrician and a prominent member of the Union Club, Whipple was, despite his squat physique, a formidable athlete. Like most gentlemen of his station, he could shoot and sail and ride a fast horse. But Whipple's greatest prowess was reserved for the esoteric sport of speed walking. In fact, he was a walking *champion*. He was reputed to be the fastest pedestrian in all the country. In walking matches held over the years, no one had bested him. This morning, attired in black breeches and a black cap, Whipple prepared to confront his latest challenger.

A few minutes before the appointed hour of seven, the ponderous door to the double brownstone at 425 Fifth Avenue cracked open, and Whipple's rival emerged on the stoop. He wore a tweed sport jacket, a white cap, and ankle-high leather boots. As he left his mansion behind and bounded down the wet steps, the crowd gave a cheer for James Gordon Bennett Jr.

Bennett had never tested his mettle at the sport of speed walking. He was frankly dubious of Whipple's talents and wanted to knock him off his pedestal. One night in early April, in the halls of the Union Club, the two men had agreed to a match. The purse was arranged at $6,000, and a ten-mile course was mapped out, starting at Bennett's brownstone and ending at the racetrack clubhouse at Jerome Park, across the Harlem River in the Bronx. Champion and challenger then began a strenuous regimen of training. The match date was set for May 5, rain or shine.

Now Bennett stepped into the crowded street, accompanied by his trainer. A correspondent from the *New York Times* stood on the curb, scribbling notes. The contrast between the rivals, he reported, was most striking: "Bennett was nearly half a head taller than his competitor. His opponent was of a more compact build, though to all appearances well endowed with muscle and wind." Two judges, with fob watches in their hands, assumed their places beside the starting line, while the referee greeted the athletes and reviewed the match rules: No jostling, no deviation from the designated route—and, of course, no breaking into a run.

The campanile at a church two blocks away began to chime the hour, and the contestants crouched beside each other. The church bells pealed: *five . . . six . . . seven.* The referee cried out, *"Go!"* And the walkers took off, heading north on Fifth Avenue, striding past the Croton Reservoir, past the turreted mansions of several Gilded Age barons, past the lower reaches of Central Park, which had officially opened the previous year. Sheep grazed in the park's meadow, and occasionally the roars of the big cats could be heard coming from the menagerie near the armory at Sixty-fourth Street.

The contestants continued north on Fifth Avenue, with their trainers jumping in front from time to time to exhort their racers or point out flaws in their technique. The "pace of both men was terrific," said the *Times* reporter, "each putting his best foot foremost, evidently with an intention of tiring out the other, if possible, at an early stage of the race." The street was so sloppy with mud that the two walkers had trouble establishing a smooth gait—the strain on the contestants was "almost pitiable."

Meanwhile, the crowds at the starting line scrambled for their waiting carriages and soon came "driving up the avenue at a trot, nearly abreast of the two pedestrians." Bennett flailed his arms with each stride. "In fact," noted the reporter, "it might be said of him that he walked as much with his arms as with his legs." The technique seemed to be working for the *Herald* publisher; by the end of the first mile, Bennett had inched a few feet ahead. Whipple appeared disheartened by this, but he "kept up the same steady gait, hoping to wear out his rival in the long run."

Bennett tossed off his hat and tweed coat and "set to work with fresh energy." Though complaining that gravel was accumulating in his boots, he continued to outdistance his opponent. Whipple "struggled manfully," but as the two men turned left at 110th Street and then headed up St. Nicholas Avenue, it seemed possible that Bennett might pull off an upset. It appeared to the *Times* man that Whipple was "slowly but surely giving in." He became so winded that at one point he had to sit down on the sidewalk.

By the time Bennett crossed over the Harlem River at the Macombs Bridge, he had extended his lead by three hundred yards and was pressing toward the finish "with unflagging energy." He breezed through Fordham and up Central Avenue, then passed triumphantly through the entrance to Jerome Park at 8:46:55. Seven minutes later, Whipple staggered across the finish line. When asked what had happened, the former champion could only guess that he had "over-trained."

Bennett was casual about his victory. He was a man used to winning, a man who *expected* to win, and yet he also seemed bashful about being the center of attention. When the *Times* reporter asked him how he had pulled off his upset, he was at a loss for words. "Oh, I am always walking, you know, more or less," he said. Bennett and Whipple shared a light meal at the Jerome Park clubhouse and then headed back to Manhattan—leaving the followers of the race to collect what was later estimated to be $50,000 in bets.

THE MULTIMILLIONAIRE WHOM the guests at Henry Grinnell's dinner party had advised De Long to go see was nothing if not a lover of spectacle. To James Gordon Bennett Jr., life was a perpetual escapade, a test of wits, a bravura performance. Bennett liked fast walking, fast ships, fast carriages, fast women, fast decisions, fast communications, and any bold new development or design that promised to quicken the pulse of the national blood. Therefore, when George De Long came to New York in early 1874 and paid a visit to Bennett's white-marbled offices at the corner of Broadway and Ann Street, he found a receptive audience. De Long professed his desire to reach the North Pole. He laid out why he felt this was the time. He explained how he believed it was America's destiny to take the lead in Arctic exploration and noted that Grinnell had grown tired of underwriting voyages. Given the anemic state of the U.S. Navy, any American-led exploration would need a benefactor to replace Grinnell. De Long understood that any professional expedition to the High North would have to be a unique hybrid enterprise—a national project backed by private largesse.

Bennett warmed to the idea of an ambitious Arctic expedition, so much so that he even flirted with the notion of personally venturing out with De Long. An Arctic push would be good for the nation, good for science, good for sport, and, most important, good for his paper. It dovetailed perfectly with his interests.

The playboy-publisher liked De Long, liked his persistence, the aspect of hard discipline that seemed to inform his fervor, the intensity that burned within his bespectacled eyes. After his magnificent performance in Greenland, De Long was the logical man to lead the next major assault on the High North. When he did, he would do so under the auspices of the *New York Herald*. It would be a story that Bennett's paper could milk in many ways—an exploration that could trump Stanley's accounts from Africa. De Long himself would write the main narrative, of course, but there would also be a *Herald* staff correspondent on board to file reports. Bennett would pay for everything.

It was agreed that De Long would hunt for a sturdy vessel, one that could survive the Arctic crush, and begin to assemble a team of explorers. Bennett, meanwhile, would consult with the best scientists and geographers in Europe to gather the latest ideas about how to solve the Arctic problem.

Then De Long left. He and Bennett parted not as friends, exactly, but as co-conspirators in a quest. "The two men were attracted to each other from the first, and Bennett promised to back the project to the limit," Emma De Long later wrote. "Bennett realized at once that he had found the man he was looking for."

They surely made for an odd couple. Yet although various obstacles would combine to delay their mission to the High North, De Long and Bennett would never turn loose their dream.

GEORGE DE LONG had found his Medici, but he could not have possibly imagined, in this short initial visit in New York, how spectacularly weird Bennett was. De Long could not know of Bennett's many obsessions, his peculiar prejudices, his random gusts of spite or whimsy. Bennett may have been New York's most eligible bachelor; he was also New York's moodiest brat.

He was "Bennett the Terrible, the mad Commodore, the autocrat of the transatlantic cables," one biographer wrote; he saw himself as "one of the lords of creation." A longtime *Herald* editor later remarked of his boss that he "was a ruler over a domain of romance; he himself at times a romantic ruler. If impulse called he obeyed, and no rule existed but to be broken."

Bennett had a habit of strolling into one of the finest establishments in Paris or New York and snatching the table linens as he proceeded down the aisle, smashing plates and glassware on the floor, to the horror of the dining patrons, until he reached his reserved table in the back. (He never failed to write a check for the damages.) Once, after a musical show in Amsterdam, he invited the beautiful lead actress and the entire cast to tour his yacht. Then he quietly slipped out to sea and for several days cruised the Atlantic, essentially holding the cast hostage and demanding repeat performances—all the while attempting to seduce the young starlet. Upon returning to shore, Bennett gladly paid an enormous sum to the Amsterdam theater to cover its losses.

It was difficult to keep track of all of Bennett's fiercely held likes and dislikes. For breakfast, he insisted on plover's eggs. He would not allow facial hair to be worn by any man serving on his yachts. He owned hundreds of thermometers and barometers and was fascinated by the slightest changes in the weather. He had a doting love for Pomeranians—he kept dozens of them and served them only Vichy springwater to drink. Bennett believed his yappy little pooches were such astute judges of human character that he would sometimes hire editors, or choose not to, purely on the basis of his dogs' reactions when the prospective employee walked into the room. (Some job candidates, having learned of Bennett's odd deference to his dogs, would arrive at interviews with their coat pockets stuffed with morsels of raw meat.) Bennett also had a fetish for owls—he kept them everywhere: living owls, pictures of owls, busts of owls, owls on cuff links, owls on stationery. They decorated his brownstone, his yachts, his country houses. Something about their winking, swivel-headed, nocturnal ways struck his deepest fancy.

What all of these eccentricities added up to was hard to say, and might not be worthy of recounting were it not also true that James Gordon Bennett was, in his own incomparable way, a brilliant publisher with electric sensibilities and a profound intuition for what moved and mesmerized the American public. He was one of the fathers of the communications age, and though he was a terror to work for, he created one of the great institutions in American journalism.

De Long would never understand his patron, but he was lucky to have him. He had found a man who possessed not only a limitless reserve of cash but also a bottomless appetite for a story that could usher in the modern world.

4 · For You I Will Dare Anything

America's newest Arctic hero was a young man of myriad talents and deep contradictions. Emma De Long thought there was within her husband an "incessant friction"—a contrast between impetuosity and patient striving, between a love for adventure and a compulsion to accomplish something ambitious and sustained. De Long could be a romantic, sometimes an extravagant one. He had what Emma called "a hungry heart." But he willingly confined himself for most of his life to a straitjacket of absolute discipline. He knew what he wanted with nearly perfect clarity, and he pursued it with unswerving conviction—resistance only intensified his resolve.

De Long was a lover of opera, symphonies, and fine novels, an exacting correspondent who wrote beautiful letters in a delicate, florid hand. He doted on his baby girl, Sylvie, and hated the assignments that took him away from the daily joys of their family life. Letting Emma supervise the details of the household and most of their finances, De Long was casual about his domestic affairs. When in command of a ship, however, he could be a harsh disciplinarian with a granite disposition. One historian called his commanding style "monolithic." Though a complete creature of the Navy, he hated nothing in the world more than naval hierarchies, naval politics, and naval rules, all of which he found an aggravation and a bore.

De Long blamed the Navy for some of his worst traits. He once wrote, "Ship life is a hard thing on the temper. Mark Twain in his

Innocents Abroad says that going to sea develops 'all of man's bad qualities and brings out new ones that he did not suppose himself mean enough for.' I wonder if that accounts for all the rough edges of my character." He admitted that he could be "hard on men," but such was the nature of a naval officer's life. "I can only say I never allow any argument," De Long once wrote. "It is my office to command and theirs to obey."

The United States in the 1870s was, De Long knew, far from being a world-class naval power. Although the U.S. Navy was slowly making advancements, many European nations viewed the tiny, antiquated American fleet as a joke. According to naval historian Peter Karsten, it was "a third-rate assemblage" of "old tubs" in "various states of disrepair . . . the laughingstock of the world." Far from an adventurous existence, life in the American Navy was marked by cramped quarters, low pay, draconian discipline, and jealous competition for rank in a promotion process that could be stultifying and slow.

Most of the assignments consisted of "showing the flag" in foreign ports and performing mind-numbingly dreary tasks aboard ship. It was a life of "crushing hopelessness," said a junior officer at the time. "The most aspiring years of our lives" were consumed by "the dullest, the most uninteresting, the most useless duties." Like many young officers, De Long often felt that he was wasting away his brightest days. "A stagnant navy," noted one maritime scholar, "was no place for a man on the make."

George De Long was nothing if not a man on the make, driven by big ideas. It was no wonder, then, that the Arctic, for all its hardships and dangers, exerted such a powerful pull on him. Here was a way for him to circumvent some of the drudgeries of naval duty, to achieve fame if not fortune, and possibly to hasten his ascension in rank while also doing something consequential for science and the nation. It offered a path to glory that an ordinary Navy career—at least during peacetime—seemed incapable of offering. A risky Arctic expedition carried some of the dash and distinction of a wartime assignment without the necessity of being in a war. Most important, it provided a faster track to commanding a ship, something to which De Long, even in his youth, had always aspired.

GEORGE FRANCIS DE LONG was born in New York City on August 22, 1844, the only child of a lower-middle-class couple in Brook-

lyn. George's father, a cool, quiet, indifferent man of French Huguenot roots, exerted little influence over him. It was George's Catholic
mother, loving but overprotective in the extreme, who dominated—
and quite nearly suffocated—his adolescence. Forever fearful that he
might be injured, she refused to let George play outside or pal around
with neighborhood kids. Always expecting him to be punctual, she
ordered him to make long, straight marches to and from school.
Emma said that De Long's mother was "morbidly solicitous for him"
and strictly forbade his skating, swimming, or boating, so that he was
"jealously guarded from outdoor influences, and restrained from the
ordinary sports of boyhood."

One day a gang of neighborhood kids who mistook his aloofness
for elitism waited in ambush and pelted him at close range with snow-
balls. In the melee, George's eardrum was damaged by ice shards,
and his inner ear became infected. The family doctor, worried that
George might lose his hearing, attended to him for several weeks. An
Arctic historian later noted, half facetiously, that this incident seemed
an augury—"De Long's first encounter with hostile ice."

Driven indoors throughout his youth, George became intensively,
if resentfully, bookish. "His spirit and energy, hemmed in upon the
adventurous side, found exercise in an intellectual ardor," noted a
biographical sketch published by Houghton, Mifflin in the 1880s.
George practically lived at the Mercantile Library in midtown Manhattan, and he even became a librarian there in his mid-teens. He read
deeply in history and was drawn to stories of great monarchs, politicians, and generals. In contrast to the drab safety of his own boyhood,
he began to yearn for a career of adventure. When he was sixteen,
thinking his middle name, Francis, to be a bit feminine, he got it into
his head to formally change his name to George *Washington* De Long.
His parents were puzzled, but George insisted, and the name change
became official.

Around that same time, George became a connoisseur of the
naval battles of the War of 1812 and a devotee of Frederick Marryat's
swashbuckling tales of the high seas. These books ignited in him a
profound desire to enter the Naval Academy. He imagined himself
sailing the world and living a life of stirring sea battles, with anchor-
ages in exotic ports. "Because of the repression to which he was so
constantly subjected," observed the Houghton, Mifflin biography,
"he was restless and filled with an uneasy desire for larger liberty."

George's mother was dead set against the idea of her only child pursuing a life in the Navy, with all its perils. Instead, she wanted George to become a lawyer, a minister, or a doctor. But he would not budge on the issue. Through remarkable persistence that involved, among other things, taking a train down to Washington and personally pleading his eligibility before the secretary of the Navy himself, he secured an appointment to the U.S. Naval Academy for the fall of 1861.

During the Civil War, the Lincoln administration thought it prudent to move the Naval Academy from its Annapolis campus to a hodgepodge of buildings in Newport, and so Rhode Island is where De Long spent his years as a midshipman. (Newport was also young Gordon Bennett's summertime haunt and the place where he often kept his yachts.) At the Naval Academy, De Long proved a serious scholar and a meticulous cadet. He thrived there—"I was in my proper element at last," he later said. He graduated tenth in his class in the spring of 1865, just as the war was drawing to a close.

It was not unusual to find among the young men of the immediate post–Civil War generation a kind of inferiority complex, a sense that history had passed them by, that their brothers and fathers and uncles had participated in something momentous while they had not. The magnitude of the previous generation's sacrifice made young men like De Long feel inadequate—and irredeemably green. If De Long could not win glory on fields of battle, then perhaps he could earn it in fields of ice.

De Long's early naval assignments, however, were anything but glorious. He first served aboard the USS *Canandaigua,* a seven-gun sloop of war that had seen considerable action during the Union blockade of the Confederacy. On the day he reported for duty at the Boston Navy Yard, where the *Canandaigua* was docked, De Long did something amusing. Inspecting his quarters aboard ship, De Long observed that there were only two berths even though four midshipmen had been assigned to the compartment. The two others, presumably, would have no beds at all—or else would have to swing in hammocks. So De Long boldly marched to the office of the commandant of the Boston Navy Yard, an august rear admiral named Silas Stringham, to lodge a complaint.

"Admiral," he said, "I am Midshipman De Long of the USS *Canandaigua.* Sir, I have been inspecting my quarters on board. I came to ask you to have two more berths put in before we start."

Admiral Stringham peered at this impertinent young man. "So you are Midshipman De Long of the USS *Canandaigua?*"

"Yes, sir."

"Well, Midshipman De Long of the USS *Canandaigua,* I advise you to return to the USS *Canandaigua,* and consider yourself lucky that you have any bunks at all in the steerage."

Chastened, De Long did as he was told. The crew of the ship ridiculed him for the temerity he had shown, but the joke was on them: Just before the *Canandaigua* left port, a team of carpenters came aboard and constructed two more berths. Admiral Stringham had taken De Long's suggestion to heart. (Years later, Stringham and De Long shared a laugh over the story.)

Throughout his career, De Long would prove to be a man unafraid to badger his superiors in order to get things done. "He got what he wanted," Emma said, "because he dared to ask for it."

DE LONG SAILED aboard the *Canandaigua* for three years. As part of the European Squadron, the sloop of war cruised the North Atlantic and the Mediterranean, protecting American interests and showing the flag at ports all over Europe, North Africa, and the Middle East. In June 1868, the ship was brought into Le Havre, France, for repairs. Le Havre, its waterfront an extensive network of piers, dry docks, and shipyards, was a pleasant international city near the place where the Seine emptied into the English Channel. It was surrounded by the green rolling hills of Normandy, which gave way to precipitous cliffs that swept down to the cold sea.

De Long, now twenty-four years old, was given leave and spent a week carousing in Paris with fellow officers before returning to Le Havre. There he attended a dinner party at the home of a successful American steamship magnate named James Wotton. Captain Jimmie, as he was known, was part owner of the New York and Havre Steamship Company. He and his wife, Margaret, had a large family and lived in a mansion high on a hill, called La Côte, that overlooked the busy port city and the whitecap-streaked English Channel beyond. The Wottons liked to fill their home with interesting people, good food, and dancing, and they were known for generously entertaining American naval officers when they sailed into port. They had a billiards room and a large ballroom, where musicians frequently played waltzes.

On this evening De Long became entranced by the Wottons' daughter, Emma. She was seventeen years old, pretty, with big, perceptive eyes, an often insouciant expression, and lustrous curly brown hair. Emma had been raised in both New York and Le Havre, had been well-schooled at a French lycée, and considered herself "a finished young lady." De Long took a liking to her immediately, and when the waltzing began, he went straight to her dance card and jotted his name in all the spaces not already taken. Emma was intrigued by the young officer—she found him "dashing, tall, and broad-shouldered" but a little "aggressive," as she later put it, noting, "Evidently he intended a conquest."

A week later, the Wottons held another soiree. At the close of a dance, De Long led Emma to a sofa in the middle of the ballroom and, without preamble, asked her to be his wife.

Emma was stunned. "But we've scarcely met!" she protested.

The skirts of the whirling dancers brushed against De Long's face, but he appeared unperturbed. "I feel as though I've known you always," he told her. "As though I've simply been waiting for you to appear."

Emma did not quite know how to respond to his ardor. On the one hand, she liked him. "I was gradually being drawn to George De Long," she wrote, "and I recognized in him many qualities which I admired." But she found his "violent feelings" intimidating. "The energy of his courtship," she said, "was inexhaustible." When the evening was over and George left with the other officers of the *Canandaigua,* she was confused. "I felt completely lost," she said. "I did not understand myself at all."

The shipwrights had completed their repairs of the *Canandaigua,* and the sloop of war was scheduled to leave for the Mediterranean in a few days. Growing desperate, De Long wrote to Emma:

> As I may not be able to speak to you alone before my departure, I have been bold enough to ask you to read the[se] few words . . . trusting you will accept them as the offering of an honest and loving heart. I am writing despondently. I am going away from you and placing an immense barrier between me and all that I love. I cannot lose you without a struggle. For you I will dare anything.

Though Emma was moved by his letter, she did not reply. She was determined not to succumb to his overtures. But the day before he left, she gave him a farewell present—a blue silk bag she had sewn, in which she had placed a lock of her hair and a gold cross inlaid with six pearls. In preparing this little gesture, she surprised herself. "I did not want him to go away empty-handed," she later wrote. "Love, even then, was playing tricks upon one who thought herself immune!"

Pleased by her present, De Long took her in his arms and kissed her for the first time. The next day the *Canandaigua* sailed out to sea.

A FEW MONTHS later, De Long, after being assigned to another ship, found himself in New York City, where he arranged to meet with James Wotton, who was in the United States on business. De Long wanted to formally ask Mr. Wotton for permission to marry his daughter.

The meeting started off surprisingly well. "Your father spoke to me kindly and feelingly, perhaps more kindly than my merits deserve," De Long wrote Emma. "He said in the first place that love was much too sacred a thing to interfere in lightly and that generally speaking the parties most interested were the best ones to decide such matters for themselves. But nevertheless it was necessary for parents to exercise such a care over their children as to insure them a happy life."

Wotton refused to give his consent to the marriage. Instead, he issued a test. De Long, who had just been promoted to the rank of lieutenant, would soon be headed out to sea for a new cruise—this one aboard the USS *Lancaster.* The steam-powered sloop of war would head for the Caribbean and South America and would likely be away for three years. If, at the end of those three years, George and Emma still had feelings for each other, Wotton said, then he would give the marriage his blessing.

De Long was crushed by this enforced probation, but he accepted it with bulldog tenacity. "I am firmly resolved," he wrote Emma from Brazil, "to remain a wanderer from my own land. I love you with all the strength of my heart and soul, and I am going forth to make myself worthy of you or give way under the pressure."

In the torpor of the tropics, the little memento Emma had given George was looking a bit worse for wear. It had become a sorry mascot of his deferred love. "Poor little silken bag!" he wrote. "Salt water, salt air and heat have faded it sadly. You will hardly recognize it when you see it."

ONE YEAR WENT by, then two, and De Long remained steadfast as he continued his long cruise in South American waters. His correspondence with Emma was interrupted in 1870, when the Prussian army stormed across France and laid siege to Paris. The Franco-Prussian War gave the world an ugly glimpse of what total warfare might look like in modern times. For five months, the trapped Parisians subsisted on rats, dogs, and cats and were able to communicate with the outside world only through messages sent by carrier pigeons or hot-air balloons. The Wotton family, fearing that Le Havre would soon fall to the Germans as well, filled a few chests with silver and other valuables and moved across the English Channel to the Isle of Wight.

George, deprived of news, did not understand why his letters were not reaching Emma. From Rio de Janeiro, he wrote in despair:

> For this long, long year I have waited and waited and waited in vain. I have overestimated my strength. I am sick and unhappy all of the time and my life is a burden to me from day to day. I have no aim, no object in life. A kind word from you may save me yet.

By the turn of the year, the Prussian scare was over, and Emma moved with her family back to Le Havre, where she was finally able to reply to George's letters. "My great regret," she wrote, "is the severe and long test you have been subjected to and the suffering it has caused you. I only hope and pray it has not injured you permanently. Please consider yourself absolutely free." Then she wrote a somewhat cryptic closer: "I have not changed."

George optimistically interpreted this to mean that she still loved him and that she was declaring their long probationary test to be over. He was so sure of this sanguine interpretation that in two days he had secured leave and packed his bags for the six-thousand-mile voyage, via New York, to Le Havre. He sent a note ahead to declare his intentions: At long last, he was coming to claim her as his bride.

Yet Emma's true feelings were more ambiguous. She admired him—that much was true—and she did not want to cause him any more suffering. But on the subject of marriage she still vacillated. Mostly, she entertained doubts, fed by her father (a former steamship captain himself), about the hardships of being married to a naval officer; she was not certain she could endure the long absences, the doubt-ridden interludes, the years of hypothetical companionship. She saw for herself a life of waiting.

When George arrived at Le Havre in February 1871, foreign warships were anchored in the harbor to protect their nationals should the Prussian forces, still encamped around Paris, suddenly advance on the port city. Representing the United States was the USS *Shenandoah,* a sloop of war staffed by many officers De Long knew well. The Wottons invited De Long to stay in a guest room in their mansion on La Côte. Upon seeing Emma, George promptly reached into his vest pocket, produced a handsome diamond ring, and slid it onto her finger. "I melted somewhat," she wrote, "but still felt full of turmoil. I could not make up my mind."

For several weeks, they pursued a frantic courtship. They had much catching up to do—the two young lovers were nearly strangers, despite more than two years of fitful correspondence. George and Emma spent long afternoons strolling the pier, and at night the Wottons held their usual rounds of dinner parties and balls. Emma began to see George in a different light. "I was falling in love with [him] fast," she said. "The better I came to know him the more I admired him." He had an "adventurous spirit," she thought, but was "innately refined." As the days went by, she came to understand his "insistent wooing of me, and I gave him full credit for having foreseen that we really were suited to each other. I [had] found a companion who could assure me complete happiness."

A date was set: the first of March. It would not be a white wedding; because of the war, the supply of white satin and silk had been exhausted in Le Havre, so Emma would have to improvise. The wedding's location would have to be improvised as well. In France, marriage was a civil contract, and no official could be found in Le Havre who had the legal authority to perform the ceremony—they were all in Paris, where the armistice talks were under way. But then an ingenious solution presented itself: The USS *Shenandoah,* still docked in the harbor, was technically American soil. They could be married upon her decks. It seemed only fitting that a Navy lieutenant and a young woman from a steam-liner family would be married aboard a ship.

On the evening of March 1, 1871, the *Shenandoah* was decorated with festive flags and Chinese lanterns. The guests, in evening gowns and naval dress uniforms, waited on the pier as the *Shenandoah*'s boats rowed over from the ship. Finally the crowd had assembled, and then the bride and groom stepped onto the deck. A priest with the forthrightly American name of George Washington presided over the ceremony. When Emma and George were married, at precisely ten o'clock, wild cheers went up and echoed across the darkened harbor.

The quest on which George De Long had embarked after returning from Greenland was built on a grand and seductive idea, one that had taken hundreds of years to evolve. It was a concept with an elegant symmetry and a beguiling pull. De Long, who had read everything he could that pertained to the Arctic, knew every turn and wrinkle of the idea: the procession of explorers who had tested it, the thinkers who had contemplated its larger possibilities. De Long believed in the idea with such conviction that he was prepared to risk his career and even his life on it, for he knew that if he could take it out of the realm of the theoretical and into the world of fact, he would be judged one of the greatest exploratory heroes of all time.

The idea, widely believed by the world's leading scientists and geographers, went like this: The weather wasn't especially cold at the North Pole, at least not in summer. On the contrary, the dome of the world was covered in a shallow, warm, ice-free sea whose waters could be smoothly sailed, much as one might sail across the Caribbean or the Mediterranean. This tepid Arctic basin teemed with marine life—and was, quite possibly, home to a lost civilization. Cartographers were so sure of its existence that they routinely depicted it on their maps, often labeling the top of the globe, matter-of-factly, OPEN POLAR SEA.

Gerardus Mercator's beautiful, if completely hypothetical, map of the Arctic published in 1595 showed an iceless polar sea that, although ringed by mountainous lands, freely communicated with the Atlantic and Pacific by means of four symmetrically arranged river channels. Emanuel Bowen's late-eighteenth-century map called this apparently ice-free body of water the Northern Ocean. The British Admiralty had produced numerous maps throughout the 1800s that showed a largely iceless sea, and charts commissioned by the U.S. Navy showed much the same thing.

No one had ever seen this fantastical Open Polar Sea, but that did not seem to matter. Somewhere along the way, the idea had gathered a logic of its own. Fixing it on maps had fixed it in people's minds. Like Atlantis or El Dorado, it was a beautiful vision based on legends, rumors, and tenuous scraps of information. Layer by layer, decade by decade, scientists and thinkers had contributed to the plausibility, the probability, and finally the *certainty* of this chimerical notion. No amount of contrary evidence could dislodge it from the collective imagination.

Many improbable ideas had been floated to explain the Open Polar Sea. Some people said it was due to the churning effects of the earth's rotation. Others said it was caused by heat vents, or by some extreme magnification of the sun's rays that occurred at the poles. Still others insisted that basking in sunshine twenty-four hours a day for six months of the year was more than enough to keep the pole ice-free. Then, too, many scientists at the time believed that a deep body of salt water *could not freeze,* that only shallow seawater, close to coastlines, was capable of forming ice—therefore, the polar sea was necessarily an open one. There was a desperation in these explanations, like trying to prove the existence of God by employing elaborate teleological arguments. It was extraordinary how much energy had been expended over the centuries in attempts to explain a thing that, although widely believed, had never been seen.

To be sure, the Open Polar Sea theory had its skeptics. At the time that De Long was coming into the story, the most prominent and vocal of these was Sir Clements R. Markham, the secretary of the Royal Geographical Society. In *The Threshold of the Unknown Region,* Markham called the Open Polar Sea a "mischievous" idea and insisted that it had done "much harm to the advance of discovery and the progress of sound geography." Arguments supporting the Open Polar Sea were "all so obviously fabulous," Markham scoffed, "that it is astonishing how any sane man could have been found to give credit to them." But Markham's naysaying was a minority view; the

Open Polar Sea was a collective obsession, an idée fixe that tickled the human fancy. It *had* to be true.

Since the beginning of Arctic exploration, whenever an adventurer sailed north, the same thing invariably happened: He was thwarted by ice, usually somewhere in the vicinity of the 80th parallel. But the theory of the Open Polar Sea held that this Arctic ice barrier was merely a ring that encircled the large warm-water basin—a "girdle," this ring was sometimes called, an "annulus," an "ice-belt." If an explorer could bust through this icy circle, preferably in a ship with a reinforced hull, he would eventually find open water and enjoy smooth sailing to the North Pole. The trick, then, was to find a gap in the ice, a place where it was thinner or weaker or slushier, a natural portal of some kind.

That portal was what George De Long was determined to find—and to do it, he would employ the best maps, the most up-to-date equipment, and the latest ideas from the fields of oceanography, meteorology, and navigation.

DE LONG WAS heavily influenced by a lengthy article that had appeared in the November 1869 issue of *Putnam's Magazine*. The article, tantalizingly entitled "Gateways to the Pole," enlarged upon all the theories supporting the Open Polar Sea, then went on to propose a surefire method for locating an easily navigable passage to these mythical warm waters. "There is reason to believe," the piece began, "that the perilous question of a way to the Pole has been at last answered."

The article focused on the ideas of a well-known Navy officer, Silas Bent. Captain Bent had occupied much of his life sailing the Pacific, where he had undertaken extensive hydrographic surveys for the U.S. Navy. Bent, who had sailed with Matthew Perry on the commodore's historic voyage to Japan in 1852, was particularly intrigued by a massive current known as the Kuro Siwo, a kind of Pacific analogue to the Atlantic Ocean's Gulf Stream.

Although the Kuro Siwo had been well known among Japanese, Korean, and Chinese fishermen for centuries, it had not been formally studied until Bent turned his sharp eye on its murky vastness. The Kuro Siwo (Japanese for "Black Current") swept up from tropical waters, brushing past Formosa and Japan, before heading out into the open Pacific. Like the Gulf Stream, it was a warm current and, thus, a kind of conveyor belt for nutrients, plankton, krill, and other food sources consumed by the marine mammals of the North Pacific. Out in the open ocean, the current could be seen as a clear line of demarcation; it had a distinctive blue-black color, deep and dark, that sailors found vaguely spooky. The current moved inexorably northward, a temperate river in a cold sea—aiming, it seemed, for the Bering Strait.

Precisely where the Kuro Siwo went was the subject of much speculation among scientists, but Bent had his own ideas. He felt certain that it flowed through the Bering Strait, burrowed under the Arctic ice, and worked its way to the Open Polar Sea. On the Atlantic side, Bent thought the Gulf Stream did much the same thing, sweeping past Norway and far to the northeast. (In fact, the Gulf Stream is potent enough to render the Russian port of Murmansk ice-free year-round.) Bent believed that the Gulf Stream continued north and eventually burrowed under the Arctic pack.

The confluence of these two mighty oceanic currents, Bent argued, was what kept the Open Polar Sea warm and ice-free. As Bent saw it, the Kuro Siwo and the Gulf Stream reflected a graceful planetary symmetry; they were dual strands of a massive distribution system that transferred heat from the tropics to the northern regions, from the Torrid Zones to the Frigid Zones. The earth, Bent reasoned, was like a rarefied organism, with its own exquisitely designed circulatory system.

Wrote Bent: "There is a circulation in the air; there is a circulation in the bodies of all animals; there is a circulation in the oceans— all of which are governed by laws, immutably fixed, and which in all their modifications and conditions they rigidly observe and obey. The sea, the atmosphere and the sun, are to the earth what the blood, the lungs, and the heart are to the animal economy. There is an equilibrium in all nature." The Kuro Siwo and Gulf Stream, Bent argued, pumped and flowed northward "like blood from the heart of the animal system, to carry their life-giving warmth and nourishment along their path to the earth's extremities."

Taken together, the Kuro Siwo and the Gulf Stream packed enough thermal wallop, the *Putnam's* article suggested, to "abolish the climate" of certain parts of the Arctic: "Armed in their tropical birthplace with the potential energy of the sun's heat, they, and they alone, can pierce the polar ice and carve routes to the Pole itself." Bent suggested an interesting idea: If his theory was right, an explorer could best rely on a thermometer instead of a compass to reach the apex of the world.

SILAS BENT'S IDEAS were largely predicated, in turn, on the work of the eminent American oceanographer, astronomer, and meteorologist Matthew Fontaine Maury of the U.S. Naval Observatory. Maury, who was sometimes called the Pathfinder of the Seas, had spearheaded comprehensive studies of ocean winds and currents, compiling huge amounts of data, which he assembled into copiously detailed charts that are still studied to this day.

Maury, along with superintendent Alexander Dallas Bache of the U.S. Coast and Geodetic Survey, was one of the stalwart American proponents of the Open Polar Sea. Maury's belief in it was largely based on anecdotal evidence: driftwood from Siberian rivers that had washed up on the shores of Greenland. Whalers high in the Arctic who had reported seeing huge numbers of birds migrating north, in autumn, over great stretches of ice pack. Russian explorers who had noted the existence of polynyas, large open-water areas in the ice cap, far to the north of the Siberian coast. (Between May and July, Maury noted, a sizable expanse of open water often formed at the extreme north end of Baffin Bay—off Greenland's west coast. It was first described in the early 1600s and had come to be known among whalers as, simply, the North Water.)

In his masterwork, *The Physical Geography of the Sea*, Maury wrote about a right whale that had been caught near the Bering Strait. Embedded in the whale's flesh was an old harpoon bearing the stamp of a vessel that operated only near Greenland. This wounded whale had thus somehow made its way from the North Atlantic to the North Pacific. How was this possible?

"It is known that these whales can not travel under the ice for such a great distance," Maury correctly observed. Nor had it swum clear around Cape Horn and then made its way up the Pacific to the Bering Strait. "The tropical regions of the ocean," he pointed out, "are to the right whale as a sea of fire, through which he can not pass, and into which he never enters." As far as Maury was concerned, this whale's capture near Bering Strait constituted "irrefragable proof that there is, at times at least, open water communication through the Arctic Sea from one side of the continent to the other."

Maury's near obsession with the Open Polar Sea was intimately connected to his interest in another important oceanic phenomenon, one he'd spent much of his career studying: the Gulf Stream. Far better than anybody then alive, Maury understood the current's breadth, velocity, power, and thermal properties. When he talked about it, this master of charts and minutiae could be quite poetic. "There is a river in the ocean," Maury wrote in *The Physical Geography of the Sea*. "The Gulf of Mexico is its fountain, and its mouth is in the Arctic Sea. There is in the world no other such majestic flow of waters. Its current is more rapid than the Mississippi or the Amazon, and its volume is more than a thousand times greater. Its waters, as far out as the Carolina coasts, are of an indigo blue. They are so distinctly marked, that their line of junction, with the common sea-water, may be traced by the eye."

Silas Bent believed that his Kuro Siwo was every bit as powerful as Maury's Gulf Stream. "In volume, velocity, and dimensions, they are almost identical," the *Putnam's* article noted. Their salinity, temperature, and larger climatic influence were comparable. If anything, Bent surmised, the Kuro Siwo was more potent, since the Pacific was a considerably larger ocean than the Atlantic. For this reason, he thought that the next big push for the pole should come from the direction of the Bering Strait—an angle of attack that had never been tried before.

THE THEORIES OF Silas Bent and Matthew Fontaine Maury, while buttressed by the science of their day, tapped into wellsprings of myth, fable, and belief. Variations of the Open Polar Sea idea had existed since prehistoric times. The notion of a safe, warm place at the roof of the globe—an oasis in a desert of ice, a polar utopia—seems to have been deeply embedded in the human psyche.

The Vikings spoke of a place at the world's northern rim, sometimes called Ultima Thule, where the oceans emptied into a vast hole that recharged all the springs and rivers on the earth. The Greeks believed in a realm called Hyperborea that lay far to the north. A place of eternal spring where the sun never set, Hyperborea was said to be bordered by the mighty River Okeanos and the Riphean Mountains, where lived the griffins—formidable beasts that were half lion and half eagle. The notion that Saint Nicholas—a.k.a. Kris Kringle or Santa Claus—lives at the North Pole seems to have a much more recent vintage. The earliest known reference to Saint Nick's polar residence comes from a Thomas Nast cartoon in an 1866 issue of *Harper's Weekly*—the artist captioned a collection of his Yuletide engravings "Santa Claussville, N.P." Still, the larger idea behind Nast's conceit—of a warm, jolly, beneficent place at the apex of the world where people might live—had ancient roots, and it spoke to America's consuming fascination with the North Pole throughout the 1800s.

A number of early scientists imagined that the poles must have giant vortices or vents from which large amounts of thermal or electromagnetic energy escaped. Newton postulated that the planet was a spheroid flattened at the poles—which, if true, meant that polar lands and seas were closer to the earth's warm inner core and therefore could be quite temperate. Eighteenth-century British astronomer Edmond Halley, famous for calculating the orbit of the comet that bears his name, believed that the earth was hollow, suffused with luminous gases, and inhabited by animals and even a race of humans. Halley thought the planet's crust was so thin at the poles that it emitted plumes of radiant gases far into the atmosphere—this was his explanation for the aurora borealis.

Much of the theorizing about an ice-free polar sea was fueled by a practical desire: If a clear route could be found over the pole, the commercial implications would be enormous. For centuries, the British and the Dutch had been particularly keen on finding a northern passage to Asia that would allow them better to compete against the Spanish and Portuguese, who had all but monopolized the southern sea routes around Cape Horn and the Cape of Good Hope. Consequently, finding an ice-free northern passage became a holy grail in the sixteenth and seventeenth centuries. William Barents and Henry Hudson, among other prominent explorers, became big believers in variations of the Open Polar Sea concept, although in their far-flung travels they never found compelling evidence for its existence.

One of the earliest and most dogged theoretical champions of the Open Polar Sea was an eighteenth-century lawyer and naturalist from England named Daines Barrington. Barrington's evidence was dubious at best—it seems to have consisted mainly of a tall tale from the 1600s, spun in a tavern in Amsterdam, in which a Dutch whaler claimed to have once sailed to the North Pole and back on a "free and open Sea" in "fine warm Weather, such as was at Amsterdam in the Summer time." As far as Barrington was concerned, this was proof positive that the Arctic was ice-free and navigable at least part of the year, and he tirelessly agitated for his government to mount an expedition to the North Pole.

OVER THE NEXT century and a half, Barrington's cause was taken up by a long procession of rogues, explorers, scientists, pseudoscientists, and outright kooks. In the 1820s, a colorful crank from Ohio named John Cleves Symmes Jr. toured the United States, arguing that there were large holes at the North and South Poles that connected to networks of probably inhabited subterranean cavities. Scientists scoffed, but his "holes at the poles" concept, encapsulated in his best-selling book *Symmes' Theory of the Concentric Spheres,* struck a chord with large audiences and eventually helped influence Congress, in 1836, to appropriate $300,000 for an ambitious voyage toward the South Pole.

Two years later, Edgar Allan Poe, apparently influenced by Symmes's hollow-earth theories, published a strange and fantastical novel called *The Narrative of Arthur Gordon Pym of Nantucket.* In Poe's narrative, the eponymous main character sails to unexplored Antarctic regions and passes through an ice barrier only to emerge in a warm polar sea, where he encounters an island inhabited by a lost race of humans.

Still, throughout the nineteenth century, most of the action and most of the literature pertaining to the Open Polar Sea remained fixed on the Arctic. The theory's most indefatigable proponent was Sir John Barrow, the longtime second secretary of the British Admiralty. Throughout the first half of the 1800s, Barrow sent numerous expeditions into the waters around Greenland and Baffin Island to prove the Open Polar Sea's existence, or at least to find some seasonally ice-free route—a Northwest Passage—over the top of Canada that would lead to the Pacific.

The largest and most famous of the voyages promoted by Barrow was the Franklin expedition of 1845. Captain John Franklin and his crew set sail from England in two absurdly well-provisioned vessels, the *Terror* and the *Erebus.* After making stops along the coast of Greenland, Franklin and his men—129, all told—ventured into the unknown. They were never heard from again. Although numerous search expeditions were launched in the late 1840s and early 1850s, the mystery of what happened to Franklin remained unsolved, and it endured as an international cause célèbre for decades. One of the leading ideas was that Franklin and his men were still sailing around in the Open Polar Sea—unable to find a way out.

In 1853, a swashbuckling American explorer named Elisha Kent Kane launched an expedition with the dual purpose of rescuing Franklin and finding the Open Polar Sea. The following year, while pushing along the northwest coast of Greenland, members of Kane's party came upon what appeared to be open ocean. In fact, it was only a small, seasonal gap in the ice pack, but Kane felt sure his team had made an epic discovery.

"Seals were sporting and waterfowl feeding in this open sea," he later wrote. "Its waves came rolling in, and dashing with measured tread, like the majestic billows of [an] old ocean, against the shore. Solitude, the cold and boundless expanse, and the mysterious heavings of its green waters, lent their charm to the scene." Kane said that laying eyes on the Open Polar Sea "was well calculated to arouse emotions of the highest order . . . I do not believe there was a man among us who did not long for the means of entering upon its bright and lonely waters." Maps later published on the basis of the Kane expedition's reports depicted an "OPEN SEA" labeled in unequivocal bold letters, stretching across the pole.

In 1860, another American explorer, Dr. Isaac Israel Hayes, led an Arctic expedition up the coast of Ellesmere Island, where he, too, thought he glimpsed Kane's Open Polar Sea. "The sea about the North Pole," Hayes reported, "must lie within the ice belt known to invest it." But by the time Hayes returned to the United States, the Civil War had ignited and no one seemed much interested in his claims.

The Open Polar Sea idea took a bit of a hiatus, yet the notion of a hollow planet with vents in the Arctic gained new currency with the publication, in 1864, of Jules Verne's fantasy novel *Journey to the Center of the Earth*. In Verne's story, the protagonist, a German professor named Otto Lidenbrock, drops into the crater of a dormant volcano in Iceland and soon encounters a warm subterranean sea whose shores are populated with mastodon herds and a giant proto-human creature that might be described as the missing link. In literature, at least, the concept of the polar sea had moved underground.

AFTER THE CIVIL WAR, American public interest in the theory slowly rekindled. Charles Francis Hall believed in the Open Polar Sea with an almost religious fervor, but the abject failure of his expedition caused many to doubt the sanity of flinging even more men and ships at a fanciful abstraction. Silas Bent's theories, however, injected new life into the argument: Maybe the Open Polar Sea existed after all. Maybe it was just that explorers like Hall had chosen the wrong route and had encountered the ice in an infelicitous place. They had not understood that powerful warm-water currents could do the hard work for them.

And so, with Bent's new theory, the centuries-old obsession with the Open Polar Sea was given one last reprieve. All Bent's hypothesis needed was a young explorer who was bold enough to test it.

Bent had written a letter (quoted in the *Putnam's* article) to the president of the American Geographical Society of New York in which he drove home his point. The Gulf Stream and the Kuro Siwo, Bent said, "are the only practicable avenues" by which ships can reach the Open Polar Sea and, from there, sail to the North Pole. A future voyager would simply have to follow one of these two currents to the precise place where it meets the ice; here he would find the ice cap softened and weakened by the steady pulsing warmth of a tropical sea-river—and there he could pass through a slushy portal that would lead straight to the Open Polar Sea. Bent had an intriguing name for this theoretical portal; he called it the Thermometric Gateway to the Pole.

Putnam's rhapsodized that "a great and solid mind has successfully bridged this polar chasm." The article cried out for a young man like De Long to come along and prove the soundness of Bent's ideas. "This profound and beautiful hypothesis may boast no sanction of high authority, nor count as its advocate any Arctic explorer. For a while, it may have to rest its claims on deductions of science, and be ushered into notice on the quiet authority of mathematical calculation."

But eventually some challenger would come along, some Arctic hero, to find the "Thermometric Gateway" and pursue the grail. From the standpoint of pure discovery, the prize could not have been any richer, nor the stakes any higher. "Who shall say," *Putnam's* concluded, "that within the Arctic circle, there may not yet be found some vestige of humanity—some fragment of our race, wafted thither by these mighty currents we have heard of, whose cry of welcome is yet to greet the mariner who finds them, and amongst whom there may be found some of God's elect?"

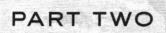

PART TWO

The National Genius

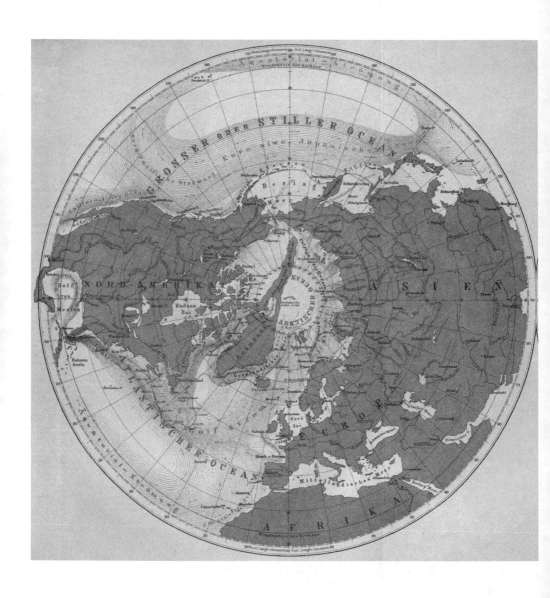

6 · The Engine of the World

Throughout the first week of July 1876, the week of America's hundredth birthday, the nation's attentions were focused on Philadelphia. Not only was the City of Brotherly Love the place where the Declaration of Independence had been signed a century earlier; the city was hosting a world's fair, which, on this sultry summer week, was drawing hundreds of thousands of visitors from around the globe. The Centennial Exhibition, host to thirty-seven nations, was situated on a campus of nearly four hundred acres in Fairmount Park, across the Schuylkill River from Philadelphia. It was America's first world exposition, and by summer's end nearly ten million people would have come to gawk at the nearly thirty thousand exhibits nestled inside the fair's 250 pavilions and halls. The grounds were so sprawling that a newly devised elevated rail system—an early type of monorail—was used to shuttle crowds back and forth between two of the most popular buildings.

The crowds had come to be dazzled, and they were not disappointed. Among the many new creations on display were the Remington typewriter, an intricate stringed apparatus called a Calculating Machine, and a curious gizmo that a bearded Scotsman named Alexander Graham Bell was calling his "telephone." (Bell would read from Hamlet's soliloquy at one end of the hall, and attendees at the other could plainly hear the inventor's voice issuing from a little speaker. "My God, it talks!" exclaimed one prominent visitor, Emperor Dom Pedro of Brazil.)

All summer the exposition had been the talk of the land. James Gordon Bennett had been to the fair several times, and he'd made sure his best reporters stayed in Philadelphia to work the grounds and cover the comings and goings of dignitaries from around the world—the lords and monarchs, the authors and artists, the scientists and railroad magnates. The *Herald* ran Centennial Exposition stories every day—in fact, by special arrangement, thousands of copies of Bennett's paper were printed on an enormous press right on the grounds. Young entrepreneurs like George Westinghouse and George Eastman could be seen at the centennial, hungrily prowling the exhibits for ideas cross-fertilized with other ideas. The twenty-nine-year-old Thomas Edison was there, too, showcasing a strange little device called the electric pen. Another brilliant American inventor, Moses Farmer, drew crowds with his electric dynamo, which he used to power a set of artificial lights—called arc lamps—that blazed through the Philadelphia night.

There were other puzzlements and oddities. At the Japanese pavilion, a miraculously fast-growing pea plant called *kudzu* was unveiled to an unsuspecting Western world. Elsewhere, the crowds could gaze upon new works by Rodin, listen to concerts played on the world's largest pipe organ, or marvel at the immense handheld torch of Frédéric-Auguste Bartholdi's Lady Liberty (the rest of her was still under construction in France). It was here, at the Centennial Exhibition, that the American masses were introduced to a new condiment called Heinz ketchup, to a fizzy sassafras concoction sold under the name Hires Root Beer, and to the perfect novelty of a tropical fruit, served in foil with a fork, known as a *banana*.

BY FAR THE most popular attraction of the exposition, however, was Machinery Hall, a cavernous greenhouse structure that covered fourteen acres—nearly three times the square footage of St. Peter's Basilica at Vatican City. The hall was a temple to machines of all kinds, and it thrummed and whirred and whined with the operation of countless pumps, turbines, generators, lathes, saws, and ingenious new fixtures of tool-and-die equipment. The floor was packed with aisle after aisle of inventions—most of them American, many of them revolutionary. There was, for example, the Line-Wolf Ammonia Compressor, a contraption for making ice. There was the Brayton Ready Motor, a practical early prototype of the internal combustion engine. There was a seven-thousand-pound pendulum clock manu-factured by Seth Thomas that was calibrated to control twenty-six other clocks interspersed throughout the hall. There were new kinds of locomotive brakes, new kinds of elevators, and improved versions of the rotary cylinder press.

But the most extraordinary thing about Machinery Hall was the great motor that powered everything else. The Grand Central Engine, sometimes simply called the Centennial Steam Engine, was the larg-est engine in the world. Weighing more than 650 tons, constructed by the brilliant American engineer George Corliss, it supplied free steam power, via a network of underground shafts totaling a mile in length, to the more than eight thousand smaller machines on display throughout the hall.

On the fair's opening day in May, surrounded by crowds of more than 150,000 people, President Ulysses S. Grant had tugged on a lever that set the behemoth in motion. As it sprang to life, the immense engine gave off a purr that seemed to emanate from the soul of the thing itself—a correspondent for *Scientific American* described it as a "murmuring sound . . . what may aptly be called mechanical music." The machine dwarfed the president. Standing more than five stories high, parked on a platform in the center of the gargantuan hall, it was a living sculpture of plunging arms, nodding cranks, and fine-toothed gears. Its flywheel alone, turning at a stately thirty-six revolutions per minute, weighed fifty-six tons.

Over the summer, the Grand Central Engine had proved to be the sentimental favorite of the crowds and, in some eloquent way, had come to symbolize the exposition itself. It was, said *Scientific Ameri-can,* the fair's "great pulsating iron heart." On the day he visited, Walt Whitman sat down in front of the elegant monstrosity and stared at it for a half hour without uttering a word. The author William Dean Howells called it "an athlete of steel" and thought that it was through new machine creations like this that "the national genius most freely speaks."

Writing in the *Atlantic Monthly,* Howells noted how "the mighty walking-beams plunge their pistons downward, the enormous fly-wheel revolves with a hoarded power that makes all tremble, the hundred life-like details do their office with unerring intelligence." The polished colossus was so perfect in its design that it practically ran itself. "In the midst of this ineffably strong mechanism," Howells said, "is a chair where the engineer sits reading his newspaper, as in a peaceful bower. Now and then he lays down his paper and clambers up one of the stairways that cover the framework, and touches some irritated spot on the giant's body with a drop of oil, and goes down again and takes up his newspaper."

Visitors from other countries were enchanted by the technological prowess marshaled in Machinery Hall—and, specifically, in the Corliss engine. Something was happening in America, some new energy, an efflorescence of native talent. An American style of manufacturing seemed to be emerging—one that relied on automation, on interchangeable parts, on machine-made machines that fed still *other* machines. The *Times* of London gushed, "The American invents as the Greek sculpted and the Italian painted: it is genius." Other English observers struck notes of quiet despair. "If we are to be judged by the comparison with the Americans in 1876," a prominent British engineer named John Anderson wrote in an official report on the Centennial Exhibition, "it would be to confirm . . . that we are losing our former leadership and it is passing to the Americans."

ONE OF THE most distinguished visitors at the Centennial Exposition that sweltering week in July was a German professor named August Petermann. Although Petermann was arguably the most famous and most eminent geographer in all the world, he had traveled little throughout his hermit's life, and he had never been to America before. On a trip up and down the Eastern Seaboard, he spent ten days in Philadelphia, wandering through all the exhibition pavilions—and he was stunned and exhilarated by what he saw. The Centennial Exhibition was, he thought, "a grand achievement, eclipsing all former expositions in Europe. Here can be clearly seen what position the United States holds in the culture of the world."

Herr Doktor August Heinrich Petermann was a grave, introverted man with small hands, wire-rimmed spectacles, and a full trim beard. He usually wore a formal dress coat with tails, accompanied by a silk vest and a cravat. Fifty-four years old, he had a jeweler's eyes, tiny and hard, and he moved and conversed with an exactitude that many found intimidating. A polymath in the Humboldtian tradition, he could hold forth, with grandiose argumentation, on just about any topic of world science. Beneath his controlled exterior, though, he was a bit of a hothead, and had long suffered from bouts of manic depression. At times a yearning sentimentality weighed upon his face, a tug of melancholy, a Weltschmerz. He constantly fell into quarrels, the ardor of his views sharpened by the fact that he often carried a small revolver in his vest pocket. Petermann spoke impeccable English but with a slight British accent, for he had lived for many years in London, where he been a powerful, if controversial, member of the Royal Geographical Society. He had worked at the Royal Greenwich Observatory and had briefly served as the "physical geographer and engraver in stone" to Queen Victoria herself.

In the 1850s, Petermann had returned to his native Thuringia, in the forest-mantled heartland of Germany. It was there, in the tranquil medieval city of Gotha, that he had created a geographical institute that published the world's most meticulous and beautiful maps. His operation was run like a finely calibrated machine, respected by scientists and adventurers around the globe. Among other projects, he was editor of the influential monthly journal *Petermanns Geographische Mitteilungen,* which published the latest maps and articles from the front lines of exploration.

The Sage of Gotha, as Petermann was widely known, had a reputation as one of the world's leading "theoretical cartographers." Which is to say, he concerned himself with those few remaining voids on the planet that were still unknown, places man had never touched or described. He viewed it as his personal and professional responsibility to fill in those holes, bit by bit. Petermann made a habit of systematically interviewing explorers fresh from, say, the African bush or the Australian outback, and after synthesizing their reports and field maps, he and his armies of cartographers were able to shade in the planet's gaps with a little more detail. J. G. Bartholomew, the eminent British cartographer, wrote of Petermann's passion for terra incognita, "The filling up of the blank spaces of the unknown in his maps had such a fascination for him that rest seemed impossible to him while any country remained unexplored."

No place captivated Petermann more powerfully than the Arctic. For decades, in both England and Germany, he had agitated for Arctic exploration. He wrote dozens of academic treatises and delivered countless speeches on the topic. He believed that an understanding of the North Pole was central to understanding the larger workings of the planet—its currents, its winds, its systems of heat regulation, its subterranean tumults, its geomagnetic aberrations. The pole was the linchpin, the master key to solving greater mysteries. "Without a knowledge of the North Pole," he wrote, "all geographical knowledge remains fragmentary."

Petermann was probably the world's most vocal and indefatigable advocate of the Open Polar Sea theory. He was quite sure that somewhere beyond the moving "girdle" of Arctic pack, explorers would find what he called a "polar basin" filled with relatively warm water. Indeed, his own company's maps of the Arctic clearly showed an iceless pole. "The ice pack as a whole forms a mobile belt on whose polar side the sea is more or less ice free," he argued. "Ships that break through this ice belt will find a navigable sea in the highest latitudes and to the pole itself." It was a question of locating the right gateway, the perfect portal, through the ice. Attaining the pole, he insisted, would be a "very easy, trivial thing. A suitable steamship, at the right time of year, could carry out a trip to the North Pole and back in two to three months."

Petermann was a big believer in the role steam engines would play in reaching the polar basin. Eventually, he felt, breakthroughs in technology would lead to an engine powerful and efficient enough to send a ship through the pack and into the Open Polar Sea beyond. This was one of the reasons Petermann was so mesmerized by the might and mastery on display at Machinery Hall. The hum of George Corliss's Centennial Steam Engine was music to the German professor's ears. Americans, it seemed, now had the technology to produce a motor that could propel mankind to the North Pole.

WHEN IT CAME to the Arctic, Petermann had given up on the British. English explorers, refusing to heed his theories, had stubbornly tried to penetrate the Arctic by way of the west coast of Greenland, only to meet with hardships and disasters he easily could have predicted. In recent years, Petermann had placed all his Arctic hopes on his own recently unified nation. In 1868, and then again in 1869, he had personally organized and championed two ambitious German-led expeditions that sought to reach the pole by way of the east coast of Greenland, a route he felt sure would provide a more favorable gateway to the "polar basin." (Petermann himself did not venture on these voyages; he preferred to direct the odyssey from his study in his villa at Gotha.)

The two German expeditions, though heroic efforts, met with

limited success. Still, Petermann clamored for his countrymen to make further pushes into the Arctic. By the early 1870s, however, cash-strapped Germany had begun to quail at the costs and risks of the whole Arctic enterprise.

But after his week at the Centennial Exposition, Petermann was certain that the Americans were next in line to lead bold thrusts into the Arctic. Petermann had followed the *Polaris* expedition closely, and where others saw disaster, he saw promise. "The Americans have eclipsed all other nations in Polar research," he wrote. The British, he said, have "talked loudly for nine years, criticizing all other endeavors and opinions, while doing nothing themselves." In the wake of the *Polaris* expedition, Petermann called on America to lead an ambitious new voyage into the Arctic. Such "high-toned acts of the United States government," he said, "would shame the British into silence."

"America," he declared, "has given the names of Kane, Hayes, and Hall to the roll of Arctic heroes, and I am sure others will follow."

The polar project would entail enormous risks, he admitted. There was no getting around the fact that men would probably die in the process of reaching the pole, but the benefits to society made such a hazard worthwhile. Sacrifice for the sake of discovery was infinitely more rewarding to humanity than sacrifice in battlefield trenches. "I hardly believe that this great work will be brought to its conclusion without the loss of ships and human lives," he wrote. "[But] why should thousands of noble lives be slaughtered only in inhumane wars? Is not such a great affair also worth a few lives?"

Petermann could not understand why the same European societies that freely endorsed ambitious exploratory tromps through the malarial jungles of Africa could not countenance the periodic deaths of their adventurous sons in the High Arctic. If anything, he insisted, the polar regions were far safer than the Dark Continent. "For decades," he said, "our explorers, one after the other, have let themselves be slaughtered in the interiors of the most dangerous continents, especially Africa, perhaps by fanatical inhabitants, perhaps by the deadly climate, while such dangers and sacrifice occur with Arctic expeditions, at the most, only as rare exceptions."

But everything Petermann had seen in America—and especially in Philadelphia—had convinced him that the United States had the national nerve for this endeavor. After attending the Centennial Exposition, Petermann visited Washington, Baltimore, and the Naval Academy at Annapolis. He toured Boston, various towns in

New England, and then Niagara Falls. Everywhere he went, he was celebrated. The country's leading scientists feted him. In Washington, he met with the presidential candidate Rutherford B. Hayes, and officials threw a formal reception. Reporters followed him and quoted his pronouncements at length. His American tour was like a victory lap at the end of a prestigious career. It was all a pleasant surprise: Petermann had not realized he had such an adoring public in the United States.

ON JULY 10, Petermann was invited to speak before the American Geographical Society in New York. The event was held at Chickering Hall, at the corner of Fifth Avenue and Eighteenth Street. The auditorium was oppressively hot and humid—a historic heat wave was suffocating the Northeast—and yet crowds came in droves to see the famous German. "I was almost killed by the heat," Petermann later said. A classical organist played a short concert, and then Petermann took the stage.

He could not say enough about this extraordinary nation and its raw energy, and he thanked his hosts for their many kindnesses. "I am altogether most happy that I have lived to see this great country and people," he began. He was impressed by Washington, D.C. The capital, he said, had been "built on a magnificent plan, and the extent of its squares and parks surpass those of any other city in the world." He especially loved New York, where he had been staying in the plush Brevoort Hotel. "This city," he said, "and especially its Broadway, appears to me a kind of prime meridian, where two worlds meet, the eastern and the western."

When he visited Annapolis, Dr. Petermann happened to be at the Naval Academy during graduation, and he was thrilled by the sight of the happy midshipmen collecting their diplomas and tossing their caps in the air. He was convinced that America would one day have a powerful navy—a navy that would play a role not only in war but also in peacetime exploration. "When I learned at Annapolis that only one man-of-war is in service now," he said, "it struck me how essentially a country of peace this mighty nation is."

August Petermann would be returning to Germany soon, but he would arrive a changed man. "All my expectations have been surpassed," he said. "All I have seen has filled me with admiration." The United States was now, he thought, the new engine driving the world.

It was "at the head of any human progress and culture that may be found on the globe. This is a highly favored and rich country, a land of wonderful natural capabilities."

Then, alluding to the wondrous Centennial Exposition, he concluded: "I wish you and this country the same progress and prosperity as has marked your first one hundred years."

7 · SATISFACTION

J ames Gordon Bennett Jr. liked to give the impression that he had sprung fully formed into the world—an original creature, with no past, no allegiances, indebted to no one. But to understand his extraordinary place in the social milieu of New York, as well as in the rough-and-tumble world of American newspapers, one has to reach back and recognize the equally extraordinary career of his father, James Gordon Bennett Sr.

Bennett the Elder was a dour, bookish man who had immigrated to the United States from Scotland in 1819 and, through a combination of shrewd business instincts and a nearly masochistic work ethic, managed to found the *Herald* sixteen years later. From the start, he wanted his penny paper to be "impudent and intrusive," and at that he more than succeeded. His attacks on politicians and businessmen were so scathing that he frequently incurred death threats, and he was beaten in the streets on several occasions. He received a bomb in the mail. One enemy tried to drown him. But adversity only egged Bennett on. He was fearless, and he loved playing the role of a bothersome Jeremiah. His paper named names, and his reporters freely ventured into the city's vice-ridden netherworlds. In 1836, he drew outrage for his front-page coverage of the brutal hatchet murder of a prostitute; for this salacious story, he had conducted what is generally regarded as the first full-length interview ever published in a newspaper. (Genteel sensibilities were especially offended by the fact that he had interviewed the victim's madam.)

While the financial pages of rival papers often turned a blind eye to shenanigans on Wall Street, Bennett Sr.'s *Herald* regularly published investigations into the latest stock market frauds and scams. A speculator named A. A. Clason, incensed by a particularly hard-hitting piece that had run in the *Herald,* ambushed Bennett in the street and lashed him with a horsewhip. Bennett's biographer reported that "the whip broke at the first blow, however, and fell to the sidewalk; Bennett politely picked up the pieces and handed them to his assailant."

Bennett the Elder was the city's most notorious grump, and he certainly looked the part: Prematurely gray, he was a slouching, badly cross-eyed man with a beak of a nose and a craggy face that danced with nervous tics. His distressing appearance once got him kicked out of a bordello—the girls, chasing him from their establishment, told him (or so he later claimed): "You are too ugly a rascal to come amongst us."

Bennett's paper was as sought after as he was shunned. The *Herald* soon grew to be the largest-circulation daily in America. As its sole owner, he became a multimillionaire, though his money did nothing to gain him entry into New York social circles. Bennett remained a pariah, blackballed from the best clubs and salons. But what did he care? "American Society," he boasted, "consists of the people who don't invite me to their parties."

Bennett Sr.'s views were never tepid on any subject. He was, for example, a vigorous opponent of women's rights—"motherhood is the best cure for the mania," he said, "and we would recommend it to all who are afflicted." His outlook on life was unencumbered by even a trace of altruism. "Lofty editorials and public-spirited crusades, in his view, were a lot of nonsense," observed one biographer. "All men were selfish, greedy, and intrinsically worthless; the human condition could never be bettered, certainly not through the medium of journalism." Instead, Bennett busied himself solely with "getting out the liveliest sheet in town and watching his acumen reflected in the balance sheets, the circulation tallies, and the advertising revenues."

One day in 1840, however, Bennett suddenly felt the tug of an unfamiliar emotion: *love.* He became smitten with an Irishwoman, half his age, named Henrietta Crean. A fashionable social climber who was fluent in at least six languages, Miss Crean taught piano and elocution and was widely described as one of the most elegant young women in New York. Bennett certainly thought she was; he fairly gushed about her in the pages of his own paper, noting that her "figure is most magnificent—her head, neck, and bust, of the purest classic contour."

No one thought it possible, but Bennett had fallen head over heels. They were soon married, and in May 1841, a boy, James Gordon Bennett Jr., was born. (The *Herald*'s nemesis, the New York *Sun*, duly noted the arrival but insisted that the handsome child could not be Bennett's.) Although three more children were born in quick succession, only one, a lovely daughter named Jeannette, survived past early childhood.

Henrietta Bennett hated her role as the trophy wife of the most controversial misanthrope in American publishing. One day in November 1850, while she and her husband were out for a stroll down Broadway, Bennett was assailed by a gang of vigilantes led by a man named John Graham, whose run for district attorney Bennett had opposed. Henrietta watched in horror as her husband was beaten nearly to death in the street, while a pair of policemen standing nearby failed to intervene. After Bennett's recovery, Henrietta informed him that she was finished with New York. She had no taste for her husband's tempestuous, ink-stained life and thought it was no world for their children to grow up in. She collected young James and Jeannette and decamped to Paris; except for a few brief visits, she never came back. Bennett effectively returned to his ways as a crotchety bachelor, running his paper alone.

James and Jeannette thus grew up as expatriates—raised by an indulgent Irish mother, taught by the best French tutors, and sheltered by an ocean from the grim, hard man who made their lavish existence possible.

AS JAMES BECAME a teenager, he made more frequent trips back to the New York to be with his father. Bennett Sr. wanted his son to take over the paper eventually, so he gave him a desk and at least the appearance of a few responsibilities. But the princeling had no interest in journalism—or work of any kind. He had discovered that the world of New York high society, which had shunned his father, warmly embraced him, and he began to run with a fast crowd. He became admired, said an editor of the *Sun,* as "the beau ideal of the man of the world and all around daredevil." An early biographer remarked that "it would take an Arabian Night's volume to chronicle all the mad doings of the young man and his 'set.'" When he wasn't frequenting taverns and fleshpots, he spent most of his time on yachts, and he proved to be a formidable, if reckless, sailor. His father built him his own yacht, the *Henrietta,* in 1860, and James began to sail it competitively, winning races in both America and England.

When the Civil War broke out, James wanted to serve in the Union Navy, even though he had no naval training. When that proved impossible, he effectively bought himself an officership in the U.S. Revenue Cutter Service, in which he was commissioned as a "third lieutenant" and served on his own donated yacht, the *Henrietta.* He patrolled Long Island and then participated in the naval blockade off the coast of Florida. Bennett's service to his country proved short-lived, but it helped forge a close relationship between the *Herald* and the U.S. Navy that would last for decades.

In 1866, Bennett won the first transoceanic yacht race, sailing the *Henrietta* from Sandy Hook, New Jersey, to the Isle of Wight in thirteen days, twenty-one hours, and fifty-five minutes. When he wasn't on the high seas, Bennett began to show much more interest in the *Herald,* and later that same year, the ailing elder Bennett turned the paper's reins over to his son. (Bennett Sr. died in 1872 at the age of seventy-six.)

From the start, Bennett Jr. was a tyrannical and thoroughly unpredictable boss. "I am the only reader of this paper," he often told his editors. "I am the only one to be pleased." But his instincts for a good story were nearly pitch-perfect, and the circulation of the *Herald* increased dramatically. Unlike his miserly father, Bennett Jr. was willing to spend huge sums of money to gather the news, and he sent his reporters farther and farther afield to do it. In 1869, he came up with the idea of sending a reporter to search for David Livingstone in Africa, and he is said to have dispatched young Henry Morton Stanley with an almost laughably laconic command: "Find Livingstone." Stanley did, of course, and the exclusives he sent back expanded the *Herald*'s circulation even further.

Bennett was unlike any other publisher in the world. A playboy, a breakneck sportsman, and an absolute autocrat, he had a high-wire management style that drove reporters crazy but often spurred them to find extraordinary stories under impossible deadline pressures. Somehow the whole delicate construction worked, and under Bennett's incomparable personality, the *New York Herald* became the most interesting and influential newspaper in America, if not the world. One reporter and editor who labored under Bennett for many years compared working at the *Herald* to serving in the French Foreign Legion: "There was something compelling about the tigerish proprietor with his fickleness and brutality. Women are said to be fascinated by such characters. Certainly, newspaper men were."

IN THE MIDST of a snowfall on New Year's Day 1877, James Gordon Bennett Jr. pulled his sleigh up to 44 West Nineteenth Street, told his coachman to wait for him, and then staggered up the stairs to join the holiday party that was well under way at his fiancée's house. The rumors that had been buzzing around New York were true: James Bennett, after a history of dalliances with stage girls and women of questionable repute, had finally fallen in love and was engaged to be married to a proper debutante. The nuptials were scheduled to take place in just a few weeks.

The lucky lady was Caroline May, the daughter of a prominent doctor who lived in Baltimore, summered in Newport, and kept this fine town house in Manhattan. Caroline was described as "a slender, fair-haired girl with a proud tilt to her chin" and, according to another account, was a woman of "unusual beauty . . . noted for charm and daring." She must have been extraordinary, for she had managed to accomplish something many New Yorkers thought impossible. Wrote one biographer: "Jimmy Bennett, veteran of fleshpots, terror of polite society, naked coachman, reckless polo player, high-living and free-spending clubman, was about to be tamed by domesticity."

For as long as anyone could remember, fashionable Knickerbockers had observed a tradition of "calling" on New Year's Day. Families would hitch up their horses and sleighs and, amid a happy din of song and jangling harness bells, move about the city, attending open-house parties where the brandy and bourbon eggnog flowed freely. These gatherings were "the excuse for much drunkenness," one Bennett contemporary later wrote. Bennett had been "calling" all day, and by four in the afternoon, as he rapped on the Mays' front door, he was well into his cups.

Bennett was welcomed into the warm parlor and, with his accustomed alacrity, made his way to the bar. He was always delighted to be at the May home, and the Mays seemed happy to have him for a future son-in-law. Caroline had become a close friend of Bennett's younger sister, Jeannette, which further solidified the bond.

By all accounts Bennett loved Caroline, and his intentions to marry her appeared genuine. The previous summer, the social pages of the newspapers had noted that in Newport she'd "had the seat of honor" on the box of his carriage and that he often took her out on his yacht. In New York, the couple was frequently seen at the opera, at dinner parties, and at the theater.

"The match was regarded a brilliant one by the young lady's friends," noted one newspaper, "[and] the friends of Mr. Bennett and his father were equally pleased." At Caroline's request, Bennett had ordered an elaborate trousseau of clothes, jewelry, and linens from the finest shops in Paris, and when the shipment arrived in New York, customs officials reportedly charged him $9,000 in duties. The wedding was to be a small, private affair, after which Bennett and his new bride would board the steamer *Russia* and sail for Europe, where an extensive newlywed tour had been arranged.

On this festive first day of the New Year, the wedding plans remained intact. Yet there seemed a part of Bennett that was not ready to settle down. He had doubts about matrimony, even if he had no doubts about Caroline. Several times during their engagement, she had been forced to break things off when Bennett drank too much and scampered away with his sporting friends, pulling off some idiotic and thoroughly embarrassing stunt. One gossip columnist asserted that Bennett was liable "at any moment to go on a spree" and observed that liquor had a way of "intensifying his impulsiveness . . . and deadening the many noble qualities of head and heart which characterize him when he is 'himself.' "

Still, hope sprang eternal within certain social circles. One New York society columnist noted optimistically that it "had been some time" since Bennett went on a bender and that he seemed "so assiduous in his attentions to his fiancée that all his friends began to hope this time there would be a marriage."

Now Bennett barged into the drawing room of the May home and greeted Caroline, her parents, and her several sisters. The room was also packed with many of Bennett's friends from the Union Club, and there was much teasing and backslapping as he circulated among them. A fire crackled in one corner, and a grand piano sat in another, with carolers gathered around. Bennett made some ribald comments, and when a servant proffered a tray of fortified punch, helped himself to another drink.

About this time Bennett took full leave of his senses. Standing beside the grand piano, he unbuttoned his trousers and, in plain view of the guests, began to relieve himself, arcing a stream into the innards of the instrument. (Other accounts say he pissed into the fireplace.) Whatever the case, Bennett clearly felt it was time to "pump out the bilge," as one chronicler put it, and he had no compunction about doing so inside a high society salon. "Bennett forgot where he was," a *Herald* editor wrote years later, "and became guilty of conduct unbecoming a gentleman—or any one else."

The drawing room was suddenly plunged in chaos. Genteel guests recoiled in horror and bolted from the scene. Women screamed and swooned—or feigned swooning. As Bennett shook off, a clutch of his friends encircled him and demanded to know what in God's name he was doing. He seemed oblivious to the enormity of his offense, even when two strong men briskly escorted him out of the May residence and tossed him into the street, beside his waiting sleigh.

IT WAS NOT until the next morning, when he had sobered up, that Bennett began to fathom what he had done. The May family sent a message informing him that, once again, the engagement was off—and this time, for good. When he wandered over to the Union Club, he detected a new coolness of tone among his chums. On the streets, passersby cut him awkward glances. People throughout the city expected Bennett to misbehave in colorful, outlandish ways, but this time he had gone too far.

Bennett must have sensed this, yet he was too proud to issue an apology to the May family or make amends with Caroline. Perhaps he did not believe he had done anything wrong. What business was it of anyone else's how and where James Gordon Bennett Jr. chose to empty his bladder? He lay low for a day in his house, causing a few of his rival papers to surmise that he had left town—the *Sun* reported that he had "fled to Canada."

But the scandal did not die down. On January 3, Bennett walked out of the Union Club after lunch and was just about to step into his waiting sleigh on Fifth Avenue when he was menaced by a dark figure standing at the curb. It was Frederick May, Caroline's brother, up from Baltimore. A stout man of twenty-six, May was an old-fashioned southerner who believed in chivalry and family honor. He had come to avenge the public disgrace of the May household (not to mention the May piano) and to restore his sister's good name.

May brandished a horsewhip and commenced to flog Bennett with it. At first Bennett put up no fight. May kept at it, knocking Bennett to the ground and beating him nearly senseless. There was a strange déjà vu about the scene—it was just like the old *Herald* days, when Bennett's father had been on the receiving end of many a public thrashing.

"Why don't you kill me while you are about it and get it over with?" Bennett eventually managed to say. He grappled with his assailant and wrestled him to the ground. By now, the windows of the Union Club were befogged by eager spectators. For a minute or so, the two men rolled around together, pummeling each other until "blood stained the snow from the sidewalk to the gutter," as one newspaper put it.

Eventually a few Union Club members dashed down to the street and disentangled the grunting opponents. May took off down Fifth Avenue, while Bennett crawled onto his sleigh, holding his jaw and grimacing in pain, with a nasty gash across the bridge of his nose.

The nose was the least of his injuries. Bennett's pride smarted terribly, and for the next few days, he stewed in his own juices. Then he devised a solution to his discomfort, one that he knew his southern opponent could well appreciate. Jeannette, who was staying with her brother at the family mansion on Fifth Avenue, tearfully tried to intervene, but it was no use. Bennett's mind was made up: He was going to challenge May to a duel.

The messenger Bennett sent to throw down the gauntlet was his friend Charles Longfellow, son of the great poet. May told Longfellow he would accept Bennett's challenge, and a secret location was decided upon along the border between Maryland and Delaware, near a place called Slaughter's Gap. The duel would take place on January 7.

BY 1877, DUELING was illegal everywhere in the United States and, indeed, was widely considered an archaic, if not barbaric, custom. Bennett and May both knew that any district attorney who got wind of the affair would prosecute to the fullest; whoever emerged alive from the episode would likely face a lengthy jail sentence. So it was agreed that the details of the duel would be held in absolute secrecy.

Traveling under assumed names, the two contestants and their retinues—including surgeons—took a train to a rural stop called Slaughter's Station, then set out on foot over the snowy ground. The cover story they used to reassure suspicious locals was that they were officials dispatched by the Pennsylvania Railroad to scout a new spur line. After an hour they came to a secluded pasture that straddled the border between the two states, not far from the musky banks of the Choptank River. A lookout was posted on the surrounding high ground to ensure that the dueling parties had not been followed.

At about two o'clock, the two men removed their overcoats and took their positions, twenty paces apart. Each man selected and loaded his pistol, while their seconds stood alongside, issuing words of encouragement. May had come dressed in dark clothes, but his second, thinking that black would stand out in bold relief against the snow, gave him a light-colored jacket to slip on. A story in the New York *World* later reported that May stood sideways, with his back to the wind, and covered his flank with his pistol arm, holding his elbow against his hip—while Mr. Bennett "gave full front, which exposed him to more danger, but enabled him to take better aim."

"Are you ready?" an attendant called out, and when the contestants nodded their assent, he gave the count: "One, two, three . . . *fire!*" The two men raised their weapons and took aim.

Precisely what happened next is disputed, but the likeliest version is that May pulled the trigger first. His pistol apparently misfired (although some accounts say he deliberately aimed into the air). This left Bennett the opportunity to take his time and aim with the utmost deliberation. A few tense moments passed—witnesses thought Bennett, his mustache quivering and bristling, seemed tremendously nervous. He is said to have felt a pang of mercy for his vulnerable opponent. He fired, but his ball only nicked May, striking him a few inches below the shoulder of his pistol arm. The wound was just serious enough for May's surgeon to declare it "disabling." Fred May could not continue the duel.

Bennett and May both declared their "satisfaction," and that was it—the affair was over. Both parties were relieved by this most fortunate outcome, but the two men did not shake hands or even speak to each other as they shuffled back toward the train tracks in the snow.

Along the way, Bennett fell in with his second, Dr. Charles Phelps. "Well, Doctor," he asked. "Do you think I did right?"

"I would have been very sorry to have killed any man who was at my mercy," Dr. Phelps replied. Then, seeing the hideous swollen scar across Bennett's nose, he added, "But I would have been terribly tempted to wing him."

May reportedly was taken to an uncle's home in Maryland, where a physician soon gave him a clean bill of health. Bennett and his party checked into a nearby inn and ordered many pitchers of beer. His *Herald* did not cover the duel, but the *New York Times* carried several reports—one of which happily noted that the matter had ended "amicably" and that "both parties left the field evidently in high spirits at the pleasant conclusion of what promised to be a bloody tragedy." Neither man, asserted the *Times,* was seriously hurt "as to life, limb, or digestion."

THE BENNETT-MAY AFFAIR has been called the last formal duel fought in the United States. If that claim seems doubtful, certainly it was *one* of the last, and, because of the prominence of the individuals involved, it drew a great deal of scrutiny across the nation and the world. Law enforcement officials in several states investigated the incident but could not find enough evidence to prosecute; all the eyewitnesses kept to their vow of secrecy. Dr. Phelps even went to jail for his refusal to testify before a grand jury assembled by the New York district attorney. Members of the two dueling parties, hoping to downplay matters and thus throw prosecutors off the scent, anonymously floated to the press a version in which May had not been injured at all—and this was the story that generally stuck.

Still, when Bennett returned to New York, he found that his blunder at the May house was neither forgotten nor forgiven, and his having fought a duel in its aftermath only added a legal dimension to the snickering notoriety of a social crime. He was now persona non grata, just as his father once had been, though for very different reasons. Fifth Avenue hostesses decided that they "did not care to entertain a fellow who apparently had not been housebroken," said one Bennett biographer.

Bennett's reaction to being ostracized was curious, or perhaps it was just Bennettesque. If the May family did not want him, if New York society shunned him, if the district attorney was determined to pursue him, then Bennett would take a plague-on-all-your-houses approach: He would leave New York forever. Just as his mother had done, with him and little Jeannette in tow, he would forsake his life in America and exile himself to Paris. He would have nothing to do with the city affixed to his newspaper's name and would instead run his business empire from an ocean's remove, relying on exorbitantly expensive transatlantic cables to communicate daily with his editors and convey his every bizarre wish. "It was not so much a case of Bennett banishing himself," a biographer later wrote. Rather, it was a case "of New York being banished from his cosmos."

One day in mid-January he quietly slipped down to the docks and boarded a steamer bound for Le Havre, France. He soon ensconced himself in Paris, in a grand belle époque apartment on the Champs-Élysées. But after he'd been there for a while, he heard through friends that Fred May had come to France, still bent on avenging his sister's good name. Bennett, fearing an ambush, ordered what was described as a "resplendent" cuirass—a coat of mail—and wore it beneath his clothes for weeks. Finally, maddened by the suspense and growing tired of wearing the hot, heavy armor, he sent friends to confront May and make him state his plans. One of Bennett's close Paris acquaintances later wrote, "Mr. May declared that he had no homicidal intentions, so, to his great relief, JGB discarded the cuirass."

For a time, Bennett took up with a Russian mistress who went by the name "Madame A" and was said to be the "most disagreeable woman in Paris society." He did not revive his love with Caroline May—and would spend most of the rest of his life as a bachelor. He never again lived in New York.

In March 1877, James Gordon Bennett, his interest in an Arctic expedition quickening, decided it was time to pay a visit to Dr. August Petermann, the Arctic expert. Bennett took a succession of trains from Paris east across the French countryside, then burrowed into the hinterlands of Germany. The train ride was, Bennett groused, "a tiresome journey," and it cramped his style to clatter across such soporific expanses, to a realm his newspaper could not reach and his yachts could not penetrate. He passed through the Thuringian Forest, the ancient land dipping and heaving like a dark green sea. The train dropped into a fertile basin, a patchwork of cow pastures and mustard fields, and then chuffed into the prim village of Gotha.

Gotha was a medieval burg of about fifteen thousand people, quaint in the extreme, with winding cobblestoned streets and crisp church spires and forthright buildings of stone and brick. The fountains in the public squares were fed by a canal that brought fresh water from a river fifteen miles away. Looming over the town was an enormous baroque fortress—the Friedenstein Palace—built in the 1650s. A newspaper reporter at the time described Gotha as a "dreamy drowsy town . . . It looked as if an event had not happened for a hundred years."

Bennett made his way to the Justus Perthes publishing house, where Dr. Petermann ran his geographical *Anstalt,* or institute. Although Gotha was in the middle of nowhere—certainly from Bennett's jaundiced perspective—it had long been one of Germany's preeminent publishing centers. Incongruously, this rustic town was also a bookish town. Not only were maps and atlases produced here, but also encyclopedias, dictionaries, almanacs, magazines, and all manner of specialty publications. It was steeped in the fine art and delicate machinery of design, lithography, copper engraving, color printing, bookbinding, and other facets of the trade. A studious perfectionism governed the rhythms of town life, and late into the night one could feel the vibrations of the steam-powered rotary presses.

Petermann greeted Bennett in the drafting room of his institute, where teams of apprentice cartographers sat hunkered over their tilted tables, working with compasses and horsehair paintbrushes and hachuring pens. Petermann liked to bring visitors here. His monthly journal, *Petermanns Geographische Mitteilungen,* was designed and prepared here—as were his numerous atlases. Although the Duke of Gotha had awarded Petermann a professor's chair with an honorary doctorate at the University of Göttingen, about seventy-five miles to the northwest, the position was little more than a sinecure, and he rarely set foot on the campus. This busy workshop in Gotha was his real home. He kept an open office in the midst of the scratching, scribbling deskwork. Bennett, not quite knowing how to address the eminent cartographer, simply called him "Your Doctorship."

Petermann's *Anstalt* had long been a kind of clearinghouse for the latest geographic knowledge. Exploration fueled his atlases; his atlases, in turn, fueled exploration. The Latin motto of his magazine was *Ubique terrarum*—"All around the world"—and the slogan was often accompanied by the ancient ouroborous symbol, a serpent consuming its own tail. The image reflected the kind of circular reasoning that lay at the heart of Petermann's enterprise at Gotha: Knowledge of the world would feed ever more knowledge of the world.

PETERMANN ALWAYS TOOK pleasure in showing off his little empire, which he ran with an exacting efficiency. He was often cruel to the underlings who labored for him, and he was stingy with compliments. "He knew how to teach, but it was difficult for him to praise his students' work," one Perthes colleague later wrote. "He rose to world renown on the backs of his co-workers."

Still, there was a wonderment to the operation he had established. Here in his busy atelier, a remarkably accurate portrait of planet Earth was steadily taking shape and sharpening into ever-clearer resolution. Here every feature of the world was given a name and a contour and a coloration—every river, cape, fjord, glacier, swamp, and isthmus. No detail was too small for Petermann's mapmakers. Every major elevation differential was noted, every prevailing sea current, every road and railway, every oasis and caravan route, even the known locations of the telegraph wires that had been strung across continents and the braided cables that had been submerged along the ocean floor.

Petermann's maps were second to none. They were reliable, up-to-date, technically brilliant, and intricately beautiful, usually colored by hand. They were chock-full of data, with complex renderings of relief and gradient, and endless loops and whorls of isotherms showing subtle differences in climate, population densities, and changes in oceanic temperature. His staff could execute a new map extremely quickly. Larousse, the French publisher of popular dictionaries, had a few years earlier doffed its hat to Petermann's work: "Today Petermann is regarded in all civilized nations as the premier authority of our epoch on the subject of geography."

After giving him a tour of his *geographischer Anstalt,* Petermann led Bennett through the Perthes publishing plant, with its copper engraving machines and large presses. Then they strolled over to Petermann's villa near the train station. They passed through his garden and repaired to his study, where the shelves sagged with nearly every Arctic book that had ever been written. Petermann, said one Arctic historian, had come to be viewed as the world's "Polarpapa," a kind of "international president of the geographical world." People from around the globe came to Gotha to sit with him and hear his views on Arctic exploration. He had won numerous accolades and honorary degrees, and the royal houses of Italy, Austria, and Spain, among others, had awarded him prestigious medals.

Yet there was something wacky about August Petermann. Many of his views on the Arctic were, we now know, absurdly off base, or just odd. He recommended, for example, that explorers kidnap at least one male and one female Eskimo from every High Arctic native tribe they encountered and bring them back, in the fashion of Noah's ark, so that scientists might study the captives and send them on tour for the viewing public. He had a pet theory, based on no particular evidence, that Greeks and Italians were, genetically speaking, the two nationalities best disposed to withstand the rigors of Arctic travel. (Possibly, this was because he genuinely believed it was balmy up there.) He also maintained that salty ocean water could not freeze, at least not to a degree sufficient to mantle the entire pole in ice; ice packs hugged only the Arctic coastlines, he believed, and were primarily the product of freshwater rivers meeting the Arctic seas. At other times, he put forward a slightly different argument: that salt water *could* freeze, perhaps, but that when it did, all of its salt content was leached out or excreted in an "efflorescence." In any case, he insisted, ice packs contained little or no salt—so Arctic explorers could rely on the ice cap as an unfiltered source of fresh water.

When it came to the Arctic, Petermann was a man "with an undeviating affinity for the wrong guess," noted David Thomas Murphy, a historian of German Arctic exploration. "Such notions strike the modern reader as so unlikely, so spectacularly counterintuitive, and in retrospect so wrong that they seem to border upon the deranged."

Petermann had never ventured to the Arctic himself. Indeed, his sojourn to the United States was by far the most ambitious trip of his life. He was, said another historian, "the supreme armchair rover." Yet he grew only more stubborn in the face of contrary evidence provided by men who *had* been to the Arctic. In many ways Petermann was an enigma—a combative romantic, a meticulous dreamer with a taste for the spectacular. "His character combined outstanding virtues with disastrous faults," Murphy wrote. "He was undoubtedly a visionary, energetic and determined, gifted in his field, and possessed of public relations skills." But he was also a " 'hare-brained' eccentric whose fanciful misconstruction of Arctic geography led a succession of polar explorers to disaster."

All the same, Bennett was fascinated by Petermann and wanted to hear everything he had to offer. Bennett made only sketchy notes of their three-hour meeting, so it is not known precisely what was said, but he later sent a *Herald* reporter back to Gotha to recapture the conversation and present the professor's wide-ranging views on the state of the art of Arctic exploration.

THE SAGE OF GOTHA applauded Bennett for his willingness to underwrite a new polar push. "This Arctic business belongs to the world at large," Petermann told the *Herald* reporter. "Now that the Congo and the Nile sources have been settled, this is the one great thing that remains to be done." And the Americans, he said, were the ones to do it. If he'd ever had any doubts, his trip to the Centennial Exposition had clinched his views.

England, of course, still had the most expertise in the field of polar exploration, but he had deep misgivings about the Brits. Petermann had a love-hate relationship with the United Kingdom. Although he had been born and raised in nearby Bleicherode and schooled in Potsdam, Petermann had worked in London throughout the first part of his career, and he remained infatuated with English culture. He had moved back to Germany in the mid-1850s, but he still read the London papers every day, drank English tea every afternoon, and closely followed the bulletins of the Royal Geographical Society. His wife, Clara, was British, and they spoke English in their home. Their three daughters had been raised as proper English girls.

If Petermann was an Anglophile at heart, England had nonetheless rejected him. This had partly to do with burgeoning nationalism and xenophobia in England after the rise of Bismarck and the Franco-Prussian War. It also had to do with style: The leading explorers and Arctic thinkers in Great Britain didn't *like* Petermann. They found him increasingly fanciful and stubborn. The *Times* of London had taken to snubbing him, as had the Royal Navy. On the subject of the Arctic, Petermann had a horrible temper and tangled with anyone who disagreed with him. The officers of the Royal Geographical Society, where he had long been a leading member, had blackballed him. Petermann, it seemed, had become an unwanted child.

Petermann's staunchest enemy in Great Britain was Clements R. Markham of the Royal Geographical Society. Markham had come to regard Petermann as a charlatan and a windbag. "Dr. Petermann has done serious injury to the cause of Arctic exploration," Markham had argued. He thought Petermann's favorite subject, the Open Polar Sea theory, was pure rot. (The Brits, through hard experience, had begun to abandon the idea of sailing to the pole; thinking there was nothing but ice up there, Markham and other leading British advocates of exploration believed sledges and supply depots, not ships, would provide the way to the top.)

"All experience," Markham wrote, "seems to prove that the polar basin, when not covered with compact, unbroken ice, is filled with closely-packed, unnavigable drift-ice, in which some apertures may be found." Markham warned that Petermann's notion of smoothly sailing to the North Pole would send young sailors to their deaths. Petermann, he scoffed, thinks sailors can "penetrate through the belt or girdle of ice which encircles the open polar basin of his imagination . . . and then sail across it. All very easy to write at Gotha."

Sherard Osborn, a Royal Navy admiral and explorer, and another distinguished member of the Royal Geographical Society, had piled on: "I think it utterly mistaken to try to penetrate with ships to the North Pole," he wrote, "and I would be part of an expedition sent out to this goal only if Herr Dr. Petermann personally came along for the journey."

Feeling spurned by the adopted nation he'd once loved, Petermann clung to his wizardly world in faraway Gotha and all but ignored the Arctic doings of the Brits.

But the Americans intrigued Petermann more than ever. They had a most peculiar and interesting way of doing things, he thought. The Americans seemed to ignore hierarchy and the stifling weight of ages. In supple and energetic ways, they could combine national interest with commercial interest, government sponsorship with private funding, military glory with civic pride. The Americans, with their dazzling inventions and their organizational élan, would reach the North Pole, he felt sure. Petermann was impressed by how quickly the United States had bounced back from its Civil War and thrown its efforts into the polar game. "The world will not fail to recognize," he had written, "that the Americans, after they have ended and paid for a costly war, have had something left over for science."

Petermann, of course, was well aware that Bennett had sent Stanley to Africa. He understood that it was a stunt to sell newspapers, but still, Stanley's trek had produced sound knowledge while whetting the public appetite for further discovery. Afterward, Stanley had met with Petermann in Gotha, and the professor had incorporated knowledge the explorer had gleaned on the ground to create the latest maps of the African interior. Bennett had made a real and lasting contribution to science, for which Petermann was grateful.

Petermann felt that Bennett and De Long should approach the North Pole with the same directness and can-do pragmatism that had characterized Stanley's tromp through the Dark Continent. "Some day," Petermann told the *Herald* reporter, "the Pole will be found by a navigator who goes to his work with the common sense and determination Stanley showed in Africa. I look at the Arctic explorations in the general interest of science. All expeditions raise new questions. The more we see the more we want to see and know. Success is only relative."

———

WHAT BENNETT REALLY wanted to consult with "His Doctor-ship" about was the angle of attack: How should De Long approach the pole? What was the best route for smashing through the ice and reaching the Open Polar Sea?

Predictably, Petermann had elaborate theories on the subject. First of all, he said, give up on Greenland. The route through Smith's Sound had produced nothing but heartache. Charles Hall's expedi-tion had been only the latest example of what would befall any expedi-tion headed in that direction. Explorers there would always encounter what Petermann and others called the Paleocrystic Sea, the ring of hopelessly impassable ancient ice encircling the pole.

"Smith's Sound has become a habit," Petermann said. "People believe in it because twenty or thirty years ago they were told to believe in it. Franklin went in that direction, and so did Kane and Hall and Hayes, and other glorious, famous names have thrown a romance over all that region. So the illusion has grown that if the Pole cannot be reached over this route, it cannot be reached at all. There was the same illusion about African discovery. Think of the expedi-tions that have gone into Africa, following old and beaten tracks, to come to the same end—destruction and death."

Most assuredly, it was time for an entirely new route. Petermann had read Silas Bent's treatises on the Kuro Siwo and was familiar with his ideas about a "thermometric gateway." Petermann agreed with Bent. The place to strike for the pole was the Bering Strait, just as De Long had been thinking. Not only had the route never been tried before, but the Kuro Siwo was likely to be a warm-water current powerful enough to soften up a pathway through the ice that would lead to the Open Polar Sea.

But there was another compelling reason for going by way of the Bering Strait, Petermann suggested. Lying off the coast of northeast-ern Siberia, not far from the Bering Strait, was a mysterious landmass marked on some maps as Wrangel Land. For centuries, it had existed as little more than a rumor, a mirage, a fog-gauzed dream. People weren't sure what it was. Perhaps it was an island, perhaps a continent, perhaps a magical portal to the pole. Perhaps it didn't exist at all. Before it came to be called Wrangel Land, it had gone by a succession of other names scrawled on whaling charts: Tikegan Land, Plover Island, Kellett Land.

In 1822, Chukchi natives on the northeast Siberian coast told the Russian-financed explorer Ferdinand von Wrangel about a land to the north that could sometimes be seen when atmospheric conditions were just right. The Chukchis had never been there, but once every few years, on sharp, clear days when the mists and fogs opened up, and when the vagaries of Arctic refraction were favorable, a mountainous land seemed to rise up from the sea like a dream. The Chukchis called it the Invisible Island, and they spoke of legends of a forgotten people who lived there. They had seen herds of wild reindeer clomping north from the Siberian mainland across the ice, presumably to graze on the strange land during their seasonal migration. Flocks of geese and seabirds, too, had been seen aiming in that direction. The animals seemed to know something the humans did not.

Enticed by what he heard, Baron von Wrangel sailed for the mythic land, but he was thwarted by ice and failed to snatch even a glimpse of it. Nearly thirty years later, the captain of an English vessel searching for Sir John Franklin's lost expedition thought he spotted a large Arctic island in the distance. Later, various whaling captains insisted they'd seen it, though their claims were disputed. A German whaler, Eduard Dallmann, was even said to have briefly landed on it in 1866.

Something was there—Petermann was convinced of it. And this land, he believed (on the basis of anecdotes from Arctic whalers and ancient reports from Russian explorers), was surrounded by open water. "It is a well-known fact," he had written, "that there exists to the north of the Siberian coast, and, at a comparatively short distance from it, a sea open at all seasons."

Now Petermann drove home his point: Bennett and De Long should utilize that open sea and make Wrangel Land the target of their expedition. What a contribution to science it would be to finally learn what this land was about! On their way to the pole, he said, Bennett's party should try to land on Wrangel, explore it, and claim it for the United States.

PETERMANN HAD HIS own unorthodox theory about Wrangel Land. He thought it was an extension of northern Greenland—that Greenland wrapped across the Arctic, forming a massive transpolar continent. Petermann had produced a rather preposterous-looking map that showed this fancied piece of real estate, which he liked to call

Transpolarland. As Greenland stretched north into the unexplored High Arctic, it tapered and became a long proboscis that extended for more than a thousand miles, up and over the pole, ending at Wrangel Land. This exceedingly long, thin peninsula, with an open polar sea lapping at both sides of its apparently ice-free coastline—this elephant's trunk of hypothetical land—looked absurd on the map. But Petermann stuck to his theory all the more zealously for the ridicule it invited.

Petermann's idea was for Bennett's explorers to work their way up the Wrangel coast and see where it led. They could overwinter on the landmass if they had to and hunt for reindeer or any other game that might be living on it. They could use Wrangel Land as a kind of ladder to climb toward their ultimate goal. If they reached the Open Polar Sea, they could dash for the pole in their ship. If they didn't, they could sprint toward it with dogs, sleds, and small boats. Either way, they were sure to make a major contribution to science—proving or disproving his Transpolarland hypothesis. And while doing so, they would likely go farther north than anyone had ever been before.

This was the most viable path toward the North Pole, Petermann insisted. "Perhaps I am wrong," he told the *Herald* reporter, "but the way to show that is to give me the evidence. My idea is that if one door will not open, try another. If one route is marked with failures, try a new one. I have no ill will to any plan or expedition that means honest work in the Arctic regions."

But make no mistake, Petermann said, an Arctic voyage was dangerous work. He always underscored that point. "A great task must be greatly conceived," he had written before one of the German polar expeditions. "For such tasks, one must be a great man, a great character. If you have doubts or scruples, back out now."

Petermann pledged to give Bennett's expedition a full set of charts and maps of the Arctic and to help the expedition any other way he could. But beneath his enthusiasm for Bennett's new endeavor, an undertow of sadness pulled at Petermann, a sense of resignation. It was as though he were in mourning—and in a way, he was. Two years earlier, one of his three daughters had died of an unspecified condition, brought on, according to one account, "from mental overexertion."

His daughter's death had upset the equilibrium of his existence. His mood had grown dark. Manic depression ran in his genes; several male members of his family—reportedly his father and a brother—

had taken their own lives. Now Petermann and his wife, Clara, were on the verge of separating. He had thrown himself into his work as though it were the only thing he had left. Petermann held on to his Arctic dreams with a frantic desperation; Bennett's proposed expedition, Petermann realized, might be his last chance to vindicate his polar theories in the public eye. He longed for Bennett and De Long to succeed.

As soon as Bennett returned to Paris, he dashed off a spirited note to De Long. "I have just returned from a hurried trip to Gotha, on a visit to Dr. Petermann. You have no doubt heard of him by reputation. I can assure you the three hours I spent with him fully repaid me for the tiresome journey. He told me he had been studying the North Pole problem for the last thirty years and that he feels certain it can be reached."

The Bering Strait, Bennett reported, was the way to go—De Long had been right all along. "Petermann says it can be done in one summer . . . with a suitable vessel and a commander experienced in ice navigation."

Petermann had made it sound so tantalizing, and so easy, that Bennett had contracted the Arctic bug himself. It was just a passing fancy, but now *he* was thinking of going to the pole, in his own ship. In closing, Bennett must have given De Long a start when he wrote, "I have been seriously thinking of getting another vessel in addition to the one you will have and starting myself by Dr. Petermann's route."

From Gordon Bennett's first meeting with George De Long, the publisher's desire to sponsor a North Pole attempt had only grown keener. Throughout 1876 and 1877, he had kept in close communication with De Long by mail and cable, seeking reassurance that the young officer's ambitions had not changed. "He is more than ever disposed to carry the affair through," De Long wrote Emma. In the fall of 1876, Bennett persuaded De Long to seek a leave of absence from the Navy Department and come to England to hunt for just the right ship in which to voyage to the Arctic. Bennett, of course, would pay for everything.

De Long leapt at the opportunity. He was growing concerned about a new effort recently floated before Congress by a U.S. Army Signal Corps officer named Henry Howgate to establish an American colony somewhere in the High Arctic, from which an assault on the North Pole could be a staged. The idea that a North Pole attempt could be land-based, as opposed to nautical, worried De Long. In such a scenario, the Army would likely lead the effort, not the Navy, and De Long's leadership role would thus be supplanted. For his own sake, and for the Navy's, he felt tremendously motivated to find a ship—and find it soon.

De Long took a steamer to England in December, and found polar exploration circles there in an uproar about a British-led Arctic expedition that had recently returned from a nearly disastrous attempt to reach the North Pole via the west coast of Greenland. Led by British naval officer George Nares, the expedition had achieved a new "farthest north" record but had developed scurvy and a host of other problems before retreating home. The Nares debacle was much on De Long's mind when he met with Bennett at Somerby Hall, a classic country mansion the publisher owned in Lincolnshire, but the two men agreed to forge ahead with their proposed mission. Then De Long set to work. He roamed up and down the length of England in search of a vessel, sending teams of hired agents ahead of him to snoop around the country's major ports and make confidential inquiries. For three weeks, De Long traveled almost constantly, catching occasional naps or snacks on the train. "I have astonished my stomach with tea," he complained to Emma, "and what with that and the loss of sleep I am as nervous as a cat."

He particularly focused his efforts on the ports of Scotland, where, with that country's well-established whaling and sealing industries, he felt certain he could find a craft that was "adequate for battling the ice." He prowled the docks in Dundee and Peterhead and hobnobbed with captains—trying, at times, to loosen them up with a little whiskey. But he could find no owners who were prepared to turn loose their ice-proven ships. "The demand for whalebone is something fabulous," De Long wrote in disgust, and "everything that can be put together is going this spring and summer to hunt whales."

De Long had planned to travel on to Hamburg and other major ports in Europe. But first he made a stop at Cowes, the prominent yachting capital on the Isle of Wight, in the English Channel. There he got word of a certain vessel called the *Pandora* that had successfully returned from a difficult voyage to the Arctic—a voyage, in fact, which Bennett had helped fund, and on which one of Bennett's *Herald* correspondents had tagged along to write dispatches. The little ship was not currently being used, De Long was told, and might be for sale. On a "fearful day," with a gale blowing rain and snow, De Long promptly went to the marina and nosed around until he found the craft in question.

De Long loved the *Pandora* as soon as he laid eyes on her. She was, he thought, a "tidy" ship. A three-master, but also equipped with a steam engine that powered a screw propeller, the *Pandora* was 146 feet long, with a beam of 25 feet. Fully loaded and rigged, she drew 15 feet of water. She was bark-rigged and carried eight boats, including a steam cutter and three whaleboats. She had a sharply pointed bow— reinforced for the ice—and a narrowly rounded stern. The *Pandora* could sleep thirty comfortably, which was precisely the number of men De Long thought he should take to the Arctic. Her displacement was 570 tons.

What most impressed De Long about the *Pandora* was her felicitous history: She seemed to be a vessel imbued with good luck. Built in Devonport, England, and launched in 1862, she had ably served as a Royal Navy gunboat off the coast of Africa for four years before passing into private hands. Then, stripped of her guns, the *Pandora* had been outfitted for the Arctic and had made two trips to Greenland, where she had acquitted herself magnificently as a survivor of the ice.

De Long liked the fact that the *Pandora* was a former Royal Navy ship. Up until that time, most of the exploration in the Arctic had been undertaken by the Admiralty. De Long was fairly in awe of the English legacy in this arena, and as an officer in a weakling navy, he felt a certain reverence toward a nation that had long exerted such a sweeping and sophisticated command of the seas. He found something satisfying about the notion that he, an American, might command a former Royal Navy gunship in the High Arctic—as though the exploration torch were being handed off, across the Atlantic, to a younger, hungrier aspirant.

THERE WAS ONLY one problem with the *Pandora:* She wasn't for sale. Her owner, an accomplished yet somewhat eccentric gentleman adventurer named Allen Young, doted on his exploring yacht. Young had personally captained the *Pandora* during both of her voyages to Greenland. He loved the little ship's lines, her reliability, and the ready way in which she "answered her helm," as he put it. The *Pandora* had become his second home, and he had fond memories of the days he'd spent upon her decks.

At times, his adventuring style had been a little odd. Once, while skirting the floes in Baffin Bay, Young had captured a live polar bear, chained it to the quarterdeck, and, after feeding it a cocktail of chloroform and opium, tried to tame the beast and make it his ship's mascot. (He also kept a pet pig aboard ship for a while.) For his gallant and colorful services to his country while sailing the *Pandora*, Young recently had been knighted.

Sir Allen had ventured along the east coast of Baffin Island in pursuit of that age-old obsession of the British Admiralty: finding a

Northwest Passage across the top of Canada to the Bering Strait. Predictably, thick ice had foiled his efforts, as it had all previous Northwest Passage expeditions. But the *Pandora* had performed impressively well while trapped in the grinding pack. At one point during the voyage, the ship became "hopelessly beset," as Young described it. He could hear the vessel's timbers groaning and cracking. The pressure became so great that he had his crew blast the surrounding pack with gunpowder, yet "the floe still pressed sadly on our poor little ship. We were all ready to leave the *Pandora* should she show any further signs of succumbing. I felt that she was in her icy tomb, and that escape was hopeless."

But the *Pandora* had held firm. Young later found that despite the "severe battle she had endured," the ship had suffered nothing more serious than a bent propeller blade. It was as though this happy little yacht had a guardian angel. "We were all in good health," Young boasted to the secretary of the Admiralty about his voyage. "We rode in perfect safety and comfort."

During those adventures in Greenland, the owner had formed a seemingly permanent and inseparable bond with his ship. Although De Long offered him a fair price, Sir Allen would not sell. He had no particular use for the *Pandora* now; he wanted to hold on to her—for sentimental reasons.

Or so he said. A year later, on an impulse, Young decided that he *did* want to sell and contacted Bennett immediately. Bennett came over from Paris and bought her then and there, for a sum of $6,000. Allen soon regretted his rash decision and reapproached Bennett, attempting to buy the *Pandora* back. Bennett wouldn't budge.

AS SOON AS he could obtain an extended leave of absence, De Long, who had spent the year engrossed in Arctic reading while serving in New York on Navy duty, returned to England to supervise the *Pandora*'s cleaning and refitting. This time, De Long brought Emma and their five-year-old daughter, Sylvie. They rented a room in a modest hotel at 15 New Cavendish Street in London's West End. Every day for nearly four months during the spring and early summer of 1878, De Long went down to the Thames, where the *Pandora* was in dry dock at a place called Walker's yards in Deptford. He wanted to oversee every detail of the ship's overhaul. "A small omission now," De Long wrote, "may cost us the success of the expedition in the end."

To improve the ship, Bennett cannibalized parts and fixtures from his own racing yacht, *Dauntless*. De Long was, said Emma, "unremitting in his attentions to the *Pandora*'s preparations," and she, too, found herself "drawn into the maelstrom" as plans for the expedition began to accelerate.

The late spring saw a whirlwind of dinner parties and gatherings that had the feeling, to the De Longs, of an extended send-off. De Long considered himself an ingénue in the Arctic department, and yet during his final weeks in London, he was treated like a VIP. He met with the Royal Geographical Society, as well as all manner of British scientists and explorers. Veteran polar adventurers inundated him with requests to join his expedition. A relative of England's greatest Arctic martyr, Sir John Franklin, held a gathering to fete De Long's coming journey—during which De Long promised to keep a lookout for any tidings of the long-lost explorer and his large expedition (who at this point had been missing for thirty-three years). Sir Allen Young also entertained the De Longs and donated a large part of his Arctic library and maps to be kept on the *Pandora*.

With so much discussion about the expedition, little Sylvie could tell that something big was afoot, but she was too young to understand what it was about.

"Where is Papa going?" she asked at one point.

"To the North Pole," Emma replied. But Sylvie shrugged her shoulders, thinking it was a joke, as though her father were going off to some mythic storybook place—like the center of the earth or the surface of the moon.

The *Times* of London took notice of the activity along the Thames. "The *Pandora* is being thoroughly refitted in Walker's yards," the paper announced, "and may be said to be almost a new vessel. She will be ready for sea in a short time."

De Long and Bennett had decided that further refitting work would be done in Le Havre, where the *Pandora* would dock for another month—and where the ship would be formally rechristened and placed under American registry. Bennett, who had returned to Paris, was trying to come up with a new name for the vessel, one that was not freighted with so much ominous mythology. He felt he could not in good conscience send a full crew of men to the Arctic in a ship that was named after a Greek story about a box containing all the world's evils and plagues.

De Long had decided that he himself would sail the *Pandora* from England to France, and then all the way around South America to San Francisco, where still further repairs would be undertaken at a U.S. Navy yard. Emma and Sylvie would accompany him in the *Pandora* as far as California, with a small crew. In midsummer of the following year, the expedition would commence in earnest, aiming for the Bering Strait—and the North Pole.

On a fine bright morning in late June, the *Pandora,* which had been briefly docked in the heart of London to take on supplies, eased away down the Thames. Westminster Abbey and St. Paul's slid from view as she turned downstream. In high spirits, George and Emma made for the place of her youth, the place of their courtship, and the place where they had been wed—Le Havre, France.

James Gordon Bennett paced alongside his ship, studying her lines in the bright salt air. The *Pandora* wasn't as sleek or as fast or as big as the several yachts he had owned, and not nearly as beautiful. But she was a "staunch" little ship, he thought—and one that enjoyed the advantage of having already survived several odysseys in the ice. There was still more work to be done on her. Yet Bennett, who liked to think he could sniff out nautical flaws with the most casual of inspections, felt confident that his new acquisition was nearly ready for the High North. What he saw in this sturdy yacht can only be guessed, but he knew this: Her voyage was going to make headlines.

It was July 4, 1878. The *Pandora* lay moored in a slip safely tucked behind the jetty in Le Havre, in precisely the same place where the *Shenandoah* had been moored the night George and Emma De Long were married upon her decks. Today, in effect, was the last day of the *Pandora*'s existence—she was to be rechristened in a ceremony that afternoon.

Bennett had decided to rename her the *Jeannette,* after his sister. He had chartered a train from Paris and brought along his usual entourage of fashionable rogues and sportsmen, plus a few newshounds from the *Herald* to cover the proceedings. Jeannette had come as well, and traveling with her—or as close as Victorian courtship protocols would allow—was her beau, Isaac Bell, a wealthy New York cotton broker and investment tycoon.

The best-known guest in the group, however, was Henry Stanley, the Welsh-American explorer who had tromped across the jungles of Africa as a *Herald* correspondent and had become even more famous for his book about that adventure, *How I Found Livingstone.*

Everyone met for a luncheon at Frascati's, a resort hotel and casino on the waterfront. It was a place of languid luxury on the coast of upper Normandy, where wealthy Parisians came to escape the city's summer heat. On the strand, little cabanas of striped canvas billowed in the sea breeze. Musclemen in unitard bathing suits dipped into the cold Atlantic, while children erected sand castles and women in bloomers drowsed beneath sun parasols (public swimming then being generally considered an ill-advised activity for the fairer sex).

Inside Frascati's reception hall, Bennett sat at one end of a long banquet table, De Long at the other. The publisher suffered through many toasts and testimonials, watching the proceedings with cool assessing eyes, his trim mustache bristling, a mischievous grin growing across his face as the alcohol took hold.

But he did nothing, said nothing. It was as though he were following the festivities from afar. Bennett was strangely bashful around large groups of people and uncomfortable with the spotlight even when the spotlight was manifestly *his*. He was like a disinterested watchmaker, the sort of man who preferred to set situations in motion—and then sit back and amuse himself with the results.

De Long and Stanley sat next to each other and "kept up a running fire of conversion all through the luncheon," Emma later recalled. De Long was a very different sort of person from the flamboyant, egomaniacal, and sometimes ruthless explorer, yet he and Stanley had much in common, and much to talk about. The poles and the African interior—the Frigid and the Torrid Zones, as they were sometimes called—remained the two great geographical mysteries left on the planet, and both men had the same curious patron to sponsor their probes into the unknown regions.

Stanley had something De Long badly wanted: lasting fame, the kind that comes from a significant achievement capped by literary success. De Long had every intention of writing a book about his Arctic odyssey. But Stanley, only half-facetiously, insisted that *he* would pen the definitive account of the expedition. It was an adventure scoop that Bennett dearly longed to duplicate for his newspaper—a kind of encore.

"See here, De Long," Stanley said, "I intend to write a companion volume to *How I Found Livingstone.* It will be called *How I Found De Long!*"

Afterward, the party dispersed and strolled to the marina, where the *Pandora* lay moored. It was a warm, bright, hazy day. Sylvie, wearing a straw hat affixed with a hand-drawn legend that read "Jeannette," ran up and down the docks, eating apricots and innocently playing along the same waterfront where her mother had grown up. As the crowd slowly gathered, Jeannette Bennett wandered off with Isaac Bell for a short while—"the lovers," said Emma, "were very much engrossed"—until it was time for the ceremony to commence.

FROM THE STANDPOINT of the sea gods, rechristening the *Pandora* could be seen as a dubious exercise. As though her original mythological name weren't already heavy enough, a superstition had long held among some mariners that no ship should ever be renamed. Some claimed that it insulted a vessel's very soul; others said it was just a bad idea, the epitome of tempting fate.

But Gordon Bennett had spent his life thumbing his nose at convention. He had plenty of nautical superstitions of his own, odd crotchets and bugaboos, yet this was not one of them; Bennett would call his ship whatever he pleased.

To be sure, *Jeannette* was far from a commanding name for an Arctic icebreaker. But it was in keeping with the times. There was a growing trend in those days to name ships (even ones destined for bitter hard duty) after wives and mothers and nieces and aunts—as though summoning a favorite female, however dainty or dotty or dowager-like, would somehow temper the ordeals ahead.

Most likely, Bennett's choice for the name sprang from a certain familial guilt. Since he had left New York for a perpetual high life in Paris, Bennett scarcely ever saw his sister. Other than covering Jeannette's bills, he had done little to honor the pleas contained in their father's will to look closely after her welfare. Jeannette herself did not particularly like ships and had never asked her big brother to name one after her. Yet, dutifully, she had steamed over from America and taken the train from Paris to grace the ceremony with her presence.

De Long helped Jeannette to the bow of the ship, and a bottle of the finest champagne was produced. (Bennett, of course, had spared no expense in that department.) A ribbon was cut, and then, with a sweet, coquettish smile, Jeannette smashed the bottle across the freshly painted hull.

The *Pandora* was now the *Jeannette*. By a special act of Congress that Bennett's representatives in Washington had succeeded in pushing through, she had been placed under American registry, in preparation for her being declared a Navy vessel. An American flag flew proudly from her mast.

Henry Stanley stood before the crowd and offered a toast, then coaxed De Long into saying a few words. "I would have preferred not being called upon," De Long said. "You, Mr. Stanley, have the right to speak—you've accomplished your task. Mine is still before me." As De Long had always said, he did not wish to make any promises "to achieve wonders. We have hard work ahead of us, and no romance. While we may be gone three years, we may be gone for eternity."

BENNETT WATCHED THE ceremony from his usual remove. He remained "in the background," said Emma, "and it was impossible to make him come forward and take an active part." Perhaps the publisher's mind was already somewhere else—he was scheduled to sail for New York the next day for one of his unannounced inspections of the *Herald* offices.

The small crowd left from the *Jeannette* and returned to Frascati's for an evening of celebrations and toasts of brandy amid blue clouds of cigar smoke. After this night, Bennett and all his guests would disperse and return to their lives, leaving De Long more or less alone to plan and commence his voyage. Jeannette would hasten back to New York with Isaac Bell. Within a few months they would marry, and soon they would start building one of Newport's elegant "cottages." Stanley would return to further exploits in Africa, and to a career that would see him both knighted and demonized, his brutal adventures partly inspiring Joseph Conrad's *Heart of Darkness*.

Bennett wished De Long a safe journey and said he'd see him at the *Jeannette*'s embarkation in San Francisco. When De Long reported that Emma was joining him for the entire eighteen-thousand-mile voyage to California, Bennett was surprised and a little shocked. Then De Long thought he detected a stab of sadness in the lifelong bachelor. "Your wife must think a great deal of you," Bennett said. "No woman ever would do that for me."

Bennett had supplied three men to join De Long for the journey; if all went well, they were eager to sign on to the expedition to the pole. Two of them, Alfred Sweetman and John Cole, had worked for years on Bennett's yachts. Sweetman was a gangling British carpenter and mechanic, reliable but almost drearily precise. (He reported his age to De Long as "38 and 5/6 years.") Cole, an Irishman, was an agile boatswain scarcely over five feet tall who, it was said, could scramble over rigging like a monkey. Cole, who was known as Jack, had been at sea since he was thirteen. "You'll find Cole one of the best sailors you ever had," Bennett told De Long. "In times of danger, he's worth his weight in gold."

For navigator, Bennett had suggested a peculiar but perspicacious fellow named Danenhower. Master John Wilson Danenhower was twenty-nine years old, a Chicago-born graduate of the Naval Academy who came highly recommended by none other than former president Ulysses S. Grant, who'd recently gotten to know him while cruising around the Mediterranean on the USS *Vandalia*. Danenhower was a tall, formal man of dashing good looks, with thin, elegant hands, a full trim beard, and a thatch of dark hair that stood up on end. His face quivered with an intelligent sensitivity; his large, scooplike ears and piercing dark eyes contributed to the impression that he was a man who missed nothing. Danenhower had long burned with an ardent desire to reach the pole. He told De Long that he wanted to go to the Arctic "with all my heart."

De Long liked him immediately. Danenhower was a brilliant conversationalist with a sardonic sense of humor. He'd read widely in astronomy, magnetic phenomena, physics, and Arctic exploration history. His navigational knowledge seemed unimpeachable. Among other assignments, he had done a stint at the United States Naval Observatory, in Washington. Still, there was something in his manner that gave De Long pause. One day in Le Havre an American officer told him a juicy piece of gossip: Danenhower, he'd heard, had once suffered some "brain trouble" and had been pronounced insane. When De Long shared this disturbing report, Bennett replied, blackly, "If anything might make a man insane, it would be a freezing up in the Arctic."

Even so, De Long had decided to hire Danenhower as navigator for the trip around South America—and let the voyage serve as a test. De Long thought that if Danenhower's mind was still "disordered," the long sail to San Francisco would surely reveal "any lurking effects of his old complaint."

Bennett agreed with the plan. In parting, his only request for De Long was, as usual, strange: When he and Danenhower sailed from Le Havre in the *Jeannette,* it was imperative that no one ever leave her, even for a moment, until they reached San Francisco. Although the voyage might take more than two hundred days, under no circumstances was anyone to set foot on dry land until the *Jeannette* passed through the Golden Gate.

Bennett offered no reason for this odd command. It was one of his kooky notions—and, of course, he expected it to be obeyed.

THE *JEANNETTE* WAS set to sail from Le Havre on July 15. That morning, a large send-off party of Emma's childhood girlfriends came out to the docks, with assortments of French cheeses and other delicacies, to wish her bon voyage. "They wondered at my daring," she recalled, noting that most Frenchwomen "love their homeland too much to leave it without great hesitation."

As a going-away present, her friends gave her an array of flowering potted plants to enliven her quarters at sea. She placed them all around the mizzenmast that penetrated her cabin—turning the room, in effect, into a miniature tropical jungle—and lashed together the dozens of terra-cotta pots with ropes.

The first weeks of the journey were easygoing, as the *Jeannette* angled southwest along the coast of Portugal and Morocco and then passed the Canary Islands before heading out into the broad Atlantic. The weather remained fair, the seas calm, and the winds so favorable that De Long never had to fire up the steam engine. "As we were under sail," said Emma, "there was no jar, no noise, only the ripple of the water as the *Jeannette* cut through it." The steward, Samuel, a Swiss-born thespian with impeccable diction, would sing beautiful arias while he fluttered about the galley. (It turned out he had spent a season with New York's Metropolitan Opera Company.)

Emma and George had never enjoyed such a prolonged interlude of happiness. They spent a great deal of time reading from the *Jeannette*'s splendid library, which contained nearly every book ever published on polar travel. Sir Allen Young had donated many of his old

titles, and Bennett had handed over his entire library of Arctic literature. De Long also had amassed an astonishing collection of charts
and maps, many of them from Petermann's atlas company in Gotha,
including every known chart of the world north of the 65th parallel.

"We were utterly absorbed in the study of the Arctic," said Emma,
and in "the great objective ahead." Danenhower would often join
them in the chartroom for animated discussions about the best route
to take through the Bering Sea, the probable winds and currents in
the Arctic, and what would happen once they reached Wrangel Land.
Immersed in these conversations, Emma began to realize "what a powerful thing science is and how absorbing a devotion to it becomes."

Sometimes, George would pull Emma from her reading chair and
they would saunter arm in arm along the decks, conversing in the
briny mist, with Sylvie scurrying to keep up. "Though Sylvie and I
were about to part with father and husband for long," Emma wrote,
"not one word—I believe not even a thought—of regret or apprehen-
sion came to us."

II · A Benediction

On July 15, the same day the *Jeannette* set sail from Le Havre, the *New York Herald* took special note of the occasion by running a lengthy article about August Petermann. In the piece, entitled "The Unknown Arctic World: An Interview with Dr. Augustus Petermann, the Distinguished German Professor," the writer and his subject both fairly trembled in anticipation of the discoveries the *Jeannette* would make in the High North. By now, Petermann had become the guiding spirit behind the expedition—its primary theoretician, its éminence grise. While neither De Long nor Bennett took Petermann's word as gospel, the professor's ideas had come to form the scientific and intellectual framework for the whole enterprise. Petermann had given Bennett his best Arctic charts and maps, and, to a curious degree, the Sage of Gotha had placed all his highest hopes on the success of the expedition as a way of confirming his hypotheses about the Arctic.

And so Bennett, seeing merit in publicizing Petermann's attachment to the voyage, had sent a *Herald* reporter down from Berlin to spend a day with "the liberal and enthusiastic scholar of Gotha." It was a warm summer day, market day in Gotha, and the town bustled. Farmers were selling bushels of cherries and slabs of freshly butchered veal, and trysting lovers could be seen scuffling down the shady paths. "Tow-headed children were romping in the streets," the *Herald* reporter noted, and "the beer shops were filled with people, in the oddest country costumes, drinking beer and eating cheese."

Petermann invited the reporter into his villa. He began the conversation with a discussion of his interviewer's employer. "I am very glad Mr. Bennett proposes a Polar expedition," he said. "From what I know of the *Jeannette,* she is just the vessel for such an undertaking." Petermann stuck by his notion of an Open Polar Sea. "The central area of the Polar regions is more or less free from ice," he said, although he conceded that it probably would not be "like the Mediterranean or the Gulf of Mexico, always passable." Still, he said, "I am persuaded that it could be navigated by such a boat as the *Jeannette.*"

Petermann believed in the romance of ships, and he did not think that the North Pole would be reached by sledges. Although a dog-pulled sled might serve as a "useful auxiliary," it should not be considered an "essential element of an expedition," he contended. "It is not what dogs can do, but what men can do, that will gain results in the Arctic regions. I am in favor of the sea. You want a good boat and a steamer. I am disposed to pay honor to the men who bring their ships home."

The Sage of Gotha was excited by the possibility that De Long would find human civilization at the North Pole. "I should not be at all surprised," he said, "if Eskimos were found right under the Pole. It is not at all unlikely."

From the standpoint of weather and health, he predicted, the *Jeannette*'s voyage would prove surprisingly easy. "So far as health is concerned the Arctic regions are a hundred times more preferable than where Stanley was on the Congo," he said. Light deprivation might try some men's nerves, he thought, but Arctic weather was really not as hard as people believed. "The cold you can stand and thrive under," he said. "It is that long night that tells on the body and mind."

"Then," asked the *Herald* correspondent, "you have no doubt the Pole will some day be found?"

Petermann replied, "No more doubt than that we have found the Congo. And I hope Mr. Bennett's expedition will find it."

The *Herald* interview ended there. "These words," the reporter concluded, "were spoken as a benediction in a cheerful way as we walked from the Doctor's house through the garden to the gate. The afternoon shadows were falling, and as night came on the old town seemed to hum and buzz and nod and roll itself to sleep."

ALTHOUGH PETERMANN HAD put on a good face that day, he was suffering terribly. The manic depression that had gripped him for the past two years had worsened. Several months earlier, in May 1878, he had divorced his wife, Clara, and, within days, had impulsively married a German woman, Toni Pfister, from the town of Bernburg. His friends and acquaintances thought this was an act of pure madness, for he hardly knew the woman, and within weeks, it was clear to all that the new union would fail.

He was miserable, and so was she. Petermann missed his familiar life with Clara and their daughters, who had moved back to England. "Pangs of conscience gnawed at his marrow," said an early biographer. "An ominous melancholy cast a pall that darkened day by day."

Petermann's nerves were frayed. He couldn't sleep, couldn't eat, couldn't concentrate. He'd lost his zest for life. He could no longer sit at the piano or follow the international news in the papers. He seemed despondent about his work, too. Berlin had begun to eclipse Gotha as a center of cartography, map publishing, and exploration debates. Petermann had a sense that he was losing his edge, that his preeminence in the field was fading.

On September 25, 1878, he was found in his villa, hanging from the end of a rope. Suicide had evidently been on his mind for some time, for he left behind a three-week-old note. In his final months, he had made a number of cryptic remarks to his friends—remarks that, in retrospect, made chilling sense.

When she received the news of his death, Clara, in London, dashed off a letter to a family friend: "I often think how things are going at Villa Petermann," she wrote. "Oh God, it all appears to me to be like a bad dream." Hers was an "awful fate," Clara said, but she still considered herself "his poor little wife, whom he so seriously misjudged."

Petermann was buried as a local hero in a shady green park at the edge of Gotha, and he was heralded, internationally, as a kind of martyr to cartography. In his final hours, there was no indication that he had been thinking particularly of the Arctic. On his desk lay a new manuscript he'd been writing that concerned some aspect of African exploration. Yet even as he'd cinched the noose, he'd known that the vessel that carried the hope of validating his fondest dreams was en route to San Francisco—and then to the pole.

The interview he gave for the *New York Herald* was the last public utterance August Petermann ever made.

A
s the *Jeannette* drew nearer to the equator, the waters became oily calm and teemed with eels, tortoises, and dolphins. One morning, several flying fish hurled themselves on board—"just in time," said Emma, "to be served up for breakfast."

A few hundred miles off the coast of Brazil, the *Jeannette* sailed into a massive tropical storm. At the height of its fury, with the swells combing over her decks, the *Jeannette*'s main boom snapped off. The canvas mainsail danced madly in the rigging, and the ship came dangerously close to capsizing. De Long and Danenhower eventually got the runaway boom lashed down, but the storm continued to howl all night, leaving the cabins sloshing with water.

Emma stayed in her berth, clutching little Sylvie tightly, expecting a "clean swift death." As the ship rolled in the high seas, the potted plants Emma's friends had given her toppled to the floor. In the pitch-dark cabin, she could hear "one flower pot after another taking a plunge." Surveying the wreckage the next morning, Emma realized that all the mangled plants and potsherds had to be "consigned to the deep."

Alfred Sweetman, the dour carpenter, jury-rigged a new boom from a spare piece of timber, and soon the *Jeannette* was limping along nicely. Later in the morning, a pair of songbirds that evidently had blown in on the storm circled the ship and landed on the deck. They were probably from Brazil, two beautiful passerine birds of a species no one aboard recognized. One of them perched right on Danenhower's thick crew cut. "It must think it's in the brush!" Emma said with a laugh. Obviously exhausted, beaten up by the storm, the birds likely had flown many hundreds of miles.

The two "little visitors" became mascots of the ship—the focus of everyone's affections, embraced as an augury of some kind. Emma tried to nurse them back to health in her cabin. She offered them grain, bread, and condemned cheese to eat, but the birds would not touch a morsel. One soon died, presumably of hunger and exhaustion. Samuel, the steward, penned a poem to "its melancholy fate." After a solemn ceremony, he sealed the verses and the dead bird in a bottle, which he threw overboard.

The other bird seemed to improve. But a few days later, it flew out of Emma's cabin, the door having inadvertently been left ajar. The crew scrambled over the decks trying to catch it, but the bird eventually soared off the ship and out to sea. "It made three attempts to get back on board and we thought it would succeed," wrote Emma. "But its strength soon gave out and it fell into the water and was drowned, much to our sorrow."

ONE DAY, AS the *Jeannette* was approaching the southernmost coast of Argentina, not far from Tierra del Fuego, Master Danenhower pulled De Long aside to say there was something he needed to confess.

Danenhower said he had once suffered a bout of "melancholy." It had occurred three years earlier, when he was sailing aboard the *Portsmouth* near Hawaii. He could not definitely say what had triggered his depression, but he had been having "domestic troubles" back home in Washington. While at sea for six months, calling at various ports, he had not received an important letter he had been expecting. It sounded to De Long like a matter of the heart; Danenhower struck him as someone who, like himself, possessed a certain romantic streak.

In any case, Danenhower's melancholy had deepened. The ship's surgeon placed him on the sick list. When he did not improve, he was eventually sent home to Washington, where he agreed to put himself under the care of a physician at the Government Hospital for the Insane.

Danenhower committed himself with the understanding that he would not be detained in any way. However, once the asylum door slammed shut, he was treated as a lunatic—confined, isolated, his complaints ignored, his letters to the outside world tossed away. He tried to escape but was overpowered and thrown into a padded cell. He probably would be there still, Danenhower thought, but for the fact that his parents, in Washington, personally knew the secretary of the Navy—who, upon learning of Danenhower's detention, had had him immediately released.

"I thought you ought to know the whole truth," Danenhower told De Long. "I believe I'm as sound as any officer in the Navy. I was never out of my mind for a moment."

This was a lot for Captain De Long to take in, but he appreciated Danenhower's candor, and the fact that he had come forward and told his story of his own volition. "I believed him," De Long wrote. Because Danenhower's troubles had happened three years earlier, and had apparently not recurred, De Long was inclined to give the navigator the benefit of the doubt. Almost to a fault, De Long believed in the principle of giving a man a second chance. Besides, Danenhower had come so highly recommended: If he was good enough for President U. S. Grant, he was good enough for the *Jeannette.*

Danenhower had acquitted himself well on the voyage so far, and he always made for spirited and interesting company. He seemed far from depressed. "He is bright and cheerful," wrote De Long, "attentive to his duty . . . a good seaman and a correct navigator." Unless De Long learned something different in San Francisco, he was settled in his thinking: Danenhower would accompany the *Jeannette* to the North Pole.

AFTER EIGHTY DAYS at sea, the *Jeannette* headed into the Strait of Magellan. For several weeks, De Long and Danenhower negotiated the treacherous crosscurrents that flowed through this extended tangle of fog-shrouded islands, until the *Jeannette* finally passed into the heaving Pacific. Cruising along the coast of Chile, De Long knew he needed to go ashore somewhere to repair his jury-rigged boom, but Bennett's insistence that no one touch land stuck in the captain's mind. He would keep heading north without stopping, much to Emma's chagrin. "We had been out of sight of land for so long now," she wrote, "that my desire to touch the soil was almost uncontrollable."

It was now spring in the Southern Hemisphere, but still freezing cold along the snow-dusted tip of the South American continent. George and Emma spent much of their time huddled around a fumy open-grate stove, reading by its flickering light. Gales were so frequent that Samuel had to string up guide ropes between the galley and the mess—and even then, he would often stagger "and dishes and all would go sprawling on the deck, and we would be minus that course for dinner."

Farther up the Chilean coast, a squall suddenly enveloped the *Jeannette*. The Pacific swells "reared themselves mightily," Emma wrote, and the *Jeannette* would "quiver when the waves struck her." In a horrible instant, the ship heeled over so dramatically that her starboard gunwale skimmed the sea. "The horizon had tilted crazily and the squall was black all around us. We simply hung on and trusted to the ship." The *Jeannette* began to take on water and seemed on the brink of swamping.

Then, within a minute, the squall passed, the wind eased, and the *Jeannette* returned to an even keel. In the mess, Samuel served the nervous crew nuts and coffee, and an unperturbed De Long came down from the bridge and acted as though nothing had happened. "Of how close we had come to eternity," Emma wrote, "no one said a word."

Off the coast of Peru and Ecuador, the weather moderated, and the temperatures warmed. Emma and George whiled away most of their evenings on deck, luxuriating in the tropical air. She would never forget those October nights spent together—"the brilliant southern constellations, the ship sailing along smoothly, the steward whistling so softly we scarcely dared to breathe lest we break the spell." There was only the quiet creak of the timber, the groan of taut ropes, and the wind singing through the rigging. George De Long and his bride had never been happier. For so many years, his powerful relationship with sailing had been an abstraction to Emma, an obstacle to their togetherness. Now, for this one sojourn, it united them.

The *Jeannette* cruised past the Mexican mainland, then Baja, then on toward the rugged coast of California. Two days after Christmas, she passed through the Golden Gate, with only a single bucketful of coal left in her bunker.

The eighteen-thousand-mile voyage from Le Havre had taken 166 days. The *Jeannette* had performed magnificently, De Long thought, as had Master Danenhower. True to Bennett's weird wishes, no one had set foot on dry land.

13 · The U.S. Arctic Expedition

Captain De Long scrutinized his weather-beaten ship in the golden California light, going over every valve and fitting, every strake of her long hull. He wondered where her weaknesses lurked. Were there rotten timbers? Leaky seams? The smallest flaw could mean his death, and the deaths of the men who would serve with him in the Arctic. The *Jeannette* had survived the trip—had performed admirably, in fact—but he knew she was not ready for the coming battle with the ice. There was still much work to be done, and only a few months in which to do it. To withstand the pressures of the pack, the *Jeannette* would have to be reinforced in a way that no Arctic-bound vessel had ever been reinforced before.

For most of the month of January 1879, the ship lay moored at the Mare Island Navy Yard, near San Francisco, awaiting inspection from a specially appointed board of naval engineers. Mare Island was the only Navy shipyard on the West Coast, a place where new vessels were sometimes constructed and where the existing ships of the Pacific Squadron routinely came in for maintenance and inspection. It was a complex of foundries, pipe shops, machine shops, pitch houses, sawmills, smokestacks, and derricks clustered around a floating dry dock, all of it set on a marshy island where the Napa River emptied into a remote estuary of San Francisco Bay.

Each morning, the bell announced the start of the shift, and the crews of tradesmen—carpenters and coppersmiths, tinsmiths and teamsters, plumbers and painters, caulkers and coopers—went about their smoky, cacophonous work. Mare Island was the western outpost of America's burgeoning might, the well-equipped repair shop of her still tiny but soon to be ascendant Navy, which was slowly converting from canvas to steam, and from wood to metal. Perched atop the headquarters building was a copper-sheathed statue of an American eagle, the huge bird cocked at an angle toward the water, as if to bid farewell to the nation's ships as they ventured to the far reaches of the Pacific.

Many great ships had been launched or overhauled at Mare Island—brigs, monitors, corvettes, schooners, sloops of war. But the shipyard's most storied fixture throughout much of the nineteenth century was the old Boston-built fifty-four-gun frigate the USS *Independence,* which, according to one Navy historian, was for nearly seventy years "as much a part of the Mare Island waterfront as the seagulls."

Among the warships moored beside the yard, the slender *Jeannette* looked fragile and unobtrusive. When Navy engineers commenced a formal study of her, they were not impressed. To withstand the ice, they thought, the *Jeannette* still needed a considerable amount of work—on her hull, especially. How this exploring yacht, as the *Pandora,* had survived three journeys in the Arctic was a mystery to them.

Of course, these men were paid to be cautious, and they knew their recommendations would carry little consequence within the Navy hierarchy, especially since Bennett would be covering all expenses. Still, the engineers' assessment was sweeping: Decks would have to be ripped out, they declared, bulkheads constructed, new boilers installed, coal bunkers rearranged, the entire hull reinforced with additional layers of planking. They talked of adding ambitious networks of beams and braces. As their checklist of repairs and renovations kept growing, they envisioned a price tag as high as $50,000.

De Long was shocked, even though he knew many of the repairs were necessary, and even though he and his men would be the beneficiaries of the contemplated improvements. He saw deep trouble in the engineers' recommendations. "We must stop them," he wrote, "or they will ruin us." While Bennett rarely blanched at a bill, De Long believed it his duty to make sure the engineers did not concoct unnecessary repairs in order to swindle the faraway—and notoriously profligate—publisher. "I consider your interest identical to my own," De Long wrote Bennett not long after his arrival in California. "I am laboring to keep down expenses with as much zeal as if I were to foot the bills instead of you."

The work would all be done here at Mare Island, but De Long knew that the real power behind the ship's repairs, as well as its equipage, provisioning, and staffing, was concentrated three thousand miles away—on the East Coast. He wanted to consult with the Navy Department, with the Smithsonian Institution, with the Naval Academy, with the nation's best scientific minds and Arctic theorists, not to mention with Bennett's representatives at the *Herald*. August Petermann's death in Gotha, which De Long had learned about shortly after landing in San Francisco, left a void in the very soul of the expedition, one he felt he needed to fill with varieties of expertise and authority that could only be found back East.

Mainly, though, De Long hated being at the mercy of political forces he could not personally confront. Here in California, he said, "I do not carry enough guns to make a noise." Thinking Washington "undoubtedly the place to do the most good," he wrote to the secretary of the Navy and arranged an extended cross-continental junket.

De Long would leave Master John Danenhower in charge of monitoring the day-to-day operations at Mare Island. His admiration for Danenhower had only grown since they had arrived in California. De Long advised the navigator to summon as much tact and delicacy as possible when conferring with the engineers—but also to watch expenditures like a hawk. "Little things run away with the money," De Long told Danenhower, noting that he wished to be more careful about spending Bennett's cash than if it were his own. "I will now leave the matter in your hands, asking you to use your best discretion to accomplish my wishes."

During the first week of February, De Long, with Emma and Sylvie at his side, boarded a Union Pacific train in Oakland, bound for Washington, D.C.

DURING THE WEEKLONG ride east, De Long began to turn his attention to another pressing question: Who would accompany him to the pole? Thus far, he'd made fitful progress in filling out the expedition's roster, and he hoped to spend much of his time in Washington interviewing candidates. The voyage would require about thirty men. This would include a crew of twenty seamen with various specialties, presided over by five Navy officers, plus an ice pilot, a doctor, a pair of civilian scientists, and one or two dog drivers.

But why would anyone—officer, seaman, or scientist—volunteer for such a risky and difficult mission in the Arctic? Some of the attraction was generational: Most of the applicants, like De Long, had just missed out on the greatest conflict in American history. These young men thirsted for some of the glory their fathers had won on the battlefields of the Civil War, and they yearned to test their manhood in some daunting and adventurous endeavor—if not war, then something roughly analogous to it.

A few of the applicants had been to the Arctic before and had fallen in love with its strange light, its howling solitudes, its haunting and beautiful *otherness*. These were men who, like De Long, had been touched by a kind of polar madness and, for reasons they often could not fully explain, had to go back.

Then there was the essential allure of exploration itself. It was impossible to exaggerate how significant, how glorious, how glamorous the *Jeannette* expedition seemed to certain quarters of the American public. Add to all this the element of nationalism—of beating other countries to the pole—and De Long's voyage exerted an irresistible pull on a certain kind of young man.

De Long had already received hundreds of applications from people all over America and the world, and throughout the long, jouncing train ride, he scribbled scores of letters in reply to the most promising applicants. (Many of the seekers were more than a little dubious, however. De Long was besieged with letters from a precocious teenage boy who said he would go to the Arctic for free and claimed he could "edit a newspaper and get up a variety show for the entertainment of the company during the long nights of an Arctic winter.")

Ideally, De Long was looking for unmarried men in perfect health—candidates who were prime seamen, drank very little, and were willing to work for Navy pay. Foreigners were welcome, as long as they could read and write in English. He favored Scandinavians, but he thought Englishmen, Scots, and Irishmen acceptable. Spaniards, Italians, and, especially, Frenchmen should be "refused point blank," he scribbled in a note—an odd bias given that De Long was married to a French-American woman and was himself descended from French Huguenot stock. He would like to have a good musician on board, to cheer up the lonely hyperborean nights. The cook must be excellent and, given the weird food he'd be forced to prepare, ever resourceful.

More than anything, though, De Long was looking for a quality of absolute fealty to naval discipline—"unhesitating obedience to every order, no matter what it may be," as he put it—a quality that had been sorely lacking on the *Polaris* and so many other ill-fated Arctic expeditions.

JOHN DANENHOWER WOULD serve as the *Jeannette*'s navigation officer—of that De Long felt certain. Alfred Sweetman, the British carpenter, and Jack Cole, the Irish boatswain, had both performed so well on the voyage around South America that De Long had decided to take them on, too. Samuel, the Swiss thespian and opera singer who'd been such a breath of fresh air on the voyage, would *not* be coming to the Arctic. His days as a ship's steward were over; he nursed ambitions to return to the New York stage. This left De Long to hunt elsewhere. Before he'd departed San Francisco, he had started to look among the city's growing Chinese population to fill out the *Jeannette*'s galley staff. Danenhower would soon be interviewing candidates in Chinatown.

De Long already had decided on his executive officer and second-in-command: his old friend Lieutenant Charles Winans Chipp. De Long had not forgotten Chipp's valiant performance and wise counsel aboard the *Little Juniata*. Chipp's naval experience ran wide and deep. During his more than ten years at sea, he had served on sloops, frigates, and gunboats and had been everywhere, it seemed: not only the Arctic but Siam, Cuba, Norway, Formosa, the Levant, Korea, North Africa. Chipp was a native of Kingston, New York, a historic town on the Hudson some ninety miles north of Manhattan, and he'd graduated with honors from the Naval Academy in 1868. Slight of build, he had thinning dark hair swept back from a blocky forehead, a magnificent full beard, and steady, deep-set eyes. His temperament was taciturn in the extreme. "He smiles rarely and says very little," De Long wrote, but Chipp was "ever true and reliable," an officer of consummate loyalty. It took nothing more than a cable from Bennett to the Navy Department, and Chipp, then serving in China, was promptly reassigned to the *Jeannette*. As De Long was on his way to Washington by train, Chipp was steaming across the Pacific for San Francisco.

De Long had also made up his mind about another Navy officer: George Melville would serve as the *Jeannette*'s engineer. Said to be distantly related to the great author, Melville was an improvisational genius with machines—a greasy-fingered savant who seemed most at home among thumping boilers and sharp blasts of steam. The engineer, thirty-eight years old, had a booming voice, a stout physique, and an enormous bald head that rose imposingly from a low scraggle of curly hair, like an egg that was too big for its nest. He was a native of New York City—like De Long, he had been raised in Brooklyn. Melville cursed in torrents but eschewed drinking, gambling, and most other vices. He had distinguished himself in both the Boston and the New York Navy yards, had become an expert on torpedoes, and had sailed on various warships, several times with De Long. All told, Melville had spent more than a third of his lifetime afloat. An autodidact, he was proficient in mineralogy, zoology, and many other subjects.

So prized were Melville's multifaceted talents that the Navy hierarchy was quite reluctant to give him a leave of absence, as was Melville's long-suffering wife, Hetty, who lived with their three children in Sharon Hill, Pennsylvania, a small borough near Philadelphia. Hetty was a beautiful woman, but she was also an alcoholic, with a terrible temper and a history of mental instability—which may help explain Melville's tendency to accept long assignments that took him far away from home. "The secrets of his home and fireside hung over him like a cloud," one acquaintance said. But like De Long, Melville had been bitten by the Arctic bug while on an assignment in Greenland and was determined to return to the High North. He had read widely into the "Arctic problem" and had his own ideas about how to solve it. De Long considered Melville "a No. 1 man and a brother." He would be reporting to San Francisco within the month.

The only other slot De Long had devoted attention to filling was that of expedition surgeon. Inquiries throughout the ranks had produced only one name of a first-rate Navy physician who was ready and willing to go to the Arctic: Passed Assistant Surgeon James Markham Ambler. A quiet, handsome man of thirty-one, Dr. Ambler came from a prominent family (his father was also a doctor) in Virginia's Fauquier County, in the foothills of the Blue Ridge Mountains near Washington. As a teenager, he had served as a cavalryman in the Civil War, but he had spent much of his service languishing in a squalid Union prison camp. Ambler had been educated at Washington College (now Washington and Lee University) and was a graduate of the University of Maryland medical school. He had practiced for three years in Baltimore before entering the Navy in 1874.

Among his assignments, Ambler had served on a corvette for an extended cruise of the West Indies. He had recently become engaged—and was thus, according to one historian, "conspicuously lacking in enthusiasm for an Arctic cruise." But as a survivor of a prisoner-of-war camp, the young doctor seemed in no way daunted by whatever horrors the Arctic might bring. De Long looked forward to meeting Ambler in Washington; the doctor was on furlough in nearby Virginia, staying with his family.

THE DE LONGS arrived in Washington and checked into the Ebbitt House, a distinguished hotel at Fourteenth and F Streets that was popular among high-ranking Army and Navy figures. It was a six-story establishment with a mansard roof and a continental restaurant that served such delicacies as "broiled redhead duck with currant jelly sauce." General William Tecumseh Sherman occupied a suite in the hotel, as did Civil War admiral David Dixon Porter. Ebbitt House would be De Long's residence and base of operations for the next three months.

Within a few days, De Long met with the secretary of the Navy, Richard Wigginton Thompson. A country lawyer and politician from Indiana, Thompson was a gangling, apparently humorless man of seventy with white hair, bug eyes, and a huge beaklike nose. A civilian appointee who had no experience at sea, he was said to be laughably unprepared for the post of Navy secretary. A telling though possibly apocryphal story had it that soon after Thompson was hired, he conducted an inspection of a new warship; when he ventured belowdecks, the incredulous landlubber blurted out, "My God, the durned thing's hollow!"

Clueless though he may have been, Secretary Thompson declared himself completely committed to De Long's quest for the pole and pledged to do whatever he could to give the young captain the authority necessary to make it a national undertaking. "When you sail I intend for you to have the same power that is conferred upon admirals commanding fleets," Thompson told De Long. "This expedition must succeed, and you shall be forearmed against all disaffection, insubordination, and disaster." Thompson was an optimist who believed that with the Bering Strait route, De Long had "struck the gateway to the Pole."

At Thompson's urging, Congress acted promptly, on February 27 passing a bill that formally declared De Long's voyage an American enterprise, while acknowledging that a private citizen, James Gordon Bennett, would be paying for nearly everything. The bill noted that every man serving aboard the *Jeannette* would be "subject in all respects to the Articles of War and Navy Regulations and Discipline." De Long, while technically only a lieutenant in the U.S. Navy, would serve as the expedition's captain and head for the Arctic under naval orders, flying naval colors, and he would be given full authority to hold his crew "in subordination in the event of any insurrection among them." The project, now fully cloaked in the Stars and Stripes, was given a new official name: the U.S. Arctic Expedition.

For weeks, De Long would continue to hound various figures within the chambers and corridors of the Navy Department—"prodding them up all the time," as he put it—and he seemed to win everything he wanted. In regular contact with Danenhower via telegraph, De Long oversaw every detail of the *Jeannette*'s reconstruction from afar, while also communicating almost daily with Bennett in Paris. "A word from San Francisco is enough to enlighten me and I immediately open fire on the Department," he wrote the publisher. Bennett, in turn, cabled back that he was pleased that "you are getting your way in Washington."

All in all, De Long was tremendously pleased with his efforts. Secretary Thompson promised to intervene when necessary to prevent the Mare Island engineers from making frivolous or exorbitant repairs on the *Jeannette*. Thompson also said the Navy would provide a man-of-war to haul extra coal and other provisions as far as Alaska, "if there is a suitable ship at San Francisco at the time."

In short, everything De Long had sought by traveling east was coming to pass. Washington, it seemed, was opening up to him and his expedition—not only the Navy Department but Congress, the Smithsonian Institution, even the White House. One night the De Longs were invited to meet with President Rutherford B. Hayes and the First Lady. Emma thought the president a "quiet, pleasant gentleman who did not impress me very much"—a description that more or less mirrors what everyone said about the milquetoast Ohioan. A Civil War hero, wounded five times, he had been elected—some said "appointed"—in one of the most acrimonious presidential elections in American history, losing the popular vote but winning the White House only after Congress awarded the Republican candidate twenty disputed electoral votes. (Because of this, many Democrats refused to consider his presidency legitimate, calling him "Rutherfraud.")

The De Longs' meeting with President Hayes was largely a pro forma affair. "He knew nothing about Arctic exploration," Emma said, "and was only doing his duty in having us." If the evening seemed dreary, it may have been partly the result of First Lady Lucy Hayes and her alcohol-free policy—a policy that had earned her the sobriquet "Lemonade Lucy." (It was said that in the Hayeses' temperate White House, "water flowed like wine.")

Given how bored President Hayes seemed by the coming polar expedition, Emma hoped that the marginally more vivacious Mrs. Hayes would rescue their little soiree, "but even she did not manage to make the evening very exciting." As the De Longs took their leave, Lucy presented them with a large formal bouquet, a gesture that Emma appreciated but found extremely "stiff."

A FEW DAYS later, De Long finally met the man who would serve as the *Jeannette*'s physician, James Ambler. The Navy doctor came over to the Ebbitt House and introduced himself. De Long liked him immediately, but Dr. Ambler, it turned out, had bad news to report: He had discreetly done some medical sleuthing into the case of John Danenhower's "disordered intellect," and the situation appeared much more troubling than De Long had realized.

Ambler had visited the Government Hospital for the Insane, where he'd interviewed physicians who had treated Danenhower for "melancholia." They seemed to think it highly likely that Danenhower's insanity would recur, especially in an environment as harsh as the Arctic.

Then Ambler had dug a little deeper. At the Navy's Bureau of Medicine and Surgery, he'd found Danenhower's medical logs from his time aboard the *Portsmouth,* the ship on which he'd been serving, near Hawaii, when his condition first emerged, in 1875. These records indicated that Danenhower had been declared "unfit for duty," noting that in addition to suffering from a debilitating depression, he was also afflicted with neck abscesses. (These unsightly lesions, Ambler thought, could possibly be an indication that Danenhower had syphilis—and, in fact, the *Portsmouth*'s physician noted that their genesis was "not in the line of duty.") The physician went on to note that the "gloomy" and "despondent" Danenhower "repeatedly expressed to me that he had a strong inclination to jump overboard and end his misery."

Ambler told De Long that his unequivocal assessment was that a man who had been declared not only unstable and depressed but also suicidal had no business serving as an officer of an Arctic ship. Ambler thought that Danenhower's symptoms—whether physical or mental—could reappear at any time. "It is my considered opinion," he later wrote, "that the insidious disease is not unlikely to return after many years."

This was a bombshell for De Long, as he had grown fond of Danenhower, and had come to rely on him for everything back at Mare Island. Indeed, Danenhower knew more of the intimate details of the expedition than anyone but De Long himself. "I cannot replace him," De Long wrote Bennett. He worried that removing Danenhower from the roster would send him into a spiral of despair from which he might never recover. "To unship him now, if he is at all shaky, might bring about the climax we all desire to avoid." On the other hand, De Long knew Ambler was right. "My duty," he wrote, "seems clear."

Uncertain how best to go about it, De Long confided in Danenhower's brother, a prominent Washington attorney. De Long asked him to invent some family excuse for why his brother could not journey to the Arctic, some story of a "domestic nature" that would spare Danenhower any personal or professional embarrassment. De Long told the brother that he was "endeavoring to temper justice with kindness to all concerned, and that strange as it may appear to you, I have your brother's interest quite as nearly in my heart as his family." But the brother refused to participate in the ruse. Danenhower was "bent on going," his brother said.

The Danenhower family had political connections high within the Navy Department, and John's parents began to work behind the scenes to ensure that their son was formally declared fit for Arctic duty. Within a few weeks, the Navy Department issued a notice that all doubts about Danenhower's sanity were hereby declared "groundless, officially." De Long was told to take "no steps to imply distrust in the ability of any officer to perform his duties when he seems in every way capable." Reading between the lines, De Long understood this to mean that removing Danenhower from the roster would be viewed as persecuting a fellow officer—and could result in a court-martial.

De Long's hands were tied. Whether he liked it or not, Danenhower was coming to the Arctic.

DURING HIS THREE months at the Ebbitt House, De Long was so immersed in minutiae that he scarcely had time to sleep or eat. "I have been working like a beaver," he wrote, "and in such a turmoil of difficulties." He spent long hours tracking down provisions, expedition equipment, and scientific paraphernalia for the *Jeannette*. He shopped for a portable observatory that could be set up on the ice pack to take astronomical and meteorological readings. He bought a small darkroom to develop the expedition's photographs. He investigated the latest in desalination distillers. He collected magnetic and meteorological equipment and vats of chemicals to be used in preserving biological specimens.

He ordered fifty-four thousand pounds of pemmican (a jerky-like mixture of dried meat, berries, and fat) and assorted canned goods. To combat scurvy—the classic bane of Arctic expeditions—he experimented with a concoction called *koumis,* made from fermented mare's milk, which was said to be widely used by nomads on the steppes of Kazakhstan. Finding this impractical, he tested a formula for concentrating lime juice, then had a dozen barrels of the sour, viscous stuff shipped to San Francisco.

De Long wanted the men of the *Jeannette* to lack nothing in the way of comfort and equipment. The ship would have a well-stocked library, a first-class infirmary, an arsenal of modern rifles and revolvers, a choice collection of games and entertainments, even a small organ for musical concerts. De Long prided himself that "everything the *Jeannette* might need in the polar wilderness seem[s] to have been thought of." Emma had never seen her husband lost in such a whirl of activity. De Long's nudgings and proddings were "incessant," she wrote. "His watchfulness was comprehensive and minute; no detail escaped him."

He procured telegraph keys, batteries, and miles of copper wire, which he planned to string over the ice pack to enable his officers to communicate with parties that might be sent out far from the ship. At the suggestion of the Smithsonian Institution, De Long conferred with Alexander Graham Bell about the "telephones" that had made such a splash at the Centennial Exposition. De Long procured two of them, in the hope of aiding long-distance communication over the ice.

De Long was interested in taking hot-air balloons to the Arctic, as well. This idea captivated Bennett, who was always wild for any novel contrivance or contraption. De Long speculated that a balloon attached to the *Jeannette*'s mast could "attain an increased height above the ship to command a larger horizon." A lookout perched in the balloon's basket would help De Long select the best water channels through tricky passages of ice. "One ascension," he wrote, "may save many days' weary work in a wrong direction." De Long thought that balloons might also be used to supply "lifting power" to heavy sledges and thus "lessen the difficulty of dragging them over floes and hummocks."

But after consulting with two of the greatest "aeronauts" then living—the American balloonist Samuel King of Philadelphia and his eminent French colleague, Wilfrid de Fonvielle—De Long relinquished the idea. Both experts indicated that prohibitive amounts of coal would be required to heat enough gas to keep a balloon inflated and aloft. Disappointed, De Long wrote to Bennett that unless he were to fortuitously "strike a vein of coal" somewhere in the High Arctic, "I cannot recommend you to adopt it on either the score of usefulness or economy."

Balloons may have been out of the question, but what about electric lights? De Long observed that for decades, Arctic expeditions "have suffered and men have pined for light during the long winter months." He had an idea that electric lights—then called "artificial suns"—would be a tremendously useful, at times almost miraculous, amenity for his crew. He imagined stringing a network of bright lights high up in the ship's rigging, by which the men could work, exercise, even play ball games out on the ice.

At that time, Thomas Edison, conducting experiments out of a ramshackle laboratory in Menlo Park, New Jersey, was trying to work out "the bugs," as he put it, in the incandescent lightbulb. The technology still had a ways to go, but an inferior form of illumination, arc lighting, was already in limited use, mainly in industrial settings. Arc lighting, which involved sending a high-voltage current across a small gap between two carbon bars, produced a light that was extremely bright but also extremely harsh. Robert Louis Stevenson detested the welder's-torch glare thrown by the arc lamp. "A new sort of urban star now shines out nightly," he wrote. "Horrible, unearthly, obnoxious to the human eye; a lamp for a nightmare!"

Still, De Long was keen on taking lights to the frozen north. "I should like to illuminate the ship from time to time, during the Arctic winter," he wrote Edison, "and subject the crew to the benefits morally and physically arising from [it]." Light at the North Pole—it was a romantic notion but a practical one, as well. Did the young inventor have anything that could work for De Long's purposes?

Edison responded enthusiastically and, of course, saw the enormous public relations benefit that might derive from sending his lamps up to the North Pole. His incandescent lightbulb was still only in a test phase, he said, but his system of arc lamps was ready to go. He wrote De Long right back and suggested that one of Bennett's representatives from the *Herald* come over to the laboratory and examine his arc lights and generators for himself.

The *Herald* promptly sent its chief science correspondent, Jerome Collins, and a demonstration was arranged in an upstairs lab. The arc lamps, a circuit of fifteen of them, blazed brightly—almost *too* brightly. They were kept illuminated by a hand-cranked mechanism Edison had devised. It would function well, Edison explained in a letter to De Long, "so long as your sailors keep their muscle. You can belt and crank the dynamo on it when you have no steam, and your crew can take a hand driving the machine. It will keep them warm." Should De Long's men tire of this hand-cranked device, Edison could provide a small, two-horsepower steam generator that would give the crew some relief.

De Long agreed to the transaction and placed his order with the Edison Electric Light Company: four circuits of fifteen carbon lamps (that is, a total of sixty arc lights), plus all the necessary wiring, a dynamo, and other equipment. A clerk at Menlo Park noted that the "machine for lighting the North Pole has been sent away." The arc lamp system shipped by train to San Francisco promised to produce light greater than three thousand candles. "Plants," De Long observed, "have been made to grow by it."

14 · ALL THAT MAN CAN DO

While De Long had been away in Washington, the shipwrights at Mare Island had slowly brought a new *Jeannette* into existence. From her insides out, she had been revamped,
refurbished, reengineered.

In her hold, the Navy designers had placed a network of double
trusses and iron box beams to withstand the crush of the ice. The
Jeannette's bow was filled in with solid timber and strengthened outside with new planking of the stoutest American elm. Her bilge was
reinforced with strakes of Oregon pine six inches thick. Hot pitch
was squeezed into every flaw and crevice. New decks were laid. The
cabins were rearranged and berths installed to accommodate thirty-
three men. Her bunkers were significantly enlarged to carry more
than 132 tons of coal. Heavy-duty pumps were added. Engines were
overhauled. A fresh suit of sails sewn. New rigging strung. The entire
ship painted and caulked.

On the spar deck, the engineers installed a steam-powered winch
that, in times of heavy ice, could hoist the rudder and propeller out of
harm's way. The winch could also be used to "warp" the ship—that
is, to advance the vessel, by means of ropes or chains attached to ice
anchors, through leads in the pack. The Mare Island machinists built
two new state-of-the-art boilers and installed a desalination apparatus
that could distill more than five hundred gallons of fresh water a day.

The *Jeannette*'s living quarters were thoroughly retooled for cold
weather. Her cabin and forecastle were insulated with thick felt. Car-

penters built new overhangs and porches, and the poop deck was layered with multiple sheets of thick painted canvas. A new heating system was installed. Orders were placed ahead in Alaska for a full complement of fur suits, boots, mittens, and blankets. Sleds were procured, as well as alcohol stoves and eight warm tents, designed for camping in the Arctic.

The *Jeannette* had become, according to one naval historian, "more sturdily fortified for ice encounter than any previous exploring ship." When De Long arrived in California with Emma that May, he went straight down to the yard and feasted his eyes on his new ship. He was smitten by the transformation that had taken place during his absence. "I am perfectly satisfied with her," he wrote. "She is everything I want."

De Long had to congratulate Danenhower on a job well done. "He has attended to everything with which I charged him," the captain said. As ambitious as her overhaul was, the final tally would come in under $50,000. De Long attributed this largely to Danenhower's vigilance, and he now felt guiltier about having considered removing the navigator from the ship's company.

In June, De Long, accompanied by a board of officers from the shipyard, took the *Jeannette* into San Francisco Bay to test her new engines and her turning power. She had been rebuilt with an eye toward structural integrity, not agility or speed. Though she was quite sluggish, the *Jeannette* passed her trials beautifully.

Through the months of May and June, the merchandise and provisions De Long had purchased on the East Coast began to arrive at Mare Island. Edison's arc lights were brought on board, as were Bell's telephones and telegraph equipment. The portable observatory was partially assembled. A darkroom was delivered, along with boxes of glass plates and other photographic paraphernalia. Stevedores hauled the *Jeannette*'s weapons on deck—Remington rifles and shotguns, Winchester repeating rifles, English self-cocking revolvers, two whale guns, ten muzzle-loading rifles, twenty thousand cartridges of ammunition, five hundred percussion caps, six kegs of blasting powder, and seventy pounds of shot. Next came the navigational and scientific equipment: chronometers, hydrometers, ozonometers, magnetometers, aneroid barometers, transits, sextants, pendulums, zenith telescopes, microscopes, test tubes, Bunsen burners, theodolites.

The possibilities for Edison's invention notwithstanding, De Long knew that the primary source of illumination during the expedition's long winters would be lamplight. So the *Jeannette* took on 250 gallons of sperm oil, hundreds of pounds of tallow, thousands of wicks, and all manner of lamps—bull's-eye lanterns, globe lanterns, bunker lanterns, hand lanterns.

Last to be loaded was the food, drink, and medicine—enough provisions to keep thirty-three men alive and healthy for three years. Anyone closely observing the manifests could tell there was drab eating ahead: The *Jeannette* took delivery of 2,500 pounds of roast mutton, 3,000 pounds of stewed and corned beef, 3,000 pounds of salt pork, and 100 pounds of tongue. Mostly the men would be drinking coffee, tea, and consommé, as well as daily rations of lime juice. But lovers of more ardent spirits could take heart: One of the ship's storerooms had been filled to the ceiling with barrels of brandy, porter, ale, sherry, whiskey, and rum, plus cases of Budweiser beer.

DE LONG, MEANWHILE, had made much progress filling the remaining positions for the *Jeannette*. From all quarters, the various officers, scientist specialists, and seamen had begun to arrive at Mare Island to get acquainted with one another—and with the reinforced ice ark they would call home for the next several years. Among the crew were three young Cantonese men Danenhower had hired in San Francisco to serve as cook, steward, and cabin boy. Officers Charles Chipp and George Melville had reached California a month earlier, and they had been helping Danenhower at the shipyard with the final improvements on the *Jeannette*.

Now other key players were making their way to Mare Island. De Long had known he would need an "ice pilot," someone intimately familiar with the behavior of the pack and the harsh peculiarities of the Arctic Ocean. Prowling the San Francisco wharves, the captain had eventually found his man. He was an experienced whaling captain, originally from New London, Connecticut, named William Dunbar. Forty-five years old, his leathery face cured by sun, wind, and salt, Dunbar was a grave, dutiful man who kept his prematurely white hair clipped close and bristly. He had been at sea since he was ten. As a sealer and whaler, Dunbar had spent much time in the treacherous waters around the Bering Strait, where he had developed "great tact in dealing with the frozen foe," said one newspaper account, "and a most valuable fertility of resource."

Dunbar had been to the frigid waters off Antarctica and all over the South Pacific, where he'd once had to be rescued from a deserted coral island after his vessel wrecked on a reef. Though Dunbar was the oldest member of the expedition, Melville described him as "hale and hearty and a fine example of a seasoned Yankee skipper." Dunbar would be the eyes of the ship—he was expected to spend much of his time perched in the crow's nest, scouring the icy seas. De Long felt lucky to have found him.

To serve as the expedition's naturalist, De Long had hired a civilian scientist from Salem, Massachusetts, named Raymond Newcomb. A shy, pasty, gnomelike man of twenty-nine years with a scruff of chin hair that gave him an adolescent look, Newcomb came strongly recommended by the Smithsonian Institution. He had worked for the United States Commission of Fish and Fisheries and described himself as "a student of natural history, ornithology, and zoology—the lower orders." He was descended from a distinguished New England family (his grandfather was a Revolutionary War hero who fought in the Battle of Lexington). De Long found Newcomb an agreeable, if mousy, sort of man who possessed a meticulous intelligence. The naturalist had traveled very little, though, and had spent almost no time at sea. He seemed most at home working among the scalpels, glycerin pastes, and fumy acids of the taxidermy trade. He would have much to prove in the Arctic.

The other civilian scientist who had signed up, an Irishman named Jerome Collins, cut a more formidable figure. Trained as an engineer in Cork, Collins was a big, voluble raconteur who served as the chief meteorologist for Bennett's *Herald*. He was the science correspondent Bennett had sent to Menlo Park to confer with Edison about the electric lights. A pioneer in weather forecasting, Collins had done much to advance the science of international meteorology and the understanding of prevailing wind patterns. From New York, he would analyze storm fronts as they headed east over the Atlantic and then cable alerts to the *Herald*'s offices in London and Paris so readers in Europe could prepare for the coming weather. His improvements in weather prediction had earned him accolades at the Meteorological Congress in Paris.

Collins was no staid weather nerd. As a younger man, he had been a prominent Irish Republican activist, one of the founders of the militant secret society Clan-na-Gael. Before coming to New York, he had lived briefly in England, where he'd hatched a plot to spring several incarcerated Fenian comrades from a London prison—an operation that had gone awry, forcing him into hiding for a time. He'd then led a study into the feasibility of using submarines to sabotage the British navy.

Collins's politics apparently had mellowed, and his career had taken many turns. Prior to his work as a meteorologist, he had been involved in harbor construction, bridge building, railway surveying, and an ambitious land reclamation project in the New Jersey salt marshes near Manhattan.

It was Bennett who had suggested Collins for the voyage. The Irishman would serve as the expedition's meteorologist, photographer, and "chief scientist" and would also be a "special correspondent" for the *Herald*. Collins was a droll, versatile man who could sing and play the piano—and could converse intelligently about almost any subject. As would later be revealed, he also had an incorrigible weakness for puns.

Danenhower thought Collins the very definition of a dilettante— an overly loquacious sort, as the navigator put it, "who knows a little bit about everything in general and not a great deal about anything in particular." But De Long, while somewhat skeptical, seemed pleased with the addition of Collins. "He has a large fund of general information," the captain wrote Bennett, "and will make a name for himself in the Arctic, I am sure."

ONE OF THE questions that had weighed heavily on De Long as the date of the *Jeannette*'s departure approached was when, and how, James Gordon Bennett would arrive in San Francisco to bid the men of the *Jeannette* bon voyage. Bennett had agreed to come over, with the caveat that he would have to remain incognito until he reached California. The publisher insisted that the newspapers—even his own—would have no knowledge of his arrival on the East Coast of the United States.

He would take a White Star Line steamer from Liverpool to New York. Then, under cover of night, he would transfer from the liner to a waiting yacht, where he would "steal ashore like a phantom," as one account put it, and board a chartered train car in New Jersey whose windows were completely shaded. According to the plan, Bennett would take the train as far as Omaha, then switch to another special car on the Union Pacific line that would speed him to California just in time for the departure.

De Long did not understand Bennett's obsession with such elaborate stealth. It was all so strange. "No matter how carefully you kept yourself in the background," he protested to Bennett, everybody would still know "you were sending the ship and paying for the expedition." There was no hiding the fact that Bennett was, as De Long put it, "the head and promoter of the expedition to the end."

What De Long failed to see was that Bennett's need for aloofness and mystery lay at the very heart of his personality. He yearned for the shadows, like the owls that decorated his villa, his yachts, his newspaper offices. He was incapable of doing anything directly or earnestly. Bennett really *was* a phantom—and an impossible patron for a straightforward man like De Long to figure out. Bennett would get there when he got there. All De Long could do was make a few discreet inquiries with the White Star Line and the Union Pacific Railroad, and wait.

Bennett's cloak-and-dagger shenanigans were responsible for an odd development that began to prey on De Long's peace of mind. In 1878, Professor Nils Adolf Erik Nordenskiöld, a prominent Finnish-Swedish explorer, had begun a multiyear journey to complete the Northeast Passage—that is, sailing along the entire length of Eurasia's northern coast, from Finland to the Bering Strait. Nordenskiöld and his vessel, the *Vega,* had not been heard from for the better part of a year, and Bennett, with his visions of repeating a "Stanley finds Livingstone" triumph for his newspaper, got in his head that De Long should search for Nordenskiöld along the northeast coast of Siberia before dashing off for the pole. Even if Nordenskiöld wasn't lost, Bennett sensed that the meeting of the two explorers could be an electric moment that would make headlines and sell papers around the world. Yet searching for the Scandinavian constituted an entirely separate errand, a detour that would likely occupy the *Jeannette* for weeks, if not months, and prevent her from making full use of the brief summer window of Arctic ice melt.

Although De Long found this new request exasperating, he was not privy to its source. Bennett conveyed his wishes for a Nordenskiöld search not directly to De Long but through Navy secretary Thompson. "I am sure you will agree with me," Bennett wrote Thompson, "that motives of humanity suggest as the very first object the rescue and aid of Professor Nordenskiöld." In reply, the secretary vowed that "rescuing Professor Nordenskiöld will be kept constantly prominent," and then he issued a formal command to De Long.

"On reaching Bering Strait," De Long's new orders read, "you will make diligent inquiry at such points where you deem it likely that information can be obtained concerning the fate of Professor Nordenskiöld. If you have good and sufficient reasons for believing that he is safe, you will proceed on your voyage toward the North Pole. If otherwise, you will pursue such course as, in your judgment, is necessary for his aid and relief."

De Long was furious. He did not understand why the Navy would jeopardize the mission's success by seeking to rescue another nation's expedition that was, he felt, neither lost nor in any significant danger. There was "unnecessary alarm" about the Scandinavian explorer, he thought, and most Arctic experts around the world agreed. Nordenskiöld's plan all along was to hug Siberia's icy coastline, never far out of sight of land—and anyway, he was not *expected* to be heard from for another four or five months. "I am as satisfied of Nordenskiöld's safety," De Long said, "as I am that tomorrow's sun will shine." He never guessed the real reason—Bennett's desire for another sensational newspaper scoop—that hovered behind the orders. What concerned De Long was that the hunt for Nordenskiöld could drain away the whole summer. "We may find them too late in the season for us to work north," he fretted. As a consequence, the *Jeannette* would effectively lose an entire year.

De Long's response to this wrinkle was the same one he instinctively summoned whenever he faced a new obstacle: He dug in, with his peculiar mingling of stubbornness and optimism. "I believe my resolution increases," he wrote Emma, "in direct proportion to the difficulties thrown in my way." Nordenskiöld was fine—of that he was sure. De Long would make cursory stops at a few villages along the Siberian coast and quickly dispel all doubts. With any luck, the detour would set him back only a week or two. He would fulfill his Navy orders, then be on his way north.

TEN DAYS BEFORE his departure date, De Long held a commissioning ceremony at Mare Island that bound the expedition under Navy discipline and officially pronounced the *Jeannette* a U.S. Navy ship. De Long gathered all the officers and crew on deck to read the Articles of War and the *Jeannette*'s official sailing orders. The captain wore his dress uniform with gold lace and epaulets. His pince-nez glasses caught glints of light reflecting off the bay, and a polished sword dangled at his side. Chipp, Danenhower, Melville, and Ambler stood beside him, their hats cocked at rakish angles. Emma was there, too, holding a blue silk flag she had sewn for the expedition—a flag to be hoisted over newly discovered lands and the North Pole.

Twenty-three crewmen, wearing Navy blues, took their positions on the deck, along with ice pilot Dunbar and the two civilian scientists, Newcomb and Collins. De Long read aloud portions of a cabled letter from Bennett, who promised that if the *Jeannette* were to become lost or stranded, he would rescue them. "I will spare neither money nor influence to follow up and send assistance," the publisher vowed. Should the men of the *Jeannette* perish, those who were married could at least take comfort that "the widows will be protected by me."

Emma ran the blue silk flag up the mast, and it snapped in the breeze along with the American flag. The vessel would now sail over to San Francisco, for final provisioning. But it was official. The ship was duly commissioned, her name buttressed by a new designation: She was now the USS *Jeannette*.

De Long swelled with pride in his vessel and his men. "My heart is set on this thing," he wrote to Bennett. "We shall keep at it as long as the *Jeannette* floats and we are able to stand up . . . We have a good crew, good food, and a good ship, and I think we have the right kind of stuff to dare all that man can do."

15 · THE NEW INVADER

Late one night during the first week of July 1879, De Long was lingering with Emma in the sitting room of their suite in San Francisco's Palace Hotel. Books, charts, ledgers, and ship blueprints lay about the place, and De Long's head swam with vexing details as the day of his departure loomed.

The Palace, which had opened four years earlier at a cost of $5 million, was reputed to be the largest and most opulent hotel in the world—"built to whip all creation," in the words of Andrew Carnegie. The Palace's ceilings were fourteen feet tall, and each of its 755 suites boasted private baths, an early form of air-conditioning, and electric call buttons that allowed guests to make their wishes known, via intercom, to the hotel's armies of servants. The Palace was also equipped with the novelty of hydraulic elevators, paneled in redwood; they were known as "rising rooms."

George and Emma tried to savor their time together in this luxurious hotel. (Sylvie was temporarily living with Emma's sister in Iowa.) But the stress of their imminent parting weighed on both of them. For days, George had been distracted, unable to focus on the thousand pieces of minutiae associated with the voyage. Emma had been at his side through most of it, reading his correspondence, strategizing with him, serving as his sounding board—all the while "taking good care not to let my feelings get the better of me." During the trip around South America, Emma had come to know every inch of the

Jeannette, and she was so immersed in the planning that George had come to regard her as a vital member of his expedition.

Part of Emma wished she could join him in the Arctic, but she knew that was impossible. Her husband's dream of reaching the pole was his and his alone. His obsession with the Arctic was clear and constant, like a steady flame. Everything he had done for the past five years, all his efforts and travels and preparations, came down to this week. "For years, his mind had been turning to this point," she wrote. "He never imagined that he was to win a high reputation by some happy turn of fortune. He belonged to the men who have cared for great things, not to bring themselves honor, but because doing great things could alone satisfy their natures."

Later that night, De Long looked up from whatever he was reading and gazed at Emma. She was wearing a black velvet gown and a clair de lune necklace. He stared at her with a wistful expression that Emma found puzzling.

"I've been thinking," he said, "what a pretty widow you would make."

Emma's heart skipped a beat. It was uncharacteristically morose of him. It was not like George to entertain dark thoughts or wallow in sentiment. Her impulse was to rush to him, to give in to the emotions they both felt. But then she thought better of it. As she later wrote, "I was afraid the sluices would give way and we might both break down." She worried that if either of them faltered, "untold misery would have stalked beside us . . . and ruined our last days together."

Yet George pressed her. "If such a thing should happen," he said, "don't smother yourself with heavy mourning things." Should he die in the Arctic, he wanted her to dress simply and elegantly—and to look as beautiful as she did tonight.

Composing herself, Emma replied, "I *shan't* be a widow."

George left it at that. There was nothing to be done. Even if he had dark presentiments, the voyage could not be halted now. As he later wrote to her, "I am engaged in a great undertaking from which neither of us would have me retreat."

Later, George beckoned her and drew her upon his knee. "My arms went around his neck and my head rested on his shoulder," Emma recalled. They tried to prolong the moment, caressing each other, as carriages sped by the windows of the Palace and the noise of the city rose up from the hilly streets. "For an hour or more we talked quietly, holding ourselves rigidly in control."

OVER THE PREVIOUS few weeks, something remarkable had happened: George Washington De Long had become a national hero. Newspapers across America and the world had sung his praises. He could feel the hopes of the nation at his back, and that had helped to buoy him in his darker moments. What he hadn't reckoned on was pure celebrity. His sudden notoriety vaguely embarrassed him. It was not in his training or nature to hold the limelight—and he shrank from it.

De Long was a man, said the *San Francisco Examiner,* who dared to "force the Northern Sphinx to disclose its secrets." A reporter from Bennett's *Herald* lauded De Long for taking "his life in his hands and offering it up on the shrine of Arctic discovery." The *New-York Commercial Advertiser* declared, "Should success crown the efforts of the gallant commander, it will be one of the most brilliant geographical adventures ever won by man. The solution of the Northern Mystery would be the event of the century." A newspaper in upstate New York went further, stating that with the *Jeannette* expedition, "man is on the verge of a discovery before which the discovery of America by Columbus would pale."

As these overheated declarations began to suggest, the *Jeannette* carried the aspirations of a young republic burning to become a world power; the hubris at the heart of the endeavor was a quality of the times. "What the *Jeannette* will find, with the bold De Long commanding her, remains to be seen," wrote the *San Francisco Chronicle.* "He follows a new route, and will essay ingenious means hitherto untried. Will the new invader succeed in wresting from the Arctic her long-kept secret?"

A special correspondent for Bennett's *Herald* was in San Francisco to cover every detail of the departure, but there was still no sign of Bennett himself. The benefactor's absence was immensely disappointing to De Long, and he took it as a bad omen. In typical fashion, Bennett delayed answering De Long until the last possible moment, giving only vague indications that of course he would like to see his project commence.

Then, from somewhere in Europe, came the following cable: "Regret exceedingly I cannot be there to bid him Godspeed, but hope to be on hand to congratulate him upon successful return," it said. "Tell him I have greatest confidence in his energy and pluck, and I thank him sincerely for his fidelity to me. I wish this to be an American success." Should De Long fail, however, Bennett reiterated, he would spare no expense to find and rescue him.

It was vintage Bennett: brusque, aloof, pompous, and yet nearly limitless in its promises of financial generosity. Here was a cool man sitting on a warm pot of money. Bennett had probably never had any intention of coming to San Francisco—he hated crowds, hated emotion, hated, above all, to do anything that was "expected" of him. He had said his good-byes in Le Havre, and that was good enough. He would show his faith to De Long by writing checks.

In fact, he had written a big check that very week. The secretary of the Navy, Richard Wigginton Thompson, had earlier suggested to De Long that a fast ship full of good coal would be sent as far as Alaska so that the *Jeannette* would not have to carry such a large load. Navy officials also had suggested that a man-of-war might escort the *Jeannette* as far as the Bering Strait. But then a war had broken out between Chile and Bolivia, which made it "necessary to increase our force in the South Pacific."

Late in the game, the secretary of the Navy sent De Long a final message wishing him luck on the voyage and commending his fair ship "to the protective care of Almighty God." He also informed De Long that there was no longer a vessel available for hauling coal or escorting the *Jeannette*. This incensed De Long and left him scrambling to find an alternative. "The Government had shaken us adrift," he wrote, "and left us to paddle along by ourselves . . . we are beam-ended." In a moment of extreme pique, he wrote that the fate of the voyage was "hanging by a thread."

With scarcely a grumble, Bennett cabled to say he would foot the bill for a private vessel, the *Frances Hyde*. The chartered ninety-two-ton schooner, with its additional stores of coal, would cost Bennett tens of thousands of dollars, but that was not a problem. From Paris, he cabled De Long: "Any draft of yours will be honored."

De Long wrote back in gratitude: "Thank God I have a man at my back to see me through when countries fail." Still, Bennett's decision not to attend the bon voyage ceremonies cut to the quick. "I was electrified," De Long wrote Bennett. "When you finally telegraphed you would not come, it was like a blow aimed right at the success of the expedition."

————

IN THE LAST days before the *Jeannette*'s embarkation, De Long was the toast of San Francisco. Everywhere he went, he was met by cheering crowds, salutes, and doffed hats. At the Palace, he was deluged with letters. Friends and well-wishers sent him good-luck trinkets and talismans to take on board—including a flute that was said to have magical powers. "If you play it anywhere near shore," an accompanying note said, "I am sure the wolves will all come down to howl." A tract society provided a box of Bibles for the crew. The governor of California, William Irwin, arranged a luncheon. The San Francisco Chamber of Commerce passed a resolution praising the "brave and accomplished commander" and his "picked band of reso-lute men." A popular local medium who claimed to "see with eyes not material" conducted a well-attended séance during which she claimed to have learned that De Long would "get farther than any man living has been" and that he would survive the adventure to "die quietly" in his bed.

De Long received innumerable letters from Arctic theorists and cranks. One predicted solemnly that at the 87th parallel, De Long and his men would "enter a region . . . where a tropical heat would meet them issuing from the hollow centre of the earth." Another writer was convinced that De Long's expedition would prove "the feasibility of trans-oceanic communication for commercial purposes between the Pacific and England" via the Bering Strait—all De Long had to do was chart the way and the route could be easily marked with a system of lighthouses and buoys.

Meanwhile, newspapermen from around the country clamored to secure "exclusive" interviews with De Long. The captain refused all comers, often with a gruff reply: "I have no information to give upon the subject." De Long had long ago learned the value of reticence—and besides, he had no time to fritter away on interviews. "He is fro-zen already," lamented one reporter, "and can't be thawed out."

One afternoon, the California Academy of Sciences held a recep-tion in honor of De Long and his officers. Noted scientists from all over the West Coast attended. They were curious to know what De Long sought to learn in the Arctic and what he hoped to accomplish there. Responding to their queries, De Long rose diffidently and spoke a few brief words. "It is one of the most difficult things," he began, in fact, it is an *impossible* thing—for one starting out on an expedition of this kind to say in advance what he is "going to do." After reaching the seventy-first parallel of latitude, we go out into a great blank space. You will excuse me, therefore, from attempting to explain what we are "going to do." If you will be kind enough to keep us in memory while we are gone, we will attempt to tell you "what we have done" on our return, which, I dare say, will be more interesting. I can only return to you my sincere thanks for the interest you manifest in our peculiar undertaking.

The scientists of the academy offered a toast, and then De Long and his officers departed the reception to a rousing ovation.

A few days later, De Long visited San Francisco's Merchants Exchange to confer with a very different society of experts—a large group of Arctic whaling captains who happened to be in port. The meeting had been arranged by De Long's good friend William Bradford, an acclaimed painter known for his dramatic Arctic scenes who was well acquainted with the world of the whalers. Bradford thought it would be good for De Long to avail himself "of whatever information their experience might afford and suggestions they might have to make."

The get-together turned out to be a seminar on Arctic conditions, with Bradford serving as moderator. One by one, the whaling captains stood to speak. They were greasy, grizzled men, most of them from New England, who understood the perfidiousness of the Arctic better than anyone else. They were from the same fraternity of men that De Long had met with in New Bedford a few years earlier, when he had learned that a North Pole attempt via the Bering Strait would essentially be "going downhill." Now the captains told De Long what they knew of the prevailing currents and the violent winds and the weird behavior of the ice around the Bering Strait. They shared their wisdom and legends and rumors, relating all that they had heard about the mysterious Wrangel Land.

De Long was grateful for their advice, and he questioned them closely. They did not mince words about the dangers of the ice pack. In the summer of 1871, thirty-two whaling vessels, carrying more than a thousand men, had entered the pack north of the Bering Sea and were destroyed. Still, many of the whalers believed that if he kept going, De Long eventually would find the Open Polar Sea. "How we envy Captain De Long," one whaler, Captain Benjamin Franklin Homan, would write. "How beautiful and warm and pleasant it will be in that warm sea around the north pole whare thare [*sic*] will be found all sorts of life and sumer [*sic*] fruits. What a lovely vineyard to live in."

Another whaling captain remained "ominously silent," Bradford recalled, "not venturing an opinion or offering a suggestion." This taciturn fellow was Ebenezer Nye, a legend among whalers. He was the wealthy captain of the *Mount Wollaston* and had significant stakes in many other whaling vessels. A fifty-seven-year-old man from New Bedford, Massachusetts, Nye had been a whaler since he was nine, and he had a reputation as a nearly miraculous survivor of the high seas. He had been shipwrecked three times in the Arctic and had once drifted for twenty-one days in a lifeboat across the South Pacific, losing seventy pounds of his body weight. Bradford thought Captain Nye was "one of the oldest, bravest, and best men in the service . . . There was no man sailing to the frigid seas who knew more of their perils than he."

Disturbed by Nye's reticence, Bradford finally stood up and singled him out. "Captain Nye has not given us his opinion," Bradford announced, "and we would like to hear from him."

Nye rose reluctantly and rendered his thoughts. "Gentlemen, there isn't much to be said about this matter," he began. He noted that he himself would be heading up to hunt for whales along the very same ice pack where De Long would be, not far from Wrangel Land. "Lt. De Long," Nye asked, "you have a very strong vessel, have you not?"

Yes, De Long replied. After all the reinforcements that had been completed on Mare Island, he thought the *Jeannette* was "strong enough to fight her way to the Pole."

"And she is magnificently equipped?" Nye continued.

Yes, De Long said.

"And you will take plenty of provisions, and all the coal you can carry?"

De Long said he would.

Captain Nye mulled over everything he had heard. "Well, then," he said, "put her into the ice and let her drift, and you may get through. Or, you may go to the devil—and the chances are about equal."

JULY 8, THE day of the *Jeannette*'s departure, dawned with a gravity that seemed in keeping with Captain Nye's pronouncement. All
morning the skies over San Francisco churned with storms. Over at
the Merchants Exchange, the skippers scowled at the gloom and predicted "dirty weather" for the *Jeannette*. "She'll have it devilishly thick
all the way up the coast," one captain was heard to say. But by the
forenoon, the sun had begun to burn through the clouds and the
winds had settled down to a steady light breeze from the southwest, a
favorable direction for the *Jeannette*. Soon it was crisp and clear, with
only a scrim of fog over Mount Tamalpais. Said one reporter: "Nature
relented."

As church bells clanged throughout the city, crowds began to
swarm along the piers and high on the flanks of Telegraph Hill, which
by early afternoon looked to one observer like the "bristling back of
a huge porcupine." The decrepit Meiggs Wharf, at the end of Market
Street, teetered from the weight of the throngs. On the Embarcadero,
police formed barricades and wielded billy clubs to keep the crowds
at bay.

The object of the public's attentions lay at anchor, just off Yerba
Buena Island, bobbing gently in the shallows, her yards squared,
her stack occasionally issuing wisps of black smoke. "The taut little
bark," said the *Daily Alta California,* was "the cynosure of thousands
of eyes." From the *Jeannette*'s mainmast flew the American flag and
the blue silk expedition flag Emma had sewn. The ship was freshly
painted and scrubbed clean. It sat noticeably low in the water from
the stores of coal and provisions she'd taken on board. Some of the
expedition members could be seen walking the decks or scrambling
over the rigging. Other crewmen leaned over the bulwarks, wrote a
reporter, "gazing with sorrowful eyes at the city of wealth and luxury,
whose streets they might never tread again."

Dozens of yachts skimmed along the bay—sleek pleasure craft
with pert names like *Frolic, Magic, Lively, Virgin,* and *Startled Fawn*.
The entire fleet of the local yacht club had answered its commodore's
call to appear en masse and escort De Long to sea. Mingling with
the yachts were tugs, fishing boats, and chartered steamships loaded
down with well-wishers. The captains of these motley vessels were
stalling, idling, circling, in anticipation of the moment of departure.

By two o'clock, the *Jeannette*'s officers and crew were all on
board—everyone, that is, except for De Long. The captain was still

in his suite at the Palace Hotel with Emma. In full uniform, he was at his desk, working on an official letter to Washington—

San Francisco, CAL, July 8th, 1879

Hon. R. W. Thompson,
Secretary of the Navy—

Sir,
      I have the honor to inform you that the Jeannette, *being in all respects ready for sea, will sail at three o'clock this afternoon on her cruise to the Arctic regions. While I appreciate the grave responsibility entrusted to my care, I beg leave to assure you that I will endeavor to perform this important duty in a manner calculated to reflect credit upon the ship, the navy, and the country. I desire to place upon record my conviction that nothing has been left unprovided which the enterprise and liberality of Mr. James Gordon Bennett could suggest.*
      Your obedient servant,
      George W. De Long

Shortly after completing the letter, De Long nodded to Emma, and together they rode one of the Palace's "rising rooms" down to a carriage waiting outside. The driver sped them to the wharf at the end of Washington Street. When the De Longs emerged from their carriage at precisely three o'clock, a roar went up from the crowds, which were estimated to number more than ten thousand people.

It was "quite a mob," De Long said, and Telegraph Hill was "black with people." He turned and removed his hat in acknowledgment; then he and Emma squeezed through a press of dignitaries, making their way to the water's edge. There, with thousands of spectators whistling and waving hats, the couple stepped into a small boat and were briskly rowed to the *Jeannette*. The plan was for Emma to accompany George as far as the Golden Gate, where she would finally bid her husband farewell. She and the De Longs' close friend William Bradford, already aboard the *Jeannette*, would hitch a ride back to the city on one of the convoying yachts.

At around four o'clock, the *Jeannette* weighed anchor and her screw propeller spun in the water. The ship slowly turned toward Alcatraz. So burdened was she with coal and provisions that some skeptics questioned how De Long would outrun even the most sluggish Arctic icebergs. The ship "moved so slowly," noted the *Chronicle,* "as to excite satirical remarks regarding the possibility of her escaping the slowly-closing jaws of ice-pinch in some future hour of peril." At her present rate of speed, noted the Vallejo paper, "it will not take over ten years to reach the North Pole . . . if the wind is favorable."

As the *Jeannette* steamed into the bay, yachts flitted around her, and people clung to the rails of chartered steam ferries, shouting farewells amid clouds of handkerchiefs. Melville, the engineer, thought it "right royal," with so many "jolly tars huzzaing and firing guns with deafening effect." De Long was nearly brought to tears by the "immense demonstration."

Yet the captain couldn't help noticing that the Navy's presence was missing from the celebrations. "Not a sign of a naval officer was seen in the departing ovation," De Long wrote. "It was a mortification to me." The absence was especially conspicuous because he knew that three ships from the Pacific Fleet—the *Alert, Alaska,* and *Tuscarora*— lay at anchor only a few miles away. If this wasn't insult enough, a Navy tug on some separate errand cut across the *Jeannette*'s wake and angled off for Mare Island without so much as a toot of its whistle. As far as Emma was concerned, this was "shabby treatment" from a Navy that had become jealous of the international attentions the *Jeannette* had received and whose entrenched political hierarchies were uncomfortable with the hybrid public-private nature of this project.

But just as the *Jeannette* was about to slip through the Golden Gate, the Army redeemed the Navy's slight: The Fourth Artillery fired an eleven-gun salute from the ramparts of the Presidio. The resounding boom carried over the water, delighting the men of the *Jeannette.* Collins reveled in the spectacle of the big guns "belching away and the fat lumps of white smoke rolling down to the sea below." Melville called it a "solemn amen to the godspeeds of the people . . . Never was a departure more auspicious."

De Long answered the Army's courtesy by dipping his colors, and from the "brazen throats" of the accompanying tugs came a chorus of steam whistles. "We now see the old flag waving high on its mast over the stronghold of Uncle Sam," wrote Collins. "Farewell, brave boys, may your guns always salute friends and terrify enemies. Not a man on board has the shadow of a melancholy thought on his face. We are happy in the knowledge that millions bear us friendly wishes."

SOON THE *JEANNETTE* was on the open Pacific, pitching in the swells as she turned toward the northwest. The sky ahead appeared foggy, and there was a stiff breeze. Collins tried to lighten the mood in the wardroom by sitting at the small pump organ and regaling Emma and George with stanzas from the new Gilbert and Sullivan comic opera, *H.M.S. Pinafore*. Around six o'clock, a yacht called the *Frolic* pulled up close to their stern. De Long knew its purpose: The time had come for Emma and Bradford to return to San Francisco. "The hour is at hand . . . time's up," Collins wrote. "We part company with civilization for the present."

Emma found a private moment with Dr. Ambler, whom she had come to regard as a confidant. "Will you be a close companion to my husband?" she asked the surgeon. "You know how lonely a commanding officer must necessarily be."

Ambler vowed that he would, but then he qualified his statement. The Arctic was a peculiar place, he said. "No doubt we'll lose our sense of proportion. Please be lenient in your judgment of us."

De Long intervened to say, "It's time to go." As a small boat was lowered from the davit, Emma shook hands with the other officers, greeting each one, thought Collins, "with a fortitude that was fairly heroic." Then she turned to speak to some of the crew. "Stay good friends and pull together . . . you must succeed!" she said. "I beg you to stand by your captain."

George and Emma climbed into the boat, with Bradford following them. As the sailors rowed away for the *Frolic,* there were, said Collins, "few dry eyes upon the quarter deck of the *Jeannette*." Bradford found the brief trip excruciating. "The silence was oppressive," the artist later wrote, "the only sound being the thump of the oars in the rowlocks and the swash of the water." Reaching the side of the *Frolic,* De Long pressed his wife's hand and said, simply, "Good-bye." She put her arms around his neck, and they kissed. It was only then, De Long wrote, that "the full force of my going away struck home . . . I felt stunned."

Emma climbed aboard the yacht, then turned and gave George a look that seemed to Bradford a "devout silent prayer for his safety." Bradford could see that the "pang of separation was heightened by her regret that she could not share his trials." De Long seemed to hesitate, "as if for a moment unnerved." Then, regaining his composure, he turned to the sailors and said, in a sure voice, "Pull away, men." Then he returned to his ship.

Emma watched the *Jeannette* until it was merely a gray dot on the horizon. When it was gone from sight, she went belowdecks, as the *Frolic* turned back toward San Francisco. "I craved only solitude," she wrote. "A complete apathy took possession of me. It seemed . . . the end of everything."

Aboard the *Jeannette,* De Long sat at his desk. The U.S. Arctic Expedition, he was pleased to write in his log, finally had commenced. He noted, "The ship is now beginning her voyage to that unknown part of the world lying north of Bering Strait. May God's blessing attend us all."

The *Jeannette,* a *Chronicle* reporter wrote, became a "long dark pencil of shadow standing up straight against the vivid sunset." Then she was gone. "Three years hence, De Long will probably announce his return. For the present he is lost to the world. He is sailed out into the dark, and the world can only watch the edge of the darkness for the first glimmer of the *Jeannette*'s whitening sails."

PART THREE

A Glorious Country to Learn Patience In

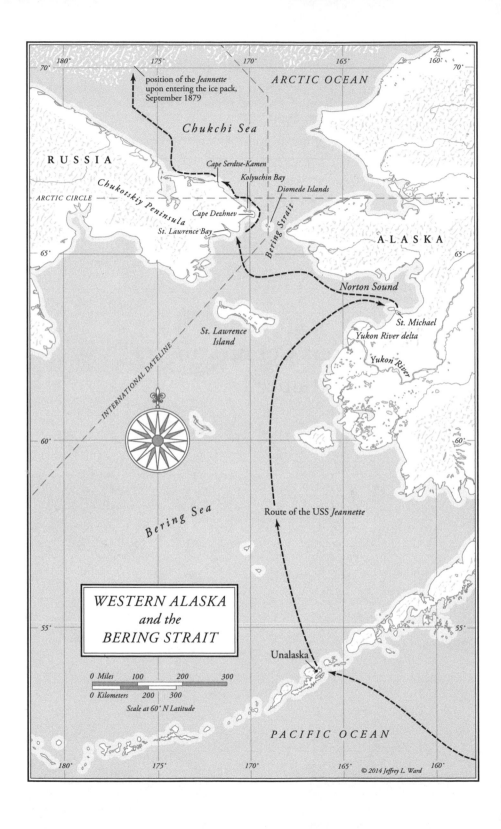

position of the *Jeannette*
upon entering the ice pack,
September 1879

ARCTIC OCEAN

Chukchi Sea

RUSSIA

Cape Serdtse-Kamen

Kolyuchin Bay

Diomede Islands

ARCTIC CIRCLE

Chukotskiy Peninsula

Cape Dezhnev

St. Lawrence Bay

Bering Strait

ALASKA

Norton Sound

St. Michael

Yukon River delta

Yukon River

St. Lawrence
Island

INTERNATIONAL DATELINE

Bering Sea

Route of the USS *Jeannette*

WESTERN ALASKA
and the
BERING STRAIT

Unalaska

0 Miles   100   200   300

0 Kilometers   200   300

Scale at 60° N Latitude

PACIFIC OCEAN

© 2014 Jeffrey L. Ward

Even while the *Jeannette* steamed north toward the Bering Strait, another world-renowned vessel was steaming south out of it, and down the North Pacific coast of Russia. It was the *Vega*, Adolf Nordenskiöld's exploring ship. The world didn't know it yet, but the Finnish-Swedish scientist and explorer had emerged, a month earlier, from his winter quarters in northeast Siberia and was well on his way to Japan, where he would announce his considerable accomplishment: Nordenskiöld had become the first navigator to make a complete Northeast Passage—that is, a journey across the top of the entire continent of Eurasia. Hugging the land for the most part, the *Vega* had successfully worked its way along the eight-thousand-mile coastline of the Russian Arctic.

De Long had guessed from the start that Nordenskiöld was safe—that, indeed, he had never really been in any danger. The Scandinavian didn't need to be "found," any more than Livingstone had needed to be hunted down in Africa. But Bennett had wanted his "De Long meets Nordenskiöld" moment, and that was the end of it.

But the timing of Nordenskiöld's emergence from the ice was particularly bad for De Long. He had missed Nordenskiöld by only a week. By the time De Long approached Alaskan waters, the *Vega* was making for the Kuril Islands of Japan. As one Arctic historian put it, "Somewhere in the fog-wreathed Bering Sea between the Aleutian Islands and Norton Sound, the USS *Jeannette* and the ship she was supposed to look for passed each other on opposite courses."

Meanwhile, another bit of rotten luck was brewing in Washington. Earlier in the summer, a schooner commissioned by the U.S. Coast and Geodetic Survey had made its way out of the Arctic after an ambitious multiyear study of the North Pacific and the Bering Sea. The hydrographers and meteorologists hired by the geodetic survey had been conducting painstaking analyses of oceanic currents, depths, salinities, temperatures, and prevailing windpatterns. Specifically, the survey was interested in learning about the Kuro Siwo—the Black Current of Japan. Much of the data had yet to be analyzed, but already clear patterns were starting to emerge.

The Kuro Siwo, the findings suggested, was not nearly as strong or as warm or as reliable as the Atlantic's Gulf Stream. As it swept up from the coast of Japan and out into the open ocean, the Kuro Siwo frayed into numerous subsidiary currents, and its power steadily waned. If anything, the prevailing tendency at the Bering Strait was that of cold-water currents flowing *south.*

The survey's final report would be written by an eminent Harvard-trained naturalist, William Healey Dall. Dall was a scientist of wide-ranging interests—he had published papers in the fields of ornithology, anthropology, oceanography, and paleontology and had conducted numerous meteorology studies for the Smithsonian Institution. Dall had traveled extensively in Alaska, and his name would become well known throughout the region.

Dall's report on the Black Current was unequivocal. "The Kuro Siwo sends no recognizable branch northward, between the Aleutians and Kamchatka," he wrote. "No warm current from Bering Sea enters Bering Strait. The strait is *incapable* of carrying a current of warm water of sufficient magnitude to have any marked effect on the condition of the Polar Basin just north of it. Nothing in our knowledge of them offers any hope of an easier passage toward the Pole, or, in general, northward through their agency. Nothing yet revealed in the investigation of the subject in the least tends to support the widely spread but unphilosophical notion, that in any part of the Polar Sea, we may look for large areas free from ice."

By the time these devastating findings were released, De Long had sailed from San Francisco, and thus he never saw them. They called into question nearly all the scientific theories on which the *Jeannette* expedition was based—theories that had been endlessly reaffirmed in the popular imagination. (After the *Jeannette* set sail, the *Herald* had declared that it was "undebatable that a warm current of water from the Pacific flows into the Arctic Ocean at Bering Strait.") But as the U.S. Coast and Geodetic Survey results were showing, there was no warm current tunneling under the ice cap. There was no thermometric gateway to the pole. And, likely, there was no Open Polar Sea. The theories of Silas Bent, Matthew Fontaine Maury, and the late August Petermann were resoundingly wrong.

While the *Jeannette* wallowed ever northward, scientists and bureaucrats in Washington slowly digested the new data. Everything they learned seemed to suggest that De Long's voyage, before it had even begun in earnest, was a fool's errand.

Another scientist who would closely study the survey data was a respected physician and chemist named Thomas Antisell. Dr. Antisell, in an address before the American Geographical Society in New York, was ruthless in his conclusion. The portal De Long was aiming for offered "no real gate of entrance into the Arctic Ocean," he said. "The North Pacific Ocean has, practically speaking, no northern outlet; Bering Straits is but a *cul de sac.*"

17 · NIPPED

On August 12, a little more than a month after she crossed the Golden Gate and steamed out to sea, the USS *Jeannette* eased into the bay near St. Michael, Alaska. As she dropped anchor in Norton Sound, a lookout at the fort loaded a decrepit cast-iron cannon, dating back to Russian days, and fired a few salvos in the *Jeannette*'s honor.

St. Michael, a trading post established by Czar Nicholas I in 1833, was the collection point and business hub for much of America's dealings with her raw new territory in the Far North. There was not much to the place—several crumbling storehouses, an ammunition depot, a few clusters of small houses, and an old Russian Orthodox church. But this would be De Long's final supply stop before heading into the unknown. Here he would take on stores, replenish his coal bunkers, collect furs, purchase dogs, and send off correspondence.

The settlement was located less than a hundred miles from the northernmost mouth of the Yukon delta, where a plume of reddish-brown river sediment reached far out into the sea. St. Michael was frequented by whalers, sealers, miners, trappers, merchants, and commercial agents who sold supplies for anyone venturing into the Alaskan interior. Massive quantities of furs and skins—more than a million dollars' worth—were said to be shipped out of St. Michael each year.

This was the season when the ships from San Francisco arrived, when hundreds of Indians and Eskimos camped outside the fort to meet with representatives of the fur companies, to trade pelts and skins and dried fish for calico and guns and rum. Clusters of Indians huddled around bonfires of driftwood that had floated down the mighty Yukon. It was a time of roistering and wrestling and tug-of-war contests under the midnight sun, a time of "mallemaroking," as the whalers called their drunken sprees.

De Long wanted his men to savor a few days of the Arctic summer and to enjoy the festiveness of this bustling fort on the outermost, uppermost edge of the American empire. Even so, he found St. Michael to be "a miserable place." There was an air of decay here, De Long thought, of corruption and licentiousness fueled by liquor and greed. Yet he knew that this was likely the last they would see of civilization, or of what passed for it, for several years. "We may yet look upon [St. Michael]," he wrote, "as a kind of earthly paradise."

IT HAD TAKEN De Long thirty-five days to cover the nearly three thousand miles between San Francisco and St. Michael. The ship, overburdened with coal, had "rolled and wallowed like a pig," he said, but for the first few days they had enjoyed mostly smooth sailing, and the mood on board was merry. At nighttime, Collins would sit at the organ and pick out tunes, and the men, some banging tambourines or plucking fiddles, would break into song.

At other times, Collins, tepidly at first, would try out a few puns on the crew. Once the floodgates opened, the waters flowed: Collins could not stop himself. "Some of them were good," De Long judged, "and some wretchedly poor." Just as often, his puns were incomprehensible, turning on a joke, perhaps Irish in origin, that the others just didn't get. "For a while we steadily refused to see his puns," De Long wrote, "and would all look at him as innocently and inquiringly as babies when he got one off, asking him to explain it two or three times over, until he finally exclaimed that our intellects must be weakening in proportion as we increased our distance from San Francisco. Now, however, we let him pun away, praise the good ones, and condemn the bad."

All in all, De Long could not have been happier with his men. They were "our little family," he said, "as fine a crew as ever went on board of a ship. There has not been a sign of a disagreement or a suspicion of a growl." They were a cross section of Gilded Age America— which meant an *immigrant* America, tough, self-reliant men who were hopeful and hungry for lives better than the ones they'd left behind in the Old World. There were Germans, two Danes, two Irishmen, a Finn, a Scot, a Norwegian, a Russian. There were French-Americans, Dutch-Americans, a few Scotch-Irish, and three Chinese.

De Long was particularly pleased with the Chinese cook, Ah Sam, and the steward, Charles Tong Sing, both of whom had been hired out of San Francisco's Chinatown. Ah Sam's cooking was good, De Long thought, and getting better all the time. He was a prodigious baker of breads—and though he made coffee far too weak for the men's liking, he was getting the hang of things and seemed to be enjoying himself. Sam and Charley were "impervious to all" and "ever cheerful," De Long thought, and seemed to have "no concern for the future, no cares for the past."

But the third Chinese crew member De Long had hired—Ah Sing, the cabin boy—was proving to be a disaster. Nervous, uncoordinated, and clueless, Ah Sing spoke no English and was forever stumbling about the ship, spilling food and liquids over the mess-hall diners, smashing plates and cups on the floor. He was "simply waste lumber," De Long thought. "He has already, by his stupidity, almost made me grow gray." Ah Sam and Charles Tong Sing were constantly correcting the boy, scolding him in torrents of Chinese. Something about Ah Sing's smile was unsettling. Sickly sweet and unchanging, it was a smile that drove everyone crazy—Melville, especially. Said De Long: "Melville would take him ashore now and shoot him if I passed the word."

On Unalaska Island, in the Aleutian chain, De Long had briefly stopped to take on some cargo, including furs, sealskins, deerskins, blankets, six tons of dried fish, and 150 tons of coal. He'd posted some correspondence with a southbound steamer, then turned north into the foggy Bering Sea to resume the long journey toward St. Michael.

For several days, the *Jeannette* encountered heavy seas that plunged the less experienced hands into horrible bouts of seasickness. Ah Sing looked "like a corpse resurrected," said De Long. "He was a shadow of his former self, his long pig-tail all in a confused mass of hair flying in the wind. I really feared he might die." But the Irish punster had the worst time of it. "Poor Collins was so sick that he could easily have lost his mother and not have known it," De Long wrote; though, he noted brightly, "His puns died out for a few days." Yet much to the captain's regret, as the *Jeannette* approached St. Michael, a restored Collins was "getting back to them again."

DE LONG HAD to wait in St. Michael for nearly a week for the *Francis Hyde,* the supply schooner Bennett had chartered back in San Francisco, to catch up, bringing his last stores of coal. So the captain busied himself with other matters. He bought smoked fish and raw meat. He commissioned the native Inuits to sew fur suits and sealskin blankets. He bought deerskin boots and an assortment of wolf and mink pelts. He inquired among the villagers for any tidings, or even rumors, of Nordenskiöld's whereabouts (though no one here knew anything). Representatives from the Alaska Commercial Company gave him more weapons and ammunition. From the Inuits, he bought forty sled dogs—"fine animals, young and active, and they took to me very kindly today when I visited them on shore."

Bringing dogs along had always been part of De Long's plan, but he realized that neither he nor any of his men knew how to drive or care for the animals. He went among the villagers to hire two knowledgeable hands to join the expedition. He quickly found two young men willing to sign on—Alexey, who listed himself as a hunter, and a friend named Aneguin. Though both spoke some English, the two young Inuits understood little about the expedition—where it was headed, what it was seeking to do, or the risks involved. They were mainly lured by what seemed, to them, exceedingly high pay. Alexey would receive $20 a month, plus a small stipend for his wife and child. Not only that: At the end of the expedition, he would take home the extraordinary gift of one Winchester repeating rifle with one thousand cartridges. The younger, unmarried Aneguin would receive slightly smaller wages.

The *Francis Hyde* finally arrived with the much-awaited coal shipment, and De Long set a departure date of August 21. That morning, the two Inuit dog drivers came on board and acquainted themselves with the *Jeannette.* An Inuit girl also boarded the ship for a short while. She was Alexey's wife—a stout, shy young woman whose broad smile could not mask the worry she felt for her husband. Their young boy came along, too. The scene of their farewell moved all the men of the *Jeannette,* many of whom were no doubt lovesick for their own wives or girlfriends. The couple held hands as they sat on a pile of potato sacks near the cabin door.

Collins, who caught the moment in a dispatch for the *Herald,* thought Alexey's wife "behaved with great propriety under the circumstances," showing "stolidity tempered by affection for her spouse." They lingered for a while, speaking softly to each other, tears pooling in their eyes. Seabirds wheeled overhead, and the ship banged and rattled as the last pieces of cargo were hoisted aboard. As the Inuit couple "exchanged vows of eternal fidelity," said Collins, "I was greatly touched."

De Long, perhaps thinking of his own farewell with Emma, was similarly moved. He tried to find something he could give the Inuit woman as a memento of the ship on which her husband would live for the next two or three years. The best he could scrounge up was a china saucer and teacup marked UNITED STATES NAVY in gilt letters. De Long also gave a harmonica to their boy. Alexey's wife accepted the gifts with gratitude. She "seemed overpowered with emotion at the possession of such unique treasures," Collins wrote, "and at once hid them in the ample folds, or rather stowage places, of her fur dress."

When De Long announced that it was time for all visitors to leave the ship, Alexey was reluctant to let his wife go. "Clinging together hand in hand, they wandered and wondered about the ship," said Melville, "until at last with many doubts and fears, they affectionately parted."

BEFORE DE LONG could head north in earnest, he had one more errand to accomplish: He still had to solve the mystery of the whereabouts of the Scandinavian explorer Adolf Nordenskiöld. He didn't necessarily have to *find* Nordenskiöld, but he did have to turn up convincing evidence that his ship, the *Vega,* had wintered safely and was in no need of assistance. De Long still chafed at this assignment, but since it had been issued by the secretary of the Navy himself, he could not shirk his responsibility. Of course, De Long didn't know that the mystery had already been put to rest. He feared he would have to waste weeks, maybe months, on this wild-goose chase. On the evening of August 21, the *Jeannette* weighed anchor and, with the *Francis Hyde* following behind, headed west, toward the Siberian coast, in search of tidings of the "lost" explorer.

While the *Jeannette* was crossing the Bering Sea in a heavy gale, a huge wave broke on board and struck the front of De Long's cabin. Instantly, the window was smashed, and his room flooded. "I was sitting dozing in my chair," he wrote, "when suddenly I was buried by the sea, covered with broken glass, and everything I had was afloat."

They approached Russia's St. Lawrence Bay, where De Long sent a party ashore to inquire about Nordenskiöld. The Chukchi natives there seemed to know something about a foreign ship that had spent the winter in an ice-locked bay farther up the coast. Some of the other natives recalled seeing a steamer working its way south along the coast in July.

Not wasting any time, De Long turned north, sailing toward the Diomede Islands and the strait. On August 27, somewhere in the open waters near the Bering Strait, the *Jeannette* and her coal tender, the *Francis Hyde,* prepared to part ways. De Long took on a last load of coal, then transferred his correspondence—including his final letter home to Emma—to the other ship. He had also decided to send Ah Sing, the hopeless cabin boy, back to San Francisco. There was no use keeping him. "I discharged the Chinese boy," De Long wrote. "He went on board the schooner with the same childlike and bland smile that has ever characterized him, accepting the inevitable as a philosopher."

Then the *Jeannette* turned north, and the *Francis Hyde* turned south. In the bundle of mail that the *Francis Hyde* carried was a dispatch Collins had written for the *Herald,* in which he concluded, "Feeling that we have the sympathy of all we left at home, we go north trusting in God's protection and our good fortune. Farewell!"

De Long made straight for East Cape—now called Cape Dezhnev—the easternmost point on the Eurasian continent. There, employing his new dog driver Alexey as a translator, De Long learned from an old woman in a local village that an exploring ship had indeed wintered at a place called Kolyuchin Bay, farther up the coast.

After crossing the Arctic Circle, the *Jeannette* next touched land at a place called Cape Serdtse-Kamen. The natives there led some of De Long's men on a hike over mossy tundra for several hours, until they came to a protected spot where, according to them, the foreign party had safely spent the winter. There, in tents, De Long's men rummaged among some tin cans marked STOCKHOLM, as well as through scraps of paper scribbled in Swedish. The men also found what Danenhower described as "some interesting pictures of Stockholm professional beauties." The Chukchi natives showed the crew some engraved navy buttons that had been given to them—which proved to be Swedish, Danish, and Russian. The Chukchis conveyed through sign language and pantomime that the foreign steamer had passed safely out to the east as soon as the ice had melted.

As far as De Long was concerned, all of this constituted evidence compelling enough to call the mystery closed—and to absolve him of any more detective responsibilities. "I believe all our hearts were thankful," he wrote, "that at last we knew Nordenskiöld was safe, and we might proceed on our way toward Wrangel Land . . . we will go on our way rejoicing."

So De Long was finally free to push north. On August 31, he turned the *Jeannette* out of Kolyuchin Bay and aimed in the presumed direction of Wrangel. He had to make up for lost time, using the last of the summer window to achieve as high a latitude as possible. At long last, said Danenhower, "we felt that our Arctic cruise had actually commenced."

FOR THE FIRST two days, they made good headway under sail, moving through ice-free seas. But then they began to encounter larger and larger pieces of drift ice. The weather turned sharp and cool, with the temperature ranging around twenty degrees Fahrenheit. A squall blew over the ship and left the rigging coated in a slick white film— a sudden harbinger of what was to come. "It was one mass of snow and frost," De Long said, "a beautiful sight." The snow didn't worry him, but the ice did. "We observe a gradual closing in of large floes around us," he noted. "The pack surrounding us seems to have a uniform thickness of about seven feet."

This unexpectedly early buildup of ice was offset by a turn of good news: On September 4, Dunbar, standing in the crow's nest, sighted Herald Island, a tiny crag in the Chukchi Sea well known among whalers. (Unrelated to Bennett's newspaper, the island had been named in 1849 by the man who first sighted and landed on it, Sir Henry Kellett, captain of the HMS *Herald*.) Herald Island was clearly marked on De Long's sketchy charts, but he knew that just beyond it, some fifty miles in the fog to the west, was supposed to be Wrangel Land, Petermann's elusive transpolar continent. It was the literal and figurative goal De Long had been aiming for, yet still he could not see it.

The next day, the men *did* snatch a glimpse of Wrangel—or at least they thought so. "During the forenoon," De Long said, "there were several occasions when we distinctly saw land beyond and above Herald Island, to the southwest. I should at first have been inclined to think [it] was a kind of false island made by mirage; but as it was in the shape of high snow-topped mountains with clearly defined edges, such as could not have been caused by mirage, I am strengthened in my belief that we really saw [Wrangel]."

After several more sightings, everyone was convinced: *Wrangel Land!* They rejoiced at the thought that they were so near the place where they could find winter quarters and begin exploring terra incognita.

The celebration was short-lived, however, for now the ship was thudding into ever-larger cakes of ice, sending them spinning sluggishly off to the sides. De Long, who had moved up to the crow's nest, tried to read the swirling patterns as best he could and pressed ahead, threading through the shrinking leads. "Our sides are scraped and scratched and cut," he wrote, "but they are the scars of honorable wounds received in action with the ice."

DE LONG FOUND the navigating reminiscent of his time aboard the *Little Juniata* off Greenland. He often had to push into a lead and ram the ice again and again until he had finally snubbed his way into a little crevice. The butting of the ship would often shoot elaborate spiderweb patterns of cracks well ahead of the bow. The *Jeannette* was usually able to "shove the floes apart enough to squeeze through," De Long said. More and more, as he pushed through these tight passages, De Long came to rely on Dunbar's advice. The New England codger could see things others couldn't, could discern patterns in the ice that were inscrutable to the other men. He was, said Melville, "our ancient mariner and Arctic authority . . . with that keenness of vision that comes from forty years' experience at sea."

At times, the men had to use the steam winch, with ropes and block-and-tackle pulleys attached to claws planted ahead in the ice, to jerk or "warp" the *Jeannette* forward. There were clanking noises and spewings of smoke and hot vapor as the *Jeannette*'s steam engine pushed full throttle and the steam winch cranked. Sometimes, to save on coal, De Long had the men and dogs hop onto the ice and make herculean attempts to tow the vessel. The heavy, moist air resonated with the sound of grunting and growling as man and beast tried to guide the ship through promising gaps in the floes. The men dug in their heels, straining at their ropes, and the howling dogs pulled with all their strength.

But De Long's options were dwindling. Ice lay in every direction now, clotting the way forward; the lanes and gaps were closing up. "Every opening in the pack with the least northing to it had been tried," Melville said, and the "ice cut off all chances of retreat." As soon as the ship knifed open a crack and passed through it, Melville would look astern and see the crack closing up again, snapping shut like the jaws of an enormous steel trap.

The pressures building around the ship were terrific. Explosions detonated in all directions, as the jagged jigsaw pieces smashed into one another with brutal force, sometimes causing pressure ridges to form. Here and there, geysers of surf hissed through cracks in the ice. There were scraping sounds, too, rasping sighs and raw squeals, as a giant slab would crunch up onto another one and then, bobbing in the swells, slowly grind it to pieces.

De Long was trying to find a lane that would lead him toward Wrangel, but it was no use. The pack kept shunting him aside, toward the northeast, farther and farther from his grail. They spotted Wrangel several more times—"a table land, with a range of peaks," in De Long's estimation—but it was fading out of reach. "This is the land which, two months ago yesterday, we sailed for from San Francisco, hoping to explore this winter," De Long despaired. "Man proposes but God disposes."

Now the *Jeannette*'s hull shuddered more than ever as she banged into and caromed off ever-more-imposing slabs. The ice was now fifteen feet thick in many places. Several times the bow drove high up onto an ice floe, creaked to a point of stasis, and then, properly chastened, slid back down into the water.

Still, through all this, the *Jeannette* held firm. De Long had to place his trust in the Mare Island engineers who had so painstakingly reinforced her hull; for now at least, their hard work seemed to have paid off. "She shook very badly," Danenhower remarked, but "it did not do her any damage. Indeed the ship stood the concussions handsomely."

ON SUNDAY, SEPTEMBER 7, the men felt a new pressure working on the starboard side, and then suddenly a large floe shoved the *Jeannette* onto a shelf of ice, causing her to list crazily. Other floes tightened around the ship. Under the pressure, her timbers began to tick and groan. Within minutes, the *Jeannette* was completely imprisoned. Her overtaxed steam engine wheezed, and her stack spat thick plumes of smoke, but she could not budge an inch. The ship had been "nipped," as the old Arctic whalers put it, in their profession's curious lexicon of understatement.

Wrote Danenhower: "We banked fires, secured the vessel with ice anchors and remained. We could proceed no farther." The *Jeannette* remained cocked at a queer angle, so that the men could not stand straight, or sit normally, or lie in their bunks without fear of rolling out. The ice was still settling, burbling, releasing bubbles of air, collapsing on its own pockets and voids. But it was turning into cement.

De Long looked over the pack and tried to think where he could have gone so wrong. His water thermometer readings had shown no evidence of a warm-water current pushing north. Where was the Kuro Siwo? The thermometric gateway, if it existed, certainly was not here. The Open Polar Sea seemed farther away than ever. "As far as the eye can range is ice," De Long wrote. "Not only does it look as if it had never broken up and become water . . . it looks as if it never would. It would take an earthquake at least to get us out of our besetment."

He had known all along, of course, that the *Jeannette* would become locked in ice like this; he just hadn't thought it would happen this far south, or this early in the season. He had hoped to reach the 80th parallel before winter set in, but here they were, icebound, at the 72nd. It was almost embarrassing. His plan had been to touch land somewhere along the coast of Wrangel, and there find a protected cove in which to safely anchor his ship for the winter, away from the violent crunch of the larger ice pack. But now the *Jeannette* was left vulnerable to much more powerful forces—subject to whims and wiles he could not begin to calculate. Now, more than ever, he cursed the delays caused by his pointless search for Nordenskiöld. De Long believed, probably correctly, that his one lost week on the Siberian coast had cost him his chance of landing on Wrangel and prevented him from accomplishing anything significant in the way of exploration, or reaching a "farthest north" record, until the following year.

Still, the ship's entrapment didn't discourage the captain. He hoped that this pack was a temporary aberration, an oddity out of the usual seasonal pattern. Arctic whalers had told him that "in the latter part of September and early part of October there is experienced in these latitudes quite an Indian Summer," he wrote, optimistically. Another blast of warm weather "will liberate us," he felt sure. "I consider it an exceptional state of ice we are having just now, and count on September gales to break up the pack and open leads."

But at other times, De Long appeared to accept that he was locked in for the winter. He seemed, indeed, to embrace adversity—and to hunt for its possible meanings. "This is a glorious country to learn patience in," he said. "My disappointment is great, how great no one else will probably know. There seemed nothing left but making a virtue of necessity and staying where we were."

AS THE ICE was closing around the *Jeannette,* an American whaling fleet was working along the southern margin of the same pack, hunting for the season's last prizes before heading home to San Francisco. The captains of these three whaling ships spotted a vessel off toward the north, some ten miles away, not far from Herald Island. Even from a distance, Captain Bauldry, of the whaling bark *Helen Mar,* could see that it was a steamer, and that it was struggling.

Bauldry studied it with a glass and tried to make sense of its movements. It was not a whaling ship, he felt sure. It was far too late in the season for a ship to be heading that way, slipping off the edge of the known world. But an ever-shifting trail of black smoke told him that the vessel was fighting her way through the pack, bumping and butting this way and that, aiming for the north and the west but apparently failing to reach her goal.

When the *Helen Mar* and her companion ships, the *Sea Breeze* and the *Dawn,* returned to California, the observations of their captains were reported in the San Francisco newspapers. It was the last sighting anyone ever had of the USS *Jeannette.*

That August, as De Long struggled north, James Gordon Bennett was in Newport, Rhode Island, summering with some of his cronies and visiting his sister, Jeannette Bennett Bell. He kept his yacht anchored at the marina and spent the better part of the month sailing, coach racing, and carousing with the white-flannel set. His faux pas against the May family had been forgiven, and he was once again accepted among the Newport "cottagers." Indeed, Bennett had come to be considered the life of the party, a welcome provocateur. Noted the *Newport Mercury* upon his arrival on August 2: "Everyone at once looked for the opening of the festivities and sports of the season, for Mr. Bennett has the energy and push needed to give the coach of gaiety a good start."

Bennett was a member of the staid and proper Newport Reading Room, a club that admitted only the most prominent and affluent gentlemen. He found the place dreadfully boring, and one day in mid-August he decided to ruffle the club's feathers. He apparently had been on a drinking binge with an old polo-playing chum from England, Henry Augustus Candy, a captain in the British cavalry. Bennett dared Candy—apparently sweetening the challenge with a bet—to do something guaranteed to shake up the stodgy membership of the Reading Room. Candy accepted, and a plan was hatched.

Later that afternoon Captain Candy, dressed in full polo regalia, mounted his pony and headed over to the Reading Room's prim yellow clubhouse on Bellevue Avenue. He rode the animal up the front

steps, through the double doors, and into the front hall of the establishment itself. A white-coated steward is said to have shouted, "Sir,
you cannot ride a horse in here!" But Candy paid him no mind and
continued into the salon, through the bar, and in and out of other
rooms, ignoring the perplexed club members who sat reading their
magazines and sipping gin and tonics. Then Candy expertly wheeled
his horse around, exited through the front door, and galloped off.

Candy had won his bet with Bennett and demonstrated impeccable equestrian skills, but the Reading Room membership promptly
censured him and vowed that neither he nor Bennett would ever enter
the clubhouse again. The Reading Room's icy reaction to the prank,
while predictable, threw a switch in Bennett's curious circuitry. In a
pique of indignation, he decided to build a rival clubhouse, one that
would be decidedly sportier, rowdier, and less hidebound by tradition.
He would call it the Newport Casino.

Bennett bought a big piece of land just down Bellevue Avenue
from the Reading Room. The Newport Casino, he decided, would be
an immense palace of fun—a rebuke to anyone who called Newport
stuffy. It would have a bowling alley, a billiards parlor, lawn courts, a
theater, a restaurant, several bars, and a ballroom. He hired the best
architect he could find: the young Stanford White, from New York's
famous firm of McKim, Mead, and White. Blueprints were drawn
up, and ground breaking commenced within months. A grand opening was planned for the following summer.

An idea began to take shape in Bennett's mind: The Newport
Casino would hold competitive tennis tournaments. Having successfully introduced polo to the United States, he would now introduce
the nation to England's hottest new racket sport. As he envisioned it,
his casino would become the cradle of American tennis.

Bennett spent the rest of the year immersed in blueprints. He
was almost giddy with excitement. He would show the killjoys of the
Newport Reading Room. Bennett's thoughts seemed to race in every
direction that summer, but they were a million miles from the Arctic.

19 · If by Any Mischance

After the *Jeannette* left San Francisco, Emma De Long knew she had to "steel myself," as she put it, "for a long, long vigil." That day, she had returned to her room at the Palace Hotel and had fallen into a stupor. She had no energy, no willpower, no interest in the world. "I did not want to do anything," she wrote, "or even to think." She had no pressing responsibilities, since Sylvie was staying with her sister in the Midwest. Her parents, who had been in Australia, were supposed to have met her in San Francisco in time for the departure, but their steamer had been delayed, and they were not due for another week. For several days, she turned her room into a dark cave and wouldn't come out.

William Bradford, the De Longs' close friend who had escorted her back to shore from the Golden Gate the day the *Jeannette* set sail, lived in San Francisco part of the year and kept a studio there. One day he checked in on Emma and saw that she was suffering. So he proposed a diversion: How about a trip to Yosemite?

Emma brightened immediately. She had never been there, and had never seen any of the magnificent country of California. He would bring along his paints and his photographic equipment, and while his wife and Emma picnicked and toured the valley, he would look for landscapes to capture.

Emma always found comfort in the company of William Bradford. He was a serene man with a kind face, curly ginger hair, and extravagantly frizzy sideburns. Fifty-six years old, he had made nine trips to the Arctic, mostly around Greenland, and had safely returned home from each, not only healthy but exhilarated. He was one of the most eloquent and convincing evangelists of the frozen world. His Arctic paintings, meticulous in detail, had sold well on both sides of the Atlantic. Queen Victoria had commissioned one of his works. He was also an esteemed member of the American Geographical Society of New York, and his lectures all over the world had done much to fire the public imagination about the High North. Bradford made the Arctic seem exotic and adventurous, a domain touched with a particular grandeur. The way he described it, and depicted it in his paintings and photographs, the Arctic had an aesthetic all its own; even when it was terrible, it was transcendent.

"There is no phenomenon . . . more sublime in its aspects than a storm spending its fury on the edge of the ice-pack," Bradford had written. "The water, breaking with terrific weight and power, wave after wave, is hurled against the pack which it breaks, and tears, and rips up, throwing huge blocks upon the stubbornly resisting surface. It is a tremendous war of the elements, never to be forgotten."

At its essence, Bradford's work was concerned with man's yearning for the unknown. He was an explorer at heart, and he shared and appreciated George De Long's northing impulse. A native of a little town near New Bedford, Massachusetts, and a devotee of the Hudson River school, Bradford was known for his pictures of stranded whaleships, freakishly shaped icebergs, furred men confronting polar bears, and glacial fjords lit by the midnight sun. Though the scenes were lonely and sometimes desperate, he managed always to instill wonder and beauty in them.

Emma took solace in being with a friend who found a land so severe also so inviting. She tried to think of George as heading for the romantic realm Bradford described. The tranquility in his paintings, and in his demeanor, made her more tranquil, too.

So Emma joined the Bradfords and, by rail and horse carriage, they headed east toward the High Sierra. They ambled among the sequoias of the Calaveras Forest—one of the giant redwoods would be named Jeannette in the expedition's honor. They made their way to Yosemite and reveled in the waterfalls and the immense scallops of granite: El Capitan, Half Dome, Sentinel Rock. The excursion was just what Emma needed. "Although at first I felt so apathetic," she said, "I gradually fell under the spell of the scenery." It was "good for my deadened state of mind, and I began to enjoy myself again."

BY THE TIME she returned to San Francisco, Emma was restored. Her parents had arrived from Australia and were waiting at the Palace Hotel. Emma was happy to reunite with her family and tour the hilly city together. Then they took a train to Burlington, Iowa, where Emma's sister lived with her husband, General S. L. Glasgow. Sylvie had been staying at their home for the past few months, and now the Glasgows invited Emma and Sylvie to live with them for the duration of the *Jeannette* voyage. This steamboat town, built on a bluff overlooking the Mississippi River, was where Emma would spend much of her "long, long vigil." She diligently wrote letters to George, knowing that they probably would never reach him; she called them her "letters to nowhere," and they became a therapeutic ritual. She penned them in triplicate so that they could be sent to multiple Arctic locations at once—whaling and trading outposts in Alaska, Greenland, and Spitsbergen, Norway. She included the latter two destinations on the hopeful premise that the *Jeannette*, after reaching the North Pole, might sail across the Open Polar Sea and pop out of the ice on the other side of the Arctic.

Soon after she set up quarters at the Glasgow house in Burlington, Emma contracted a mysterious virus that kept her bedridden for several weeks. So far, she had heard no reports from the Arctic, and she was starting to worry. But just as she grew well enough to sit up in bed, a sheaf of correspondence arrived from Alaska. Finally, George's letters to her had gotten through.

In one of them, he mentioned that he had hung a photograph of her, as well as a portrait of Sylvie, at the head of his bed. After their long voyage together around South America, George was so used to having them both on board the *Jeannette* that he kept imagining they were still around. "Half a dozen times a day I blunder into the port stateroom," he wrote, "with what a disappointment at finding you are not there! I wonder if I will ever get used to your not being with me." On August 9 he wrote: "Sometimes I make the calculation that all the glory of all the Arctic expeditions in the world is not worth the happiness of having you with me for five minutes."

George still had the gift Emma had given him during their courting days in Le Havre, the little memento he had carried with him, as a bachelor, for all those years at sea. "I came across the little blue bag with a lock of your hair and the cross," he wrote, "and now I carry it around in my pocket, as lovesick as I was eleven years ago." In one of the envelopes was a picture of himself, with a note that said, "For my wife to look at when she is wondering where I am."

Mostly, the letters were brusque and businesslike, filled with minutiae about the voyage—which was natural, for George had come to regard Emma as a fellow officer of the expedition. But in the last letter, dated August 27, his tone softened. Included in the season's final batch of Arctic mail, it was the very last letter he would write before entering the ice.

August 27

We are now hoisting the last of the supplies and shall leave at seven o'clock this evening. The weather is beautiful—light southerly breeze and smooth sea, and I am anxious to be off. And yet it seems like saying good-by once more. However, I am in this thing, and I am going to see it through.

Good-by, with a thousand kisses. With God's help I shall yet do something to make you proud of bearing your husband's name. Do not give me up, for I shall one day or another come back to claim my wife and child. May God keep and bless you, wherever you are, and save your love for me.

If by any mischance we should never meet again in this world, be assured that in everything, word and deed, you have always been to me the truest, best, and most loving wife a man ever had. My whole heart and soul go out to you . . . my precious, darling, good-by.

20 · A Delusion and a Snare

For the whole month of September, and all of October, too, the *Jeannette* remained trapped in the ice. De Long harbored no more illusions: They were beset for the season. It was time to dig in. He had the men unship the rudder and hoist it up on deck, out of harm's way. He had them coat the engines with white lead and tallow and drain pipes to forestall freezing. He issued fur clothing. He had the carpenters hammer together an addition to the deckhouse and cover it with layers of insulating felt. To reduce heat loss from the hull, he ordered the men to pile snowbanks all around the *Jeannette,* up to the rails.

The *Jeannette* was drifting mostly in a northwestern direction, though the pack could be erratic, shifting day by day, even minute by minute. Many times they found that they had circled back to the same spot, weeks and sometimes months later. The ship was heeled over to starboard at a sharp angle, and she trembled at times in gusts of wind, but otherwise she seemed quite stable, congealed in her slab of ice. Melville thought the ship was "embedded . . . as in a mould." To De Long, the *Jeannette* felt "as steady as if she were in a dry dock."

As they drifted, they always kept an eye on Wrangel Land. Passing north of it, they obtained views of Wrangel that had never been seen by man. It was as though they'd crossed over to the dark side of the moon. As they cut across the top of it, two things became apparent to De Long. First, they would never reach Wrangel—the floes were sweeping them too far away from it, and too quickly, for them to attempt a safe landing.

De Long's second realization was that they'd made a substantial discovery. Seeing Wrangel from its north side and drifting across any possible connection it might have had with other lands farther north, he now knew the truth: Wrangel Land was a good-sized island, but it was no continent. Petermann's idea of a transpolar landmass was wrong. "Dr. Petermann's theory was no longer tenable," Danenhower wrote, "for its insularity was evident." Wrangel had nothing whatsoever to do with Greenland. (So much for "the much-boasted continent," Melville scoffed.) The maps could now be altered: WRANGEL LAND had been demoted; it was now just WRANGEL ISLAND.

De Long had effectively consigned another myth to the scrap heap: the thermometric gateway. The ice in which they were so stubbornly locked had certainly caused De Long to doubt Silas Bent's celebrated theory, but it was the *Jeannette*'s slow and careful accumulation of scientific data that clinched the captain's opinion. Every day, his men had gone out and hacked holes in the sea ice to take studious measurements of ocean depth, current, salinity, specific gravity, and temperature. Not once had they found the slightest evidence of a warm-water current flowing north—or, indeed, flowing in any direction. The Kuro Siwo was nowhere to be found. As De Long gazed out over the endless expanses of ice, he cursed the lustrous idea that had led him to their present fix. Said the captain: "I pronounce a thermometric gateway to the North Pole a delusion and a snare."

De Long was even starting to doubt the cherished concept of the Open Polar Sea. This implacable ice did not appear to be a mere "girdle," or an "annulus," that one could simply bust through. It seemed to stretch out forever, and the pressures locked up within the pack suggested unimaginably huge expanses of even thicker ice. "Is this always a dead sea?" he wondered. "Does the ice never find an outlet? Surely it must go somewhere. I should not be surprised if the ocean had frozen over down to the equator. I believe this icy waste will go on surging to and fro until the last trump blows."

During late-night smoking sessions in the wardroom, De Long and Danenhower had begun to guess at the truth: that the pole was covered by a huge and permanent though ever-shifting carapace of ice. There were no large landmasses, and no basins of open water, but this ice sheath *did* move, seemingly in a clockwise fashion, powered by the vagaries of current and wind. Said Danenhower: "Some of us talked about the polar region being covered with an immense 'ice cap' which seemed to have a slow, general movement in the direction of the hands of a watch; the direction of the drift, of course, being different in the different segments."

The *Jeannette* expedition had thus begun to shed its organizing ideas, in all their unfounded romance, and to replace them with a reckoning of the way the Arctic truly was. This, in turn, led De Long to the gradual understanding that an endlessly more perilous voyage lay ahead. They might reach the North Pole yet, but almost certainly they were not going to *sail* there.

FOR NOW, DE LONG had to focus on establishing a workable shipboard economy. A daily routine started to form: All hands up by seven. Galley fires roaring by seven-fifteen. Breakfast at eight. Onboard chores performed through the midmorning. Soundings at noon.

Then they headed out to the ice for two hours of exercise. Sometimes they put on snowshoes and clomped around the ship, often with rifles in hand, in case they spotted walruses, seals, or other game. Other days, if there was a nice flat spot in the ice, they laced up their skates. Often they held football games out on the floes.

Dinner was served at three p.m., after which the galley fires were put out to save coal. Tea and a light meal were taken between seven and eight. At night Danenhower led a class in elementary navigation for all comers, while other officers met in the wardroom for a smoke and a review of the day. Lights out by ten.

No rum or spirits were allowed except on a few festive occasions determined by De Long. The first of every month, Dr. Ambler conducted a medical examination of every officer and crew member—no exceptions. On Sundays, De Long would recite the naval Articles of War, then lead a short devotional service.

Day by day, this was the general choreography, but certain individuals had specific tasks. Danenhower spent most of his time taking meteorological and astronomical observations. Dr. Ambler, when he wasn't examining patients, roamed the cabins testing for excess carbon dioxide and subjecting the drinking water to silver nitrate tests to ascertain its salinity.

The two Inuits, Alexey and Aneguin, mostly occupied themselves dealing with what De Long called "our hoodlum gang" of dogs, which were nearly always fighting, whining, and fouling the decks. Alexey and Aneguin hated the stuffy cabins of the ship so much that they constructed their own lean-to on the deck. They were formidable hunters—every other day a few fresh seals could be seen hanging up in the rigging—but the two Alaskans sometimes did strange things out on the ice, mystical things that spooked the other men. They spoke to the moon. They offered gifts of tobacco to the ice. They made predictions about the dogs' behavior that often played out with astonishing accuracy. Once, after shooting a giant walrus, Alexey bared an arm, shoved it down the throat of his prey, and, pulling it out, wiped the warm blood on his forehead. "For good luck," he said. Another time, after killing a seal, Alexey removed small pieces of each hind foot, as well as the gallbladder, and placed them carefully in a hole in the ice. "Make um more seal," he explained. Still, De Long was impressed by the two Inuits and thought a "quiet dignity" pervaded everything they did.

The two Chinese immigrants, Ah Sam and Charles Tong Sing, kept to the galley, where they had learned to prepare such delicacies as seal fritters, roast "squab" of seagull, and the company favorite, walrus sausage. ("A rare good thing it is," De Long pronounced it. Seal and walrus, he insisted, "are not to be despised.") Sam and Charley slept in their cookhouse, too, in a little curtained-off area they kept spotlessly clean. Aside from singing and playing cards, they seemed to enjoy only one other diversion from their pots and pans: Out on the ice, they loved to fly colorful kites with long paper streamers, a spectacle that amused and delighted the other men. Sam and Charley were "seemingly emotionless," De Long noted, in "all weathers, all circumstances . . . as impenetrable in this cold weather as if we were enjoying a tropical spring. They hold no communion with their fellow-men, but are nevertheless cheerful and contented with each other's society."

Newcomb, the Smithsonian-recommended naturalist, spent his days shooting birds, scavenging curiosities from the ice pack, and dredging the blue mud of the sea floor for marine specimens. His study had become something of an abattoir, piled high with the carcasses of decaying animals—or parts of animals—which, when mixed with the astringent chemicals his work required, gave off a nauseating stench. His collection already included a walrus fetus, numerous starfish and bivalves, various species of Arctic fish, several puffins, an albatross with a seven-foot wingspan, and two rare Ross's gulls. Most of the men found Newcomb—some called him Ninkum—morbid and strange. Said Melville: "The less I had to do with him the better."

De Long thought Newcomb a tad odd, too, but was impressed with his zeal. "Natural History is well looked out for," De Long had to concede. "Any animal or bird that comes near the ship does so at the peril of its life." Newcomb rarely mixed with the men. "He may be deemed to be our silent member," De Long wrote. "But he has his little place in the port chart-room all fixed up with his tools, and is as happy as can be."

All in all, the crew seemed more or less content. De Long called them "our little colony" and was pleased to note that "everybody is in good health and in good spirits . . . They have their musical instruments every night and play and sing. There are so many good voices that I am thinking of getting up a choir."

Inevitably, though, a certain monotony began to set in. "It is unnatural for us to have this enforced close companionship," De Long wrote, "and we seem to get in each other's way." He admitted that on some days, a few of the men seemed "mentally 'out of sorts,'" and felt "the time hang heavily"—but that was to be expected. "If life within the Arctic circle were perfect comfort," De Long reasoned, "everybody would be coming here. We must be thankful that our discomforts are no greater."

If the daily routines and rituals ran smoothly, the credit for that belonged to one man: Lieutenant Charles Chipp, the ship's executive officer. Chipp was a loner, and so laconic and cheerless-seeming that he sometimes made the other men uncomfortable. He spent most of his free hours studying the auroras that often danced across the night skies. But De Long had become utterly dependent upon his number two. "Chipp is putting everything in order quietly and steadily," De Long said, "and he has everything reduced already to a system. Today when I inspected the ship she was as neat as a pin, the men nicely dressed, and everything looking more like a man-of-war."

Chipp was good for keeping things right, but when things went wrong, De Long had come to place his deepest faith in Melville. There was nothing, it seemed, the engineer couldn't fix, no problem he couldn't solve. "More and more a treasure" was how De Long described him. If a piece of machinery was ailing, he would tear it apart and rebuild it, cannibalizing components from other machines. Back in the summer, when a pump rod had broken on the engine, Melville had blithely told De Long that he could make a new one—or, if the captain preferred, he could make *twenty* new ones; it was all the same to him.

Melville, who usually had a pipe fitting or soldering iron or welding torch in his hand, was always tinkering, inventing things to improve life on the ship. He devised a new method for recording wind velocities. He designed a little machine to crimp the soles of the fur boots the men had been sewing from pelts purchased in Alaska. When the distiller started putting out water that was too salty, Melville ripped the whole apparatus apart and built it anew, so that it produced a perfectly pure liquid. Whenever De Long asked him if such-and-such contraption could be built, Melville would go to the drawing board and madly sketch out diagrams. Usually the answer was "Yes, it can be done," and that became Melville's mantra.

Melville sang lustily in a stentorian voice and cursed with such gusto that De Long had to formally reprimand him for profanity. But he was "bright as a dollar and cheerful as possible all the time," said De Long. He seemed to have "indomitable energy" and a "splendid . . . fertility of device."

"Melville is one of the strong points in this expedition," De Long said. "I believe he could make an engine out of a few barrel hoops."

PART OF THE *Jeannette*'s daily routine involved baiting the bear traps, usually with the bloody entrails of some seal Alexey had shot. So far, the crewmen had spotted a few polar bears at a distance and had seen innumerable pawprints on the ice, but what De Long wanted was fresh *Ursus* steaks for the mess table. In the first weeks, the only prey they had caught in the bear traps were two of the expedition's sled dogs—which were pulled howling from the steel jaws, hurt but not irreparably maimed.

Early on the morning of September 17, Chipp and Dunbar, the New England whaler and ice pilot, went out to examine the bear traps. About a mile from the ship, they came upon one that had been sprung. The caught bear had managed to yank the trap away from its ice anchor, and Dunbar could see a trail of blood on the ice. As the bear had dragged the trap along, it had left a broad scrape across the ice, which rendered the animal's path of escape unmistakable.

Chipp and Dunbar hastily returned to the ship to report their find and to gather supplies for a full-scale bear hunt. Melville and De Long joined them, and soon the four men were dashing over the ice. After an hour of following the bloody trail, they began to see the tracks of two *other* bears, one on either side of the injured animal. To De Long, it appeared "as if two friends had remained by him to encourage him in his retreat."

For six miles they tramped across the ice, puffing and sweating in their heavy furs. Finally they came to a low place in the ice and saw their quarry, still entangled in the trap, growling in pain. It was a young male; only a small part of his left forepaw had been snagged. One of his companions remained with him—a young she-bear. "The female made no attempt to desert him," said De Long, in admiration, "but ran ahead and back to him as if to coax him on. Upon sighting us, both rose on their hind legs and howled dolefully."

Melville said the bears dashed across the floe "with the ungracefulness of a cow but the speed of a deer, causing the snow to fly like feathers in a gale." Sometimes the male bear's "curiosity [would] get the better of his judgment, and he [would] stop to inspect these strange creatures that dare put him to flight, for he is the monarch of the polar regions."

When the trapped bear and his companion turned to make their final stand, Dunbar and Chipp opened fire with their Winchesters, and Melville took a crack with his Remington breechloader. De Long's shot proved the coup de grâce, and, as he put it, "the thing was soon over."

Chipp and Dunbar were sent back to the ship to fetch men and sleds for hauling their prizes. A few hours later they returned, with nearly the entire crew of the *Jeannette* in tow. Everyone wanted in on the blood sport, it seemed, and the afternoon soon "turned into a holiday," wrote De Long. The men rigged up scales and weighed the two animals: The female was 422 pounds, the male 580.

They were small bears, in fact—Dunbar, a month later, would kill one that tipped the scales at half a ton—but these were the *Jeannette*'s first bear kills, and so would be remembered fondly. Collins, who had brought his photographic equipment, captured images of the hunters and their trophies. Then the bears were skinned and dressed, and the meat and furs piled upon the sledges. By afternoon, everyone was a greasy, gory mess. But "all hands were jubilant," said De Long, "as after a victory," for they knew that fresh meat was in store for dinner that night.

Newcomb, the serial bird killer, was not to be outdone by the big-game hunters. A little ways off by himself, out on the ice, he shot "seven beautiful young gulls," he proudly noted, and added them to his growing collection of carcasses to be stuffed.

BY MID-OCTOBER, AS the Arctic darkness steadily descended over the crew, De Long decided it was time to try out Edison's electric lights. He looked forward to the morale boost they would provide—blazing over the ship at night, a dazzling novelty of American ingenuity.

The task of making Edison's lights work was tremendously important for Jerome Collins. His title was chief scientist of the expedition. He was the one who had conferred with Edison at Menlo Park, and he had personally ordered the arc lamps, the dynamo, and other equipment. Collins, even more than De Long, believed in the restorative powers the lights would have on the men.

But De Long had started to entertain doubts about Collins. Among his other duties, the Irish meteorologist was supposed to be the official expedition photographer, and indeed he had exposed numerous plates with his American Optical Company double-swing cone bellows camera—like the ones he had taken on the day of the bear kill. A problem had presented itself, however: Collins had brought the exposed plates to the darkroom, but no finished images had ever emerged. The reason was embarrassing for Collins, almost mortifying: He couldn't find the developing chemicals he had ordered in San Francisco. He searched frantically in the holds, ransacking the boxes in which the photographic plates had been stowed. Apparently, they had never made it aboard ship. This oversight, he knew, was entirely his fault.

Luckily, Melville had thought to bring his own photographic equipment, including developing chemicals. In the future, it was Melville who would take most of the expedition photographs.

Another task specifically assigned to Collins was the erection of an "observatory" on the ice—a portable canvas structure, stabilized by ice anchors, that would be kept full of meteorological instruments. At De Long's request, Collins and Lieutenant Chipp had strung telephone wire so the ship could stay in regular communication with whoever might be in the observatory. But when Collins connected Bell's new inventions, they worked only briefly before the signal flickered out. The brittle copper wire wouldn't conduct properly once it got wet, and it was constantly snagging and breaking on the crusty ice. Evidently, the bare No. 24 wire that Bell's lab had provided was the wrong gauge. In any case, the telephones were a bust. The blame for this could not rightly be put on Collins, but somehow it registered with De Long as yet another illustration of the chief scientist's general fecklessness.

Melville was proving to be the *real* chief scientist, more knowledgeable, more resourceful, and more proficient with the instruments Collins was supposed to have mastered. Collins truly was an expert on weather, but what he seemed to care most about was the "science" of puns, and by now he had exhausted his repertoire. The men had grown sick of his wordplay—"You give me an earache!" Newcomb had cried at one point—and yet Collins wouldn't quit. He'd run out of musical numbers, too. When he sat at his little organ, playing sprightly Gilbert and Sullivan selections for the hundredth time, he could not see how he was grating on everyone's nerves.

What Collins could see was that Melville had usurped his role. Hurt and resentful, Collins increasingly withdrew to his room, and he began to flout De Long's rules. He would not go out and exercise, and he refused to let Dr. Ambler examine him for the monthly medical report. He would sleep late, smoking through the midmorning, dawdling with his chores. With each passing day, he became more marginalized.

Collins found himself in an impossible situation. Most likely, he wasn't cut out for this kind of work. He was a man of many talents, but they did not run in the direction of nautical life. He had never been on a prolonged cruise before, to the Arctic or anywhere else, and he had never been under the watch of a man as formidable or as rigorous as George De Long. He fundamentally did not understand that De Long was the absolute master of this ship, and of everything that went on inside and around it. Then, too, Collins had an Irishman's well-honed sense of persecution—once slighted, he could not easily shake it off. His frictions with De Long were inevitable.

Part of the problem was his ambiguous status: Neither an officer nor a seaman, Collins was something in between—a highly trained civilian who, though allowed to eat with the officers, enjoyed no official naval rank. He thought this situation inherently placed him in "a trap," and probably he was right. As perhaps the best-educated man on board the ship, and as Bennett's handpicked correspondent for the expedition, Collins felt he should be allowed to skirt Navy discipline, but De Long had other ideas. Certainly Collins thought he was entitled to more respect.

For all these reasons, the success of Edison's lights loomed as an all-important test of Collins's true place on board the USS *Jeannette*.

ON OCTOBER 15, Collins fished the sixty carbon lamps from their boxes, and De Long had them hoisted high in the rigging. A small steam engine, called a Baxter boiler, was fired to provide steam power, and Collins connected it to Edison's "dynamo" device, which was, in turn, connected to the circuits of lamps. For several hours, Collins worked with the nest of machines and wires. But even when seventy pounds of steam pressure was applied, he could not get Edison's device to make a spark. The little galvanometer needle on the contraption hardly budged.

The men peered up into the rigging with hopeful expressions, but the circuit of lamps failed to produce a wink of light. No one could hide his disappointment. It was as though the country had let them down.

Collins was befuddled. It was true that he had never tested the lamps in San Francisco, but in Menlo Park he had seen with his own eyes how brilliantly they worked, illuminating Edison's lab with a "light greater than three thousand candles." Why weren't they working now?

De Long put Melville on the problem. After taking Edison's device apart, the engineer concluded that it must have gotten doused during the turbulent crossing of the Bering Sea. He dried out the apparatus, then tried uncoiling all its wires and reinsulating them, but it was no use: Not even Melville, the *Jeannette*'s crafty Vulcan, could get the thing to work.

A few days later, Dr. Ambler told De Long of a curious dream he'd had about Edison's lamps. In the dream, Sir John Franklin, the long-lost British explorer, had come aboard the *Jeannette* for a tour. Dr. Ambler led Franklin all over the ship and told him excitedly about Edison's electric lights, an invention that, of course, wasn't even dreamed about in Franklin's day. But Franklin bluntly interrupted him. "Your electric machine," he said, "is not worth a damn."

"I begin to fear that Franklin is right," De Long wrote. "Edison's light is irretrievably worthless. Time enough has been lost in trying to make this machine of use." Perhaps it was Edison's fault, but De Long placed much of the blame on Collins. In any case, the lamps had "gone 'where the woodbine twineth,' " as De Long put it—which was to say, into the junk pile of oblivion. Disgusted, he told Collins to box up the lamps and stow them in the hold. Collins was despondent, his mood as black as the unlit Arctic.

And so the days grew shorter and colder—and the natural light ever more feeble. The sun slowly slipped from the polar skies. On November 16, it left altogether and would not return for several months. Spermaceti candles and oil lanterns would have to suffice. So much for Thomas Alva Edison and his company's pledge about "lighting the North Pole."

For the next seventy-one days, the *Jeannette* would be cloaked in darkness.

Scarcely a week after De Long declared Edison's lights "irretrievably useless," the inventor's lab in Menlo Park, New Jersey, made a historic breakthrough. For several months, Edison had been homing in on an incandescent bulb that would be reliable and safe—a lamp that would throw steady, pleasing light without flickering or flaming out. The trick had been finding the right substance to serve as a durable filament. He had tested platinum, carbon, wood splints, cotton and linen thread, even fishing line. But now, Edison boasted to reporters, he had the principle in his grasp. It was, he claimed, "so simple that a bootblack might understand it."

On the night of October 21, 1879, Edison was experimenting with a filament made from carbonized sewing thread. A vacuum bulb fitted with the new filament was arranged on a small platform in the lab. When power was supplied, the lamp burned, unflickering, for an hour, then two hours, then three. Edison, having grown tired of the experiment after slightly more than forty hours of steady light, ramped up the power until the filament finally sizzled and burned out.

"The electric light is perfected," Edison crowed to the *New York Times*. Although this wasn't quite true, his incandescent bulb was now well on its way to reality—and already it represented a quantum leap over the arc lamp system he had sold to De Long. His company had also made significant improvements in the reliability of its dynamos: The model Edison provided for the *Jeannette* expedition had caused endless problems for his customers, but after he overhauled the design, subsequent generations of his dynamo had proved admirably dependable.

By November, having applied for a patent for his incandescent lamp, Edison tried out a new filament made of carbonized bamboo. It burned true for more than twelve hundred hours. By December Edison was making public demonstrations and taking his first commercial orders. "We will make electricity so cheap," he said, "that only the rich will burn candles."

A new era was at hand. De Long had missed it by only a few months. When a reporter from Bennett's *Herald* asked Edison how long his bulbs would last, the inventor, his mouth full of chewing tobacco, replied, "Forever, almost."

About the same time the sun vanished, the ice began to move again. The noise was terrible—first the sounds of the ice warring with itself, then the more dreadful sounds of the ice warring with the ship. The turbulence started early on a cold November morning. De Long was awakened by a "grinding and crushing— I know of no sound on shore that can be compared with it," he said. "A rumble, a shriek, a groan, and a crash of a falling house all combined might convey an idea."

He went outside to study the pack, which he likened to "a marble yard, adrift." Soon others joined him on the deck. To Melville, it sounded at first like "distant artillery" but then it grew louder. "Giant blocks pitched and rolled as though controlled by invisible hands, and the vast compressing bodies shrieked a shrill and horrible song."

Danenhower thought the pack was "in a state of greater confusion than an old Turkish graveyard." The men watched in horror as great pieces of ice were "pushed about like toys," Newcomb said, occasionally causing the ship to groan like "some leviathan in death agonies." The noise was so unnerving that it set the dogs to whining; Newcomb found their "choruses of howls most unearthly."

Then the ice began to squeeze the ship—literally, to strangle it. Beads of oakum tar and pine pitch oozed from the seams. At one point, the decks *bulged*. The wooden planks were so obviously stressed that De Long expected them to rupture.

Several times, he prepared to abandon the ship. Supplies were stockpiled on the deck, the boats made ready for lowering, and the sleds stuffed with forty days' worth of provisions. De Long instructed the men to sleep with their clothes on and to pack their knapsacks and bedrolls. There wasn't much else they could do but listen—and wait.

"We live in a weary suspense," De Long wrote. "Wintering in the pack may be a thrilling thing to read about alongside a warm fire, but the actual thing is sufficient to make any man prematurely old. A crisis may occur at any moment, and we can do nothing but be thankful in the morning that it has not come during the night, and at night that it has not come since the morning. Living over a powder-mill waiting for an explosion would be a similar mode of existence."

There was one moment when De Long thought he surely was witnessing the death of the *Jeannette*. Out on the moonlit ice, the men could see and hear an eruption taking place. Two giant plates of ice were colliding, creating a pressure ridge. Along the leading edge of this collision, the floes were smashing and telescoping, setting off a chain reaction of upheavals that seemed to be building straight for the *Jeannette*. De Long, Chipp, and several of the crew stood on the roof of the deckhouse and watched it come, as though it were an onrushing train. De Long grabbed a mainstay and yelled, "All hands hold firm!" As it approached, the wide-eyed men fumbled for the handiest rope or shroud and, muttering prayers, braced for the collision. "On came the frozen wave, nearer and nearer," wrote Melville, "while silent and awestruck we watched its terrible progress."

Then it hulked across the rails, smashing a hole in the starboard bulwark and covering the decks in skittering shards. The ship lurched and shuddered. The men twisted on their dangling ropes. Some had been smacked in the face with missiles of ice. Yet the violence, terrific as it was, passed in seconds, and the eruptions continued on the other side of the ship, as though some giant beast were tunneling just beneath the ice. The men grew silent, leaving only the whimpering of the terrified dogs.

Miraculously, the *Jeannette* was not mortally injured. "The ship is all right now," Newcomb marveled, "but for how long no one knows. I have my gun and knapsack ready to leave at a moment's notice for . . . *God knows where*." Melville was astounded that the ship had survived. "Her time had not yet come" was all he could figure. He credited the work done at Mare Island—"the powerful trusses sturdily withstood the pressure," he noted.

Like sinners who'd been granted a reprieve, the crew cheerfully got to work repairing the ship. "The men sang and joked with apparent *sang froid*," said Melville, "while they cleared the decks of ice or pushed away the overhanging masses that were crushing the light bulwarks. The discipline of the ship's company was perfect."

De Long saw the *Jeannette*'s salvation as nothing less than providential: "The pack is no place for a ship, and I wish with all my heart that we were out of it. But a man must be a hard unbeliever who does not recognize a divine hand in these wonderful escapes."

BY THE END of November, the ice had settled down at last. On December 2, De Long felt comfortable enough with the conditions to try sleeping normally again. "I shall undress before retiring tonight," he wrote, preparing for a luxury he had not enjoyed for three weeks. Something of an insomniac anyway, he had hardly slept an unbroken hour during the whole ice siege.

Now he took to walking out on the ice at night before bed. He relished these midnight strolls. They were the only moments he got to spend alone, immersed in his thoughts. He would pull on his furs, light up his meerschaum pipe, and traipse about the ship, out where the pack was clean, beyond the garbage dumps and the ash heaps. Under the crisp moon and stars, safely embedded again in solid ice, the *Jeannette* looked as though "she had dropped out of fairyland," he thought. Standing a hundred yards from the ship, "one has a scene of the wildest and most awful beauty." The "majestic silence" made a man "feel how trifling and insignificant he is in comparison with such grand works in nature." As he walked, De Long was often treated to light shows of auroras, meteor showers, lunar halos, or the oddity of a mock moon. One night a mysterious ball of light danced on the floes near the *Jeannette*—it blinked and pulsed, intensified, waned, extinguished itself, then returned brighter than ever to dance some more.

"I think the night one of the most beautiful I have ever seen," De Long wrote after one of his strolls. "The heavens were cloudless, the moon shining brightly, and every star twinkling; the air perfectly calm, not a sound to break the spell. The ship and her surroundings made a perfect picture. The long lines of wire reaching to the tripod and observatory, round frosted lumps here and there where a dog lay asleep. The *Jeannette* standing out in bold relief against the sky, every rope and spar with a thick coat of snow and frost—simply a beautiful spectacle."

But then De Long would catch himself, as though vaguely embarrassed by his rhapsodies. "I commence them and cannot finish them," he wrote. "I seem to know the tune but never remember the words. These poetical outbursts are too much for me."

EVER SINCE THEY'D gotten locked in the ice, De Long had worried about Danenhower's mental state. All the terrors of the ice, the melancholy of the polar darkness, the claustrophobic dread that could set in while one was living under conditions of near imprisonment—the whole Arctic experience was a perfect incubator for insanity, De Long thought. So the captain had been discreetly watching Danenhower, fearful that the navigator's depression—his "disordered intellect," his history of "brain trouble"—might return.

So far, it hadn't. De Long could not have been more pleased and impressed with the navigator. Danenhower, along with Chipp and Melville, had been a mainstay. Danenhower was resourceful, hardworking, good-humored. Many nights they lingered late in the wardroom, smoking, laughing, looking at maps, conducting their own Arctic seminars. If anything, Danenhower had cheered *him* up. "His efforts have kept us many an hour from moping," De Long wrote. "He is highly prized by all of us." Still, De Long said, "there is something about him which I cannot fathom. I cannot yet bring myself to have that *implicit* confidence in him that I would like to feel."

Danenhower's only medical issue so far was an aggravation in his left eye. He had apparently developed some sort of conjunctivitis that made his lens sore and irritated. Dr. Ambler didn't think much about it at first. The navigator worked so hard at his inadequately lit desk, poring over nautical charts, making calculations, checking precision instruments, that it seemed inevitable that his eyes would become strained. There was little "navigating" to do, strictly speaking, while the ship remained icebound, yet Danenhower was constantly making observations to determine the *Jeannette's* precise position while engaging in the larger scientific questions of the expedition. Danenhower studied so hard, De Long remarked, that "you would think the books would run away with him." Everyone agreed that the navigator should take a break and give his eyes a rest.

But after a few weeks, Danenhower's condition worsened. The pain was so excruciating he could scarcely think. When Dr. Ambler examined him again, he saw that something was wrong with his iris. It was inflamed, and it appeared "sluggish." It had turned a strange hue—more or less the color of mud—and a sticky fluid oozed from his eye.

In late December, Ambler decided to review Danenhower's entire medical history. After a lot of questioning, the navigator admitted that he had once contracted venereal disease, though he believed it had been cured. Now Dr. Ambler told him otherwise: His condition was called syphilitic iritis. It was a fairly common symptom of second-stage syphilis. Syphilis was a strange and pernicious disease that manifested itself in countless maladies of the body and mind. It often masqueraded as some other disease—and did it so well that doctors often called it the Great Imposter. Ambler had seen and treated syphilitic iritis before. The malady could be very serious. Unless Danenhower was extremely careful—or extremely lucky—he would likely go blind in his left eye. There was always a chance it could develop in his right eye, as well.

Ambler treated Danenhower with a shot of mercury in his buttocks, a standard, if dubious, treatment for syphilis at the time that had numerous deleterious side effects. (A dictum common among doctors went: "One night with Venus, a lifetime with Mercury.") To dull the pain, Ambler applied lint doused with tincture of opium. He also dropped small doses of atropine into Danenhower's eye to dilate the pupil. The goal was to keep the pupil open and to prevent the iris from adhering to the lens. If the drops didn't work, Ambler would be forced to operate, inserting a probe into the eye's tissues to release the gummy adhesions before the iris and lens melded together into a permanent scar.

For now, Ambler said, Danenhower's eye could not tolerate any kind of light—not even candlelight or moonlight. Ambler instructed the navigator to wear smoked snow goggles and keep his bad eye blindfolded at all times. As though Danenhower's quarters weren't already tomblike enough, a canvas shade would have to be put up to black out his window. His navigational and astronomical work would cease. From now on, Danenhower would keep to his dungeon.

It was as though the doctor had sentenced him to an indefinite period of solitary confinement. Ambler tendered Danenhower a favor, though: He promised that he would not tell De Long about the syphilis—at least, not now. Ambler reported to the captain's cabin and informed him only that Danenhower had been placed on the sick list and that his left eye had "broken down." Venereal disease was not mentioned, but Ambler did tell De Long that the navigator might lose the sight of his left eye.

De Long was shocked by this development, and he despaired for his friend and fellow officer. "He is now shut out from all participation," De Long wrote, "and we can do nothing but go down occasionally to sit and talk with him in the dark. He is cheerful enough, however, and having great force of character, has made up his mind to accept the situation and fight it out."

CHRISTMAS MORNING BEGAN black and bleak, the winds howling, the temperatures outside so cold that the contracting bolts and metal fasteners throughout the ship snapped and cracked in their timbers. Overnight, a sleeping dog curled up on the pack had become so firmly adhered to the ice that it had to be removed with a shovel. It was impossible to take observations because the lenses of the instruments could not be cleared of frost and vapor. Inside the ship, a green scum of long-accumulated condensation clung to the walls, ceilings, bulkheads, and nearly every other interior surface.

"This is the dreariest day I have ever experienced," De Long wrote, "and it is certainly passed in the dreariest part of the world." On this Christmas morning, he felt he had nothing to celebrate. He was unaware that in Washington that very week, the Navy Department had promoted him to the rank of lieutenant commander. As he thought of Emma and Sylvie and the comforts of home, he could hardly drag himself out of bed.

De Long's spirits lifted when some of the men came aft to distribute a bill of fare they'd secretly printed on the *Jeannette*'s small press. A Christmas feast was to be held at three p.m., with entertainment afterward. De Long's mouth watered when he read the sumptuous menu—

SOUP.

Julienne.

FISH.

Spiced salmon.

MEATS.

Arctic turkey (roast seal). Cold ham.

VEGETABLES.

Canned green peas. Succotash.
Macaroni, with cheese and tomatoes.

DESSERT.

English canned plum pudding, with cold sauce. Mince pie.
Muscat dates, figs, almonds, filberts, English walnuts, raisins, mixed
candy from France direct by the ship.

WINES.

Pale sherry.

BEER.

London stout.

French chocolate and coffee.
"Hard tack."
Cigars.

ARCTIC STEAMER *JEANNETTE.*

Beset in the pack, 72 degrees north latitude

The Christmas feast proved powerfully good, so good it brought
tears to the men's eyes. Afterward, toasts were proposed, and everyone
sipped a dram or two of what De Long called "a fine compound" that
Melville had concocted from Irish whiskey and a few secret ingre-
dients. Following the meal, Alexey did a native Alaskan dance, and
then there was clog dancing as Adolph Dressler sawed the fiddle and
Albert Kuehne worked his accordion. The festive mood had a curing
effect. There was only one sour note: Collins refused to attend. He

was holed up in his room, brooding. Since the failure of the Edison lights, Collins had slipped into a funk and could not be coaxed out of it. On this day, especially, he was in no mood to be merry.

But the men somehow managed to persuade Collins to take charge of a minstrel show being planned for New Year's Day. Collins loved the idea. He would choreograph the show, write the scenes and intervening narrations—and sprinkle the thing with all the puns he wanted.

At midnight on the thirty-first, the New Year was announced by a rapid ringing of the ship's bell by the man on the watch. Officers and crewmen assembled on the quarterdeck and sang out three cheers for the *Jeannette*. The next morning, a printed program was circulated by a crewman done up in blackface, announcing a performance that night of "The Celebrated Jeannette Minstrels." Among other acts, it promised an orchestral overture, a violin solo, a jig dance by the ever-energetic seaman Jack Cole, and a performance by "the world-renowned Aneguin, of the Great Northwest, in his original comicalities."

At eight-thirty that night, everyone assembled in the deckhouse, where a stage had been erected with a drop curtain and lanterns serving as footlights, the whole proscenium decorated with flags. Danenhower, his left eye covered with a thick bandage, sat in the back. Collins began the show with a prologue in which he read some "conundrums," as he called them. They were groaners of the first order, but his crewmates were so glad to see him back in action that nobody cared.

"Why," said Collins, "is that stanchion like Mr. James Gordon Bennett?"

Why?

"Because it supports the house."

"And why do you suppose it is that the USS *Jeannette* will never run out of fuel?"

"Because we have Cole on board!"

Collins went on in this vein, ignoring the guffaws, eventually incorporating every member of the *Jeannette* into a riddle or a rhyme. Then the show began in earnest—with songs, skits, and dances. The acts were interspersed with *"Tableaux vivants,"* as Collins called them, silent scenes depicting such themes as "Sailors mourning over a dead marine" (two men mute with grief over an empty brandy bottle) and "Our good Queen Anne" (Aneguin dressed in drag). The acts were silly and amateurish, and everyone loved them. De Long judged Kuehne's violin solo "fine indeed, especially when one takes into consideration the fact that a seaman's life does not render the fingers supple and delicate." Ah Sam and Charles Tong Sing recited a Cantonese ballad, then broke into a sham knife fight. Then, said De Long, "Mr. Cole gave us a jig with all the gravity of a judge."

Not since the day they left San Francisco had such mirth and fellow feeling run through the ranks. "We broke up at eleven o'clock," said De Long, "and we all felt satisfied with the ship, the minstrels, ourselves, and the manner in which we had celebrated the first day of the year of our Lord, 1880."

PART FOUR

We Are Not Yet Daunted

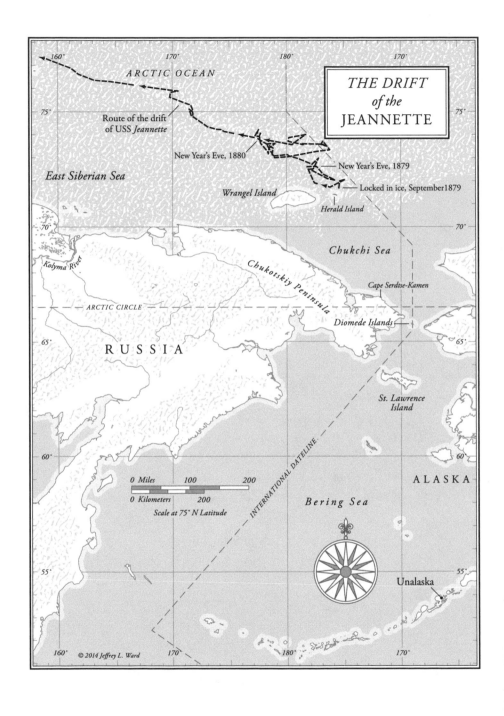

160°   ARCTIC OCEAN   170°   180°   170°

75°   Route of the drift
of USS *Jeannette*

THE DRIFT
of the
JEANNETTE

75°

East Siberian Sea

New Year's Eve, 1880

New Year's Eve, 1879

Locked in ice, September 1879

Wrangel Island

Herald Island

70°   *Chukchi Sea*   70°

Kolyma River

Chukotskiy Peninsula

Cape Serdtse-Kamen

ARCTIC CIRCLE

Diomede Islands

65°   R U S S I A   65°

*St. Lawrence
Island*

60°   60°

0 Miles   100   200

0 Kilometers   200

Scale at 75° N Latitude

INTERNATIONAL DATELINE

Bering Sea

A L A S K A

55°   *Unalaska*   55°

160°   © 2014 Jeffrey L. Ward   170°   180°   170°

My dearest husband—

    I am beginning to feel as if it were about time to hear something of you. I am in hopes you have left letters behind that may be found and brought back. I am longing for the sight of your handwriting, and what wouldn't I give for the joy of seeing you in person!

    At five o'clock every afternoon I have a feeling that you will soon be home and I must be all ready to receive you. I often imagine you in your room on board the ship, seated in your big chair, smoking your pipe after dinner, all alone in your glory, and I wish I could be with you to share it.

    Good-by for a whole year; this is the last Arctic mail for 1880 and my last chance of sending you any news. Let us hope that joy will not be too long deferred and that I will not have grown old and weary waiting.

Emma

GRAND OPENING
of the
NEW JEANNETTE OPERA HOUSE!
Corner Forecastle Ave. and Bowery

Tickets at the popular price of $0.00

Performance to commence at 8:30 p.m.

Sledges may be ordered at 10 p.m.

The best liquors may be had at Lee's Distillery,
within a few steps of the Theatre

A full year had passed, but everything was the same: The same gaslit stage, the same sun-starved actors, the same musicians playing the same instruments. The same dreary weather outside, the same stomachs stuffed on the same holiday feast, the same cracked lips sipping the same watered-down rum. Collins was again in charge, inflicting his wordplay on an audience that sat receptive for another festive night. Cole danced his furious jig, the Inuits performed their native dances, Sam and Charley sang their Cantonese ballads. Nothing had changed.

It was New Year's Eve 1880, and the USS *Jeannette* was still locked in the ice. For a brief time, in the hottest days of August, it had seemed she might break free from her prison, but then the ice closed up again, as implacable as ever. They had been trapped in the pack for sixteen months now and had drifted thirteen hundred miles—far enough to reach the pole and well beyond. Yet the route they'd taken was so convoluted, so full of jagged backtracks, that their present location was only three hundred miles northwest of the place where they'd first entered the floes.

Of course, they were grating on each other's nerves, but they were all alive and, for the most part, healthy. Though their coal supply had dwindled alarmingly, the ship remained snug and warm. A few of the dogs had died, but otherwise the *Jeannette* retained her full complement of living souls—an ark inching across the frozen sea.

But facing their second year in the pack was a sentence so crushing that it could be borne only by some stirring of levity. And so, to usher in 1881, another round of entertainments had been staged. Upon entering the "opera house," the guests were handed boutonnieres fashioned from crinkled colored paper. After a musical overture, Collins opened with a poem—

> *On the lone icebound sea we gather here*
> *To greet the dawning of another year*
> *Now for merriment we all unite*
> *And make the deckhouse ring with joy to-night,*
> *How quickly our fleet thoughts wing*
> *To distant lands and scenes, to bring*
> *A mystic spell upon our friends, who ask each other*
> *"How fares our absent ones—son, husband, brother?"*

Then the pageant began. The costumes were a little livelier than the year before, the sets a little more elaborate, but otherwise the performance was surreally familiar. Among the acts, the standout by far was the young British coal heaver Walter Sharvell, who had transformed himself into what De Long described as "a very comely young miss," complete with a wig, white stockings, and a prodigious bust stuffed into a shapely calico dress. This popular drag queen flirted and danced coquettishly, and was all too convincing to a crew of lonely men who had not seen a woman in nearly five hundred days.

The men closed the show with "The Star-Spangled Banner," and

De Long rose to say a few words to ring in the New Year. As the captain surveyed the past twelve months, he could not stifle his bitterness and disappointment. They were hardly any nearer to the North Pole than when they'd first met the ice. They had been "drifting about like a modern *Flying Dutchman*," noted De Long in his journal, "thirty-three people wearing out their hearts and souls." The year 1880 had been a blank. It had been a year of languor, of monochrome monotony—a year frozen in time. Everything, it seemed, was the same.

AND YET THAT wasn't quite true. When he looked back on it, De Long could see the highs and lows. The moments of heroism, the small delights, the work well done. There had been ingenious mechanical inventions and atmospheric spectacles too weird and wonderful to adequately describe. There had been rousing bear hunts—including one that brought home a prize male weighing 943 pounds. There had been days so warm the men had turned lobster red from the sun, and yet at one point, in February, the temperature had reached fifty-eight degrees below zero. They had played a thousand games of checkers and poker, backgammon and chess. When the warm weather came, they had scraped and repainted nearly every surface of the fair *Jeannette*. On the Fourth of July, they had dressed her up with flags and bunting and fired their guns in the nation's honor. When the short Arctic summer passed again into winter, the ice "began its horrid screeching and grinding," said De Long, "as if in celebration."

The novelty of life on the ice had long since worn off, Melville noted. "Our supplies of jokes and stories were completely exhausted, and their points had been dulled by much handling," he wrote. "The ship's company, fore and aft, had found their affinities; and congenial spirits began to walk, talk, and hunt together in couples. In the cabin there was more reading and less conversation, and the senior officers seemed daily bound by a closer band."

If they had not really gone anywhere, they had journeyed into regions of the psyche where few men had ever been, interior spaces that brought out aspects of themselves they'd never known existed. In ways few could imagine, the true grain of their characters had been revealed. In his Sunday devotionals, the captain's thoughts had inevitably run toward the story of Job. "He is recorded to have had many trials and tribulations which he bore with wonderful patience," De

Long had written. "But so far as is known, Job was never caught in pack ice."

In his lowest moments, De Long had considered quitting the *Jeannette* and heading for Siberia or Alaska. But he couldn't bring himself to do it. "I abhor the idea—we have come through so much," he said. "We shall stick to the ship as long as she sticks to us."

THE LOWEST MOMENT of all had happened on January 19, 1880. From the bowels of the ship, a dread cry had gone up from Lieutenant Chipp: *"Man the pumps!"* The *Jeannette* had finally succumbed to the cumulative wrenchings and shudderings of the ice. She was leaking badly—at a rate later estimated to be more than four thousand gallons per hour. When the trouble was discovered, her hold was already hip-deep in seawater. But it was so cold—the ambient temperature outside hovered around thirty degrees below zero—that the water turned to slush as soon as it seeped in.

Up on deck, De Long initiated emergency procedures to abandon ship. But in the hold, a crew member named William Nindemann stepped forward and exerted the full force of his personality. A thirty-year-old immigrant from Rügen Island, Germany, William Friedrich Carl Nindemann was listed as an ordinary seaman, but there was nothing ordinary about him. He had already suffered enough in his lifetime to set him apart from everyone else on board. Nindemann was a survivor of Hall's *Polaris* expedition in Greenland and had drifted with Tyson all those eighteen hundred miles on the ice floe, only to return to the Arctic to search for his lost mates. Even before the *Polaris* tragedy, Nindemann had made a name for himself as a shipwreck survivor: Three years earlier, he had been among the crew of a private American yacht that sank off the coast of North Africa. Nindemann was rescued by Tunisian Arabs, who took him hostage and demanded $15,000 ransom. Nindemann, it seemed, was a preternaturally lucky man who was not only addicted to the Arctic but was apparently impervious to hardship at sea. He had become a naturalized American citizen just a few months before setting sail on the *Jeannette*. Nindemann was signed on as the ship's quartermaster.

Practically from the day the *Jeannette* set sail, Nindemann had risen above the other seamen; he was the hardest working, the least complaining, the most resourceful, the quickest to volunteer for dan-

gerous duty. The second day out of San Francisco, a ponderous hatch-
way cover had fallen on his hand and nearly severed one of his fingers.
An alarmed Dr. Ambler stitched it up, but the German went about his
work without a whimper, refusing to go on the sick list even for a day.
"Nindemann is hardworking as a horse," said De Long, and "seems to
know no such thing as fatigue."

Nindemann was also oblivious to cold. His circulation appeared
to be different from other men's. On freezing winter hunts, he wore
hardly any clothes. He kept his cabin colder than everyone else's.
His feet were inured to frost. He was a polar creature, through and
though. As Collins said in one of his pieces of doggerel, "Not since
Adam sinn'd e'er lived a man / Who lov'd the Arctic like our Nindemann."

Now Nindemann waded into the flooded hold. For more than
twenty-four hours, he labored in the freezing gloom, cramming whatever materials he could find—felt, oakum, tallow, plaster, cement,
ashes—into the frames where the water appeared to be rushing in.
Much of that time he was joined by another stalwart, the British carpenter and mechanic Alfred Sweetman. The two men seemed not to
notice the freezing slush that came up to their knees; others who tried
to pitch in were driven away within minutes, their feet throbbing and
blue.

As they labored, Melville devised a system of steam pumps and
siphons, and other men worked hand pumps around the clock. Melville cannibalized Edison's generator for spare parts to make the system run. Then he designed a windmill to bring up even more water,
its turning blades improvised from old tin cans. The contraption soon
"rattled off in fine style," De Long remarked, and was "worthy of
being handed down to posterity."

Nindemann and Sweetman, meanwhile, didn't stop working.
Once they'd reduced the leak to a few hundred gallons per hour, they
began constructing an extra-watertight bulkhead in the forward-most
hold, the forepeak. All told, they worked for sixteen straight days,
almost without stopping, sleeping in shifts of no more than a few
hours, often skipping meals. When the new bulkhead was finished
and thoroughly caulked, it stanched the leaks further. After the crisis
was over and the ship had been saved, Nindemann and Sweetman
collapsed in exhaustion. De Long made a special notation in his logs,
recommending the two men for Congressional Medals of Honor.

Though their work was a success, the leaks would never be entirely fixed. The rattle and clunk of pumps would be a constant agitation for the rest of the voyage—a reminder that catastrophe was always just a few mechanical strokes away.

De Long tried to get to know Nindemann better. There was something remarkable about him, something about the ferocity of his work ethic, that the captain wanted to understand. He was a splendid masochist, a man who seemed to speed up in extreme cold. He had no rank, but in De Long's estimation, Nindemann had already moved to the forefront of the expedition.

Nindemann did not respond to praise, and he kept his distance. Seemingly emotionless, he had a black mustache and leathery skin and spoke forcefully in a thick German accent—a man of action, not words. He wouldn't attend De Long's divine service on Sunday, either. "I believe in nature," he said. "Nature is my God. I don't believe in the hereafter. This world is where we get all our punishment."

DURING 1880, THE dogs had become a central part of the *Jeannette* adventure. They had hunted and hauled, they had entertained, they had caused countless headaches, but they were indispensable. Once, thirty of them were used to drag a colossal walrus kill back to the ship, a prize that weighed twenty-eight hundred pounds. The men had gotten to know the dogs, had named them and picked favorites. Kasmatka. Tom. Quicksilver. Jack. Prince. Smike. Bismarck. Paddy. Skinny. Foxy. Plug Ugly. Dewclaws. Snuffy. Snoozer. Joe. Jim. Armstrong. Wolf. Bingo. They ate just about anything—rotten fish, seal entrails, walrus blubber, condemned foodstuffs, slops of all kinds— and they remained surprisingly healthy. "They are fat as dumplings," De Long said, "and as lazy as human beings in the tropics."

The dogs fought all the time, sometimes to the death, and yet they also observed subtle rules of kinship that allowed for many moments of extraordinary tenderness. Only Alexey seemed to understand them. He could see canine animosities brewing well before they came to a head.

Once, he and Dunbar went out with a team on a walrus hunt. On the way, Bingo escaped from his harness, much to the jealous dismay of the other dogs, who tried to chase him down. Alexey said to Dunbar, "*Bom bye,* other dogs him plenty whip" (for deserting). The hunting party returned to the ship in the afternoon, having enjoyed no success. About a half hour later, Hans Erichsen reported to De Long that Bingo had been killed in a vicious dogfight.

Alexey's prediction had proved eerily true. Wrote De Long: "Though three or four hours had elapsed, the dogs remembered the circumstance of the desertion, and finding Bingo at a safe distance from the ship had pitched into him and chewed him so badly before Erichsen could reach them that he died within ten minutes of being carried on board. We skinned him to have his coat for future wearing apparel, and his carcass lies frozen on the deck-house roof for possible food for his murderers."

De Long himself had grown attached to one of the dogs, a tough survivor called Snuffy. Early in the voyage Snuffy had gotten into a fight and developed an infection that caused his head and snout to swell up hideously. What De Long so admired about Snuffy was his "most wonderful power to hold on to life," as he put it. "Although I know that he will never be of use again, I prefer to give him all the life that he can hang on to in these uncharitable regions. Occasionally he seems to be going, as, for instance, today, when he was lying on an old mattress on the rubbish heap, seemingly at his last gasp. Being occupied with taking sights, I postponed his shooting until the afternoon, when, going out to see that he had not died in the meanwhile, I found him gone one hundred yards or so, and as frisky and far from death as ever."

De Long noticed that another dog, Jack, had rallied around Snuffy. "Jack watches him, protects him from the others, leads him, cleans him," De Long wrote. The captain was touched by these tender mercies—Jack seemed to derive no tangible benefit from them. But eventually Snuffy's condition worsened to the point that De Long felt it was cruel to keep him alive any longer. "For some days," De Long said, "he had wasted away to a shadow. Lying on the ice, the heat from his body had thawed away a hole, and he was sinking gradually from view."

So Snuffy was taken to the other side of the ship and shot. "The poor brute is gone now," De Long said, and Jack, his friend, seemed "unable to comprehend his disappearance." Jack lingered by Snuffy's old ice hole "in inquiring anxiety," said De Long. "What a life this is."

DANENEHOWER WAS ANOTHER kind of scrappy survivor. The navigator had spent the entire year of 1880 confined to his darkened room. His advanced syphilis had begun to manifest itself in other symptoms, including lesions on his legs and inside and around his mouth. It appeared that he would indeed lose the sight of his left eye. Even though Dr. Ambler applied atropine religiously, the gummy substance inside the eye kept reappearing, adhering the iris to the lens.

In January, when the pain had become too much for the navigator to bear, Dr. Ambler decided to operate. He gave Danenhower a little opium, and three burly men were brought in to hold down the patient's arms and legs. Then Ambler, wielding a knife and a rubber probe, cut into the cornea and investigated the anterior chamber of the eye. He used an aspirator to "let out a lot of turbid fluid," as he put it in his report. The pain was excruciating, but Danenhower endured it stoically.

Every so often, De Long would stick his head into the room and watch the proceedings. "I hardly know which to admire most," he wrote, "the skill and celerity of the surgeon or the nerve and endurance of Danenhower."

The procedure was a partial success, but over the next six months, Ambler would have to operate again, and again, to drain the "purulent matter" off the eye. All told, Danenhower underwent more than a dozen operations throughout 1880.

By now De Long had been told the truth: that Danenhower had syphilis, that he had known it even before he signed on to the *Jeannette*. Ambler had tried to keep the secret as long as he could, but when the sores had appeared, it was no use. The captain was shocked and furious to learn this news. So that explained not only his eye and his skin sores but also his "brain trouble," the bouts of depression that had cropped up in his record; it was well known that syphilis could make a man go mad. It made no difference that Danenhower had *thought* he was cured—there was no "cure" for syphilis at the time. In De Long's estimation, Danenhower, by holding on to his secret, had committed an unforgivable sin of willful deception that endangered the whole expedition. Knowing what he knew, Danenhower should have recused himself from the outset.

Still, the captain couldn't help being moved by the uncomplaining toughness and equanimity with which Danenhower suffered his plight. "The knife and probe are regular things in his case now," wrote De Long. "There is no improvement. He bears his confinement and the pain of the operations heroically. But he will never be of any use to the expedition and I seriously fear can never be of very much use to himself."

AS DE LONG thought back over 1880, what galled him most was the circularity of the voyage: For all their sufferings, they had circled back more or less to the place they'd started. It got him thinking of machines—machines that do certain repetitive tasks and will keep on functioning as long as the fuel holds out. He bemoaned what he called the "mechanical supplying of the system with food, heat, and clothing, in order to keep the human engine running." Man, he said, "is but a superior kind of machine after all. Set him going, and keep him wound up, and he can run monotonously, like a clock."

He also thought of farm animals and other beasts of burden, who plod along a narrow course and never go anywhere. "I have often wondered if a horse driving a saw-mill had any mental queries as to why he tramped over his endless plank, and what on earth there was accomplished by his so doing. The saw was generally out of his sight, he perceived no work accomplished, and ended his day in identically the same place at which he began it. And, as far as equine judgment could forecast, he would do the same thing tomorrow, and every other day thereafter. If that horse had reasoning faculties, I pity him and appreciate now his thoughts and feelings."

But even when he reflected in this maudlin way, De Long usually caught himself. "A man up here thinks a wonderful amount of non-sense," he wrote, "and commits many absurdities which he will laugh at afterwards." He was an optimist at heart, he insisted. His motto was *Nil desperandum*—"Never despair." "Over this imprisonment," he said, "a certain indefinable, inexplicable something keeps telling me all will come out right yet. Some still small voice within me tells me this can hardly be the ending of all my labor and zeal."

And so on New Year's Eve 1880, when De Long stood up in front of the men, he tried to convey some of the hope that drove and animated him each day. He had never been very good at speeches, though, and he had nothing planned. He puffed his pipe for a while, drinking in the mood of the night, and he then began. "Like every event in life," he said, this cruise may be divided into two parts: That which has been and that which is to be. We are about to turn our backs on the old year and turn our faces toward the new. During the past sixteen months we have drifted thirteen-hundred miles. Danger has confronted us each day. We have been squeezed and jammed, tossed and tumbled, nipped and pressed, until the ship's hull would have burst had it not been as strong as the hearts it held within. We have pumped a leaking ship for a year and kept her habitable. And we are all still here. We face the future with the firm hope of doing something worthy of ourselves, and worthy of the flag that floats above us. We are not yet daunted.

Something about his words caught fire with the crew. They made the deckhouse ring with their cheers. *Nil desperandum! We are not yet daunted!* At midnight, the traditional eight bells were struck for the old year, then eight more for the new. De Long said good night to the men, then lingered awhile in the wardroom with Melville and Dunbar before turning in to jot a few lines in his journal. "The year 1881 [was] officially inaugurated in the United States Arctic Steamer *Jeannette,* in latitude 73°48' N, and longitude 177°32' E. I begin the new year in this book by turning over a new leaf, and I hope to God we are turning over a new leaf in our book of luck."

My Dear Husband—I got up a Christmas tree for Sylvie and she was perfectly delighted with it. We dressed the tree that night and on Christmas morning I led her into the parlor and there stood the tree in all its glory surrounded by innumerable dolls and trinkets. We looked so few standing around the tree that bright Christmas morning, it was sad. Let us hope, next Christmas.

This is the time of year to form good resolutions, and I am making a good many, but first and foremost I am going to give up fretting and am going to be bright and hopeful and energetic. I suppose you are in total darkness now but you will see the sun by February. How you must long for it!

Your loving Emma

Through the spring of 1881, the *Jeannette* continued her jagged drift across the Arctic pack, creeping toward the northwest. The ice showed new cracks and fissures, the first signs of the coming thaw, but offered scant promise of release.

May 17 dawned flat and gloomy, but in the late afternoon, the leaden skies parted, offering views to the horizon. At seven p.m., the ever-vigilant Dunbar was in the crow's nest, watching the crunching floes through his glass as the men went about their evening routines. Dunbar had been acting funny lately—something was agitating him. Some subtle change in the wind and the drift patterns of the ice engaged his mariner's mind. For a week or more, it had seemed to him that something in the distance, to the leeward side, was obstructing the free movement of the floe, smashing and fissuring the ice into smaller pieces.

Suddenly Dunbar issued a raspy call to the men below, one so strange and unexpected that at first they could not register its significance. "Land ho!" he cried out. "Land ho! Off the starboard bow!"

It was just a vision in the distance, maybe fifty miles off, a nub of gray standing proud of the hummocks and pressure ridges. For several days, Captain De Long studied this curiosity, wondering if it might be an illusion—a refraction of light, perhaps, a fata morgana. He could not be sure what it was, for it was often obscured by mist and fog, and a low cloud clung to it. But a few days later, the cloud dissipated, and the island became clearly visible to the naked eye:

a tall conical mass, like a volcano, riven by gulches, its steep flanks speckled with snow. There was no denying it. This was land, the first they had seen in more than four hundred days—ever since they had lost sight of Wrangel in early 1880. In his journal, De Long's relief was palpable: "There is something, then, besides ice in this world."

As they drifted toward it, De Long consulted his charts. None of the maps, not even the most up-to-date ones Bennett had procured from Petermann, showed anything for many hundreds of miles in any direction. For the past year they had been drifting across a great stretch of the Arctic through which no vessel had ever passed. A smile must have spread over De Long's face, for the conclusion was inescapable. "We have discovered something," he wrote. "Our voyage, thank God, is not a perfect blank."

De Long adopted a rhapsodic tone in his journal. "What this desolate island, standing among icy wastes, may have to do in the economy of nature, I do not know, or in fact care. It is solid land, and will stand still long enough to let a man realize where he is."

He christened the new terrain Jeannette Island and began to make plans for landing on it. The crewmen were ecstatic. "At once," Melville wrote, "all the younger prophets turned out on the high hummocks to scan the discovered country. All were as elated as though a second Goshen had sprung into view." The men, studying the island with field glasses, began to imagine that they could see live game flitting on Jeannette's distant shores. "Some of the far-seeing enthusiasts," said Melville, "distinctly descried reindeer moving about; and others of still greater ken could plainly distinguish the buck from the doe."

Then, on May 25, Dunbar sighted *another* piece of land. At first he surmised that it was merely an outcropping of Jeannette Island, but by May 27, it became apparent that it was another island altogether, considerably larger than Jeannette and perhaps thirty miles beyond it, to the northwest. What was more, the ship was heading directly toward it—passing little Jeannette by.

So Captain De Long and the crew shifted their affections toward this newer, larger rock. De Long named it Henrietta Island, after both Bennett's Irish mother and the schooner that Bennett had used to win the first transatlantic yacht race. (It was, like Jeannette, a soft and effeminate name for such a hard trophy, but then again, these men had not been in the company of women for twenty-three months.) They couldn't stop looking at the island. Henrietta was, said De Long, "the cynosure of all eyes . . . as pleasing as an oasis in the desert." It became their talisman, their fetish. "We gaze at it," De Long said, "we criticize it, we guess at its distance, we wish for a favoring gale to drive us towards it, and no doubt we would accept an assertion that it contained a gold mine which would make us all as rich as the treasury without its debts."

The crewmen fantasized about finding safe harbor on Henrietta and setting up camp for a time—repairing the ship's leaks, eating fresh meat, and savoring the dimly remembered pleasures of walking on terra firma. "We shall enjoy getting our foot on solid earth as much as if it were Central Park," De Long said. "Most of us look carefully at our island before we go to bed to make sure it has not melted away."

By the end of May, Henrietta's features were sharpening into bold relief. Collins and Newcomb kept themselves busy producing sketches: There were steep headlands, rocky points, discharging glaciers. It appeared to be a circular hump of land about four miles across, a plug of creation capped by eternal snow, forged by heat, whittled by wind, and gouged by ice. But De Long held out hope that the island's interior, or hidden coves along its coast, might teem with life. Perhaps there would be bears and walruses to shoot, driftwood to salvage, fresh water to drink, rookeries from which to rob eggs. He envisioned an early summer idyll to reclaim the expedition's energies.

But with the unpredictable churn of the ice pack, De Long worried that the ship, while generally aiming toward Henrietta, might assume a different course and pass it by, just as she had missed Jeannette Island. On May 31, seeing his opportunity vanishing, he decided to dispatch a small detachment of men and dogs to make landfall and perform a cursory reconnaissance. It was an incredibly risky idea: With so much turbulence around them, with the ice cracking in all directions, the explorers could easily become marooned, drifting to their deaths on a detached floe. A lead could open and swallow them. A single storm or the untimely descent of fog could separate them visually from the ship just long enough to ensure that they would never be found again.

Yet De Long thought the rewards of the reconnaissance mission far outweighed its risks—and he picked the "flower" of the crew to make the attempt on Henrietta. The ferociously competent Melville would be in charge. Dunbar, who knew the treacherous idiosyncrasies of ice better than anyone, would serve as guide. Four of De Long's strongest, ablest men would haul the gear: Nindemann, Erichsen, Sharvell, and the fireman James Bartlett. De Long himself hankered to lead the expedition—it was, he said, "my strong desire." But Chipp had come down with some sort of intestinal ailment, forcing him to join Danenhower on the sick list. De Long concluded that it would be irresponsible for him to leave the ship and her crew for such a glorious errand.

At nine o'clock, Melville and his party gathered on the ice with fifteen dogs and a dinghy to be pulled on a McClintock sled. They were equipped with rifles, ammunition, a tent, and provisions for ten days. Altogether, they had nearly a ton of equipment and supplies. The rest of the crew circled about and cheered them, firing off a few volleys of the large brass gun. It was the first time any part of their expedition had been separated from the group in nearly two years. An immense black flag was flown from the mainmast to serve as a beacon for Melville's return.

Melville gave the sign, and in a ruckus of scraping runners and yipping dogs, they took off for white-domed Henrietta. According to their best guess, the island was only twelve miles away, but they had to pass over what looked to be the most impossible terrain imaginable— a "wild tumult," as Melville described it, "a chaos of ice."

Five hundred yards from the ship, a lead of open water halted them, forcing them to lower the dinghy into the water and ferry the sled and supplies across. But they could not coax the dogs to plunge into the freezing water—their howls of protest carried over the ice. Two of the huskies escaped from their harnesses and sprinted toward the ship. Several fleet-footed men aboard the *Jeannette* intercepted the canine deserters and hauled them back to Melville, who reattached them to the team.

All day, and through the bright polar night, De Long had a lookout in the crow's nest keep an eye on the departing men. Melville and his detail crept across the floes, their course marked by crazy detours. Their progress was nearly comical in its slowness. Watching them was like watching a column of dung beetles recede across an obstacle-filled desert. They became a collection of dots on the ice, then a blotch, then a speck—until, midway through the following day, they disappeared from view, lost behind the crusty ridges of ice.

CAPTAIN DE LONG soon became preoccupied with other worries. The ice pressure on the stern had been intensifying all week. The leaks that had bedeviled the *Jeannette* since she'd first been locked in the ice had grown worse. De Long ordered the hand pumps manned around the clock and had the windmill rigged up again. Its large, oblong blades thwanged in the fresh wind, bringing up more than 100 gallons every hour from the flooded holds. Yet with all this effort, the crew could scarcely keep pace. By De Long's calculation, the ship was taking on 4,874 gallons a day.

To relieve some of the pressure on the stern, De Long armed the men with picks, mauls, and ice saws and had them dig a trench around the rudder and propeller well. "It is hard as flint," De Long wrote, "and clings like an old and tried friend." So powerful was the ice's grip that when it was pried loose, strips of oakum caulking ripped from the seams. In some places, the grain pattern of the boards could be seen imprinted upon the chunks of removed ice.

If this weren't enough, De Long was presented with a medical crisis, the most serious one of the voyage. The morning after Melville's party left, Dr. Ambler broke the news that a good number of the remaining crew—at least seven—were now suffering from a mysterious "distemper." Whatever it was, Ambler feared it could become an epidemic. ("What *next?*" De Long jotted in exasperation.) For weeks, crewmen had been complaining of a curious range of symptoms: listlessness, sleeping difficulties, low appetite, weight loss, anemia, a metallic taste on the tongue, and, especially, sharp cramping of the bowels. Some noticed a slight tremor in their hands; others appeared to be passing blood in their urine.

The complaints had lately increased, and now Chipp, Newcomb, Kuehne, Alexey, Ah Sam, Charles Tong Sing, and even Dr. Ambler himself were suffering. Newcomb, especially, was in horrible pain—looking "as woebegone as possible," as De Long wrote. Newcomb was made all the more miserable by the fact that he had so badly wanted to join Melville's party in the attempt on Henrietta. Newcomb felt that, as the voyage's naturalist, it was his responsibility to make a study of the birds and other wildlife that might be living on the new island. Yet he couldn't get out of bed.

Dr. Ambler wasn't sure, but several long days of medical sleuthing led him to make an educated guess about the underlying cause of the strange malady. It was *lead poisoning*. If he was right, this was a grave matter. Lead toxicity could soon progress to delirium, seizures, kidney failure, and death. The doctor knew he had to find the source of the contaminant immediately; the expedition's survival depended on it.

FOR DAYS, MELVILLE and his party of five struggled over the ice. The glaciated ramparts of the island loomed ever closer, but Melville's progress proved even tougher and slower than he had imagined it would be. Dunbar led the way, carrying a black silk flag as a marker. They made only a few miles a day, straining up and down the jagged slabs. "Millions of tons of blocks were piled up," Melville wrote, "as though they were the ghastly heaps of the slain from the battle that was forever raging among the broken masses; and great bodies of ice were incessantly fleeing, it seemed, from the mad pursuit of those behind."

The dinghy, packed with their tent and all their food, wobbled on the McClintock sled. The men had strapped themselves to it with long canvas harnesses and were pulling the load alongside the dogs. At times the huskies proved more hindrance than help. They growled and snapped at each other; several times the men had to break up free-for-alls. In this jumbled terrain, the dogs kept snagging their harnesses and wrapping the lines around one another—often becoming, Melville said, as "hopelessly tangled up as a basketful of eels."

By the fourth day of their sojourn, it became obvious they would never reach Henrietta while dragging a dinghy filled with nearly a ton of supplies. So Melville decided to leave the boat and all but a single day's worth of provisions and make a "dash" for the island. It was a brilliant sunny day, and Henrietta's features shone so clearly that Melville felt he could touch them—its "black serrated rocks," he wrote, were "streaked with veins of iron" and seemed to have been forged in a "great blast furnace." Hurriedly, the men placed the dinghy on an elevated hummock and, to mark it for their return, flew a black flag from an oar stuck snugly in the ice. For good measure, Erichsen attached his bright felt hat to the top of the oar.

Melville understood that abandoning the boat and their food supply was a "hazardous expedient" and that returning safely to it might be "greatly a matter of luck," especially if bad weather were to set in. But he could think of no other way to reach Henrietta with any reasonable chance of getting back to the ship alive.

With their load considerably lightened, they made good progress.

But by the next morning, after a breakfast of pig's feet simmered in mutton broth, they got under way only to learn of a troubling development: The previous day's unremitting sun had taken a severe toll on Dunbar's eyes, and he had become badly snow-blind. The crusty old whaler had spent most of his life at sea, often in the Arctic, but never had he been struck down with this age-old malady—photokeratitis, bake eyes, welder's flash. Dunbar was supposed to be the guide, with the keenest vision in the party, moving ahead of everyone else to pick the clearest path. But he couldn't see his own hand in front of him. His eyes burned and twitched and welled with tears. His pupils were constricted, his corneas inflamed. Strange specks of light danced across his field of vision. Still, Dunbar was too proud to admit this mortifying truth—and he didn't, until it became obvious to everyone else that something was wrong.

Melville tried to comfort Dunbar and asked him to ride in the sled. There was no use in his stumbling across the pack like a drunkard—he might hurt himself. But the old ice pilot refused to be a burden. When Melville ordered him to get in the sled, Dunbar roared, "Leave me here then!"

"He begged in the most distressing manner to be left on the ice," Melville wrote. "It was the first time in his life that he had ever been broken down, and it grieved him sorely." Despite Dunbar's strenuous protests, the men placed him in the McClintock ("greatly to the old gentleman's disgust," noted Melville), and they continued on toward Henrietta, now with Erichsen taking up the silk flag and serving as ice pilot.

They could no longer see the island—it had become veiled by a snowstorm. But Melville kept them on a steady compass course, and he knew they were drawing near. They maintained a good pace, until the sled plunged through the ice and was nearly submerged in freezing seawater. Dunbar, cursing helplessly inside the sled, clutched its crossbars while Erichsen rushed to his aid. The big, brawny Dane crouched over the McClintock and lifted it from the slushy pool, setting it on the ice as though it were a child's toy. Melville, praising Erichsen's "herculean feats of strength," wondered how they would have survived without him. On this occasion, he had almost certainly saved Dunbar's life.

Sometime that evening, June 2, the six men pulled themselves onto the shores of Henrietta Island. Elated, exhausted, and relieved, they padded across a thin beach and onto a field of black rocks splotched with moss and lichen. It was the first land they had stood on in 642 days. Dunbar expressed pure joy in the sensation of what he called "sanding my hooves." It felt wonderful but also strange to amble on hard ground. It was different from walking on a ship pitched at queer angles, and different from walking on floating cakes of ice and snow; the muscles of their legs and feet were unaccustomed to it, and at first their gait was wobbly and uncertain.

Although Henrietta was an ancient place—volcanic rocks on the island date back five hundred million years—Melville and his men were by all evidence the first human beings ever to set foot on it. Knowing this ignited a complicated range of emotions in the engineer; he seemed to find the moment of discovery both beautiful and haunting. This was what explorers lived for, what animated and drove them. This was the joy that saw them through the hardships. At the same time, Melville was spooked. No one had ever been here. Perhaps no one was ever *meant* to be here. "We stood lost in the contemplation," he wrote. "The silence was awful." They had landed on "a black monster" whose steep headlands loomed "as they had for ages, like sentinels, challenging our strange advent."

They had reached the end of the earth. For more than a thousand miles to the east, and nearly a thousand miles to the west, Henrietta was the northernmost mote of land, a lonesome satellite in the High Arctic. In this part of the world, no scrap of terra firma was so close to the earth's apex.

Melville claimed this virgin land as an American possession "in the name of the Great Jehovah and the President of the United States." Then he "baptized" the island by sprinkling a few drops of corn extract from a small wicker bottle. Erichsen planted an American flag in the rocky soil. Later, higher up the island's flanks, Melville and his men looked back with satisfaction toward the ice field over which they had struggled. In the spectral light, they could see the *Jeannette* some ten miles away, still locked in the ice, its position having shifted to a troubling degree.

Tomorrow they would have to make haste. But now they pitched their tent and crawled inside and, as Melville put it, fell fast "in the arms of Morpheus."

ABOARD THE *JEANNETTE,* Dr. Ambler and Captain De Long frantically searched for the source of the contamination. Several more crew members had come down with symptoms, and Ambler was alarmed.

The ship's distilling system was the first suspect. De Long had the whole apparatus dismantled and minutely studied for any appearance of lead leaching into the water supply. A few lead pipe fittings were found, but they were in such good condition it seemed unlikely that they could be the cause of the acute symptoms being reported.

It took another day before Ambler was able to determine the culprit. At supper, the crew dug into a bowl of stewed tomatoes, as they had nearly every night for months. One of the men crunched down on something hard and removed from his mouth a metal pellet. As they picked through their portions, other men found more of the tiny gobbets. They didn't think much of it, but at one point, someone joked, "Who shot the tomatoes?"

This got Dr. Ambler's mind churning. After close inspection, he determined that the small bits of metal were lead and surmised that the natural acid in the tomatoes had, over the course of the long journey, reacted with the lead solder used to seal the tin cans in which the tomatoes were stored. Some of the cans were in bad condition, their insides coated with a residue of black oxide of lead. The crew had been ingesting small but steadily growing amounts over time.

There seemed little rhyme or reason behind who came down with the symptoms—each person's metabolism was different. "Curious that so many of us feel *no* effects," De Long wondered, "as we are all on the same diet." On the other hand, he noted, Charles Tong Sing, who, along with Newcomb, was the sickest of all the "lead invalids," was something of a tomato fanatic—"he is remarkably fond of this vegetable, and eats of it unsparingly."

From the start of the expedition, Dr. Ambler had insisted that the crew regularly consume tomatoes to help avoid scurvy; they, like citrus fruits, were correctly thought to be good antiscorbutics (although the reason why—high vitamin C content—was not then understood by science). But with this turn of events, a countervailing danger of Arctic travel had presented itself: The food that might save you could be stored in a container that might kill you.

"What use is it," De Long groused, "to secure exemption from scurvy for two years if disabling lead poison finishes you in the third?"

Dr. Ambler, even though he was quite sick, took charge. The tainted tomatoes were thrown out, and a new diet was drawn up, with increased daily rations of concentrated lime juice. Within days, Ambler began to see improvements among the sick. What most worried him was Melville and the men on the ice. They might be stricken with the same sickness and find themselves unable to move.

By this time, Captain De Long was nursing a "constant uneasiness" about the sled party's safety. Melville and his men, he calculated, should have been back by now. Over the past two days, a thick, gelid fog had set in, limiting visibility to less than fifty yards. Not only had the crow's-nest lookouts lost sight of Melville's detachment; they'd lost sight of the island entirely.

For hours, De Long stared into the fog, hoping for a break in it, scouring in vain for human forms scuttling across the pack. All they could do, he said, was "fall back on our familiar resort, waiting in blindness." Every so often he ordered the brass gun fired to send out an auditory beacon, now that all visual beacons had been rendered useless. De Long began to rue his decision to dispatch a party to explore the island. He feared he'd made a dreadful mistake.

EARLY ON THE morning of June 3, Melville and his men made a quick breakfast and then set off to explore Henrietta. Nearly half the island was covered in glaciers. There were no signs of life, other than large populations of birds—guillemots, mainly, nesting along the rocky cliffs, which were streaked with guano. The birds, never having seen a human being before, had no fear. Sharvell, shotgun in hand, walked up to their nests and shot a number of them. The guillemots sat dumbfounded, showing no presentiment of danger.

The men fanned over the island, making sketches, taking measurements, and exhilarating in the first prerogative of explorers; naming things. There was Mount Sylvie, Mount Chipp, Point Dunbar, the Bennett Headlands. Melville and the men climbed a promontory, which Dunbar declared Melville's Head but others dubbed Bald Head, in honor of the chief engineer's shiny pate. There, in a cleft in the rock 250 feet above the frozen sea, they erected a cairn of stones. Inside, Melville placed a zinc case containing several copies of the *New York Herald* and a copper cylinder, eighteen inches long, in which was stored a written record of the *Jeannette*'s voyage thus far, penned by Captain De Long.

Melville, though "flushed with the success of the undertaking," did not linger on Henrietta. He knew he had to rush back to the dinghy and the supplies, and then back to the ship before it drifted out of sight or out of range. The men collected a few souvenirs from the island—some moss, some stone samples, and Sharvell's dead birds. After less than twenty-four hours on the volcanic rock, Melville's party repacked the sled and pushed off, with Erichsen leading the way, hoisting the black silk flag.

The weather was "miserable" and "cruel," and so fogged in that they had to travel the first two days entirely by compass. Open lanes of seawater halted them, and several times the sled was completely drenched. The ice, churning and popping with concussive sounds, left the dogs panic-stricken. Worse, Nindemann had come down with a severe illness. He was doubled over with excruciating cramps, almost certainly caused by the same lead poisoning that afflicted the men back on the ship. Melville had never seen Nindemann in such a state; he had always been the toughest, most stalwart member of the crew, but now the German was "enduring the agonies of the lost," Melville wrote.

With everyone gathered inside the tent that night, Melville rummaged in the medicine chest and produced a bottle of capsicum tincture for Nindemann. Distilled from cayenne and other powerful peppers, capsicum extract was then a common antidote for cramps. But the engineer's fingers were so cold and sore that he couldn't pry open the bottle. The always cheerful Erichsen intervened, drew the cork from the vial, and gave Nindemann a few drops. Then the big Dane clumsily spilled the capsicum extract all over his hands. Thinking nothing of it, he dug into the medicine chest and fished out a bottle of sweet-oil emollient, which he liberally rubbed over his sore body, chafed groin, irritated eyes, and sunburned face.

Suddenly Erichsen's body seemed to be on fire; he'd forgotten about the capsicum oil still on his hands. "The result," said Melville, "was at once a surprise to him and a delight to us." Shrieking, smarting, eyes wide with astonishment, Erichsen hurled himself from the tent, peeled off his clothes, and writhed in the snow to cool his stinging skin—squirming, said Melville, "like an eel." Everyone in the tent, even Nindemann, broke out in raucous laughter.

Dunbar, squinting, yelled through his chuckles at the naked form outside the tent: "Erichsen, are you hot enough to make the snow hiss?"

BY JUNE 3, De Long had grown heartsick with worry. Where was Melville? The captain realized that sending out a search party in this low-visibility weather would be a fruitless, if not foolish, exercise. All he could do was keep firing off volleys of the brass gun and hope that Melville might home in on the report.

On the morning of June 4, the weather cleared. It was crisp and cold, and the windmill blades whirred in the sharp breeze. The lookouts couldn't see Melville's party, but Henrietta loomed vividly. De Long had the men build a big fire on the ice, feeding it with tar and oakum to send up a thick plume of black smoke. Surely Melville, if he was within twenty miles, would see it. Yet there was no sign of him.

A polar bear, apparently lured by the acrid smell of the smoke, came lumbering over to the ship and was seen scratching itself on a clothes pole stuck in the pack and sniffing around the few remaining sled dogs, curled on the ice behind the ship. Edward Starr was the first to react. He grabbed a rifle and fired a shot, which missed. He jumped onto the ice and chased after the bear, firing twice more. "Away ran Bruin," De Long wrote, the animal seeming to accelerate as it "heard the bullet sing across the ice. But alas!, our 600 pounds of fresh meat escaped."

At six the next morning, June 5, the watchman in the crow's nest sounded an alarm and blurted, *"Party in sight!"* De Long raced onto the deck and, sure enough, he could see the flash of a silk flag appearing intermittently between the hummocks, several miles off. He was so excited that he ran toward the bridge for a better look with his field glasses. Bounding up the steps, he was leveled by a blow to the head and knocked nearly unconscious. He stood up, dazed. Blood trickled down his face and dripped onto the quarterdeck. Ah Sam looked at the captain aghast, saying, "Oh my! Great big hole!"

De Long, in his anxiousness to learn more about Melville, had forgotten about the recently reinstalled windmill. One of its sharp blades had sliced open his head, leaving a four-inch gash serious enough that Dr. Ambler demanded to take him to the infirmary. But before he would go, the captain had to know if everyone in Melville's party was alive and safe. In the shaky lens of the lookout's glass, the men emerged from behind an ice ridge. De Long was "intensely relieved" to spot six tiny forms trudging across the pack, with Erichsen out ahead, wearing his old felt hat and carrying the flag.

"Thank God," De Long wrote, "we have landed upon a newly

discovered part of this earth, and a perilous journey has been accomplished without disaster."

Dr. Ambler stitched and plastered De Long's wound, and soon the captain joined the others on the ice to welcome the sojourners. They hugged and laughed and drank whiskey, with "the dogs yelling lustily." Melville couldn't tell "who was more pleased, the greeters or the greeted."

When Melville asked about the big bandage on the captain's head, De Long replied sheepishly that he'd had "a bout with the windmill." Then he smiled and embraced Melville. "Well done, old fellow," he said. "I am glad to see you back."

That same week, as De Long and his men rejoiced in their conquest of a new crag of land, another American vessel was working its way up the eastern coast of Siberia, across the Bering Strait from Alaska. This ship, the reinforced steamer *Corwin,* crept along the ragged margin of the pack, waiting for summer to melt the frozen gates of the Arctic.

The *Corwin*'s captain, Calvin Hooper, was a commissioned officer of the U.S. Revenue Cutter Service, a predecessor of today's Coast Guard. And the *Corwin,* which had left its home port of San Francisco in May, had many errands to accomplish during its season's cruise: carry the Arctic mail, check on the safety of the whaling fleet, interdict illicit whiskey and firearm traffic, enforce trapping and trade treaties in Alaska, and inspect the holds of ships for violations of the annual seal hunt. But the most urgent purpose of the *Corwin*'s mission, carrying the hopes and fears of the nation, was to learn the fate of the USS *Jeannette.*

As Hooper stopped at tiny settlements along the Siberian coast, a story began to emerge, filtered through multiple languages, its details distorted from having traveled by word of mouth from village to village. The Chukchis spoke of a shipwreck somewhere to the north, hundreds of miles up the coast. An American vessel had become locked in the ice and drifted for months. Finally it had been crushed, its timbers torn asunder and scattered over the ice. There had been disease and horrible tribulation. Some Chukchi natives were supposed to have seen corpses.

Hooper was guardedly interested. "Notwithstanding the well-known mendacity of the natives in this vicinity," he wrote, "the report contained a ground work of truth." Could this shipwreck be the *Jeannette*? he wondered. Was it one of several American whaling ships—among them the *Vigilant* and the *Mount Wollaston,* captained by the prophetic Ebenezer Nye—that had gone missing the previous fall? Or, just as likely, was the story a fiction, concocted by canny natives seeking a reward?

Whatever the case, Captain Hooper had to learn more. By the first week of June, he had pushed his way north to the ice's edge, on the scent of this tragic tale.

FOR THE PREVIOUS year, newspapers across the United States had called for the launch of relief expeditions to learn what had become of De Long. Some papers had gone so far as to declare that De Long and all his men were dead. Emma De Long had lobbied quietly through the winter to ignite public sentiment for a rescue effort. By early 1881, cries for a solution to the *Jeannette* mystery had intensified: People had to know where De Long and his men were. It was as though the nation had sent its countrymen down into a hole in the earth, or off to another planet, and now, for reasons of science, for reasons of national pride and emotional closure, there had to be a reckoning.

In truth, many Arctic "experts" were optimistic about the *Jeannette* and thought that the dearth of news about her was a good thing—a sign that she had made it through the impediment of the ice and was well on her way to the pole. "I cannot see any reason for being . . . anxious about the *Jeannette,*" the Austro-Hungarian Arctic explorer Karl Weyprecht opined for the newspapers. "A ship whose object is discoveries in uninhabited regions cannot be expected to remain in communication with home . . . Mr. De Long has no reason to linger about the outer ice for the benefit of those who are expecting news. The absence of news . . . must be contemplated as a symptom of success."

Bennett felt the same way. He had written to Emma De Long, "I hope the silly prophecies of outside irresponsible papers about the *Jeannette* have not frightened you. I am perfectly confident of the absolute safety of the ship and crew. The very fact of her not being heard from yet is to me the best evidence of her success." At a meeting of the American Geographical Society in New York, the Arctic explorer Isaac Hayes dismissed all worries about De Long. "I do not anticipate that the *Jeannette* has been either crushed by the ice or hopelessly beset," he said. Emma, in the audience, was given a standing ovation when she was acknowledged. "I see the face of Mrs. De Long among us," Hayes said, "and I want to express my belief that her husband is just as safe tonight, though not as happy, as if he sat by her side."

Maybe so, yet Congress was deluged with petitions for action. The American Geographical Society implored the White House and the U.S. Navy to do something. The new president, James Garfield, who had taken office in March, threw his wholehearted support behind the rescue effort. Congress appropriated nearly $200,000 to outfit suitable relief vessels, and the hastily created Jeannette Relief Expedition Board, led by a prominent rear admiral, began to oversee the effort. Bennett would kick in extra funding wherever it was needed. The search was strictly precautionary, the relief board insisted. There was no overriding cause for worry. "The whole history of Arctic exploration is marked by great dangers, wonderful escapes, [and] successes where appearances forbade any rational hope," the board's initial report concluded. "We believe that the *Jeannette* and her gallant crew are safe."

All the same, Emma De Long had grown increasingly worried about the safety of her husband and his crew. She had been receiving letters from George Melville's wife, Hetty, who was sure the men of the *Jeannette* had all perished. Hetty Melville's letters were strange. Claiming to be a clairvoyant, she declared, "I shall never see my husband in this world again." She insisted that she had been visited by her husband's ghost: "He came to me as he said he would if he died, and he was in pure white." Emma decided that Mrs. Melville was probably mentally ill, yet her own worries about the *Jeannette* only deepened as relief vessels prepared to depart for the Arctic during the spring of 1881.

The *Corwin* was the first of three American ships to be sent out. Another ship, the man-of-war *Alliance,* would leave from Norfolk with two hundred men and make for Arctic reaches far to the north of Norway, on the theory that the *Jeannette* might have traveled over the pole and popped out on the other side of the ice cap. A third rescue ship, the *Rodgers,* would leave from San Francisco later in the summer and pursue a slightly different route through the Bering Strait toward the frozen ocean beyond. Gordon Bennett made sure that both the *Alliance* and the *Rodgers* would have top correspondents from the *Herald* aboard, and Emma De Long furnished the captains of both ships with copies of all her correspondence to her husband—the "letters to nowhere" she had been writing all year.

As for the *Corwin,* Captain Hooper's instructions from his superiors in Washington were worded hopefully, brooking little possibility that the *Jeannette* might have met catastrophe. "You will make careful inquiry in the Arctic regarding the progress and whereabouts of the steamer *Jeannette,*" the orders read, "and will if practicable communicate with [it] and extend any needed assistance." Hooper's orders expressed confidence that he would "bring back some tidings" of the lost explorers. Along the way, they would put out the word among all the whalers, sealers, walrus hunters, traders, and natives they encountered to keep a lookout for De Long's men and publicize a reward for reliable information leading to the discovery of the *Jeannette.* By the end of the season's cruise, the *Corwin* would travel more than fifteen thousand miles.

Hooper's mission was to reach the Bering Strait as quickly as possible and, once the ice permitted, to steam straight for Wrangel Land. De Long had stated from the outset of his voyage that his objective was to work his way up Wrangel toward the pole. As he had told Emma, the captain planned to leave messages in zinc canisters beneath well-marked cairns every twenty-five miles up the east coast of Wrangel, for the benefit of any future searchers. Hooper's orders, then, were to hunt for these cairns and follow whatever story might be contained in the secreted messages.

The SS *Thomas Corwin* was the most seaworthy Arctic vessel on the West Coast. Built in Portland in 1876, she was a single-screw steam-powered topsail schooner 137 feet long and made of stout Oregon fir fastened with galvanized iron and locust pegs. Although not nearly as ice-strong as the *Jeannette,* the *Corwin* had done honorable Arctic duty for three years, and her hull had recently been sheathed with thick oak planking to withstand the pack.

The man at her helm was a coolheaded career mariner with little formal schooling but with a preternatural gift for mathematics and navigation. Thirty-nine years old, a native of Boston, Calvin Leighton Hooper was a stolid, no-nonsense man with shiny pomaded hair and

aggressive muttonchops. He had sailed away from home at age twelve
as a cabin boy, become a first mate on a clipper ship at twenty-one,
and, following the Civil War, dedicated his life to the Revenue Cutter
Service. His was a hybrid profession that required him to be captain,
diplomat, detective, customs officer, and frontier sheriff of the high
seas. His ship was well armed, and he had full authority to confiscate
property, impound vessels, impose fines, arrest criminal suspects—
and, if necessary, kill them. The implacable expression on his sea-
dog face seemed to say that he would have no qualms about doing
so. America's sparsely populated new possession, Alaska, was a wild
and violent territory; if there was any law to be found there, Calvin
Hooper was it.

In addition to everything else Hooper had to do on this summer's
voyage, the crew of the *Corwin* also had to perform nearly ceaseless
scientific and geographical tasks: taking soundings, making temperature and barometric readings, improving charts, sketching coastlines,
collecting specimens.

The most famous, or soon to be famous, scientific eminence on
board the *Corwin* was a Scottish-born botanist who had lately been
studying the role that glaciers had played in the sculpting of Yosemite
Valley. A wiry man with a shaggy red beard and the burning blue eyes
of a half-crazed bard, he regularly wrote for the San Francisco *Evening
Bulletin*—although, in his deepest soul, he was a poet. His name was
John Muir.

BEFORE HE BECAME America's preeminent naturalist, before he
waged the conservation battles that would inspire the national park
system and ignite the modern environmental movement, John Muir
was a restless polymath who used newspaper and magazine assignments to help pay for his far-flung rambles to places of absolute wilderness. Like everyone else living in the Bay Area, Muir was well
aware of the *Jeannette*'s voyage and the national desire to learn her
fate. San Francisco viewed itself as the *Jeannette*'s home port, and the
newspapers there had speculated endlessly on De Long's whereabouts.

Muir, however, was not especially interested in the *Jeannette* mystery. An acquaintance of Hooper's, he had decided to accept the captain's invitation to come aboard the *Corwin* for the opportunity the
trip afforded to study far larger mysteries: the role of ice in the shap-

ing of continents, the formation of land bridges, the ebb and flow of ancient oceans.

Muir had been to southern Alaska twice before, and he had fallen in love with its pristine immensity. But he had never been above the Arctic Circle; nor had he encountered permafrost or the grinding forces of the polar ice pack. A natural historian later wrote that while voyaging on the *Corwin,* Muir wanted to "see back into deep time . . . In his heart of hearts, he was a wilderness man, always looking at the biggest picture." He was interested in primordial processes of creation that, although millions of years in the making, might still be visible on a grand scale.

Muir had immigrated to the United States as a boy, but he still had a trace of a Scottish lilt. He'd grown up in Wisconsin and put in a few years at the state university in Madison before embarking on a thousand-mile walk across the American South to Florida, after which he'd continued on to Cuba. Through convoluted inspirations, Muir had landed in California, and he had been living there for thirteen years. Most of that time he'd spent in the Sierras, where he had herded sheep, discovered an alpine glacier, undertaken an ambitious field study of the giant sequoia, labored unsuccessfully on a huge book about the Ice Age, made first ascents of California's highest peaks, and served as a guide in Yosemite.

Recently married, Muir had pledged to his wife, Louisa, that he would curb his footloose ways and settle down with her on her father's extensive fruit ranch in the golden hills northeast of Oakland. But the call of travel had proved irresistible: Only two months after the birth of their first child, Muir had signed on with the *Corwin* for a cruise that would last at least six months—and, if the ship were to become trapped in the ice, for another year after that. It would be, Muir thought, a "fine icy time."

WHEN THE *CORWIN* left San Francisco, in the first week of May, the Marin hills were flecked with golden poppies, and well-wishers cheered from yachts that rode alongside the departing steamer in the bay—a miniature version of the send-off San Franciscans had given the *Jeannette.* The *Corwin* had a crew of twenty, including several Japanese cabin boys. Turning north after passing through the Golden Gate, Hooper steamed up the Pacific for two weeks, then groped through the foggy Aleutian Islands, where the ship weathered snow-storms and a battering gale.

The ship would make several stops in the Aleutian Islands. As far as Muir could see, the native Aleuts had been virtually ruined by their contact with "civilization," first Russian and now American. Whalers, sealers, and representatives of the fur companies had introduced them to new vices while sapping the vitality from their old ways of doing things. "After paying old debts contracted with the Companies," Muir wrote, the Aleuts "invest the remainder in trinkets, in clothing not so good as their own furs, and in beer, and go at once into hoggish dissipation, hair-pulling, wife-beating, etc. In a few years their health becomes impaired, they become less successful in hunting, their children are neglected and die, and they go to ruin generally."

The *Corwin* pushed into the Bering Sea and made several stops in the Pribilof Islands, where the Alaska Commercial Company was killing and flaying some one hundred thousand fur seals each year. The farther north the *Corwin* ventured—to places less contaminated by outside influences—the more things improved. On the coast of Siberia near Plover Bay, Hooper called at a tiny settlement of thirty Chukchi natives. He and his men were invited into one of the hovels half-buried in the ground, its roof little more than a network of bones and driftwood logs covered in walrus skins. Inside, Muir was surprised to find "a number of very snug, clean, luxurious bedrooms, whose sides, ceiling, and floor were made of fur; they were lighted by means of a pan of whale-oil with a bit of moss for a wick." Muir found these people happy, well fed, and seemingly living in equilibrium with their world. "After being out all day hunting in the stormy weather, the Chukchi withdraws into this furry sanctum, takes off all his clothing, and spreads his wearied limbs in luxurious ease, sleeping perfectly nude in the severest weather."

Hooper was touched by the Chukchis' hospitality around the hearth, even if the food they offered the Americans was, in the captain's mind, inedible: boiled seal entrails, fermented walrus, raw whale meat, bowls of coagulated blood, and berries floating in rancid oil. While the food "created a feeling of . . . nausea," Hooper wrote, "one cannot but be impressed with the generous nature of the natives in thus offering to divide their best, and in many cases all they have, without thought."

The Americans smoked and drank tea with the Chukchis, and

were coaxed into participating in athletic contests: footraces, lance throwing, stone putting, and shouldering huge piles of driftwood logs. For all their strength and dexterity, the natives indicated that they did not how to swim. Wrote Irving Rosse, the surgeon on the *Corwin,* "They have the greatest aversion to water," though they were most adroit with their "little shuttle-shaped canoe, which is a kind of marine bicycle." The doctor noted that they were extremely kind to their children ("who do not show the same peevishness as seen in our nurseries"), and he seemed both intrigued and repulsed by the Chukchis' sexual promiscuity—"women are freely offered to strangers by way of hospitality, showing a decided preference for white men."

Muir would write at length about the Chukchis—of their smiles and laughter, of their trusting nature, of small moments of tenderness between a father and son. He was heartened to see a way of life that, though fragile, still held an ancient integrity. Witnessing a farewell between a husband and his gently sobbing wife, Muir felt moved to paraphrase Shakespeare: "One touch of nature makes all the world kin, and here were many touches among the wild Chukchis." They were, he thought, "better behaved than white men, and not half so greedy, shameless, or dishonest . . . These people interest me greatly, and it is worth coming far to know them."

IT WAS IN late May, at a place called Marcus Bay, on the Siberian coast west of St. Lawrence Island, that the men of the *Corwin* first got wind of the story about an American shipwreck. A boatful of Chukchi natives came aboard and told the tale with animation. They said that three seal hunters had been out on the ice well to the west of Cape Serdtse-Kamen—a desolate outcropping of land several hundred miles away—and had discovered a ship beset in the pack, with its crew dead on the deck or in the cabin. The seal hunters apparently had taken a bag of money from the wreck, Muir wrote, "and such articles as they could carry away, some of which had been shown to other natives, and the story had traveled from one settlement to another thus far down the coast."

Muir accepted the narrative. He thought the Chukchis had told it "with an air of perfect good faith, and they seemed themselves to believe what they were telling." But, like Hooper, Muir also weighed the possibility that they were angling for a reward. "We listened with many grains of allowance," Muir said.

The following day, in St. Lawrence Bay, the *Corwin* encountered still more Chukchis who were familiar with the story of the shipwreck. They came aboard the ship to trade walrus tusks and sealskin boots. An old man named Jaroochah sat down on the sludgy deck of the *Corwin,* called for a drink of water, then began to relate the tale—"in a loud, vehement, growling, roaring voice," Muir recalled, "and with frantic gestures." Speaking through a Chukchi translator who spoke passable "whaler English" ("three quarters profanity and nearly one quarter slang," according to Muir), Jaroochah described how the masts of the ship had been snapped off by the ice, how the boats were stove in, how the hold was flooded with seawater. The old man went on to say that the ice all around was littered with "ghastly corpses." He seemed unsure, however, whether there were one or two wrecks.

Hooper was suspicious of Jaroochah's theatricality and the too-vivid particulars of his story—"all of which," the captain thought, "were related in such an earnest and impressive manner that it would be difficult for any one unacquainted with Tchuktchi character to realize that most of it was manufactured on the spot." Jaroochah would not shut up—he spoke, said Muir, "in overwhelming torrents . . . like a perennial mountain spring, some of his deep chest tones sounding like the roar of a lion . . . [He] could hardly stem his eloquence even while eating." Later, he inquired whether Hooper had any rum to sell and declared "with vehement gestures" that it would "greatly augment my happiness." Captain Hooper soon learned from other villagers that Jaroochah had a reputation as a teller of tales—he was, Hooper said, "one of the worst old rascals in the country." Another Chukchi flatly regarded him as "a bad fellow, like a dog."

Hooper quizzed Jaroochah about Wrangel Land, the place where he felt sure De Long was now trapped—or at least had been trapped. The captain showed the old man a chart and asked if he knew of this mysterious landmass out in the ocean to the north. Jaroochah immediately said, "Oh yes, many white foxes there." He said the natives from the northeasternmost shore of Siberia often traveled there to kill those Arctic foxes. "But when pressed hard with questions he could not answer," Hooper wrote, "he acknowledged that he had never known any one to cross there, but had heard of such things in his youth."

On the other hand, Jaroochah's story about the American shipwreck jibed, in important details, with what Captain Hooper had heard at Marcus Bay. "At the bottom of it all," Hooper thought, "there seemed to be a foundation of truth, and I became more than ever convinced that some discovery had been made by the natives to the north."

Hooper realized that he could not reach the supposed location of the ruined ship, not in the *Corwin*. The pack was choking his way and might not melt for another month. He would have to hire Chukchi guides and dog teams and dispatch a smaller party to chase the story overland along the coast of Siberia.

When Hooper announced that it was his intention to do this, Jaroochah replied that there was no use in going; everyone aboard the wrecked ship was dead, and the vessel had drifted away.

"We will seek them whether they're dead or alive," Hooper said.

But Jaroochah maintained it was no use. The ice and snow were too soft for good sledding during this season. When he saw that the Americans still intended to seek out their lost countrymen, Jaroochah "regarded us," said Muir, "as foolish and incorrigible white trash"—and kept on talking.

HOOPER SET OUT for various villages on either side of the Bering Strait in search of dogs to buy and natives to drive them. He made a successful stop at the Diomede Islands, two volcanic plugs set on either side of the international date line in the middle of the strait. Although the two islands were less than three miles apart, Big Diomede was Russian and Little Diomede was American. From the Diomede Inuits, Hooper bought nineteen dogs, paying a sack of flour for each one.

Hooper turned the *Corwin* back toward Siberia to find more dogs and guides. In one settlement, the captain was able to locate a man named Chukchi Joe who spoke sufficient English to serve as translator for the expedition. Hooper then made for a place called Tapkan, a village of twenty huts spread along a sandbar. The village inhabitants came out to greet Hooper's party, and, said Muir, "we were kindly received and shown to good seats on reindeer skins. All of them smiled good-naturedly when we shook hands with them, and tried to repeat our salutations. When we discussed our proposed land journey, the women eagerly joined and the children listened attentively." Nordenskiöld had wintered the *Vega* very near here two years earlier, and one of the villagers brought out a fork, spoon, and compass of Russian origin, which the Scandinavian explorer had presented as a gift.

Hooper's party was invited into one of the deerskin huts. A woman was nursing a baby, while another woman roasted seal liver over some coals. After conferring with a few of the Tapkan elders, Hooper succeeded in engaging a few men and several of the village dogs to accompany the overland expedition. As they started back over the ice for the *Corwin,* one of the hired Tapkan men heard a sound that made his heart ache. "His little boy cried bitterly when he learned that his father was going away," Muir wrote, "and refused all the offers made by the women to comfort him. After we had sped over the ice, half a mile from the village, we could still hear his screams."

As the *Corwin* turned away, the villagers remained clustered at the edge of the ice, many of them no doubt wondering if they would ever see their men and dogs again.

THE FOLLOWING EVENING, the *Corwin* became so ensnared in the pack ice of the Chukchi Sea that the ship's oak rudder snapped. What little was left of it was hoisted to the deck, and the crew spent a few frantic hours jury-rigging a new rudder, amid the howling of the dogs.

Dodging wind-driven ice floes, Hooper limped for Kolyuchin Island, where the overland expedition would go ashore with its dog teams and begin the long journey. The party was led by First Lieutenant William Herring, accompanied by Third Lieutenant Reynolds, a sailor named Gessler, and several dog drivers, with Chukchi Joe serving as translator. They had twenty-five dogs, four sleds, enough food to last for two months, and a skin-boat for crossing open water.

Hooper made sure Lieutenant Herring understood the orders. As Muir wrote, they were to search the coast "for the crew of the *Jeannette* or any tidings concerning the fate of the expedition; to interview the natives they met; and to explore the prominent portions of the coast for cairns or signals of any kind." They were to travel as far as possible to the northwest, at least as far as Cape Jarkin, and then return to Tapkan, where the *Corwin* would attempt to rendezvous with them in about a month's time.

The men and dogs slogged away from the ship, across the pack, and finally made landfall on Kolyuchin Island. "The dogs rolled and raced about in exuberant sport," wrote Muir, but "a more forbidding combination of sky, rough water, ice, and driving snow could hardly be imagined by the sunny civilized south." The *Corwin* turned back toward Alaska to pursue other errands and gather more intelligence. "We went on our way," Muir jotted in his journal, "while the land party gradually faded in the snowy gloom."

My own dearest husband—

We ought to be exceedingly grateful that so many efforts are being made to rescue you. So many expeditions are in the field one of them ought surely to find you. This is going to be a trying summer to us all, anticipating news from you and possibly your return, and what bitter disappointment if we have to wait another year! Still, I will hope on until there is no possible ray of hope left.

The winter passed quickly in New York. I went very little to the theatre; had no inclination to go, strange to say. I did not enjoy it as I used to when we went together.

I have sometimes pictured you surrounded by ice, unable to control the actions of the ship and worn from hope deferred. I will not dwell on this. I have hoped and prayed you are all good friends and helpful to one another, that no sickness has fallen upon the little band.

Your adoring wife,
Emma

26 · DEATH STROKES

During the first week of June 1881, as the *Jeannette* continued her westward drift, Henrietta Island faded into a wispy gray form off the stern. Although Melville had found very little about Henrietta to recommend—no large animals to hunt, no safe ports, no driftwood to burn—De Long could not hide his sense of regret. "One might call [Henrietta] a thing of the past," he wrote, "and before many days it may be lost to view."

The ship was still stuck fast within a massive slab, but the ice was cracking and softening in the warming sea. Here and there, the men could glimpse large disconnected patches of open water around them. What a sight it was for sailors so long deprived of it—moving water, waves cresting and smashing into mare's tails of spray. The open ocean was what they knew, and the open ocean, if they could reach it, remained their only clear way home.

Yet returning home was not foremost on De Long's mind. By his calculation, the ship was little more than seven hundred miles from the North Pole, and a part of him still dreamed of reaching it—or at least of making a push through open sea to claim a "farthest north" record. Given the ship's sorry condition, he knew this was quixotic, yet he couldn't let go of his northering quest, especially now that so much open water was revealing itself.

De Long's state of mind was as fixed as the spring weather was capricious. The same hour might bring bright sun, fog, gale-force wind, rain, mist, needles of blowing ice, then sun again. All around them, the men heard dramatic shudderings as the melting pack disintegrated and bashed into other floating masses of ice, young and old, sending immense shards into the air. Yet for now, the *Jeannette* was so securely lodged in the middle of her ice island—"our friendly floe-piece," as Melville called it—that she was spared all the surrounding turmoil. "We are moving along slowly and grandly," De Long said, "a dignified figure in the midst of a howling wilderness."

Through the hourly changes, one larger trend was unmistakable: Spring was sliding fast into summer. "At last," De Long wrote, "there seems to be a disposition on the part of the weather to grow warmer, and it is high time." The sun now skimmed the horizon but never vanished behind it. In the new warmth, signs of life appeared. It was as though the men could sense the groaning tilt of the earth itself.

One morning, from the crow's nest, Dunbar thought he spotted whales surfacing through a distant opening in the ice. On another day, a huge flock of eider ducks, estimated to be more than five hundred, arrowed across the sky, flying low toward the north. (Why they were headed in that direction was the subject of discussion. Could there be more islands, or even Petermann's surmised polar continent, somewhere farther north?) The dogs, roused by the sight, scampered after the flock until they were halted by open water.

WITH SO MANY signs of summer's return, De Long's spirits brightened; everyone's did. Warmth and water brought the foretaste of freedom. Any day a major lead was sure to develop, releasing the *Jeannette* at last. "We knew that the important moment was coming," Danenhower said, "when the *Jeannette* would be liberated from her cyclopean vise."

It wasn't clear, however, whether liberation was a welcome thing. Ice had ravaged the ship for so long that no one could be sure she would float when cast upon the water again. It was possible that her frozen cradle, while posing its own dangers, was the only thing keeping her afloat. Danenhower, for one, worried about "our being launched into the confusion raging about us." He seemed certain that a liberated *Jeannette* would be in far greater peril than she was "while in the monster's grip." He thought the ship would be "crushed by the impact of antagonistic floe-pieces, among which the *Jeannette* would be like a glass toy."

During the first week of June, the ice steadily loosened its hold, with results that seemed, for now, quite promising. Down below, Melville noticed that the hull was relaxing; wooden planks that had buckled and yawned apart under the pressure were assuming their old contours—lying down again, end to end. For the first time in nearly a year, the leaks slowed to a trickle.

The sun's perpetual glare revealed to crew members the full measure of their winter squalor, what Melville called "the hideous results of forty dogs and thirty-three men living in one spot for six months." Spring cleaning commenced in earnest; De Long had the crew scrub every surface, beat every blanket, shake out every animal skin. The holds, reeking like the Augean stables, were swept clean of bones, rat droppings, dander, offal, and dog feces. The men siphoned out the pools of stagnant water that, as De Long said, had for so long "greeted our noses." Every removable object was brought out on the ice, scoured, and dried in the bright light. The sun-starved crew relished this strenuous, mostly outdoor work, for during the long winter everyone had become "bleached to an unnatural pallor," said Melville, "like vegetables grown in the dark."

After the discovery of Jeannette Island and the successful landfall on Henrietta, a guarded optimism surged through the ranks. Everyone felt that the expedition, despite its grueling hardships, had made significant accomplishments—including exploring many hundreds of miles of the planet never before seen by man. Danenhower believed that they had added considerable knowledge to the geography, understanding of currents, and meteorology of the Arctic, while dispelling many wrongheaded ideas. If nothing else, De Long said, they had "exploded so many theories of other people." The Open Polar Sea had been put to bed, at last, as had the thermometric gateway. The Kuro Siwo had been shown to play no role in altering the climate or softening the ice north of the Bering Strait. Wrangel Land, they'd learned, was just an island in no way connected to Greenland. De Long's expedition, through its constant soundings of the ocean floor beneath the ice, had come close to proving an important geographical truth: The polar basin was covered by an ocean, just as Petermann had said, but an ocean sheathed year-round in ice.

They'd shown something else, too. Whether by current or wind, the gyre of the ice cap, though erratic, had a prevailing direction, and they'd been generally heading the right way all the time—toward the pole. So the whalers' idea was not entirely wrong: This was, in a way, "going downhill," nature's route to the top.

The *Jeannette* had made contributions to nutritional science and medicine, as well: Amazingly, no one had died, and no one had been touched by the horror of scurvy. "If we [can] get out safely without loss of life," Danenhower wrote, the voyage would be judged "a grand success."

By the end of the first week of June, the mood on board was suspended between this new optimism and growing angst. The men threw themselves into their usual work but couldn't ignore the tingling awareness that something momentous—possibly wondrous, possibly catastrophic—was about to happen. De Long declared, "The crucial moment in our voyage is at hand."

AROUND MIDNIGHT ON June 11, something momentous did happen. While most of the men slept away the bright polar night, the ice opened with a ragged crack, and the *Jeannette* slipped into the water. It sounded to Danenhower as though "she were sliding down hill or off the launching ways." Once the *Jeannette* settled, she righted herself and bobbed gently in the frigid water.

After almost two years, the ship was . . . floating. It was a strange sensation. All of the men rose from their bunks, threw on clothing, and streamed onto the deck to take in the moment.

Not only was the *Jeannette* floating, she was holding firm. Melville and De Long studied the ship inside and out. In the hold, the leaks were negligible. The ice-locked lagoon in which she floated was dead calm and crystal clear, affording a view of the hull they had not enjoyed since she'd been in the shipyard in California. After they'd scoured every visible inch, the captain's spirits soared: She seemed structurally sound. There was, De Long said, "no injury whatever to the after body," and he now saw "no difficulty in keeping the ship afloat and navigating her." All those months at Mare Island spent reinforcing the hull had apparently paid off; the *Jeannette* had withstood nearly two years vise-gripped by the ice.

The men cheered their good fortune. The ship, as Danenhower put it, had finally been "released from her icy fetters" and "floated calmly on the surface of the beautiful blue water . . . a small pool in which she could bathe her sides." There were nasty-looking floes swirling nearby, but for now the *Jeannette* seemed safe.

The ship looked so idyllic basking in her little pond that around three o'clock the next day, June 12, De Long asked Melville to break out his camera and make a portrait of the fair ship. Happy to oblige, Melville shambled onto the ice with a tripod and other photographic equipment. While he fussed with the camera, Bartlett and Aneguin came in from a hunt, dragging a fresh seal, which left a smear of blood on the pack.

The ice was quiet, Melville said, and the ship looked "strikingly picturesque" as she dipped and bobbed in the bright sun. Melville ducked his head under the drape and took the last photograph that would ever be made of the USS *Jeannette*.

A HALF HOUR later, while Melville was down in the darkroom developing the photograph, the floes began to close up again. The men heard a terrific grinding, and the ice worked on the ship as never before. The pressure resumed "with tremendous force," De Long said, "the ship cracking in every part." He knew the *Jeannette* was "in for a time" and hastily bundled up and rushed onto the deck. The sounds were horrendous, as though the *Jeannette* were being tortured and maimed. Newcomb distinctly felt her "groaning and shaking" and heard a "humming sound throughout the vessel, with the cracking of the deck seams and the dancing of the whole upper works." De Long ran about the ship, chasing down every new alarming turn. "The spar deck commenced to buckle up," he said, "and the starboard side seemed again on the point of coming in." Two separate shelves of ice were pinching the ship with incalculable force. The hull, instead of rising above the pressure, as it had often done, was being driven down.

De Long got on the ice with Dunbar and surveyed the situation. "Well," the captain asked. "What do you think of it?"

Dunbar's tone was grave: "She'll either be under the floe, or on top of it by tomorrow."

Melville was down in the darkroom while all of this was taking place, and he was reluctant to leave his work until his portrait was developed. He labored in the dark, listening to the rending and creaking sounds, while his image of the *Jeannette* bathed in a tray of chemicals.

Minute by minute, the pressure intensified. Then a great fist of ice burst through the starboard coal bunker, and soon the hold was flooding. "She had been stabbed in her vitals, and was settling fast," Newcomb wrote. "The ship is not yet built that can stand such hugging." Some of the men, thinking this must be the end, raced to their bunks and grabbed their knapsacks, which had been packed for a catastrophe such as this.

Finally it came, the call they had been dreading but preparing for, off and on, for many months: *"Abandon ship!"* De Long cried. *"Abandon ship!"*

There was vigor in the captain's voice but not panic. It was as though he had resigned himself to this moment long ago, as though he had made a solemn place for it in his mind. He stood on the bridge, surveying the mayhem, puffing on his pipe.

Months ago, De Long had drawn up an emergency plan for what to do in this situation—detailing which equipment and provisions would be saved, and in what order. The men had studied the plan and rehearsed it many times. Each crew member had a precise job to do and a timeline to follow. Now, with De Long calmly choreographing the operation, everyone got to work.

Large planks were angled to the gunwales to serve as ramps. The *Jeannette*'s logs and other official papers were wrapped in canvas and handed down to the ice. Dr. Ambler escorted the lead-poisoned invalids. Alexey and Aneguin led the dogs off the ship. Danenhower, removing the bandage from his eye, grabbed the navigation instruments and charts. Starr went down into the magazine, which was flooding rapidly, and hauled out case after case of ammunition. Cole and Sweetman, operating the davits, swung the cutters and one of the whaleboats onto the ice. Dunbar studied the surrounding pack for the safest place to make camp. Everyone else hauled food, furs, tents, stove alcohol, medicines, ropes, guns, oars, harnesses, sleds, and the small wooden dinghy.

Hearing commotion throughout the ship, Melville gave up on his portrait of the *Jeannette* and left the glass plate swimming in its tray. Dashing from the darkroom, he spotted a hideous crack jigsawing across the engine room ceiling. Then he climbed up on deck and threw himself into the effort at hand.

By eight o'clock, the *Jeannette* was heeled over twenty-three degrees to starboard. None of the crew could stand without clinging to something nailed down. The ice continued to strangle the ship. The wardroom was full of water. Everywhere was the sound of ripping bolts, groaning lumber, yawning metal. "Each successive shock," Melville wrote, "was transmitted to the ship as to a centre, and resound[ed] with awful distinctness upon her sides like death strokes." The gang ladders, Newcomb said, "jumped from their chucks and danced on the deck like drumsticks on the head of a drum."

De Long was satisfied that they had saved the most important belongings. Edison's useless lights were left behind, as was the equipment Bell had provided. All the photographic plates that had been exposed during the expedition—including the portrait Melville had just taken—were stored deep inside the hull and would never be retrieved. Thinking it unsafe for the crew to climb over the foundering ship, De Long directed everyone to leave the *Jeannette* and remain on the ice. The water was rising so fast that the last stragglers working below could not exit by ladder but were forced to escape through a deck ventilator.

Captain De Long seemed to want a few moments alone with his dying ship. He staggered over her slanting decks, clutching ropes and bollards, anything to give him a steady hold. He had been the *Jeannette*'s first, last, and only captain, and he hated to leave her. The ship had been his life for the past three years. He'd found her, had sailed her around the Horn, had been the father of her rebirth in San Francisco. He'd taken her thousands of uncharted miles, farther than any vessel had ever penetrated into this region of the Arctic. The *Jeannette*, in every emotional sense, was his. And his to lose.

His disappointment bordered on self-reproach. "It will be hard," he wrote, "to be known hereafter as a man who undertook a Polar expedition and sunk his ship at the 77th parallel . . . I fancy it would have made but little difference if I had gone down with my ship."

De Long lingered a few more moments in silence. The grisly concussions of dismemberment had quieted, leaving only the sound of inrushing water. De Long waved his bearskin cap in sad salute and called out, "Goodbye, old ship." Then he jumped to the floe, issuing a stern command that no one else was to board her.

THEY SPENT THE night on the ice, thirty-three men and their dogs, watching their former home slowly slip away. They organized their belongings into long neat rows and set up tents. The weather was mild—twenty-three degrees Fahrenheit—and the mood was surprisingly jovial. Melville went so far as to call it "merry"—but merry in the way that little boys might whistle past a graveyard to keep up their courage. Alexey declared that he felt "plenty good." George

Lauterbach played his harmonica, and the men sang songs and told jokes, anything to distract them from what was happening a few hundred yards away.

By midnight, the *Jeannette* was heeled all the way over, like a mortally wounded animal lying on its side. Her lower yardarms rested on the ice. De Long, seeing no point in staring at the ship's final agonies, ordered the men to turn in for the night.

Once inside their tents, they laid rubber mackintosh blankets against the ice and crawled into their bags. An hour later, the camp was roused by a loud cracking sound. A massive vent had opened up directly beneath the captain's tent, beneath the exact spot where De Long was sleeping. Had there not been numerous men lying on either side of him—holding the rubber blanket in place with their weight—De Long, and probably Erichsen as well, would have fallen through to freezing water.

Planks were placed over the crack to make sure no one fell in. Dunbar reassessed the condition of the ice around the camp and declared it treacherous. So, at De Long's command, they marched a hundred yards away, to a safer spot—relocating their food, boats, sleds, and dogs—and set up camp all over again. It was well past three o'clock when they finally piped down.

By this point, the *Jeannette* was almost gone. The tip of the smoke pipe was nearly awash. Still lying on her side, she gently swayed with the shifting of the ice. Every now and then a sigh or a groan issued from the innards of the ship, but the fight was over.

At four o'clock, at the change of the watch, something remarkable happened. With a loud rattling of timbers and ironwork, the *Jeannette* suddenly sprang up again, like a marionette, floating upright for a few long moments. It was as though she had come back to life. But then she began to sag straight down into the water, gathering velocity as she dropped. Kuehne, the watchman, called out, "If you want to see the last of the *Jeannette*—there she goes!"

As the ship sank, the yardarms snapped upward, parallel to the masts, resembling, as Melville put it, "a great, gaunt skeleton clapping its hands above its head."

Then, in a final whirl of water, the *Jeannette* plunged out of sight. Nothing remained, said Danenhower, "of our old and good friend, the *Jeannette,* which for many months had endured the embrace of the Arctic monster." She had sunk at latitude 77°15' N, longitude 155° E, a little more than seven hundred miles south of the North Pole.

The feeling was indescribable. The men were completely alone, Melville said, "in a sense that few can appreciate. Our proper means of escape, to which so many pleasant associations attached, [was] destroyed before our eyes. We were now utterly isolated, beyond any rational hope of aid."

They were almost a thousand miles from the nearest landmass—the Arctic coast of central Siberia. Even if they could reach it, dragging all their stuff and their boats behind them, their destination was one of the most remote and unforgiving landscapes on the planet. Little was known of central Siberia's sparse settlements, and its coastline and rivers were insufficiently mapped. Siberia was notorious chiefly as the place where the czar banished criminals and political exiles—forever. De Long and his men understood the fragility of their predicament: Their only hope was a place with a reputation for hopelessness.

Yet in back of the desolation and despair, the men also felt a kind of relief. They had been locked in the pack for twenty-one months, but now their period of inaction, of waiting and wondering in hapless drift, of suffering the tedium of a monotone imprisonment, was finally over. They knew what lay before them. They had only a few months to save themselves. They realized they were facing an epic struggle for survival—and yet they were anxious to get going. "We were satisfied," Melville wrote, "since we knew the ship's usefulness had passed away, and we could now start at once, the sooner the better, on our long march to the south."

The night was still and the pack eerily quiet, as though the ice were contentedly digesting the morsel it had eaten. The men stared at the hole where the *Jeannette* had been. Nothing was left of her but a wooden chest floating upside down in the water. Their ship's requiem, said Newcomb, was "the melancholy howl of a single dog."

PART FIVE

The End of Creation

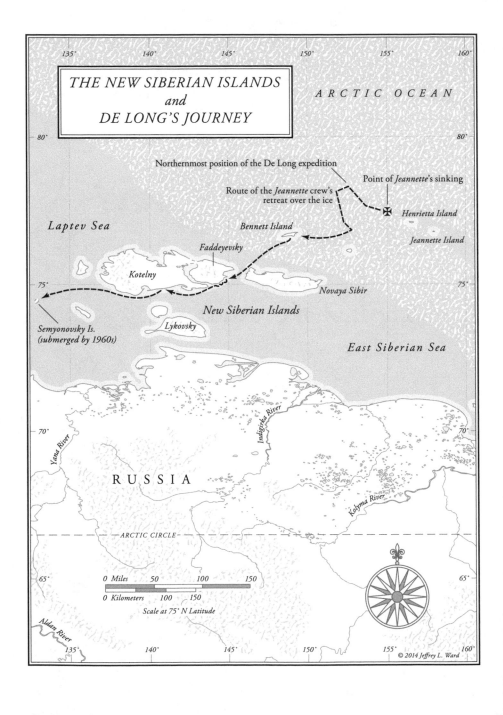

THE NEW SIBERIAN ISLANDS
and
DE LONG'S JOURNEY

ARCTIC OCEAN

135° 140° 145° 150° 155° 160°

80°

Northernmost position of the De Long expedition

Point of *Jeannette*'s sinking

Route of the *Jeannette* crew's
retreat over the ice

Henrietta Island

Laptev Sea

Bennett Island

Jeannette Island

Faddeyevsky

Kotelny

75°

New Siberian Islands

Novaya Sibir

75°

Semyonovsky Is.
(submerged by 1960s)

Lykovsky

East Siberian Sea

RUSSIA

Yana River

Indigirka River

Kolyma River

70°

ARCTIC CIRCLE

0 Miles   50   100   150

0 Kilometers   100   150

Scale at 75° N Latitude

65°

Aldan River

135° 140° 145° 150° 155° 160°

© 2014 Jeffrey L. Ward

Throughout the month of June, the rescue ship *Corwin* had zigzagged through the Bering Sea, calling at forts and villages on both sides of the strait. Creeping through fog and ice, Captain Calvin Hooper had pursued his usual rounds of errands as he waited for the sledge expedition to return from the Siberian coast with further news of an American shipwreck somewhere to the north. The *Corwin* encountered a number of American whaling ships—most of them New Bedford and Nantucket concerns—whose captains indicated they were having a banner year; after an unusually mild winter, the ice was receding farther and faster than expected, and already many of the ships had filled their holds with oil and bone. Sometimes, from a distance, Hooper could see the long black plumes of fat-fed smoke from the whalers' tryworks, as they boiled out the blubber and rendered it into barrel upon barrel of oil.

The mild winter and fast-shrinking ice gave Captain Hooper cause for optimism concerning De Long's fate. If he was trapped somewhere to the north, this was surely the year he would break free. "If the *Jeannette* is still in existence," Hooper wrote, "there can be no reason why she should not come to open water this year, as it will undoubtedly open farther than it has for years."

One of Hooper's responsibilities was to patrol the capes and islands of Alaska in search of rum merchants, whose illicit trade in alcohol was proving disastrous to the natives. It was in the service of that responsibility that in late June, Captain Hooper stopped at

St. Lawrence Island, an ice-gouged crescent of volcanic rock set in the middle of the frigid sea, directly west of the mouth of the Yukon River. Part of America's Alaskan territory, St. Lawrence Island was nearly a hundred miles long and some twenty miles wide. Three years earlier, the island had had a population of more than fifteen hundred Yupiks, living in a dozen well-established villages scattered along the coast. Theirs was an ancient, thriving culture built principally on the walrus hunt. But then, in a single winter, the populace had been nearly extinguished by some sort of disease or famine.

Around six o'clock on the evening of June 24, 1881, Hooper anchored the *Corwin* along the south coast of the island, beside a small Eskimo village. The captain, along with Muir, Smithsonian naturalist Edward Nelson, and the ship's physician, Irving Rosse, rowed toward shore in a small boat, scanning the terrain with their field glasses. The island, said Muir, was a "cheerless-looking mass of black lava, dotted with volcanoes, covered with snow, without a single tree." Landing the lifeboat, they strode across a gravel beach and then a spongy surface of snow-dusted lichen and moss. Here and there, blooming heaths and other bright wildflowers peeked through the snow. But when the men approached the village, there was no one to be seen. "We began to fear," said Muir, "that not a soul was left alive."

They were startled by a noise. Several Eskimos cried out from a cluster of summer huts on a high hill overlooking the village and came down to greet the Americans—they were, thought Muir, "quite glad to see us." Hooper asked them where all the villagers had gone. They smiled a strange broad smile and replied, "All *mucky*—all gone."

"Dead?"

"Yes, dead!"

Hooper asked where the deceased villagers had been laid to rest. The natives led the Americans behind one of the houses, to a place where eight still-decaying bodies were set out on the rocky slope. Their hosts, wrote Muir, "smiled at the ghastly spectacle of the grinning skulls and bleached bones appearing through the brown, shrunken skin."

As they stumbled about this village, Hooper and the others began to comprehend the extent of the famine. Muir counted some two hundred bodies, most "with rotting furs on them," though other corpses had been "picked bare by the crows." Many lay "mixed with kitchen-midden rubbish where they had been cast out by surviving relatives while they yet had strength to carry them."

James Gordon Bennett Jr.

The *Lysistrata,* one of Bennett's many yachts

A Shocking Sabbath Carnival of
Death.

SAVAGE BRUTES AT LARGE.

Awful Combats Between the
Beasts and Citizens.

THE KILLED AND WOUNDED.

Gen. Duryee's Magnificent
Police Tactics.

BRAVERY AND PANIC

How the Catastrophe was Brought
About—Affrighting Incidents.

PROCLAMATION BY THE MAYOR.

Gov. Dix Shoots the Bengal
Tiger in the Street.

CONSTERNATION IN THE CITY.

Another Sunday of horror has been added to those
already memorable in our city annals. The sad
and appalling catastrophe of yesterday is a further
illustration of the unforeseen perils to which large
communities are exposed. Writing even at a late
hour, without full details of the terrors of the
evening and night, and with a necessarily incom-
plete list of the killed and mutilated, we may pause
for a moment in the widespread sorrow of the hour
to cast a hasty glance over what will be felt as a
great calamity for many years. Few of the millions

The wild animal hoax in the *New
York Herald,* November 9, 1874

Dr. August Petermann

Magazine artist's depiction of John Cleves Symmes's popular hollow-earth theory

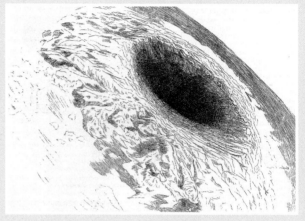

(BELOW) The "thermometric gateways" to the pole, as envisioned by Silas Bent in 1872

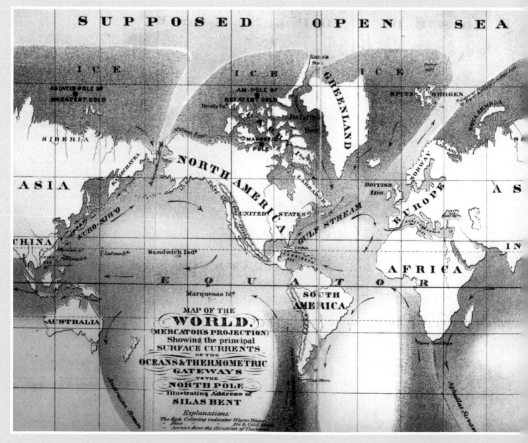

(LEFT) George and Emma
De Long and (ABOVE) their
daughter, Sylvie

Charles Chipp, executive officer

Dr. James Ambler, ship's surgeon

Lt. George De Long, expedition commander

George Melville, engineer

John Danenhower, navigator

Jerome Collins, meteorologist,
New York Herald correspondent

Raymond Newcomb, naturalist

The *Jeannette,* then known as the *Pandora,* photographed in
Greenland in the mid 1870s

William Nindemann,
quartermaster

William Dunbar, ice pilot

The *Jeannette* in Le Havre, France, in 1878, just prior to her voyage to San Francisco

The *Jeannette*'s sinking, by the popular French artist
George Louis Poilleux-Saint-Ange

De Long and his men struggle
over the ice (ABOVE), then
reach open water (RIGHT)

(BELOW)
Siberia's Lena River delta as
captured by satellite in 2000

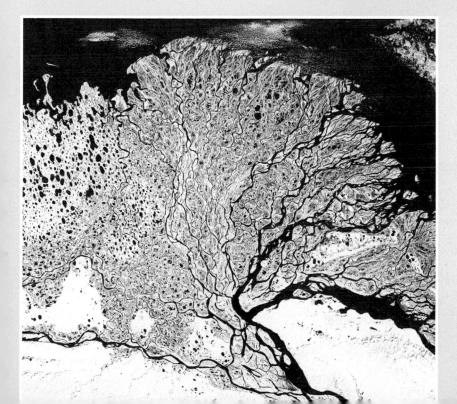

Some of the *Jeannette* crew posed for this photograph in Yakutsk, Siberia, in December 1881

Rear Admiral George Melville, photographed in 1910

The *Jeannette* monument on the grounds of the United States Naval Academy, Annapolis, Maryland

So many corpses lay on the ground or were piled inside the houses that, said Hooper, "it was almost impossible to get around without stepping over them." Muir counted thirty inside one house alone— "about half of them piled like fire-wood in a corner, the other half in bed, seeming as if they had met their fate with tranquil apathy."

It was to avoid this macabre sight that the few survivors—about a dozen—had retreated to live in the summer huts high on the hill.

WHAT, PRECISELY, HAD happened on St. Lawrence Island? Many whalers suspected an epidemic of some kind, but others believed the mass death was caused by the complete failure of the Yupiks' hunt in the summer and fall of 1878—which, in turn, was caused by an abundance of rum and whiskey illegally sold to the St. Lawrence Islanders by American traffickers. With alcohol around, Yupik life had ground to a halt—"as long as the rum lasts," wrote Hooper, "they do nothing but drink and fight." Drunkenness, said Muir, had "rendered them careless about the laying up of ordinary supplies of food for the winter." Indeed, near one of the huts, Hooper counted eight empty whiskey casks.

Then an extremely severe winter followed, with far more ice than usual, which made it harder to find seals and whales. By early 1879, the Yupiks all over St. Lawrence Island had begun to starve. They ate their own sealskin clothing, and the walrus-skin coverings of their huts, and the walrus-skin membranes of their boats. This temporarily satisfied their cravings but made them violently ill. With nothing else left to eat, they butchered their dogs until they ran completely out of food. In twos and threes, the villagers of St. Lawrence Island began to die.

The numbers across the island were staggering: More than one thousand people—two-thirds of the population—had perished in 1879, the same year the *Jeannette* had set sail and cruised right past this island on her way to the pole. The conventional explanation addressed only part of the mass starvation. Alcohol and the severe winter *were* certainly factors—alcohol, especially. But something far larger had been taking place that made this colossal famine a certainty: Over the previous decade, American whalers in the Arctic, seeking to augment the value of their cargo, had turned to harvesting walruses in astoundingly high numbers. Throughout the 1870s, American whaling vessels had taken as many as 125,000 walruses from the Bering Strait region. The slaughter had proved to be a lucrative sideline to the whaling business. The whalers cooked the animal's blubber into oil and hacked off the tusks to sell in ivory markets as far away as England and China. In a single season in 1876, more than 35,000 Bering walruses were killed.

Compared to the risky rigors of Arctic whaling, "walrusing" could be ridiculously easy. Rather than wielding lances and harpoons from tippy open boats, the whalers had discovered that they could simply clomp onto the ice with rifles and shoot large numbers of walruses point-blank in the head. Then the butchering, flensing, and boiling could begin. Firing up their try-pots aboard ship, the whalers could render more than twenty gallons of oil from the blubber of a single mature bull. In less than a decade, this industrially efficient slaughter had largely destroyed the Yupiks' primary source of food and the seasonal hunting life upon which it was based. By the 1880s, the walrus was nearly extinct in large swaths of the Bering Sea.

It was the Arctic version of a story already well known to Americans, the story of the buffalo and the Indians of the Great Plains. Here, as there, the wholesale slaughter of a people's staple prey had led, in a few short years, to ruinous dislocations, terrible dependencies—and a cultural apocalypse.

JOHN MUIR WAS haunted by what he experienced on St. Lawrence Island. "The scene was indescribably ghastly," he wrote, noting its stark juxtapositions. "Gulls, plovers, and ducks were swimming and flying about in happy life, the pure salt sea was dashing white against the shore, the blooming tundra swept back to the snow-clad volcanoes," yet the village lay "in the foulest and most glaring death."

As far as Muir could tell, the American presence in the Arctic had thus far been anything but beneficial. What had happened on St. Lawrence Island was but an extreme distillation of larger forces at work across America's northernmost frontier. Muir now could see that this icy wilderness was as vulnerable as it was vast—marked by fragile rhythms of migration, interdependencies of population, and patterns of habit many thousands of years in the making. And yet it seemed to be unraveling before his eyes.

Alaska had been an American possession for slightly more than a decade. The czar's influence, weak in the first place, had faded. While it could not be said that contact with Russian trappers and traders had improved the lives of Alaskan natives—far from it—the Russian fur concerns had rarely reached the level of entrepreneurial organization and ruthless efficiency pursued by American whalers, trading agents, and fur companies. The systematic introduction of just a few things—repeating rifles, booze, money, industrial methods of dismantling animal flesh—had caused the native cultures of Alaska to collapse at record speed.

"Even where alcohol is left out of the count," Muir wrote, "the few articles of food, clothing, guns, etc., furnished by the traders, exert a degrading influence, making them less self-reliant, and less skillful as hunters." Muir worried that "unless some aid be extended by our government which claims these people, in a few years . . . every soul of them will have vanished from the face of the earth."

ON JUNE 29, the *Corwin* anchored alongside a rim of ice a few miles from the tiny village of Tapkan. A strong wind was blowing from the north, and the ship bobbed in heavy swells. Scanning the shoreline with his field glasses, Captain Hooper was excited and relieved to see an American flag snapping in the breeze, over a white tent: Lieutenant Herring and his overland expedition had returned. Everyone on board roused into action. The anticipation was electric. "Speculation ran high throughout the ship," Hooper said, "as to what success they had met with. Had they found the *Jeannette*?"

Hooper began to make arrangements for sending a party onshore, until he noticed that Herring's men had quickly broken camp and were now struggling over the ice toward the *Corwin*. It took the better part of the day, but finally Herring reached the ship and came aboard. By then, the seas had grown so heavy that Captain Hooper realized he could no longer remain anchored where he was. Arrangements were hastily made for paying the Tapkan dog drivers—a rifle, ammunition, a bolt of calico fabric, and a few other articles; then Hooper turned the *Corwin* toward the open sea.

When the swells finally settled down, Hooper gathered Herring and the other American expeditioners in his cabin and learned the story of what had taken place over the past month.

HERRING AND HIS party of three Americans and three native dog drivers had left their landing site at Kolyuchin Island on June 2 and headed over the ice. They had an extremely hard time at first—their sled broke, the dogs quarreled, the way was hopelessly slushy—but they were fortunate enough to encounter some native seal hunters, who guided them to their settlement, some twenty-five miles to the west.

The village of Kolyuchin consisted of twenty-six dwellings and about three hundred people. The town elder received the Americans warmly and invited them into his hut, where they drank cup after cup of Russian tea. Herring inquired about the story of an American shipwreck somewhere to the west, but the elder had never heard of it. He told Herring that most of the villagers here had never seen a white man before, which explained their curiosity about the American visitors. The natives offered the travelers a feast of reindeer and fresh cod, and they stayed up until four in the morning drinking coffee and sharing tales.

After a day of rest, Herring and his party got under way again, slogging west along the Arctic coast for a week, building nightly bonfires of driftwood to dry out their drenched furs. Although they passed several villages, most of the time they trudged through expanses of absolute desolation. Along the way, they searched in vain for cairns or any other signs of the *Jeannette*. They reached a tiny settlement of five huts called Onman, where several villagers told Herring they'd heard the story of the broken vessel, adding that if he proceeded some twenty miles to the west, he would come to the village of Wankerem, where the story was better known.

So Lieutenant Herring hastened for Wankerem and was kindly invited into one of the village huts. He distributed presents of tobacco and coffee and explained the purpose of his visit. The villagers smiled and nodded and then promptly summoned three men, who were able to tell the story of the shipwreck firsthand. Pieced together by Chukchi Joe, the translator, this is the tale they told:

> Last fall, when the new ice was making, we were out sealing near the island we call Concarpio, when we saw a wrecked vessel drifting down toward the island. We went to the wreck, which was half full of water. The three masts had been cut off near the decks, to make firewood.
>
> In the cabin we found four bodies—three of them were lying in their beds, and one floating in the water. They had been dead for some time. Their skin was dried up, black, and drawn tightly

over the bones. The wind was shifting, and we were afraid to stay long. We gathered a few things and left the ship. The next night the wind changed to the southward, and the wreck drifted off shore. We never saw it again.

Lieutenant Herring inquired about the articles they had taken from the ship. Did you find any books or papers? he asked.

No, they said, *such things are of no use to us.*

Herring explained that his primary interest was in identifying the ship. Was there anything unusual about it, anything that might seem different from other ships?

The seal hunters thought about it for a while and then said: *We saw that someone had placed a pair of deer antlers, high up on the ship.* Herring was intrigued by this strange detail—it did not sound like the kind of decoration that a commander like De Long would allow on a U.S. Navy ship. By sketching out a diagram with the three hunters, Herring was able to determine that the antlers had been attached to the ship's jibboom.

Herring wanted to know more about the other things the men had taken from the ship. The three hunters disappeared and quickly returned with a small trove of loot. Among the items were two wood saws, an ax, a harpoon, a bottle of laudanum, a razor, a pair of spectacles, a candlestick, and a metal stove pan that had been stamped by its manufacturer in Philadelphia. None of the articles bore any private names, but there was a table knife with the letter *V* engraved on its handle.

Herring thanked the hunters and paid them a nice price for those items he thought most likely to help identify the ship. He asked the villagers if they had ever heard of a place called Wrangel, a mysterious land somewhere out over the ice to the north. As he later told John Muir, "They all shook their heads and said that they knew nothing of land in that direction. But one old man told them that long ago he heard something about a party of men who had come from some far unknown land to the north, over the ice."

After gaining assurances that no news had been heard of any other American vessels for hundreds of miles, Herring decided to turn back toward Tapkan before the summer's advance made the shore ice more treacherous. He and his party harnessed their dogs and headed east, reaching Tapkan in mid-June.

Waiting for the *Corwin* to return, the Americans were invited to a festival celebrating the village's first successful walrus hunt. The severed head of a walrus was brought into the chief's hut and ceremonially positioned on the ground in the center. A crowd of villagers gathered around the bewhiskered trophy, and then the chief delivered an elaborate oration and ordered his youngest son to place offerings of blessed reindeer and seal meat inside the mouth of the walrus. Then, as the ceremony continued outside, pieces of meat were tossed in the cardinal directions. Much drumming, chanting, and dancing followed; the Americans, exhausted by their long excursion, were happily intrigued by it all.

While in Tapkan, Lieutenant Herring met a group of walrus hunters who claimed they not only had seen but had briefly boarded the *Jeannette* on her way north. It was in the late summer of 1879; De Long had made a stop off Cape Serdtse-Kamen when he was looking for news about Nordenskiöld. The walrus hunters told Herring that the ship was "a steamer with three masts" and that there were two Alaskan Inuit men on board, whom they recognized by the labrets—decorative studs—in their lips. They also told Herring that there were a "large number of dogs and sleds seen on her decks."

These details were all correct and impressed Lieutenant Herring. He thought their description "goes to show that the natives . . . take notice of everything that passes near the coast. Had a vessel or party of white men visited since that time the natives would have known it, and accounts would have reached us."

CAPTAIN HOOPER LISTENED to Lieutenant Herring's story carefully. Two details leapt out at him. The first was the letter *V* engraved on the table knife, which he personally inspected. The second was the hunters' observation that a set of deer antlers was attached to the ship's jibboom. The American whaling ship *Vigilant* had had a pair of antlers attached to its jibboom. It was a kind of trademark, well known among the captains of the whaling fleet.

In Hooper's mind, that settled it. The shipwreck in question was certainly not the *Jeannette*. It was the *Vigilant,* a 215-ton wooden whaling bark out of New Bedford, Massachusetts, captained by Charles Smithers. Other Arctic whalers had last spotted the *Vigilant* in October 1879 to the southwest of Herald Island, where she'd become locked in the ice. The *Vigilant* was supposed to be carrying $16,000 worth of oil and baleen. Smithers had sailed her from Hawaii with a crew of thirty; Hooper's guess was that all hands were lost.

But there was still hope for the *Jeannette*. Captain Hooper remained convinced that De Long's expedition had survived and that the men were stranded on, or near, the mysterious Wrangel Land.

Captain Hooper felt that the fast-thinning pack and unusually mild weather offered him the best opportunity he would ever have of reaching Wrangel. In the first week of July, the *Corwin* steamed away from the coast of Siberia, headed east toward St. Michael, Alaska.

June 12, 1881

My own dearest husband—

I have such a strong feeling that I will see or hear from you this summer I can hardly wait.

May God bless and preserve you wherever you are and bring you back safely and all those with you. Remember me to my friends of the Jeannette—*I dare not say on the* Jeannette *for she may be at the bottom of the ocean and you may be struggling for your lives in boats or on the ice.*

Never mind, darling, I will bear up under any circumstances, and will meet you with open arms however and whenever you return . . .

Emma

In high spirits, De Long and his men began their long march across the frozen ocean, inching toward the familiar world, or at least a place where other human beings might conceivably be found. Stretched out for miles across the ice, they resembled, said Melville, a straggle of "vagabond insects." It was numbing, staggering work, and yet they were strangely happy—happy to be free of the confines of the ship, relieved to be moving again, eager to accept the bonds of their common struggle. They aimed for the middle of Russia and the Siberian Arctic coast, but in their minds they were heading home, to wives and mothers and girlfriends, to plump chickens and fresh garden vegetables, to soft beds and warm fires, to gossip and invention, and if not to glory, exactly, then to the cheers of an appreciative homeland.

De Long and Dunbar, equipped with field glasses and pocket prismatic compasses, clambered ahead of everyone else in the foggy distances to mark the way with black flags stuck in the ice. They called their path a "road," but the route they staked was little more than a suggestion of lesser treachery, a devious course across ever-shifting mazes of fissures, hummocks, pressure ridges, and pools of shimmering meltwater. Which is to say, the captain and his ice pilot—whose earlier problem with snow blindness had cleared up—were merely going on their best hunches.

Keep to the road! they cried. *Stay on the road!* The men could only laugh at the absurdity of the word. As Danenhower put it, there was only "knee-deep snow" and "lumps of ice that would have taken a whole corps of engineers to level." Yet they trudged on, sunburned and chapped-lipped, dressed in sour-smelling pelts, wearing slitted ice goggles, singing galley songs as they slogged over the impossible expanses of crust and rubble and sludge.

The June sun, whenever it burned through the fog, had a strange quality of penetrating intensity, as though it were training X-rays on the snow. The light revealed a dirty ice pack at times strewn with signs of life—crab claws, bear scat, mussel shells, bleached bones, goose quills, plant seeds, driftwood, ocean sponges. The gyre of the ocean and the churn of the ice had mixed everything up, old and new, animal and vegetable, into a kind of Arctic gumbo.

Dr. Ambler cared for the sick; Alexey and Aneguin tended to the dogs. But the others spent their days as draft animals, straining against their hemp ropes and canvas harnesses. They pulled more than eight tons of provisions and gear, on improvised sleds whose crosspieces had been fashioned from whiskey barrel staves and whose heavy oak runners were shod with smooth whalebone. In addition to the three battered boats, they hauled, among other things, medicine chests, ammunition, stew pots, cooking stoves, tent poles, oars, rifles, ship logs and diaries, canvas for sails, scientific instruments, the wooden dinghy, and two hundred gallons of stove alcohol.

As for food, they had inventoried, at the outset, 3,960 pounds of pemmican, 1,500 pounds of hardtack, thirty-two pounds of beef tongue, 150 pounds of Liebig's beef extract, twelve and a half pounds of pigs' feet, and substantial quantities of veal, ham, whiskey, brandy, chocolate, and tobacco. Every pound, every ounce, had been carefully weighed at the start, then just as carefully apportioned to the different sleds and crews so that everyone, aside from the sick, would pull an equal amount of weight.

There was far too much to haul in one trip, so they had to double back—and sometimes *triple* back—to bring up everything from the rear. This meant that for many of the haulers, each mile of forward progress actually represented a distance of five miles traversed. A full day of this Sisyphean business could mean twenty-five miles or more of ceaseless struggle. It would have constituted slave labor even on hard, dry ground, but this slob ice, with all its gaping holes and intervening sea-lanes, was the most trying terrain imaginable—as a landscape, said De Long, it was "terribly confused."

The men often had to launch the boats, cross a narrow lead of water, and then hop right back out again to re-stow the boats on the sleds. Other times, they would use a large cake of floating ice as a ferry, employing grappling hooks and networks of ropes to tow it, and all their belongings, across the water to the icy shore beyond. The "road-building crew" would wield pickaxes to clear a smooth groove through encrusted ice, shave off the top of a high hummock, or fashion what De Long called a "causeway" or a "flying bridge" across emerald pools of meltwater.

At the end of each day, said Melville, the men were "utterly fagged out." Some fainted from exhaustion. Others shivered from hypothermia, having plunged into the frigid water. De Long, who often chose to assume the harness with his men, said that "a more tired and hungry set of mortals could not be found . . . Every bone ache[s]." Danenhower, echoing the captain, noted that each day, every man "voted this the hardest day's work he had ever done in his life."

Yet it was extraordinary how content most of them were during the first weeks of the march, living like mules, suffering so. Nearly everyone commented on it. They slept soundly, developed ferocious appetites, and functioned each day with a clarity of purpose they had never known in their lives.

"Just now we are living royally . . . and are in glorious health," a surprised De Long wrote at the outset. "Everybody is bright and cheerful, and our camp has a lively look . . . singing is going on all around." Melville observed that the men were always "whooping" and often fell into "roars of laughter and good-natured banter . . . No ship's company ever endured such severe toil with such little complaint." As they tramped through the ice, they sang old Irish ballads and wayfaring songs, tunes like "The Rocky Road to Dublin":

I was a-hobblin' with a loud array,
   They joined me in the fray.
We quickly cleared the way
   On the rocky road to Dublin.

As harsh as it was, the icescape could also be beautiful. Seawater steadily lapped at the undersides of the floes, creating a soughing sound that was comforting in its constancy, like the flutter of a million insect wings. In places, the men encountered strange elegant monuments, made of old compressed ice, that shone an otherworldly aquamarine blue. On certain patches of the pack, a species of algae left a patina of brilliant reddish orange—watermelon snow, it was called.

De Long noted how the sun flickered through the fog; it "glimmers and blinks like a drunkard's eye." The heavy, moist air, he observed, was alive with "groans and shrieks from all directions" as large "snouts of snow" rose, inch by inch, from colliding ice pieces. Every now and then a massive floe, wallowing, glurping, would suddenly upend, trapping small fish in its pockets and divots. The fish would splutter and zag, frantically searching for a way out of their new prisons.

DE LONG AND his men had left the site of the *Jeannette*'s sinking on the evening of June 18. Before taking off, De Long jotted a note: "We break camp and start to the southward over the ice, hoping with God's blessing to reach the New Siberian Islands, and from there make our way by boats to the coast of Siberia." The captain rolled the note in a piece of black rubber and stashed it in a small water cask. He left it on the ice, hoping that it "may get somewhere."

As with nearly everything else connected with the voyage, De Long had foreseen the likelihood of this retreat—and had long ago mapped out a meticulous plan for how to proceed. He'd thought of everything, it seemed. First, he had decided to reverse their diurnal pattern: They would sleep during the days and march in the cool crispness of the evenings, when, by late June, temperatures usually hovered around twenty degrees Fahrenheit. The snow was firmer at night, and there was plenty of light by which to see—it never grew entirely dark. By avoiding the harshest glare of midday, they would minimize snow blindness and overheating. They would eat their "dinner" at eight in the morning and crawl into their tents to sleep away the day while their drenched furs were hung out to dry in temperatures that could reach well past forty degrees.

De Long had spent many hours refining a system for organizing the ranks. He divided the thirty-three members of the expedition into three parties, each with approximately eleven men. Each party was assigned to a boat, a sledge, and a camp area and was presided over by an officer. Each sled and boat had a name, a flag, and a legend affixed

to it. One legend was *In hoc signo vinces*—"By this sign you will con-
quer"; another was *Nil desperandum*—"Never despair."

This system of smaller crews would be the defining idea for the
long march home. Each team hauled together, rested together, cooked
together, ate together, slept together, and, if necessary, would die
together. De Long was quite deliberate about the arrangement. He
hoped to inject an element of esprit de corps, of group loyalty, into
this great effort: A man wouldn't want to let his fellows down, and
he'd want his own gang to outperform the other gangs. Clever in its
simplicity, it was a system that tapped into pride of person but also
pride in the group.

Subdividing the expedition into smaller teams, he felt, might also
help keep small gripes from growing pernicious. De Long, a close
student of Arctic exploration, was vigilant to the ever-lurking possibility of mutiny. He could never forget Captain Hall's fate on the
voyage of the *Polaris*. De Long understood what happened when men
under extreme duress were given the latitude to express their dissatisfactions unchecked—how quickly a wrong, real or imagined, could
magnify in men's minds, how a single misconstrued incident or comment could make its way through the ranks.

The march had started out with high morale, but De Long
knew it could quickly disintegrate, and he had to keep a firm handle
on things. He especially worried about Collins, who continued to
sulk and stew, and whose hostility to De Long remained palpable.
Danenhower, also, seemed a potential flashpoint—he did not think
his syphilitic blindness nearly so debilitating as De Long did, even
though he stumbled like a wino through the snow, and his pride had
been chafed by his being put on the sick list. Apprehending several
avenues of threat, De Long reasoned that stretching the men out in
three discrete groups over many miles of ice might diminish the possibility that the germ of insurrection would spread during the ordeal.

That it would be a long ordeal, that profound grudges and dissatisfactions would arise, De Long had no doubt. He knew that clawing
across the Arctic ice fields to open water would require "superhuman exertions." In the annals of exploration, he could not recall a
journey quite like the one on which they were now embarked. By
his estimation, they were nearly a thousand miles from the Siberian
coast, although the New Siberians, a poorly mapped and little-known
archipelago of uninhabited permafrost islands, might be encountered

along their path. There was, of course, no possibility of rescue or relief. As far as he knew, no one on earth had the remotest idea where they were, or whether they were alive.

Their survival was in their own hands. As Danenhower put it, they would literally be "working for our lives." De Long knew that "we must eventually come to open water by making due south." For months, they would be reduced to the role of beasts, slaving twelve hours a day in harness. Yet at least six men were too sick to haul—their lead-poisoning symptoms, slow to abate, left them with "no motive power." Some of the poisoned invalids were able to walk as long as they didn't haul or carry anything, while others were so feeble they had to be pulled in the hospital sled. In the worst shape of all was Chipp. He was so exhausted that he couldn't dress himself or even stand up. Plying him with brandy and opium, Dr. Ambler noted that Chipp was in a "great deal of pain & cramp & very restless . . . The circumstances are all against him . . . He is pale & his pulse is weak."

"How are we to get him through?" De Long fretted about his old friend Chipp. "Last night [he] was groaning and tumbling around all the time. I am very seriously disturbed about him."

De Long knew that they had an extremely narrow window in which to accomplish their retreat: They had only sixty days' worth of provisions. After that, they might gain a few more weeks by eating their dogs. But that was the end of it. Beyond the finite stores of food, there was the finite number of days left in the Arctic summer. Captain De Long understood that whatever happened, they would have to reach Siberia before winter set in. It was a fight against the calendar and the available calories—they had to move quickly but also efficiently. Yet they could do neither on these stretches of slurry and slop. "Our outlook," De Long wrote in fantastic understatement, "was not encouraging." He wondered when his men's essential good humor would wear off.

His mainstay was Melville. De Long knew he could not face this hegira across the ice without him. The chief engineer had proved solid as oak, his judgment always sound, his sense of fairness unerring, his improvisational wiles seemingly without limit. He seemed impervious to illness and incapable of complaint. De Long's pronouncement on Melville was all the more powerful for its succinctness: "As long as he remains as he is—strong and well—I shall get along all right."

———

WHILE ABOARD THE *Jeannette,* the men had never been in want of food. For two years, they'd always had plenty of it, and enough variety in their diet to keep them satisfied. Now, on the ice, their diet was essentially reduced to two staples. There was Liebig's beef extract, which they sipped as a warm broth, like consommé. And there was pemmican, a substantial mixture of dried meat, mashed berries, and animal tallow that had sustained many an exploring expedition over the decades. Pemmican was hearty, nutritious stuff that kept for years, weighed little, stored easily, and rarely went "off." But it was boring, boring, boring. De Long noted with disgust how pemmican had become "fish, flesh, and fowl to us." It had a sticky, salty sameness that was nauseating. It stuck to the roof of the mouth and glazed over the teeth and tongue. It radiated sour dyspeptic fumes from the stomach. It clung to their hands and fingers. It was everywhere, on them and in them: They had become walking pemmican.

Then, too—and there was no way to put this delicately— pemmican corked them up. It lingered in the system like cement and strained the nether regions. Comparative scatology became a conversation point around camp stoves. Dr. Ambler taxed his medical dignity by largely becoming a dispenser of laxatives, cod liver oil, and suppositories. (Ambler's medical logs were soon peppered with charming entries: "Lauterbach better this A.M., bowels blown out freely . . . Alexey feels quite well to-day, had movement from his bowels . . . I myself passed blood freely from bowels on one occasion. . . .")

All that pemmican also set the men to dreaming, as they never had before, about food. They grew nostalgic for the admittedly bland but comparatively excellent meals they'd eaten on the *Jeannette.* Sitting around their little stoves, picking pemmican jerky from their teeth, they fell into spirited discussions of the feasts they would prepare when they returned home. Chipp dreamed of a broiled partridge on crisp points of toast. De Long could not get off the subject of fried oysters. For Newcomb, it was pumpkin pie. For others, it was hogs' jowls and greens, corn on the cob, a plate of hash, or rich desserts. Melville fantasized about a whole canvasback duck—the engineer went on and on about how he would prepare the bird, and soon the men were all discussing the "luxury of carving and feasting on just such parts as we chose, each to his own taste—*ah!*"

Beyond their drab diet, the men suffered from a problem even more irksome: constant wetness. As the Arctic world slowly melted with summer's advance, the men found that they could never get dry.

Their skin, clammy and wrinkled, sloughed off in layers. Their sleeping bags became like pulp. Water and sludge spurted from their boots with every shambling step. Their rawhide soles, said Melville, became so soft they "took on the consistency of fresh tripe." When they tried to sleep, the heat of their own bodies would melt the mushy snow beneath their rubber blankets, and soon they would be lying in puddles of cold water. Dr. Ambler wrote that "sleeping in wet clothes in a wet bag on wet ice makes every bone & separate muscle ache in the morning. To-day I have not been able to draw a breath without pain."

As though to mock their general misery, Starr came across a handwritten note stuffed deep inside a bag of coffee—a droll message, cruel under these circumstances, evidently written by whoever had packed the container in New York City, back in the spring of 1879. Starr read the note aloud, chuckling: "This is to express my best wishes for your furtherance and success in your great undertaking. Hoping when you peruse these lines you will be thinking of the comfortable homes you left behind you for the purpose of aiding science. If you can make it convenient, drop me a line. My address, G.J.K. 10 Box, New York City."

THEN A NEW problem began to reveal itself: Something was wrong with the dogs. First it was Jim, who experienced a severe seizure one day while pulling in harness. They cut Jim from the team, and he lay on the ice for quite a while, squirming and shaking violently, as if suffering from profound cold, even though it was a bright, warm day. A few days later, Foxy suffered a similar fit and was soon discovered drowned in a pool of water. Tom experienced a different sort of attack. He became disoriented for several minutes, appearing woozy. Then, just as he seemed to return to his senses, he suddenly wheeled on his pulling partner, Wolf, and attacked him in a blind rage.

De Long could not deduce the cause of the malady. Something in their food—or not enough food? A contagious disease? Exhaustion? Whatever it was, he could ill afford to give up the services of so many dogs, as he had already lost a good number. Some had proved so mean and quarrelsome in harness that they were declared unusable and eventually shot as food for their fellows. Jack, one of the better ones, and a favorite among the men, had to be temporarily relieved from pulling so his lame back could heal. One day in the confusion of ferrying across a yawning lead, Jack was left behind on an ice floe. It was several hours before he was discovered missing, and at that point, De Long proclaimed it too hazardous to go back and mount a search. Jack was not seen again.

Soon some of the men began to experience behavioral breakdowns not unlike those suffered by the dogs. The first one to crack was the last one De Long would have expected: Edward Starr. De Long had thought of Starr as "a man whose conduct has been so uniformly beyond reproach." Along with Nindemann and Erichsen, he was always an even-tempered and eager workhorse. But one day while hauling with Melville and a small team of others, Starr reached into the boat, picked up a pair of wet boot soles, and flung them on the ice, growling in disgust. Melville turned around and glowered at Starr: The soles were Melville's, and he'd spent hours gluing and stitching them for later use. "You pick them up—and don't do that again!" Melville ordered. But Starr refused to obey. "I don't care whose soles they are, they were on my sleeping-bag!" he yelled. Melville was livid. He repeated the order, and again Starr, growing even surlier, refused to retrieve the soles.

At this point, De Long intervened and commanded Starr to obey Melville's order. Still Starr refused. He stood there by the boat, hurling expletives at no one in particular. "A nice place to put wet boot soles!" he grumbled. Summoning the full force of his personality, De Long told Starr to stop talking and repeated the order to go pick up the soles—twice, then three times. All the men in the vicinity stared in amazement. Finally, reluctantly, Starr obeyed, but he would not shut up.

"Stand apart!" De Long commanded. He approached Starr and interrogated him: "What have you to say for yourself?" Starr strangely claimed that he didn't know Melville had ever spoken to him. "Consider yourself under arrest," the captain said. He would deal with Starr later.

This was the first time anyone had openly flouted De Long's authority. It was a small crack, an incident sparked by an absurd and trifling set of circumstances. But it was a sign of things to come.

ON THE EIGHTH day of their retreat, De Long took astronomical measurements to determine the extent of their progress. It was

June 25. He entered into the enterprise hopefully, for the amount of effort thus far expended, and the optimism among the ranks, could not have been higher. Using his sextant, he took a meridian altitude reading of 77°46' N. This was curious, and surely wrong, for it was considerably north of the latitude reading he had captured at the location of the *Jeannette*'s sinking—indeed, it was the northernmost point of the entire expedition.

The next day, De Long, employing a celestial navigation method called the Sumner line of position, validated his earlier reading. He wondered if there was something wrong with his equipment—perhaps the jolts and jounces of their ice traverse had broken something, or perhaps he had made a simple mistake. He surmised that a refraction of starlight, or some other phenomenon of the High Arctic, might be interfering with the instruments. He triple-checked his calculations. He plotted more Sumner lines, then took another sextant observation at midnight. The readings came out the same.

De Long ransacked his navigational knowledge. What was the problem—where was the error? At noon the next day, he asked Melville to take an upper-meridian reading. Only then, when the latitude came back the same, did he accept the truth. For the past eight days, they had, by his guess, traveled some twenty miles to the south. But the observations indicated otherwise. In fact, they had drifted north and northwest more than twenty-eight miles. In other words, the ice pack over which they were toiling was shifting faster to the north than they were traveling south. Through all their grueling efforts, they had gone *backward*. Or, as Melville preferred to put it, they had "retroceded." It was, De Long wrote, in another vintage understatement, "enough to make one thoughtful and anxious."

De Long couldn't bring himself to broadcast his demoralizing discovery to the men. He couldn't even confess it to some of his closest officers. "I dodge [them]," he said, "lest they should ask me questions." The captain hated this evasion—it cut against his nature to prevaricate or hide anything—but given the dire circumstances, he couldn't see a way around it. He was sure that "great discouragement, if not entire loss of zeal, would ensue were such a disagreeable bit of news generally known."

The only ones he could confide in were Dr. Ambler and Melville. The engineer did not mince words in acknowledging the gravity of their predicament. "Our situation," he said, "[is] absolutely hopeless." He noticed that the men soon became "despondent and suspicious, rightly guessing the reason why the results of the first observation had been kept secret."

It was then that Captain De Long sounded his very first note of genuine despair. "If we go on this way," he wrote, "we will never get out."

Oh my dear husband—

I do so long to see you that I cannot write properly. I can hardly wait for the summer to pass, bringing its good news or bad. I have been patient so long, but it seems almost impossible for me to keep it up much longer. Still I will try my best.

How tired and weary you must be; how out of all patience at your long exile; how you must long for home and family and friends. What trials and privations you have had to undergo. I pray you may come out of them victorious and amply repaid for all your sacrifices. Sylvie and I will try to make you forget them when you return to us.

I am building all sorts of plans of future happiness when you return and you are no doubt doing the same; we must try to carry them out and fill our lives with as much joy as this earthly globe will admit.

29 · The Phantom Continent

The shamans gathered on the high grass outside the palisade fort, beneath the double cross of the old Russian Orthodox church. On a warm summer day, with Arctic flowers blossoming all around, they began a ceremony to call on the polar gods. Natives from the coastal settlements and natives from far into the interior were crowded along the shore. They danced, sang, chanted, and tapped their drums, invoking the spirits of the Far North.

Captain Hooper had called at St. Michael, Alaska, to buy coal and provisions before heading toward Wrangel and the High Arctic to look for De Long. Now, though skeptical of the proceedings, he wanted the shamans to tell him whether they could learn anything of the fate of the *Jeannette*. What did the deities know? Was De Long still alive? Was it worth the risk to steer the *Corwin* into the ice in search of the lost explorers?

These were questions of special interest in St. Michael, since two local Inuits, Alexey and Aneguin, had signed on with De Long's expedition and had not been seen in two years. The natives around St. Michael had vivid memories of De Long's men—the furs they had purchased, the dogs they had brought on board, their ambitious talk of taking their boat farther north than any man had ever dared. Alexey's wife was still waiting for him, but like all of the villagers, she was worried.

John Muir marveled at the weird energy of "the busy throng" milling about the St. Michael shore, around the fort, and among the storerooms of the Alaska Commercial Company. "They formed a strange, wild picture on the rocky beach," Muir wrote, "the squaws pitching the tents and cutting armfuls of dry grass to lay on the ground as a lining for fur carpets; the children with wild, staring eyes; groups of dandy warriors, arrayed in all the colors of the rainbow, grim, and cruel, and coldly dignified; and . . . the big bundles of shaggy bearskins, black and brown, marten, mink, fox, beaver, otter, lynx, moose, wolf, and wolverine, many of them with claws spread and hair on end, as if still fighting for life."

All around St. Michael was an extensive volcanic field, with more than fifty cones, craters, and maar lakes pocking the surrounding tundra. Inuits from far and wide believed that this seething mephitic realm was the place where the souls of the recently deceased entered the underworld. Muir walked down into one of the craters, noting the "ashes and pumice cinders strewn plentifully around the rim of the crater and down the sides of the cone . . . The rumbling sounds heard occasionally are supposed to be caused by the spirits when they are conducting in a dead Indian."

Perhaps it was the awesome power of this smoldering landscape that attracted the medicine men to come every summer to investigate matters of life and death and the netherworld. Masters of sleight of hand and ventriloquism, they wore elaborate masks and strange long gloves, their heavily tattooed bodies festooned with bear claws and animal teeth, which clanked and clicked as they moved.

The answer the shamans had for Captain Hooper was unequivocal: There was no hope whatsoever for the *Jeannette*. She was forever lost in the Arctic ice.

And what of De Long and his men? Where were they?

Their fate was sealed, the shamans said. They would never be seen again.

But there was more. The medicine men had a stern warning for Captain Hooper. The *Corwin*, if she ventured into the ice, would suffer precisely the same fate as the *Jeannette*. Go north, they told Hooper, and you will never come back.

THIS URGENT REPORT from the underworld did not faze Calvin Hooper in the least. The captain was an obstinate and straightforwardly secular man without a trace of superstition in his New England bones. The young Inuit man Hooper had hired as a translator, however, was so shaken by the shamans' pronouncement that he begged off the voyage then and there. As far as he was concerned, the *Corwin* was a ship aimed straight for hell.

As a substitute, Hooper succeeded in hiring what he described as a young Russian-Inuit "half-breed" named Andrewski, who seemed competent enough and less swayed by omens. But as a precaution, Hooper decided to take on enough coal, food, and supplies to see the *Corwin* through an entire winter, in case she should get locked in the ice, as the shamans predicted.

Muir found many of the Indians encamped at St. Michael "insolent" and "dangerous." He sensed that their relationships with traders had sapped their self-reliance: "They hunt less, and spend their idle hours in gambling and quarreling."

Muir felt sure that these Indian dissatisfactions would only fester as more and more American miners pushed into these parts of Alaska. Rumors of gold and silver were running high; in fact, a party of prospectors was reported to have been seen about a hundred miles upriver. They had come up from San Francisco in a schooner, wrote Muir, "to seek a mountain of solid silver." With the resignation of a northern Californian all too familiar with the vulgarities of "gold fever," Muir sensed what the future held. "There will probably be a rush to the new mines ere long," he wrote, and then even this distant wilderness would be invaded by men with pans and pickaxes.

Muir observed many of the same baneful American influences here that he'd seen on St. Lawrence Island. The introduction of the repeating rifle, in particular, had altered the rhythms of native hunting. A few years earlier, the hills around St. Michael had been home to thousands of wild reindeer. Now, armed with buffalo rifles, the Eskimos and other natives would slaughter caribou by the hundreds and leave them, said Muir, "lying where they fell, not even the hides being taken." The hunters would "simply cut out their tongues and leave the rest to be eaten by wolves."

Before departing for the High Arctic, Hooper deposited with representatives of the Alaska Commercial Company a sheaf of letters Emma De Long had written to her husband over the previous year. He also had a number of important items of cargo to transfer to the *St. Paul*, a San Francisco–bound steamer owned by the company. Among these were the relics the Siberian seal hunters from Wankerem had removed from the American whaling ship Hooper believed to be the wrecked *Vigilant*.

(Later that summer, the Merchants Exchange in San Francisco would put these and other artifacts on public display in the hope of identifying the doomed vessels and their lost crews. It was determined that one of articles, a pair of spectacles, belonged to Ebenezer Nye, the hard-bitten whaling captain who had ominously told De Long, "Put her into the ice and let her drift, and you may get through. Or, you may go to the devil—and the chances are about equal." This made sense, as Nye was known to have been whaling in the vicinity of the *Vigilant*. Like a prophesy turned on itself, Nye and the crews of both the *Vigilant* and the *Mount Wollaston* had perished in the very same ice pack he had so melodramatically warned De Long about.)

On July 9, when Captain Hooper weighed anchor and steered the *Corwin* from St. Michael, the seas seemed full of portent. Surgeon Irving Rosse wrote of "curious freaks of refraction and other odd phenomena." Muir described a "weird red sunset, land miraged into most grotesque forms, [and] heavy smoke from the burning tundra." But Hooper, undeterred by the ominous atmospherics, turned northwest, aiming for the Bering Strait and the High Arctic beyond. They were headed, said Muir, for the "top-most, frost-killed end of creation."

WRANGEL LAND WAS their goal, but throughout the month of July, it remained locked in ice and veiled in drizzling mist and thus could not be reached, or even seen. Muir called Wrangel "this mysterious country," "the untrodden shore," "the long-lost island." Nelson referred to it as the land "so long discussed by geographers." Rosse declared it a "problematical northern land" and began to regard it "as a myth."

Captain Hooper yearned to prove Wrangel's existence once and for all, while hunting for signs of De Long's expedition. But by the end of July, the closest Hooper could get to Wrangel was Herald Island. It was not far from Herald Island, Hooper knew, that the *Jeannette* had last been sighted, during the first week of September 1879, by three American whaling ships.

Although Herald was small—no more than six miles long—it was quite high, its rocky summit towering more than a thousand feet above the sea. If he could reach it, Hooper thought, he would have a commanding view of the Arctic ice, of Wrangel, and, perhaps, of the lost *Jeannette*. His goal, then, was to make a first ascent of Herald, and he knew that in John Muir he had a first-class mountaineer who would find his way to the top.

At ten p.m. on July 30, after what Hooper called "a good deal of bumping, squeezing, and twisting around through narrow, crooked leads," the captain anchored the *Corwin* a few hundred yards from the misty, icebound island. While most of the men leapt onto the floes and raced for the bird-swarmed rock in a spirit of mad conquest, Muir calmly scanned the cliffs with field glasses and determined the best route up. He grabbed his ice ax and took off for a steep glacial ravine a few hundred yards away from where the other men, alpine novices all, made their noisy landing. As they promptly became bogged down in heavy snow and then endangered themselves by raining boulders down on one another, Muir made good progress. He cut steps into the ice with his ax and steadily climbed past thousands upon thousands of birds "standing on narrow ledges like bottles on a grocer's shelves." Within an hour he had ascended the cliffs and was well on his way to the summit.

Muir relished his solitude. He spent several hours walking along the summit, taking notes, making sketches, hastily collecting plant specimens. He did not see a single sign of the *Jeannette*—no cairns, no relics, no evidence of human disturbance.

But the panorama was awe-inspiring, and he scanned it carefully with his glasses. In attempting to describe it, he fell into the rhapsodic language for which he would later become famous as a conservationist. "The midnight hour I spent alone on the highest summit [was] one of the most impressive hours of my life," he wrote. "The deepest silence seemed to press down on all the immeasurable, virgin landscape, [with] the frozen ocean stretching indefinitely northward."

To the west, Muir could vividly make out "the mysterious Wrangel Land . . . a wavering line of hill and dale over the white and blue ice-prairie." It was a substantial island invitingly riddled with mountains. Looking at them, he was impatient for the intervening ice to melt so he could go ascend them. The "pale gray mountains loomed," he wrote, "well calculated to fix the eye of a mountaineer."

After an hour or so, surgeon Rosse caught up with Muir on the summit, and the two men erected a cairn on a promontory to mark their arrival. "It was midnight," Rosse wrote, "and the sun shone with gleaming splendor over all this waste of ice and sea and granite." Rosse placed a bottle inside the cairn that contained an account of the *Corwin*'s landing, as well as a copy of the *New York Herald* dated April 23, 1881.

Meanwhile, the rest of the *Corwin* crew spread over the shores and headlands of the island, looking for any trace of the *Jeannette*. They found none. It was clear to everyone that, wherever he was, De Long had never touched here. "If a cairn had been built on any conspicuous point," said Muir, "we could not have failed to see it."

Just as they were pulling away from Herald Island, and beginning to grope their way through the choked mazes of ice toward open water, a young male polar bear swam right up to the bow of the *Corwin*. Hooper thought the bear was "snuffing the air as if trying by the sense of smell to learn something of this strange visitor." The captain grabbed a heavy breech-loading rifle and took aim. He wanted fresh meat for the galley, and a nice, warm skin for his quarters.

Muir found himself rooting for the bear as it tried to assess "the big, smoking, black monster" that had invaded his home. "He was a noble-looking animal and of enormous strength, living bravely . . . amid eternal ice." But he was no match for Hooper's marksmanship. "At length," said Muir, "he received a ball in the neck and stained the blue water with his blood."

FOR THE FIRST two weeks of August, the *Corwin* probed the pack, seeking a way to Wrangel. The little ship, as Rosse put it, "jammed and crashed along in a labyrinthine course," at times "completely beset by great masses of ice." It seemed as though Wrangel was taunting them—hiding behind clouds, appearing through a vent in the mist, vanishing again, then looming freakishly large through the distortions of the Arctic atmosphere. When raised by refraction, Hooper wrote, Wrangel's hills "appeared as if coming out to meet us, then faded away until nearly lost to view."

At one point the crew discovered a piece of wood on the ice— a ship's foreyard, it was determined. "Bits of rope [were] still attached to it," said Muir, and it "seemed to have been ground in the ice for a winter or two." Studying it, Hooper thought it could have been from a whaling vessel, though he couldn't rule out the possibility that it was from the *Jeannette*.

Finally, on August 12, the *Corwin* found a promising lead in the ice and drew close enough to Wrangel's southeastern shore to launch a cutter. Hooper ordered the cannon fired. Its booming report echoed from the hills and mountains and gave "notice of our presence in case anybody was near to listen," Muir said. As they approached the island in the cutter, Hooper and his landing party began to realize how substantial Wrangel was, how extensive its interior mountains, how varied its terrain. It was small wonder that mariners, snatching momentary glimpses of it over the decades, had thought it was a continent. Here was a formidable island seventy-eight miles long, its mountainous tundra flecked with the bright blooms of Arctic flowers. Winter white had given way to the briefest interval of summer's tawny gold, with only a few shrinking scraps of snow visible in the highlands.

Though they could see only a small fraction of its twenty-nine hundred square miles, Hooper and his men knew this was a far cry from Herald Island. There was something peculiarly haunting and powerful about the raw prehistoric landscape—"this grand wilderness in its untouched freshness," as Muir put it. Studying the island with field glasses, Muir could see "the small dimpling hollows with their different shades of color [and] furrows that seemed the channels of small streams . . . We gazed at the long stretch of wilderness which spread invitingly before us, and which we were so eager to explore— the rounded, glaciated bosses and foothills, the mountains with their ice-sculptured features and long withdrawing valleys."

They landed on a black gravel spit that stretched in front of the mouth of a rushing river. Not far from the skeleton of a bowhead whale, some of the men hoisted an American flag on a makeshift pole of driftwood, and Hooper declared Wrangel a new possession of the United States. He renamed it New Columbia.

Some of the men fanned out over the beach, while others disappeared into the interior. Along the coast, they found a few human-made objects: a fragment from a biscuit box, a barrel stave, a boat's spar. But all of these bits of flotsam were battered and abraded and ground up, as though they had come in on the churn of the ice pack. Hooper and his men found no signs that anyone from the *Jeannette* had lived here—indeed, no signs that a human being had ever set foot on the island.

"A land more severely solitary," Muir thought, "could hardly be found anywhere on the face of the globe." Surely, if anyone from the *Jeannette* had landed here, they would have left a cairn by this river— and they would have left footprints in the fragile tundra soil. "Had any person walked on this ground any time in summer when the snow was gone, his track would remain legible to the dullest observer for years."

Yet the men of the *Corwin* found nothing.

ALTHOUGH HE COULD not linger, Muir was in awe of Wrangel Island. He of course did not know that De Long had already determined that it was not a continent, only a fair-sized island. Whatever its size, Muir sensed that it was a primeval place where animals thrived, and where humans could not. (In fact, Wrangel boasts such an astonishing abundance of wildlife that biologists would later call it the Galápagos of the Far North. The island supports the largest population of Pacific walruses as well as one of the most extensive snowgoose colonies on earth. It is also home to snowy owls, Arctic foxes, and massive populations of lemmings and seabirds—yet in pleasant contrast to the Siberian mainland, there are no mosquitoes.)

Wrangel was a place specially made for polar bears, Muir thought (and that remains true today—it is the largest polar bear denning ground in the world). "We found bears everywhere in abundance along the edge of the ice," Muir wrote, "and they appeared to be very fat and prosperous, and very much at home, as if the country had belonged to them always. They are the unrivaled master-existences of this ice-bound solitude, and Wrangell Land may well be called the Land of the White Bear."

In a way, Wrangel was a land out of time—life here was like going back many thousands of years. Because the island was never completely glaciated during the ice ages, and never completely inundated by seawater during periods of ice retreat, the soils and plants in its interior valleys offered remnants of undisturbed Pleistocene tundra unique on the planet.

When the pharaohs were constructing the pyramids, elephants were walking around on Wrangel: This was the last place on earth where woolly mammoths lived. A dwarf subspecies thrived here as late as 1700 B.C.E., more than six thousand years after mammoth populations elsewhere became extinct. Their large curved tusks could be found everywhere on the island, lying on the gravel beaches, in ravines and streambeds.

But Hooper and his men were not able to stay long enough to stumble upon any of these petrified trophies from another epoch. The island was too large to explore in a single day, or even a single week.

Much to his annoyance, Hooper realized he had to leave. A dangerous new shift in the ice was threatening the *Corwin*. He fired off several rounds to recall the scattered parties of explorers, and they climbed into the cutter. As they worked their way back to the ship, they were flushed with the excitement of having discovered a new land—and having claimed it for their country. "The extent of the new territory thus acquired is not definitely known," wrote Muir, "nor is it likely to be for many a century, or until some considerable change has taken place in the polar climate."

Hooper had given up on finding the *Jeannette*. He turned the *Corwin* toward the Bering Strait and headed for San Francisco, not realizing that if he had continued west, skirting the ice pack along the Siberian coast for a few weeks, he might well have crossed De Long's path.

30 · A Second Promised Land

Nearly a thousand miles to the northwest of Wrangel Island, Captain De Long and his men sat nursing their wounds in soggy tents on the fast-melting ice cap of the East Siberian Sea. It was the Fourth of July—twenty-two days since the *Jeannette*'s sinking, sixteen since they had started their retreat over the pack.

The men tried to put the best face on things for their country's birthday. American flags fluttered over the tents. A bottle of brandy came out of hiding. Lauterbach tooted his harmonica, bringing on howls from the dogs, who cowered under the lee of the upturned whaleboats. But there was no disguising the fact that morale had sagged. The happy-hard delirium of the first weeks, the warm camaraderie of striving, had worn off. The galley songs had fallen silent.

The men were spent, their taut hides crosshatched with welts, their lips cracked, faces swollen, hands scabbed and blistered. All had developed variations of snow blindness, foot rot, and gastrointestinal distress. They had become little more than an accumulation of wounds moving over the ice. Every bone smarted, every sinew throbbed, every breath burned.

Dr. Ambler could no longer keep track of all the sprains, cramps, contusions, and muscle spasms he'd treated. He was running out of pain-dulling drugs. Some of the men were developing queer tingling neuropathies in their hands and feet—as well as sores from frostbite. Danenhower's eye was inflamed again, a condition Ambler found particularly worrisome. Chipp's bout with probable lead poisoning had left him near death. Heinrich Kaack's feet were covered in hideous blood blisters. The suppurating sore on Alexey's leg would not heal, even though Ambler diligently kept it dressed in collodion solution and clean bandages. Erichsen was up nights with powerful toothaches, and Lauterbach was doubled over with such piercingly painful cramps that, De Long said, he looked as though "he were going to attend a funeral at any moment."

Some men suffered frequent convulsions. Others seemed to be veering toward madness. Thirst and hunger were constant companions. Their tents leaked. Their furs stank. Their squishy boots oozed cold seawater. A new undertow of despair attended their work. The whole mission on which they were embarked—trying to reach open water—seemed increasingly dubious, for the three wooden boats they dragged were now so badly banged up ("limber as a basket," Danenhower judged them) that it was doubtful they would float once they could be launched.

The dogs, meanwhile, were so hungry they had taken to eating their leather harnesses; they had fallen into such an agitated state that they were of little use. "The knots and tangles they can get in," said Ambler, were "soul provoking and [the] cause of profound and deep swearing." The plain fact was that the dogs were slowly starving to death. "Each man had a favorite animal, and would share his rations with him," Danenhower wrote, "but this was not sufficient." Many of the sickest, hungriest dogs were experiencing epileptic fits, then dying, one by one—leaving the humans to haul even more weight.

But many of the men could no longer pull. Some couldn't walk. A few couldn't even stand. These De Long referred to as "the ineffectuals." A "sorry looking set," Melville described their encampment, a "heap of rags, bags, and old battered boats."

So far, De Long had managed to keep remarkable discipline in the ranks without resorting to force—in fact, he had not struck a single blow during the entire expedition. Still, dissident thoughts, perhaps mutinous ones, hung in the air. Not that anyone thought he could improve on De Long's leadership. Not that anyone had better ideas on what to do or where to go. If the dissatisfaction had spread, it would have been an insurrection born of general discontent. Small personality defects had magnified. Petty wrongs swelled into high crimes. Grudges became righteous and all-consuming.

De Long was having difficulties with the two civilian scientists. Newcomb was proving useless—the man wouldn't work at all aside from what Dr. Ambler called "piddling." He spent his days some-where in the back, muttering feeble obscenities at the officers. Mel-ville found Newcomb "neither useful nor ornamental." The young naturalist was the smallest, weakest member of the whole party but also the most obstinate. Ambler was nearly at his wit's end with him. "He has not yet learned to obey without speaking," the doctor wrote, "[and] will get himself hurt if he don't desist."

The situation with Collins, meanwhile, had only deteriorated. The hatred the Irishman felt for De Long, and vice versa, had become toxic. De Long kept Collins under a kind of house arrest, isolating him from the others, perhaps out of fear that he would indeed try to provoke a mutiny. The other officers seemed united in their disdain for Collins. Though a fair shot with a rifle, he was otherwise clumsy and inept, they thought, often more hindrance than help out on the ice. (Melville said he lumbered like an "Irish cow.") At one point, De Long testily yelled to Collins, "Don't let me see you put your hand to another thing unless I order you!" At least in his lonesome misery, Collins had stopped making puns.

In the face of all their trials, De Long sprinkled his journal with further gems of understatement. Gazing at a puzzle of jammed ice and meltwater that would require weeks to cross, he stoically predicted: "We are in for a time." Hopelessly disoriented by fog for the better part of a week, De Long would only allow that "we are in the dark as to our position." Halted by a lashing blizzard, he scribbled that the day's weather was "anything but satisfactory." After he plunged into a crevice and soaked himself in freezing water up to his neck, De Long wryly mentioned that the day had involved "a troublous trip."

To struggle like a spavined mule yet advance only a mile or two a day was "rather discouraging," De Long admitted. But he seemed to rise to the suffering—to thrive on it. His capacity for pain, his disdain for any kind of languor, his steel-cut work ethic—where did it come from? It was a masochism that was nevertheless warmed by sanguinity. He was nearly always able to locate some spare pocket of optimism.

Turning to his journal at the end of one nightmarish day, he wrote, "Tired, cold, wet, hungry, sleepy, disappointed, and disgusted; but ready to tackle it again to-morrow."

There were others who shared De Long's outlook and determina-tion. Among the seamen, Nindemann, Louis Noros, Bartlett, Sweet-man, and Erichsen stood above the rest. They were strong as oxen, seemingly impervious to disease, always solicitous of others, and driven by indomitable will. Among the officers, Melville continued to be De Long's rock. The engineer could do no wrong.

Still, even with men like these, De Long recognized that this tramp across the pack was quite nearly impossible—physically, mentally, and spiritually. "There is no work in the world harder than this sledging," he wrote. "The drag, drag, the slips and jerks, the sudden bringing up of the hauling belt across the chest, are fearfully trying; and the working with pickaxes through flinty ice makes every bone ache. Men *cannot* do this . . . ten and a half hours each day without breaking down."

Ambler went further, suggesting that "such work by men could never have been done before & I hope may never be done again." Recalling his days in a Civil War prisoner-of-war camp, he added, "I have seen something of men in trying times, but I have yet to see men who will equal these. For 40 days we have been under way, with all kinds of . . . hardships; but not a murmur & tonight after 19 hours of work, they are cheerful and come up smiling."

DE LONG HAD to agree with Ambler, but the captain could see that the men's good cheer was flagging. They were depleting their supply of pemmican and had not seen any wildlife for a long time. Open water was still nowhere in sight—these moving mazes of mush and rubble seemed to stretch out forever, with no landmarks to aim for, no fixed destination on the horizon to give purpose to their toil. The central coast of Siberia was still more than five hundred miles away. And, De Long knew, time was running out; the short Arctic summer would soon expire, and they would be trapped on the winter ice.

At least then, however, the ice would make some manner of sense. At least then it would freeze into something reliable, with surfaces that feet could understand. There was no order to this kind of ice, no consistency. Its every feature—its color, texture, solidity, expansiveness, crystalline structure, collapse points, tendency to shift, potential for fracturing, capacity for absorbing or reflecting light—seemed in constant flux.

This was what Petermann had called the Paleocrystic Sea. It was the product of millennia's smashing churn of the elements acting on freezing and frozen and thawing and refreezing ice. One could stare at it all day and never see coherence. Needle ice gave way to striped puddles, to thick driven snow, to rippled pockets of new ice, to mires of goop, to lagoons of open water, to ruined battlefields of shards and bricks, to spectral blue sculptures of ancient ice, and to the wind-whipped corrugations of snow that the Russians called *sastrugi*. The pack's logic, its forces of repulsion and attraction, were inscrutable. It was the very definition of random.

Splashing and stumbling over it, the men kept trying to find the lip of some pattern, something predictable or usable, some groove they could lay their thoughts into. But none was apparent. This melting icescape seemed to observe an Arctic corollary of pi—a sequence that never repeated or resolved itself. Every scalloped intricacy, every winking lane, every hummock and pressure ridge, every honeycombed crevice offered mysterious new warps of design.

At first, De Long strove for a vocabulary to characterize this exasperating quality of the ice. On page after page in his journal, he kept varying the descriptions. He spoke of "ugly openings," of fields "terribly wild and broken," "such a jam, so full of holes," "ice resembling alabaster," "lanes [that] meander away to narrow veins between piled up masses," "terrible masses of hummocks and rubble," "puzzling masses of ice and water." Finally, he seemed to tire of descriptors, settling instead on one all-purpose word: *mess*. "A fearful mess," he wrote, "the rotten and ugly mess," "such a mess of . . . rotten ice," "a confused mess," "a mess of loose pack," "one bad mess," "the sliding, shifting mess."

Another problem with this universally churned-up ice was that it was almost impossible to find fresh—*truly* fresh—water. De Long had instructed the water crew to scrape ice and snow only from the highest hummocks and, even then, to go only one inch below the surface. The water they harvested generally tasted fine. But when Dr. Ambler conducted a silver nitrate test on their supply of drinking water, it showed an alarming degree of salinity. The conclusion was unmistakable: Salt permeated this icy world, even its highest, safest places. For more than a month, they had been drinking brackish water without knowing it—adding further salt to their already salty pemmican diet. De Long was able to chalk up another one in the long tally of August Petermann's dangerously wrong ideas: The late cartographer's theory that the ice pack was a limitless source of fresh water, De Long said, "has been thoroughly exploded."

There was no telling which of their present health troubles were attributable to or exacerbated by their steady intake of brine. De Long worried specifically about scurvy, which many then thought was tied in some way to salt intake—and he increased the daily ration of concentrated lime juice accordingly. But the captain knew they couldn't go on this way much longer. They had to find fresh water.

ON THIS INDEPENDENCE Day, the men tried to enjoy themselves, happy to remove their slitted ice goggles and relinquish all concerns about navigating the "mess." But De Long, alone in his office tent, lapsed into an uncharacteristically doleful mood. He was lost in bittersweet thoughts that took him back three years. "Our flags are all flying in honor of the day, though to me it is a very blue one," he wrote. "Three years ago to-day in Havre the *Jeannette* was christened, and many pleasant things were said, and anticipations formed, all of which have gone down with the ship. I did not think that three years afterward would see us all out on the ice, and a story of a lost ship to carry back to our well-wishers at home."

On that fine day in Le Havre, with Emma at De Long's side, Bennett had spoken of sending Stanley off to the Arctic should the *Jeannette* run into trouble. But, realistically, De Long understood that he and his men were far beyond any rescuer's reach. Bennett couldn't help them, and neither could their country, which would be celebrating its 105th birthday once the sun came up on the far side of the planet. The American flags snapping over the tents seemed to mock De Long, seemed to symbolize his nation's fecklessness and his own irredeemable solitude. His only hope, he knew, was to try to redouble everyone's resolve. They would have to save themselves.

Yet the responsibility for preserving human life was beginning to weigh on him. "My duty to those who came with me is to see them safely back, and to devote all my mind and strength to that end," he wrote later that day. He had to look "misfortune in the face and . . . learn what its application may be."

EIGHT DAYS LATER, on July 12, De Long's fortunes seemed to turn. Early that morning, something flickered on the horizon. Dunbar, as usual, spotted it first. He had marched far out ahead of the others, planting his black flags in the snow. Just for a moment, in the southern distance, a vent opened in the clouds, and he swore he saw an island—a large one, luminous, bulging with mountains. Then, just as abruptly, the clouds snapped shut, leaving Dunbar to wonder if he'd really seen what he thought he had.

A little later, after supper, the clouds opened again, and this time nearly everyone saw something. "A bright vision arose before our eyes," Melville wrote. A spontaneous cheer erupted from the ranks. Danenhower described it as a "'whaleback' that looked very much like a snow-covered island," though it appeared so "greatly distorted by atmospheric effects" that "a great many would not believe that it existed at all." De Long was extremely skeptical. "There was something which certainly *looked* like land," he conceded. "But the fog assumes so many deceiving forms that one cannot be sure of anything."

Still, the captain's interest was sufficiently piqued that he broke out his Petermann charts and studied the sketchy topography of the New Siberian Islands. According to his calculations of their current position, the nearest known island—marked on his map as "Ostrov Faddeyevsky"—was more than 120 miles to the southwest. That was too far away to be the smudgy mass they had just spotted. "I cannot believe that we have seen land to-day," he concluded, and he dismissed the sighting as a mirage.

But the next day, the men spotted the island once again. This time, the details were so vivid that there was no doubt. "The sun shone clearly in the southward," Melville wrote, "and the land stood boldly revealed; its blue mountain peaks rising grandly aloft, the ice and water showing plainly below, while a white, dazzling cloud floated dreamily above." It was "the most perfect scene," the engineer said. "It inspired us with new hope," like a "second Land of Promise."

De Long reshaped his course to intercept the landmass, which he had to assume was Faddeyevsky Island after all. At that moment, the tenor of the march changed profoundly. Land could mean food, fresh water, driftwood, and the possibility of rescue. Just as important, land was something to shoot for, an impetus, a focal point. The island was still many miles off. But its effect was electrifying. Everyone rallied again around Nindemann's crisp *"Yo-Heave-Yup!"* and dug in as never before. Said Melville: "Each man straightaway became a Hercules."

As they drew near the island, wildlife presented itself. The skies coursed with guillemots, Ross's gulls, auks, pelagic cormorants, and other birds. Out on the ice ahead, the shadowy forms of sea mammals were glimpsed. On July 14, with De Long's permission, Collins grabbed a Winchester repeating rifle and took off on a hunt. An hour later he came back with a seal. The men were all so starved for fresh meat that De Long dispensed with his habit of first hanging up the carcass to dissipate the animal's heat. Instead they butchered the seal then and there, removing the blubber and the spine and slicing up the warm flesh into small chunks, which they promptly boiled in a stew of beef-extract broth.

It tasted sublime. "It was a feast I shall long remember," De Long said. "We feel as if we had dined at Delmonico's." Ambler's assessment was more equivocal. At first it "tasted very well" and he "ate a good allowance, but at the last I did not fancy it as much as when I started." Afterward, they rendered the blubber into grease, which they daubed on their leaky boots and tents.

A few days later, Collins and Ambler, hunting together, bagged an even bigger quarry: a walrus. Collins got the first shot into the swimming mammal, hitting him near the eye. "Down went the walrus," said De Long, "and we thought we had seen the last of him." Moments later, though, some in the party heard a raspy blowing sound and saw large spatterings of ejected blood on the ice pack. Then Ambler ran down the walrus and shot him five times in the skull. Dunbar, giving chase with a knife, pierced a hole through a flipper and hooked a line through it just as he was starting to sink.

A large party of men hauled the walrus to camp. He was a young bull, weighing as much as fifteen hundred pounds. De Long was thrilled by their bonanza. "The choice parts, tenderloin, sirloin, heart, liver, brain, and flippers, will more than suffice for three meals for us," he wrote, "and the dogs may eat all day if they like." When they butchered the animal, they found shrimp, anemones, sea cucumbers, and smelt in his belly. Every part of the carcass would be used. The skin would be cut into pieces for boot soles, the blubber would become grease and fuel for cooking, bones would be used to shore up the now rickety sleds, and the tusks would be given as trophies to the shooters, Collins and Ambler—but would see use as makeshift pickaxes. De Long judged the resulting stew "excellent," though "not as good as seal stew, the meat coarser and not so sweet." Newcomb thought the boiled skin "not unlike pig's feet, and with vinegar I think would be very good."

FOUR DAYS LATER, their larder grew even richer. On July 24, a young polar bear, his coat smeared dirty brown from forays on dry land, was sighted. Alexey and Aneguin stalked the animal for a while, firing two shots at long range but missing. A few hours later, Carl Görtz sighted it. The animal had come within five hundred yards of camp, apparently attracted by the scent of simmering walrus. "Görtz crawled within one hundred yards of him unnoticed," De Long noted, "and planted his two bullets with good results."

The meals they had from the bear outdid even their recent feasts. Using empty pemmican cans for stoves, they fried steaks and chops. Then, said Melville, they "roasted his paws, and made stews of his flank pieces, using his blubber for fuel." Two days later, the carcass was totally consumed. In a few sittings, they had eaten a five-hundred-pound bear.

The effect all this fresh meat had on the men could not be exaggerated. Laughter returned. Their observations grew keener. Their stamina increased. Everyone, even Chipp, came off the sick list. As they marched toward the island, the galley songs welled up again.

For a number of days, the landmass had disappeared behind thick, soupy fog. The increasing presence of animals seemed a telltale sign that they were drawing closer, but they couldn't be sure. One day, although the island remained obscured, the skies above opened long enough for the captain to take a careful positional reading. The news was so staggeringly good that while he gathered together his equipment, he told Melville to inform the men right away.

"Boys!" the engineer barked in his boldest voice. "Captain says we've made twenty-one miles the past week—and we now have a current in our favor." No longer was the ice shifting north faster than they were marching south, neutralizing all forward movement. At long last, they were making real progress.

A lusty shout went up from the men, and they took to their trudge with what Melville called "renewed vigor," picking their way through the fog.

It was during this bright but uncertain time that Dr. Ambler happened upon a live butterfly, bouncing among the floes. It was such a beautiful, incongruous thing to see out on the pack that the men could only smile in admiration. A *butterfly*—they had not seen any variety of this fluttering creature in more than two years. It could not be a "habitué" of the ice, De Long wrote, "and was certainly blown from the land"—a land that surely must be close by now, and had to offer some measure of warmth and stability to nurture such improbable life.

With this delicate inspiration, the men marched on.

AS THEY STAGGERED toward the island, one man returned to the sick list. It was Danenhower—his syphilitic eye kept worsening. Dr. Ambler had to turn more and more of his attention to the problem. The eye was, the surgeon jotted in his notes, "engorged . . . inflamed . . . flushed up." Ambler thought it might require surgery again, but most of the instruments the doctor would need to perform the procedure had gone down with the ship. All he could do was treat it with quinine and anti-inflammatory ointments and flush it out from time to time. Still, the eye would not improve.

What made Danenhower's condition even worse was that he categorically denied that it was a problem. He said he could see just fine—and apparently believed it. But on the march, he kept falling into crevices and tripping over the merest obstacle. With his bad eye bandaged and his other eye darkened by a snow goggle, and with neurological conditions caused by his syphilis that may have impaired his balance, the navigator had become, in Ambler's words, "an encumbrance." Danenhower's pride, however, and his wish not to let his fellows down, would not allow him to admit it. He insisted that he could haul—and that, indeed, he was one of the strongest men on the ice.

After a few days of quarreling between Ambler and Danenhower, De Long had to intervene. He summoned the navigator to his office tent. "You cannot see," De Long said. "It's evident from the way you stumble in the snow."

Danenhower protested. On the contrary, he said, he was strong and healthy and could see as well as the next man.

De Long cut him off: "Danenhower—you are an *impediment*! You would be a hindrance to anything you attempted to assist."

Then what will you have me do? the navigator asked.

"I refuse to assign you any duty until Dr. Ambler discharges you from the sick list. For now, you shall ride in the hospital sled."

When Danenhower tried to explain himself, De Long cut him off again: "You are dismissed."

Danenhower emerged from the tent devastated and resentful. He reported to Ambler once more and climbed aboard the hospital sled, to be hauled by others like so many pounds of pemmican. The doctor looked at Danenhower with disgust. He recalled that in Washington he had strongly recommended to De Long that Danenhower not be allowed to join the expedition in the first place. He hoped that his syphilitic patient now felt "great mortification" for coming to the Arctic when he'd known perfectly well that "he was diseased, and that he was liable to be laid up." Perversely stubborn, Danenhower had "concealed it as long as possible."

Now Danenhower's deceit endangered not only himself but all the other men. Said Ambler: "I do not think a man was ever cursed with . . . such [a] patient before." But Ambler was soon absorbed in other thoughts. Back in Virginia, he realized, it was his fiancée's birthday. He wrote in his journal, "The Little Lady . . . must be twenty-one. We had a pleasant time 3 yrs. ago to-day." Sitting alone at supper, Ambler "drank to her health in the best I had, a tin cup of tea."

THE MEN STRUGGLED onward through the fog. Several times the clouds opened to reveal the island, but the refractions were so strange and capricious that it was impossible to judge how far away it was—or the condition of the intervening ice. De Long scrutinized these kaleidoscopic changes with his glass. "The more I looked, the more confused I became," he said. Ambler jotted in his journal, "Island seems to recede as we approach." First it appeared to be surrounded by ice; moments later, it seemed to rise up from an open sea. Then it disappeared, only to return again. "I sat and studied this thing for an hour, watching every change," De Long wrote. "I was fairly staggered."

Equally baffling to De Long was the question of *which* island of the New Siberians they were marching toward. He opened up his charts again and now decided that it must be one of the Lyakhovsky Islands (Little and Great Lyakhovsky Islands are the southernmost of the New Siberian Islands). But if it *was* one of the Lyakhovsky Islands, then his maps were very crudely charted—off by more than a hundred miles. Studying the conundrum further, De Long realized that he had not considered one other possibility: Maybe this wasn't one of the New Siberian Islands at all. Maybe this was a *new* island—an island that, like Henrietta, had never been mapped or even seen before. "I am again in hopes," he wrote in a blush of excitement, "that we have made another discovery."

The fog grew thicker, and the men lost sight of the island for several days. Yet they could tell they were drawing near, because they could hear the relentless grinding of the ice on the shore, as well as the cackle and chatter of what sounded like millions of seabirds. Often they saw individual birds flying overhead with food stuck in their beaks.

On July 28, the sun shone through the clouds, and suddenly the island burst before them in magnificent detail, less than a mile away. Its highest point loomed several thousand feet over the patchily frozen ocean. The island, considerably larger than Henrietta or Jeannette Island, was draped in massive glaciers. Moss grew on the capes, and in several places there were steep cliffs streaked with bird guano. Melville could see "perpendicular masses of black basaltic rock, stained here and there with patches of red lichens, and begrimed with the decayed vegetable matter of unknown ages." All about the island were "giant rocks split and powdered by the hand of time."

The men removed their smoked goggles, let go of their drag ropes, and gasped. To Newcomb, it was a "land of rushing torrents, glaciers, huge, impregnable rocky fastnesses [and] crags of indescribable grandeur." Gulls, murres, kittiwakes, and guillemots swarmed by the thousands, flying "so thickly as to darken the sun." Just behind the deafening din of the birds' shrieking was another sound, a steady bass tone, what Newcomb called a "buzzing sound, as if from an enormous swarm of bees." This was the mingled drone of the birds' nudging, cooing, tittering, and rustling in their thousands of niches and nesting places. It was the thrum of life itself.

The men were dazzled by the spectacle; some were moved to tears. Never before had they seen or heard so many living beings crammed into one place.

As close as it was, getting to the island, De Long could see, would still be an ordeal. The ice between them and the shore was a menacing whorl of "confusion and trouble"—riddled with enough obstacles, he thought, to "hold a Goliath back." Ambler predicted that they would have "the devil to pay generally." Yet everyone was so inspired by the sight of the island that De Long decided to capitalize on the renewed energy and make a prolonged dash for it.

When they set foot on the rocky shore, on July 29, De Long gathered his bedraggled men together to make an announcement. He had to fairly yell it to make himself heard over the screeching birds. "This land toward which we have been working for so long," he said, "is a new discovery. I take possession of it in the name of the President of the United States."

Three cheers went up, and the men scattered over the island to find driftwood for a bonfire. Though they were beyond exhaustion—"everybody [is] used up," De Long said, "and could not possibly have gone further"—they relished the feel of terra firma under their feet. Except for Melville and the small party that had visited Henrietta Island, the men of the *Jeannette* had not walked on dry land for 697 days. Dr. Ambler rejoiced in the subtle sensation of what he called "renewing the electrical connections between my body and the earth."

Soon a fire crackled along the rocky beach. American flags flew over De Long's proud camp—and this time, he thought, they did not seem to mock him.

At first, the sound failed to register on the ear at all; it was more like a low vibration, from deep within the earth. Most of the men, snuffling in their sealskin bags, were too exhausted to detect it. But then the ground "rocked and trembled," said Melville, with "the roar of distant thunder." This ragged rumbling gathered strength and intensity, scattering birds from their cliff-side perches. Inside the tents, a few eyes cocked open, faces contorted into sleepy scowls of confusion. It was a noise, a sensation, like none they had experienced before. Many were convinced that it was an earthquake.

De Long and his men stumbled from their tents and stared up in disbelief through the tapered light of the Arctic predawn. On the scree slopes more than a thousand feet directly above them was a tumbling landslide of rock. The debris made "its awful way toward us with irresistible speed," said Melville.

Fortunately, the expedition was encamped on a gravel spit that was separated from the slope by a narrow channel of water. The clattering, plummeting rocks piled up in the channel, "lashing it into foam," said Newcomb, "and sending the spray fifty feet into the air." Had the water not been there to stop it, observed Melville, "we would have been buried by the rushing mass."

A cloud of dust and grit settled over the camp—choking the men and leaving them to ponder their good fortune. They had to wonder: Was the island trying to tell them something? It was as though this pristine piece of Arctic rock, never having seen human trespass before, had objected to the expedition's presence in the strongest possible terms. The avalanche deposited "a terrific amount of rotten rock," said De Long. But he seemed singularly unimpressed by the near catastrophe. After all their trials so far, he wrote, "we are prepared for everything and surprised at nothing."

De Long *was* surprised by one thing: This island on which they'd landed had proved to be a considerable piece of real estate. On their first morning, July 30, he sent reconnaissance parties scattering in all directions, and the reports they brought back were impressive. They'd found capes, plateaus, volcanic cones, several glaciers, and numerous rocky outcroppings seamed with coal. His men collected a pair of bleached reindeer antlers, samples of opals, amethyst quartz, and basaltic lava, and the bones of several marine mammals. They found traces of bear, fox, rabbit, and grouse. The island stretched for many miles—it was too large to be explored in just a day or two.

De Long, appreciating the magnitude of their discovery, decided to name the place Bennett Island. As far as he was concerned, the island was now part of the United States. "I added Bennett Island to American soil," he wrote, and then named the high escarpment beside their campsite Cape Emma.

Ostrov Bennetta, as the island is marked on Russian maps today, is about sixty square miles in area, by far the largest fragment in the uninhabited archipelago known as the De Long Islands. (By contrast, Henrietta Island, also considered part of the De Longs, is a mere crumb—only 4.6 square miles.) The summit of Bennett's highest mountain reaches fourteen hundred feet, and the island has four glaciers, one of which is 560 feet thick. Though rocky and treeless, much of the island is covered in low tundra plants—forbs, rushes, mosses, and lichens. Eons ago, Bennett was a stand-alone mountain that rose from the floor of the late Pleistocene plain of Beringia, which once connected Siberia to North America, and which now lies submerged beneath the Arctic Ocean.

During his stay on Bennett Island, Captain De Long was torn between conflicting impulses. On the one hand, he wanted to explore and map the island—this was, after all, the expedition's first significant geographical discovery. On the other hand, he knew he was racing against the Arctic clock. His survival, and that of his men, demanded that they move quickly to the south. Yet before they could do that, they had to gain strength, mend their boats, and generally reconstitute themselves for the effort ahead. De Long agonized over this delicate trigonometry—rest, explore, keep moving—knowing that whatever decision he made, his men's fate could hang in the balance. "A prolonged delay here," he recognized, "would be a serious thing for us." He could not ignore the fact that, as in a desert oasis, there was life on this island, however tenuous. But lingering here would mean sure death.

Melville urged De Long to spend time exploring Bennett Island. "Any person with manly or heroic instincts," he wrote, could see the value of exploration. On the other hand, Melville said, "the weak, timorous, or over-cautious person would avoid it."

In the end, they would spend eight precious days on Bennett Island. Their time here was, in many ways, an idyll—a "brief respite from our distressing labors," as Melville put it. They drank sweet water from streams that purled down the mountainside, fresh from a glacier. They heated the water in the fire and bathed for the first time in months. They stayed warm, thanks to the huge amount of driftwood strewn along the beaches, often piled in logjams that looked to De Long like "dock[s] fallen to decay." The rocky tundra was matted in beautiful Arctic flowers as well as an edible kind of spoonwort—De Long called it "scurvy grass"—which added fresh green relish to their diet.

And they were never in want of meat. Seabirds were everywhere, darkening the sky, and their rookeries were full of eggs. De Long sent parties up to the cliffs to kill birds by the score. Most of them were so trusting that all one had to do was ease up to them and smash them with a rock. Their flesh was rubbery in consistency, but when fried in bear fat, it could be tasty. Melville loved their "savory stews of loon, gorney, gull, murre, and other sea-fowl," and De Long wrote that a "more luxurious meal I do not recollect having had."

Others at first found the birds too rich for their constitutions. "Their effect after being eaten was like that of young veal," said Danenhower, "and pretty nearly every one of the party was made sick, the doctor included." As Ambler succinctly put it: "Bird diet— old ones tough, young tender." Newcomb, a bird lover, would only say that these winged creatures were "acceptable" as food. Yet when liberally cut with salads of scurvy grass, the rich stews went down easier.

Finding this island, De Long realized, had been a godsend, a stroke of pure luck that had come just when he'd thought his men could go no farther. Now, with each passing day, he could see their spirits reviving, a new spark in their eyes. "It seems as if Providence were directing our movements," he wrote. "There is much to be thankful for; everybody is in excellent health, in spite of our terribly hard work; the appetites are something wonderful to think of, and our sleep is sound and unbroken."

ONE OF THE other things that made Bennett Island such a pleasant refuge for De Long was that he no longer had to keep his attentions so firmly clamped on the matter of discipline. He told Chipp to "give all hands all the liberty you can on American soil." During their eight days on Bennett, De Long issued the men light assignments—to study the tides, to collect animal artifacts or gather geological specimens. But otherwise he viewed the situation almost as though they had arrived in port and were taking a brief leave of duty. This was vitally important, he felt, for everyone's morale and sanity—including his own. They all needed a respite.

Collins was free to socialize with the group again and could move about the island as he wished, so long as he brought his notebook and made detailed sketches of the topography. Danenhower, too, had freedom to do as he liked, the only caveats being that he keep his eye bandaged and try his best not to endanger himself by walking on the precarious slopes above the camp. Newcomb was fully restored to the title for which he'd been hired. He was, after all, the expedition's naturalist, with a specialty in ornithology—and here was a wild, unexplored island crowded with birds, many of them rare or little-known species.

Each morning Newcomb grabbed his notebook and his shotgun and took off on all-day "tramps," as he referred to them, usually by himself. At long last, he had arrived in *his* kind of heaven. This was why he'd signed on to the expedition in the first place; this was the first time his expertise had been called upon in any direct way.

One day, he crawled far up a valley of pinnacled rocks that "arose like some great castle of old." He was both exhilarated and daunted by the thought of being the first person ever to walk over the ancient rocks. "Probably mine was the first human foot ever there," he wrote, "and as I stood looking, I almost expected to see some gigantic knight appear and ask how or by what right I dared invade his realm."

Another day Newcomb climbed twelve hundred feet up what he called "very treacherous disintegrated rocks" to observe a colony of murres—a large species of auk. Newcomb could have lingered with the birds all day. He sat engrossed for hours, watching them from a high ledge covered in red lichen and splotched with their droppings. "I fairly envied these beautiful creatures their cozy home," he said. The murres "sat in long rows like citizens at a town meeting, and were very noisy, their voices echoing from crag to crag." It was "the most extensive breeding ground I have ever seen of any bird."

On his way down the precipitous slope, Newcomb had to bury his sheath knife to the hilt into the scree with each stride to keep from tumbling to his death. Suddenly, he heard someone crying up to him from below: *"Look out, sir!"* It was Sharvell, in a panic. When Newcomb turned around, he saw an avalanche of "huge rocks and earth coming for me." His own movements had apparently dislodged something far above that had set the mass in motion. "Seeing a chance of safety behind an outcropping, I hastily availed myself of it and barely in time, as these missiles of death hurtled down," Newcomb recalled. He pronounced it "a narrow shave" and continued his happy studies of seabirds.

BACK AT CAMP, Sweetman, the carpenter, was performing minor miracles of nautical engineering. All three of the boats, he'd found, were in bad shape. He doubted they would even float. In the whaleboat, for example, the sternpost was cracked, and the garboards—the planks closest to the keel—had been stove in. All the boats needed caulking, patching, and reinforcing, and some sort of rigging had to be devised to accept the crude sails that would power them toward the Siberian coast.

With limited tools, and with nothing for lumber save odd pieces of driftwood and walrus bones, Sweetman got working. The captain, who remained in camp taking barometric readings and astronomical observations, watched Sweetman with admiration. The man was a natural wizard with his hands, De Long thought. Of course, Melville had a few clever ideas as well, and in a few days the three boats were pronounced ready to sail.

Adding to this good news, Nindemann, on a survey of the southern coast of the island, had seen significant patches of open ocean. As he described it to De Long, there were "large lanes of water making to the southwest, and the ice was constantly separating to form new ones." Offshore from their campsite, smaller lanes were beginning to clear. De Long understood that this was their chance. The icy world was finally opening up, just a little—and just in time for the closing weeks of the Arctic summer.

De Long noticed that one of the pieces of driftwood piled beside the camp was marred by a little notch. As he studied it more closely, he realized that it was the mark of an ax, and that this stick of faded gray wood had once been a fence post. From what continent or island it had drifted was anyone's guess, but it touched him to find it here on this bleak shore; this was the first sign of civilization he had seen in two years, a subtle memento of a living world beyond his present ordeal.

With working boats and open water on which to sail them, De Long now had this piece of tooled wood to remind him that there was indeed a human society to sail for, somewhere on the southern horizon.

BEFORE HE COULD go, however, De Long had an immediate problem to ponder: What should he do with the dogs? Of the forty sled dogs they had taken aboard in Alaska, twenty-three remained. Many of them were sick, depleted, or too wild and irascible to do any real hauling. De Long saw no point in wasting any more food on them—prior to the landing on Bennett Island, they had been eating a pound of pemmican a day. In any case, there wasn't room in the three boats for all of them.

So the dogs would have to be culled. De Long went over the pack and studied each animal. He conferred with Alexey and Aneguin, who knew them best. It was terrible work, but eleven dogs were chosen. "These," De Long wrote, "were all worn out or subject to fits. The amount of food [they] eat is not compensated for by the work done, and I must think of human life first."

On August 5, he gave Erichsen the order. One by one, the Dane took them behind a hummock. Eleven gunshots reverberated off the cliffs. The men cringed at the sad thought of what was happening. ("The poor brutes" was all Danenhower could say.) De Long was particularly distressed to see Jim and Tom go; they were two of his favorites, and loyal workers. The only consolation was that he still had twelve healthy dogs left—including Snoozer, who had become the expedition's mascot.

De Long made no plans to eat any of the executed dogs. Beyond everyone's obvious distaste for consuming canine flesh, he considered them diseased animals. Then, too, after their week on Bennett Island, the men were no longer in any danger of starving.

It was nearly impossible to bury the carcasses in the flint-hard permafrost. So, after a small ceremony, the men threw them into the sea.

THE NEXT DAY, after jettisoning some of the sleds and all of the unnecessary things, the men began to load their boats. Their interlude on Bennett Island was over.

The departure came not a moment too soon. Almost literally overnight, the door to summer seemed to be slamming shut. The world of ice and snow was returning with a vengeance. "During our short sojourn here," Melville wrote, "how marked the changes! When we landed, the water was rushing in torrents from the glacier." But now, the engineer noted, "winter had really set in . . . The streams were dried up, young ice was making," and the Arctic flowers "which had looked so cheerful to our eyes were fast being clad in their winter garb." De Long noted that after a week of warm weather, everyone was suddenly "freezing all the time." Some used sticks to beat their feet "as a bastinado," to bring back their circulation. This dubious technique, "though making our feet tingle, hardly added to our comfort."

At nine-thirty on the morning of August 6—fifty-five days since the sinking of the *Jeannette*—De Long gave the order and the men shoved their three heavily laden boats into the shallows. It was, said De Long, "generally a queer day," twenty-seven degrees, with a fickle sun struggling to bore through the clouds. The boats floated low in the water under their heavy burdens, but Sweetman's repairs held firm.

Before saying good-bye to Bennett Island, De Long left a message in a rock cairn that Dunbar had built high up on the escarpment, marked with a paddle. The message said:

Bennett Island, Cape Emma.
 Latitude N 76° 38', Longitude E 153°25'. We break camp and start southward over the ice, hoping with God's grace to reach the New Siberian Islands, and from there make our way by boats to the coast of Siberia. We have three boats, thirty days provisions, and sufficient clothing,

and are in excellent health having rested here a few days. We have lost
none of our original number, and have not had scurvy. Though at times
we see much open water to the southwest, we cannot yet say whether or
not we can take to our boats to resume our journey, or shall be forced to
resort again to dragging everything over the ice.

    George W. De Long, Commanding U.S. Arctic Expedition

Then they disappeared into the squalls, three boats wallowing
forward under dingy sails attached to loose masts and clattering spars.
De Long looked fondly back one last time at his discovery, the island's
summit "towering up like a dome . . . swimming in the clouds." As
they proceeded south, threading between the ice cakes, winter seemed
to close in around them. "Our beautiful island," said Melville, "was
shrouded in white. . . . The last we saw of it was a mere shadowy contour, curved like a whale's back, and lifted into the heavens as though
to mingle its snowy purity with the silver glory of the clouds."

My dearest George—You will feel happy to know how universal is the interest in the Jeannette *and her crew. I have received telegrams and letters by the dozen. Of course papers from all over the country have been anxious for interviews with me, but I very politely but positively decline to be interviewed. I don't want my husband to go off on any more undertakings. I want him to stay comfortably at home, or I will surely get a divorce!*

—Emma

It was the time of the skeleton pack. The time of tapered pools of meltwater and cul-de-sac canals, of aquatic riddles nearly impossible to solve. The floes were too soft and hole-ridden to allow the men to make any reliable progress by sledging, but neither was there enough open water to advance by sail. So they probed and threaded among these icy labyrinths, sometimes rowing their three boats, sometimes towing them, from cake to melting cake. "So winding and intricate" were these endless channels, De Long thought, "that I am reminded of the maze at Hampton Court."

De Long called it the "skeleton pack" because he thought it resembled an entanglement of bones. A dinosaur graveyard floating upon the slate-blue sea. A reliquary of ice—clean white ribs, winged vertebrae, cracked skulls pocked with eye openings, bleached balls floating loose in their sockets.

For fifteen days they struggled over, through, and around it. Sometimes they would venture for half a day down an enticing lane, only to find that it gradually narrowed and then terminated. Other times they had to haul up on a slab and portage a half mile over to a larger channel. Or they would use chisels and picks and ropes to pry open a large floe piece in order to obtain passage to another neck of water. In this way, they made fitful progress toward the south—one day nine miles, another day five, another day twelve. "Very severe," Danenhower judged this kind of amphibious travel, "but much better than dragging the sleds over the ice." Melville called it "work for a

Titan . . . across pools, ponds, fissures, and hummocks, sinking to all depths from our knees to our necks."

De Long tried to hug the floes but not too closely, for they often had sharp tongues projecting underwater that could ground the boats—or rip a hull apart. The waves constantly gnawed at the ice, honeycombing it with tunnels and hidden voids. "The ice was very much wasted," De Long wrote, "and had numerous holes extending through to the sea." Melville described one floe piece that was "undershot by the action of the waves, which dashed madly over it, the surf flying in the air to a height of twenty feet; and, where the sea had eaten holes upward through its thickness, a thousand waterspouts cast forth spray like a school of whales."

For several days at a time, most of the men would never leave their boat. They sat huddled together, a few pulling at the oars, while others trundled ahead on the nearby ice, scouting the leads. Those down in the hulls of the boats shivered away the long hours, stamping their numb feet in the cold water that sloshed among the floorboards. At mealtimes, they chewed their pemmican or sipped a mug of beef tea that had been boiled from the stores of snow tightly packed into the ribbed recesses of the boats. Though their progress was slow and often drearily dull, the sailors could never really sleep—or even relax, for the boats were so prone to leaks, they had to be bailed frequently.

Not only that, but the three boats were so loaded down with men and provisions that they were dangerous whenever the water turned the least bit choppy. Sometimes the narrow channels opened up into whitecapped bays, on which the boats, said Melville, "capered and scampered like circus horses." De Long, worried that one of the boats would surely capsize, saw no way around it—they would have to reduce their aggregate weight by a third.

So the captain began hunting for things to abandon. He drew up a meticulous inventory of every single object carried by the expedition—every spool of thread, every glob of putty, every scrap of lumber, every hatchet, file, and awl—and then tossed out anything he felt was not absolutely imperative.

But by far the heaviest and most cumbersome objects in his inventory, aside from the wooden dinghy, were the long sleds, the ones with stout oaken runners that De Long had been using to carry the boats. Since leaving Bennett Island, he had been storing the sleds crosswise—that is, laying them athwart the gunwales of the three boats. This gave the effect of big, clumsy wooden wings that often splashed awkwardly in the water and caused the boats to stagger and wallow. "The sleds," said Dr. Ambler, "are a great nuisance towering astern, hold us back and interfere with steering."

It was obvious what De Long had to do. And yet it was a terrible gamble to have to make. In their expeditionary metamorphosis, they would have to commit to becoming entirely aquatic—which is to say, no longer travelers of the ice. They would have to dismantle the sleds and use them for firewood, with the idea that all travel hereafter would be by boat until they reached the coast of Siberia. If they encountered long stretches of ice again, the men would no longer have anything in which to convey the fragile boats; the keels would be irreparably abused as they bumped and banged and skidded across the ice. And besides, trying to drag the heavy boats without any runners would be a nearly pointless struggle for De Long's already exhausted men.

So De Long had to trust that nature would no longer clog their way with any significant expanses of pack. This was a delicate calcula-tion, he realized, as the Arctic summer was ending, the days already growing shorter and darkness slowly returning to the night skies. Still, it was mid-August, and every day they were inching southward, drawing closer to the 75th parallel, which left him room for optimism that the ice would continue opening up.

Then again, it might not. As he knew, Arctic literature was replete with stories of marooned men dying on surprisingly large packs, dur-ing surprisingly warm summers, and at surprisingly southern lati-tudes. The unpredictable Arctic had a way of squeezing in on all sides, capitalizing on any human error. Destroying the sleds, while bringing the men some measure of safety, could also be the very thing that would ensure their deaths.

Using the sleds for firewood had another urgent appeal, however: the stores of cooking alcohol had dwindled to nearly nothing. At least for a few days, this new stack of firewood would obviate the need to burn precious stove fuel. As soon as they were able to stop and haul out on a cake of ice strong enough to support a camp, De Long had Sweetman and Nindemann smash up the boat sleds, as well as the dinghy. The wood would be burned with the utmost economy— only for cooking, not for warmth. That night, as they simmered their modest dinners in crackling flames fueled by the sled wood, a few of the men wondered if they were, in effect, staring at their own funeral pyres.

DE LONG TURNED his attention to the question of the twelve remaining dogs. The problem wasn't so much their weight as their erratic behavior. They were restless in the boats, and every time they squirmed about, water came gushing in at the oarlocks. The dogs were proving a menace. Though he knew something had to be done, De Long agonized. The dogs might be needed again for hauling (though with the sleds destroyed, that seemed doubtful); or, God forbid, they might be needed for protein. A dog lover at heart, De Long ideally wanted to keep the entire dozen, as he put it, "to the end."

But happenstance soon intervened. One day, as the trio of boats eased along the edge of a large floe, four dogs—Smike, Armstrong, Dick, and Wolf—leapt onto the ice and scampered off. It took a while for De Long, who was well ahead in the first cutter, to learn what had happened, and by then it was too late. "Time was too precious," he said, to put a search party on the floe to chase down the dogs and haul them back. So the three boats crept on. Later that night, as the men cooked and ate their dinner, they could hear the "doleful howling" of the stranded dogs echoing over the pack.

A few days later, after other dogs followed suit and bolted, De Long came to the reluctant conclusion that the "most sensible thing" was to shoot *all* the dogs. He didn't want any more of them to stray off, only to suffer and starve on the ice. "Much to my regret," De Long said, he had them "led off to execution." Some of the men were terribly upset to see so many go—Erichsen was especially grieved at the shooting of his beloved Prince.

In the end, De Long elected to spare two: Kasmatka and Snoozer. They seemed to be, said Danenhower, "the only two that had sense enough to remain by us." But Kasmatka proved too clumsy and big, and after a few days he, too, was shot. Having started with forty dogs in Alaska, the expedition was down to one. "I shall keep Snoozer," De Long vowed, "until it becomes perilous to do so."

MEANWHILE, LIEUTENANT DANENHOWER'S eye continued to flare up, especially on sunny days. Although he continued wearing a patch over his left eye and a goggle over the right, his condition was worsening. His bad eye was secreting copious amounts of mucus and there was, said Ambler, an "angry look" to it, with a growing area of inflammation beneath the cornea. The doctor treated it with iodide and quinine and followed its daily progress in his journal: "inflamed," "muddy and congested," "red and congested," "vessels showing on sclerotic." Ambler dreaded the idea of operating to remove Danenhower's eye. The surgeon had neither the proper instruments nor anesthesia. The men would have to hold Danenhower down on the ice, and Ambler would have to remove the eye with a file, with nothing more than a little alcohol to see the patient through his pain.

Oddly, Danenhower continued to deny that his eye was a significant problem, insisting that he should be put in charge of one of the three boats. Although he had been assigned to Melville's whaleboat, his rank was higher than Melville's, and as a Naval Academy graduate and a navigational officer, he felt his experience and authority had been spurned. But De Long's position on Danenhower was clear: As long as he was on Ambler's sick list, Danenhower would not be allowed to lead other men, nor be placed in a position to endanger them.

The navigator fumed and sulked. He nursed conspiracy theories. He uttered threats of reprisal—suggesting that once they were back home, he would use his family connections to have De Long permanently removed from the Navy. Ambler watched Danenhower closely and began to think his behavior was bordering on the delusional. From Danenhower's "very peculiar mind," Ambler wrote, "he has gotten the idea in his head that he is being unjustly treated and has a fixed idea that there is a combination to keep him out of what he considers to be his right. He has given any amount of annoyance in his repeated attempts to get himself placed on duty. I do not consider any man who has the affliction that he has . . . [to be] a fit man to be put in charge of a boat & party of men under any circumstances."

Yet Danenhower was incorrigible. He kept going back to De Long and insisting that he be given charge of Melville's whaleboat. "You are on the sick list, sir," De Long replied. "You are unfit to take command. You cannot see."

Danenhower denied that he was the least bit blind. "I'm perfectly able to perform my duty."

"I cannot let you put other peoples' lives in jeopardy," De Long said, adding that the navigator's continual complaining was "very unofficer-like."

"Am I to take that as a private reprimand?" Danenhower demanded.

"You may take it as anything you please," roared De Long, dismissing him from his tent.

ON AUGUST 20, fourteen days since leaving Bennett Island, De Long and his men were camped on a large crust of ice after a hard night's travel. They were in high spirits, because off to the south, all they could see was unobstructed water. Finally, it seemed, they had come to the end of the skeleton pack, and to the edge of the open sea. Improving things further, during the forenoon, George Boyd cried out to De Long that he had spotted land to the southwest.

De Long, conservative as usual, raised his field glasses and studied the smudgy form himself, harrumphing that he was "not sure about it." But by two in the afternoon, "it showed plainly enough." Examining his Petermann charts, De Long surged with new optimism. There was, he said, "no doubt in my mind that it was the Island of New Siberia"—Ostrov Novaya Sibir, as the Russians called it. It looked to be about twenty miles off. Novaya Sibir was a low-lying island but fairly huge—some four thousand square miles in area. According to Petermann's notes, it was uninhabited but had been visited at times by fossil hunters dispatched by the czar to search for mammoth tusks.

De Long thrilled to the idea: Here, at last, was the known world. For the first time since drifting away from Herald Island two years earlier, De Long was seeing land that existed on a chart.

In anticipation of their first open-sea journey, they spent the rest of the day, and much of the night, patching the hulls, repairing the rigging, redistributing goods, packing snow into the boats, and jettisoning their last ounces of unnecessary things. In his tent that night, De Long wrote, "I hope for good weather tomorrow, when, with God's blessing, I expect to start on our journey afloat."

But the next morning, De Long emerged from his tent and was stunned by what he saw: To the south, there was nothing but ice. Overnight, a powerful shift in the winds had brought the ice fields down from the north and driven them against Novaya Sibir. The way to the island was now completely blocked. There were no lanes, no channels, just a churning expanse of pack. "So much ice has closed in around us," De Long said, "that it looked as if we had never been afloat at all." Melville could not hide his astonishment: "Not a speck of water anywhere," he said. "The winds had crowded the pack together, and made it appear as though we would never get out of the wilderness."

De Long sent a reconnaissance party out to test the condition of the ice. It was hopeless, they found, an unforgiving amalgam of crust and glop. There could be no forward progress through it or over it, either by boat or by sledging. And anyway, De Long had no sleds on which to convey his boats and—besides Snoozer—no dogs with which to haul them.

He couldn't believe their bad luck. A few hours earlier the way had been clear, but now De Long and his men were stuck here, prisoners, once again, of the ice. He had no choice but to stay put and hope for another shift in the winds. Said Melville: "We could do naught but await a favorable change . . . and this we proceeded to do, having accustomed ourselves to make the best of every misfortune." Dr. Ambler began to think a conspiracy was afoot. "The Fates," he said, "seem to be against us."

FOR A DAY, then two days, then three, they remained trapped on the ice. The inaction oppressed De Long. They were wasting precious time while exhausting equally precious supplies—and there was nothing he could *do* about it. Three days became a week, and still they could not budge. With each page of his journal, De Long's anxiety mounted. "Another lost day . . . The day passed in dreary stupidity . . . Another weary day dragged along . . . Seven days have been utterly lost . . . The situation is the same, discouraging, disheartening, consuming provisions without doing work."

Even though De Long put everyone on half rations, their stores were dwindling at an alarming rate. They had plenty of pemmican—some fourteen hundred pounds of the stuff—but everything else was going fast. They ran out of sugar. They ran out of hardtack. They ran out of lime juice. They boiled most of their beef extract. They brewed the last of their coffee. They burned all of the sled firewood. "Our situation worse than ever," Melville said. "Our existence [is] now a mere question of provisions."

They also ran out of tobacco, and this they missed the most. A few men had secret stashes, but for the most part the tobacco had been smoked up. In its place, many had started to smoke a mixture of tea leaves and old coffee grounds, which produced a horrible acrid smell but satisfied some of their cravings. Mainly, it gave them something to do, something to take their minds off their toil and tedium.

At first, De Long scoffed at the faux-tobacco blend, but then, as his own supply petered out, he warmed to the idea. "I expect I shall come [around] to it to-morrow," he wrote, "for my last pipeful of tobacco is to be smoked after supper to-night."

Within a few days, De Long found himself growing fidgety and irritable: "I confess I have been perfectly miserable for want of a smoke." But soon the always cheerful Erichsen came to his aid. The big Dane "tendered me a small packet of the precious article," De Long wrote. "I declined more than a pipeful, but he insisted upon my taking more, saying they had enough for some days in No. 6 tent." De Long accepted the present with profuse thanks, and promptly shared it with Ambler and Nindemann.

After supper that night, De Long sat down to a luxurious smoke. "And now," he said, with a nod to Shakespeare, "Richard is himself again."

A few days later, De Long, having used up Erichsen's gift, finally succumbed to the temptation of ersatz tobacco. "Being miserable all day without something to smoke, I had tea-leaves to-night, and, to my pleasant surprise, got considerable comfort."

THEIR SENTENCE DRAGGED on. Eight days, nine days—and still there was no movement. Actually, that was not precisely true: The sprawling ice jam before them refused to clear, but it *was* moving. The whole swirl of chunky slush on which they were encamped had been drifting all the time, and generally in the right direction: south. Whenever the fog lifted, De Long could see that their position was changing dramatically. Novaya Sibir was now off to the east, but a new island had slid into view, to the southwest.

It was Faddeyevsky, De Long determined, another vaguely charted fragment in the New Siberian archipelago. The uninhabited island had been named after a Russian fur trader, Faddeyev, who had once spent a season there hunting for pelts and had built a tiny hut. De Long realized that the winds and prevailing currents had been funneling their floe piece down into the narrow channel that separated Novaya Sibir and Faddeyevsky. Though trapped all this time, they had in fact made fair progress.

On the ninth day of their stay upon the ice, August 29, an excited Chipp reported to De Long's tent and informed him of a promising lead that had opened up toward the southwest—generally in the direction of Faddeyevsky. At once, De Long broke camp and had all the provisions and boats hauled several hundred yards across the floe to the edge of this new channel. They set up their tents at the water's edge that night, and early the next morning, seeing that the lead had yawned open even farther, De Long had the boats prepared for launch. The channel was aswirl with shards of fast-moving ice, yet after ten days of imprisonment, De Long was eager to try it. "To load boats in such a hell-gate was a ticklish thing," he wrote. But they pushed off from the floe and began their cautious voyage down the channel—hoping that, through its sinuous intrigues, it would somehow lead them to Faddeyevsky.

IT TOOK ALL day, but they wended toward the island, and though shoals complicated their arrival, they eventually beached on Faddeyevsky's desolate shores. Bennett Island had offered its rocky pleasures, but this was the first real soil they had walked on since leaving Alaska. "My relief was great after the strain of the past ten days," De Long said. "To get moss and grass under my feet again warmed me, and my freezing feet got back their usual temperature." They moved from the beach up to a kind of terrace of spongy lichen, where they erected camp and collected a pile of driftwood. "Snoozer tore around in glee, chasing lemmings, whose holes were abundant," said De Long, "while we human beings more seriously sought for eatable game."

The men found deer droppings that were quite fresh, pieces of velvety deer horn, and the tracks of a hare. A flock of black geese winged across the tundra. Another party located a pond, which immediately became their source of drinking water. Newcomb found two huge fossilized bones—he described them as the tibia and fibula of a woolly mammoth. A mile and a half from the place where they landed, Sweetman and Ah Sam discovered a hut tumbling to decay near the bank of a clean rushing stream—it was likely the hut Faddeyev himself had built decades earlier. But there were no signs of recent human presence. When De Long sent several hunters to follow the animal tracks, it was clear the deer had taken off far into the interior, no doubt spooked by the expedition's arrival. The hunters shot a dozen ducks but saw little sense in spending precious time and energy chasing down the deer; the island was too large—Faddeyevsky is more than three thousand square miles—and its boggy tundra was dotted with innumerable ponds and lakes.

So De Long decided to pitch a temporary camp on the night of August 30, then move on. The next morning, they slipped into the bay and hugged the southern coast of Faddeyevsky, heading west. There was no ice to speak of, but the water was often dangerously shallow—the three boats kept running aground on sandbars. From the boats, the men could see that the island teemed with life—ducks, geese, owls, and a few seals were quickly spotted. At around five-thirty p.m., De Long tried to land again on Faddeyevsky's coast to make supper and pitch another camp, but the approach was so rife with shoals he could not get within five hundred yards of the beach.

When darkness fell, it became apparent that they would have to spend the night in their boats—a night, it turned out, that would require nearly constant "tacking and pulling to keep in water deep enough to float us," De Long wrote. "Sleep was impossible for any-body, and we waited in wretched discomfort for the morning's light."

For the next three days, they kept nosing along the island's con-tours, covering some seventy miles of coastline. The twelve ducks that had been shot on Faddeyevsky swished around in the bottom of De Long's cutter—he was saving them for a later feast. The seas were choppy, and De Long found that unless they maintained full speed ahead, the swells would pour over the rails, causing them to lose control of the boats. "As it was," he said, "a sea would come in occasionally, wetting us to the skin and forcing us to bail as well as pump constantly." With each new wave, the men would get a thor-ough dousing. "Ye gods!" wrote Melville. "What a cold bath!"

The second cutter, captained by Chipp, proved the slowest of the three boats, and it kept lagging behind the others. Then it dis-appeared. For forty-eight hours, De Long had no idea what had become of Chipp and his detachment of nine men, which included the beloved ice pilot, Dunbar. De Long and Melville hauled up on a platform of ice and, hoisting black flags from their masts, waited for any sign of Chipp. De Long was sick with worry—Chipp, his right-hand man, his lieutenant, his old friend from their Greenland days. "Anxiety and care seem to be my steady companions now," De Long wrote, his thoughts fixed on Chipp's possible fate, "and they are doubled in intensity."

Late in the afternoon of September 3, De Long heaved a sigh of relief: Chipp's cutter was spotted, skirting the edge of the ice to the north. A cheer went up as the missing men reunited with De Long. "How rejoiced we were to see them!" said Melville. Chipp and his crew had had a horrible time of it. His cutter had grounded against a sandbank and at one point had nearly flooded. Chipp, Dunbar, and all their men looked weak and battered—Dunbar, especially. The whaler was having fainting spells and problems with his balance. Upon examination, Dr. Ambler found that he'd had "an attack of giddiness" and was experiencing heart palpitations. "Dunbar looks quite ill," noted De Long, who saw him "fall out and stagger to one side, when he sat down. I am afraid [he] has suffered more in the second cutter than he will admit. This is indeed serious, for in the hourly excitements no one can tell what may occur."

While Ambler took care of Dunbar as best he could, De Long decided to celebrate the return of Chipp's party by cooking up the dozen ducks he'd been saving. "I feared they would spoil," said De Long, "hence a good dinner was made of them." Over a savory stew, they toasted to their health and vowed never to separate again until they made it to safety.

THE FOLLOWING DAY, September 4, their old foe returned to block their way: Ice. For much of the morning they had to haul the heavy boats over a stretch of what De Long called a "rough and confused pack." Without boat sleds, the keels took the brunt of it, and the bilges were constantly exposed to gouging, thumping blows. "Long strips are peeled off the keel runners," fretted De Long, "and the boats themselves get many a scratch." At one point, De Long plunged through an ice hole up to his chin. Throughout the rest of the day his furs "clung unpleasantly," he said, "chilling me to the bone in spite of the ration of brandy which the doctor gave me."

That night they beached themselves on Faddeyevsky's adjoining island, Kotelny (the two land formations are attached by a low-lying plain). Kotelny is by far the most substantial stepping stone in the New Siberian archipelago and is one of the world's fifty largest islands. It was discovered by a Russian hunter and merchant, Ivan Lyakhov, in 1773, and had been visited by furriers and fossil ivory hunters several times during the early 1800s. Like all the other New Siberians, it was uninhabited.

Enveloped by the island's "candle-snuffer hills," as De Long called them, he and his men had a meager dinner on Kotelny's shore—but at least they found enormous piles of fuel to burn. "Long windrows of driftwood were thrown upon the beach and crowded far back from the watermark by the ice," Melville wrote. Soon they had a roaring fire going. "Though choked by smoke and scorched by sparks," said De Long, "we stood around it and steamed ourselves into partial dryness." It was, thought Melville, "the first really good camp-fire we had enjoyed since leaving the United States. . . . We warmed our fronts, froze our backs, and shriveled up considerable of our saturated garments."

Several of the sticks of flotsam they consigned to the flames bore what Melville called "marks of the friendly axe." This noticeably brightened the mood around camp. Said Melville: "How eloquently such silent signs of civilization spoke to our hearts, recalling distant scenes and friends."

De Long and his men so enjoyed the warming bonfires that they stayed two nights on Kotelny Island. De Long discovered that he was suffering from chilblains, a painful circulatory condition that produced ulcerous sores on his feet that nearly immobilized him. Others had developed incipient frostbite. For weeks, everyone had stayed wet and cold, through and through. Even more than food, what they needed was to get dry and keep warm. De Long probably would have lingered even longer on Kotelny had the hunts been more successful. But hunting was nearly impossible: A blanket of what De Long called "regulation fog" obscured everything and reduced visibility to a matter of yards. The only potential entrées they even got close to were "a few black ducks," said Melville, "paddling shyly about in the open water."

Kotelny offered far happier hunting when it came to artifacts and souvenirs. Many of the men prowled off into the mud hills, like happy kid scavengers. Nindemann brought back a hoop from a fish keg. Herbert Leach produced a perfect mammoth tusk, while others scooped up smaller specimens of elephant ivory. Alexey found a surprisingly well-built log hut, its gaps chinked with mud and rags. He returned with a wooden drinking cup, wooden utensils, and a metal coin, a Russian kopeck dated 1840. Some of these objects—the coin, especially—seemed starkly incongruous here in the misty Arctic. The concept of money, and its profound irrelevance in this lonesome wilderness, amused the men.

The only creatures that seemed to thrive on Kotelny were lemmings, the small burrowing rodents of the Arctic whose annual population cycles veer wildly from overabundance to near extinction and then back again. They must have been at the peak of their cycle, for De Long described them as running around "without number"— occasionally pursued by snowy owls. De Long's campsite was infested with lemmings, their high chirps and shrieks filling the air. The shaggy rodents skittered over everything and found their way into the tents. Wrote De Long: "Mr. Collins evidently had a bedfellow last night, a lemming, for when he went out of the tent this morning, one of these little creatures jumped out of the hood of his fur coat and burrowed his way into the sand like a flash."

ON SEPTEMBER 6, De Long and his men shoved off from Kotelny, but the conditions they faced were deplorable. The breeze had strengthened, whipping the seas into frothy whitecaps, and the swells were studded with wayward chunks of ice. "We came very near being smashed up," said Danenhower. "To have struck one of these ice pieces," Newcomb wrote, "would have been death."

Navigating these menacing waters required more effort than anything these men could have imagined. "Away we pulled for our lives," said Melville. "The sea roared and thundered . . . the sailors, blinded by the wind and spray, pulled manfully at the oars, their bare hands frozen and bleeding; and the boats tossed capriciously about with the wild waves." For the first time since the start of the *Jeannette* voyage, the crewmen were being seriously tested as *sailors,* in the direst and most fundamental sense. Melville was impressed: "Drenched to the skin by the cruel icy seas, the over-taxed men performed wonders."

They sailed day and night through the huge swells, aiming west by southwest. Those unaccustomed to sailing—including Ah Sam and Collins—got terribly seasick. For more than thirty hours, the boats pitched and yawed and, several times, came close to capsizing. The winds were so powerful that De Long had the men double-reef the sails to reduce the area of canvas; this provided stability but also slowed them down considerably. No one slept a wink; everyone stayed vigilant to what Melville called the "multi-form dangers [that] arose constantly before us." The smallest error of the helmsman, he said, "would certainly engulf us."

Melville's whaleboat came closest to disaster. At one point, wrote

Danenhower, "a heavy green sea swept over the whole port side and filled her to the thwarts; she staggered and commenced to settle, but every man with a baler in hand quickly relieved her, and she floated again. I was never frightened before in a boat, but it was a most dangerous and terrible situation. Had another sea boarded us not a man of our party would have been saved."

On September 8—eighty-eight days since the sinking of the *Jeannette*—De Long encountered a solitary floe bobbing sluggishly in the Laptev Sea. Hailing the other two boats, he decided to make for it. "I had pity on the wet and exhausted creatures around me," De Long wrote. They hauled up on the small plate of ice and camped. They were, said Melville, "perhaps the most miserable looking collection of mortals that ever crowded shivering together in a heap." Melville was so addled by the cold that he burst into song just to revive his "drowned and frozen wits." Said Ambler: "I have been so stiff & numb from cramp & cold that at times, except for my brain working, I should not know of my very existence." Yet the doctor was in awe of the men for how stoically they accepted their sufferings. "Everybody is probably in as bad a condition as myself, if not worse," Ambler wrote, "but they all stand it without complaint."

Their position was just south of the 75th parallel, a little more than a hundred miles northeast of Siberian shores. They pitched their tents and peeled off their frozen outer garments. Snoozer curled up on the ice beside the men, who mashed their hunks of pemmican and sipped tea that had been boiled on the alcohol stoves. Scarcely uttering a word, they crawled into their sealskin bags and, as Melville put it, "slept the sleep of the just."

The eight starving hunters formed a skirmish line across the narrow neck of land. With each man clutching a rifle or a shotgun, they marched in unison toward the south. They had spotted a doe and her fawn, and now they were sweeping down the length of this soggy sandbar—"on the warpath," said De Long—confident that they would eventually meet their prey.

Earlier on the morning of September 10, De Long and his men had paused here, on the blustery shores of Semyonovsky Island, a hundred miles northeast of the Siberian coast. De Long had unloaded the hunters on the island's north end and arranged to meet them a few hours later on the south. Their days of island hopping were nearly over—Semyonovsky would be their last stop, the final scrap of land in the New Siberian archipelago, before they would plunge into the wide-open sea to start their dangerous dash for the Siberian mainland.

It was charitable to call Semyonovsky an island. Only a few miles long and an eighth of a mile wide, it was a lonely, low-lying spit of mud half-submerged in the Laptev Sea, with no sign of human presence. The island was eroding so fast that Dr. Ambler predicted that this "mere strip of earth" would "probably disappear in the course of a few years and be only a chain of islets." (He was right: Over the next fifty years, Semyonovsky would steadily wash away, and by the early 1960s, it would disappear; today it is a submerged sandbar primarily known for posing a hazard to ships.) De Long was astonished by the extent of the erosion. "The southern end of this island is worn away almost to a knife-edge," he wrote. "Large masses . . . lie prostrate on the beach [and] there are huge cracks where other land-slides will occur."

Semyonovsky (sometimes spelled Semenovsky) Island was discovered in 1770 by a Russian merchant who followed the tracks of migrating reindeer that led from the Siberian coast across the pack. The doe and fawn De Long's men were now hunting were probably distant descendants of those migrating herds. The men surmised that the mother reindeer had birthed her fawn too late in the season to cross the ice bridge to the mainland, so the two had gotten stranded here for the summer.

The hunters found the two reindeer and fired several times. Though the fawn got away, the doe staggered and was finally felled by an expert shot from Noros. The men dragged her carcass to the edge of a mud cliff and hurled it onto the beach. De Long ordered the boats unloaded, the animal butchered, a bonfire lit, and a meal prepared at once. The meat was roasted, and within an hour, everything had been consumed but the bones and antlers—which they would save for a soup. Even Snoozer got to feast. "The deer dressed about one hundred and twenty pounds," Melville wrote, "and we had each a clear pound of sweet venison, washed down by a quart of tea—a royal gorge, indeed."

One of the men had found a swampy pond from which to drink. Though the water contained no salt, it was, said Melville, "discolored and unpleasant to the taste, savoring of the bog from which it was taken, and being filled with *animalculae* and red grubs." But the men were so pleased with the roaring fire and the afterglow of their venison feast, they didn't care. Said Melville: "When we at last turned in, the wet sleeping-bags troubled us but little, for now we enjoyed the delightful and almost forgotten sensation of being replete and distended with palatable food, a delicious frame of body and mind enhanced by the pleasing prospect of a jolly good soup on the morrow."

They soon dozed off to a long and contented night's sleep. "Our lesser discomforts," De Long wrote, "seemed to fade away before the warmth and security which Semenovski Island afforded."

THE NEXT DAY, September 11, the fawn was spotted at the edge of camp, no doubt looking for its mother. Alexey and a few other hunters took off in pursuit and chased it clear to the other end of the island but were unable to secure it. In the mud hills, the hunters saw the tracks of a large predator—probably a wolf, possibly a bear—and guessed that the fawn had met its fate.

The rest occupied themselves with other errands. Ambler meandered off on a geological foray, finding what he thought was a fossilized mastodon tooth, and Newcomb went on a long stroll in search of birds. Others fanned out over the island, looking in vain for any sign that a rescue party had ever set foot on Semyonovsky in search of the lost *Jeannette*. But most of the men spent the day repairing the boats and getting ready for the challenges of the coming sail. It was a calm, foggy day, the temperature hovering in the low thirties. De Long planned to leave Semyonovsky the following morning. There was much agitated discussion about how the boats would fare over several consecutive days cast in huge seas. They had already been tested enough for De Long to know that the three vessels performed very differently from one another.

De Long's boat, the first cutter, was probably the most stable, but he would be carrying the most men—fourteen, all told—and the largest allotment of provisions, in addition to all the expedition's logs, papers, and scientific specimens. Snoozer would ride with De Long as well. De Long's cutter was twenty feet, four inches from her bow to her transom stern, with a breadth of six feet at her widest point. Like the other boats, she was clinker-built—which meant that the wooden planks of her hull overlapped in the fashion of a clapboard house. She was fastened with copper, pulled six oars, and had a heavy oaken keel. Though the first cutter was slow—"a dull sailor," thought Melville—she was "an excellent sea-boat [that] stood up splendidly to her work."

Melville's craft was a whaleboat, a design slightly different from that of a cutter. Sharply pointed at both ends, she was made for the strenuous action and quick maneuvering required for harpooning whales. At twenty-four feet, four inches, the whaleboat was the longest of the three, and also the fastest when under full sail. Danenhower recalled that the master boatbuilder at Mare Island had told him "she was one of the best fastened boats that he had ever seen, and our experience proved it, for the racket she stood on the journey over the ice was almost incredible." The whaleboat needed constant mending, it seemed, but she was solid in the bones, and Melville felt sure she would hold.

The biggest worry was Chipp's boat, the second cutter. It had already been well demonstrated that she was the slowest in De Long's little fleet. By far the smallest of the three (she was only sixteen feet, three inches from stem to stern), the second cutter was soundly built, but had trouble in heavy seas. De Long sought to compensate for her weaknesses by having the other two boats take on far more than their share of the aggregate load; the second cutter would carry only eight passengers.

Despite the smaller cutter's shortcomings, some of the men favored her for the simple reason that she was the least battered of all the craft. During the long haul over the ice, Chipp's short vessel had rested comfortably, with no overhang, in the cradle of its sled, and so had taken very little abuse. In addition, Chipp's roster boasted some of the finest and most experienced sailors in the expedition—including Dunbar, Sweetman, and Chipp himself. If anyone could see her through peril, these men could.

Nonetheless, De Long brooded about the second cutter, and Chipp, too, began to express reservations. Wrote Melville: "Chipp, for the first time, complained about his boat. Until then she had been the favorite, and indeed was considered sound and efficient." Danenhower, who thought the second cutter was "a very bad sea boat," picked up on Chipp's apprehensions. Though he could hardly see, he and Chipp went out to hunt for grouse that afternoon, and the navigator found that although Chipp "was in better health than usual and was cheerful," he was "not altogether satisfied with the outlook."

On this day, a Sunday, De Long's mood was reflective and guardedly celebratory. He spent a good bit of time reading from his Bible. It was, he noted, the "ninety-first day since the ship was crushed and ourselves thrown out on the ice." After all their hardships, after more than five hundred miles of excruciating ice travel (thousands of miles, if one counted all the backtracking), they had nearly reached the Russian mainland—without losing a single man. Dunbar's heart ailments worried De Long, as did Danenhower's eye, but otherwise, as a lot, they were in remarkably good health. As long as the weather held up, they would leave in the morning.

Sanguine and satisfied with his preparations, De Long wrote a record of their landing on the island and had it buried in the cliff beneath a twenty-foot pole that was dug deeply into the mud.

Semenovski Island, Arctic Ocean

Sunday, September 11, 1881

This record of our arrival at and proposed departure from this island is left here in case of any search being made for us before we can place ourselves in communication with home. The Jeannette, *after drifting two winters in the pack ice, was crushed and sunk . . . in latitude N. 77 degrees 15 minutes, and longitude E. 155 degrees, and the thirty-three persons composing her officers and crew succeeded in reaching this island yesterday afternoon, intending to proceed to-morrow morning toward the mouth of the Lena River in our three boats. We are all well, have no scurvy, and hope with God's aid to reach the settlements on the Lena during the coming week. We have yet about seven days' provisions.*
George W. De Long,
Commanding, U.S. Arctic Expedition.

THEY ROSE AT five the next morning, breakfasted at six, and cast off at seven-thirty. The weather seemed auspicious—seas calm and ice-free, a strong breeze from the northeast, the temperature a mild thirty-one degrees. De Long instructed Melville and Chipp to stay close to him—"within hail," as he put it. Through the morning, they did just that, forming a trim single file and making good progress, covering more than sixteen miles without incident. At one point, Melville signaled that he was having trouble, and the three boats paused alongside a small floe. Melville's whaleboat had apparently thunked against a large piece of submerged ice, which had bashed in a section of her starboard bilge. But it proved a small problem for the ever-resourceful Melville, who was soon able to patch the wound.

At around noon, they stopped at an ice cake for a light lunch of tea and pemmican. Morale was high—"every one jolly," wrote Melville, "in the hope that with our present breeze, should it not grow too heavy, we might be able to reach [Siberia] after one night at sea." While the men filled the boats with snow for drinking water, De Long, Melville, and Chipp paced up and down the floe, conferring with one another about sailing strategies and how they would possibly keep their boats close, given the behavioral differences of the three craft, if the winds picked up.

De Long wanted them to make every effort to sail together. They would be aiming for the delta of the Lena River, specifically for a place marked on the maps as Cape Barkin. The three officers stood together on the ice, poring over a Petermann map of the area. De Long told Melville and Chipp that Cape Barkin was "eighty or ninety miles off, southwest true." From Cape Barkin, De Long said, they would proceed inland, following the river until they came to one of the native settlements. According to his charts and notes, there were numerous such villages all over the delta, and they should have no problem making contact with the inhabitants. They would be safe, he assured them, "as there are plenty of natives there, winter and summer."

But if they should get separated while out on the sea, each boat crew was to fend for itself. They were not to concern themselves with the survival of any other boat until they had secured their own safety. The ultimate goal was to reunite at a larger Lena River village marked on the map as Bulun, which looked to be about one hundred miles upstream from the coast. "Don't wait for me," De Long said, "but get a pilot from the natives, and proceed up the river to a place of safety as quick as you can. Be sure that you and your parties are all right before you trouble yourselves about any one else."

Right now, De Long was concentrating on the immediate sea journey ahead—and a worrisome new turn in the conditions. As he gazed over the ocean, he could see that the breeze had freshened and the seas were building. Weather seemed to be moving in. When he checked his instruments, De Long noticed that the barometric pressure had dropped. If they were to reach Siberia ahead of a storm, they had to make haste.

So the three officers bid farewell and wished each other the best of luck. Then they cast off into seas that had already become, according to Danenhower, "high and spiteful." De Long called out a reminder to stay within hail. Then the three boats cut through the swells, heading southwest.

THE ORDER OF the boats was supposed to be De Long, then Melville, then Chipp.

De Long wanted the formation to look something like a mother goose leading her two goslings, but the thickening weather soon scuttled the plan. Staying within hail proved impossible—staying even within sight was a challenge. Though De Long led off under full sail, her heavy freight caused the cutter to ride so low in the water that the waves broke continuously over the gunwales, slowing her down and thoroughly drenching her fourteen human occupants, most of whom found themselves bailing without stop. (Snoozer, cringing on the floor, soon resembled a wet rat.) Ambler, who was in De Long's boat, complained of "taking seas over our stern and quarter . . . we shipped one sea that nearly swamped us."

Chipp's boat, as predicted, trailed well behind the others, sometimes so far that she nearly slipped from sight. The little craft appeared to be stricken. Every time De Long looked back, Chipp, Dunbar, and the six others in her crew seemed to be struggling in a confusion of flapping sails and laborious maneuvers. As the seas grew throughout the afternoon, Chipp's boat would drop entirely from De Long's view each time she plunged through the trough of a wave. De Long could not imagine how Chipp could survive much more punishment.

Melville's whaleboat, meanwhile, was proving so swift that he had difficulty maintaining his designated position astern of the captain's cutter. Melville tried reefing his sail, and still he kept gaining. As the winds and seas intensified, he found that the attempts to slow his boat were dangerous. The swells, running faster than she was, repeatedly crashed over her stern, nearly overwhelming Melville and the ten other men in his boat.

By early evening, the sea had become fantastically huge. This was now a full-on gale, De Long realized, and it seemed to be growing stronger by the minute. The men in De Long's boat, though holding on for dear life, were faring better than Melville's crew. As wave after wave pummeled the whaleboat, Melville finally signaled to De Long and, pulling up close for a moment, yelled to him, "I must run or else I will swamp!" De Long seemed to wave him on, and Melville shook out his sails. Suddenly, he lurched forward and sprinted far out ahead. De Long could tell that Melville was still having trouble, but at least he was making good speed.

But when De Long looked back, he could see no trace of the second cutter. It had vanished. De Long knew in his heart that Chipp was doomed. Some of De Long's men, studying the horizon, thought they caught a momentary glimpse of a capsized boat surging on the crest of a distant wave, but it had grown so dark, they couldn't be sure. De Long knew he could not go back for his friend; in a gale like this, turning around would mean nearly certain death—and besides, there was not room in his boat for a single extra man, so any rescue was out of the question. If Chipp's cutter had capsized, he and his men would have only a few minutes. The temperature of the water was no more than thirty degrees.

Now, turning to scour the seas ahead, De Long saw nothing of Melville. He, too, had vanished. It was hard to make out anything through the foam and spray and sleet, but from the top of each wave, the men in De Long's boat scanned the gray horizon and could not find a trace. As darkness fell over the Laptev Sea and the storm howled on, De Long and his crew of thirteen men knew they were on their own.

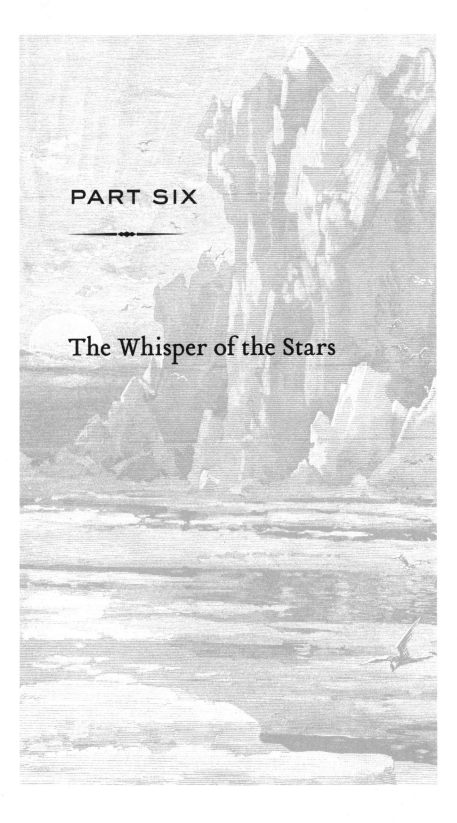

PART SIX

The Whisper of the Stars

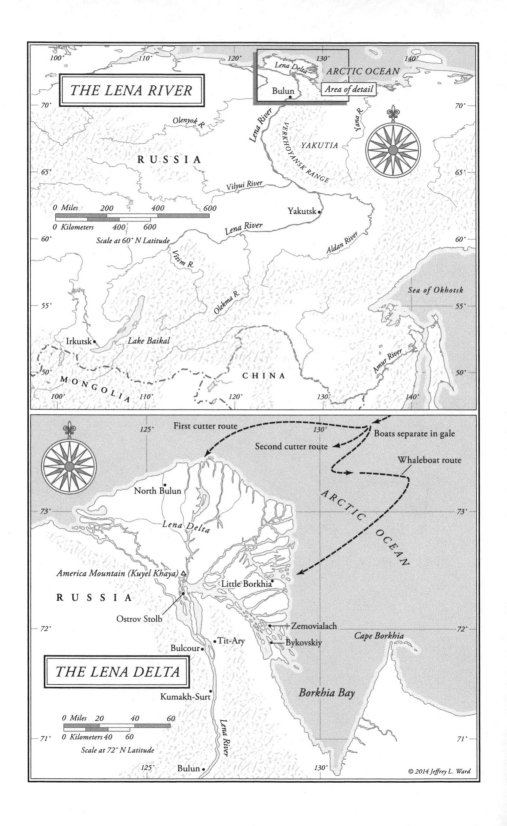

THE LENA RIVER

100° 110° 120° 130° 140°

Lena Delta
Bulun
ARCTIC OCEAN
Area of detail

70°

Olenyok R.
Lena River
Yana R.
VERKHOYANSK RANGE
YAKUTIA

RUSSIA

65°

Vilyui River
Yakutsk

0 Miles   200   400   600
0 Kilometers   400   600
Scale at 60° N Latitude

60°

Lena River
Aldan River

Izim R.

55°

Sea of Okhotsk

Olekma R.

Irkutsk   Lake Baikal

50°

Amur River

MONGOLIA   CHINA

100° 110° 120° 130° 140°

125° 130°

First cutter route
Boats separate in gale
Second cutter route
Whaleboat route

North Bulun

ARCTIC OCEAN

73°

Lena Delta

America Mountain (Kuyel Khaya) △
Little Borkhia

RUSSIA

Ostrov Stolb

Zemovialach
Bykovskiy
Cape Borkhia

72°

Tit-Ary
Bulcour

THE LENA DELTA

Borkhia Bay

Kumakh-Surt

Lena River

0 Miles   20   40   60
0 Kilometers   40   60
Scale at 72° N Latitude

71°

125°   Bulun   130°

© 2014 Jeffrey L. Ward

———————●●●———————

My dear Papa: How are you? I am taking music lessons and I go to school here. . . . I will send you my examination papers. I am trying very hard to surprise you when you get back. . . .

We must have a nice home of our own some day. Mamma is saving all her money to buy one.

We miss you very much and want you back soon . . . I pray for you every night and ask God to bless you and make you successful and bring you home safe to Mama and

Your loving daughter,
Sylvie De Long.

34 · LUCKY FOURTEEN

All through the night, the gale battered De Long's boat, tossing it about in tremendous seas. One gust ripped the mainsail in two. Another knocked down her mast. De Long and Nindemann began to jury-rig a solution but soon realized there was no use even trying to navigate in this blasting wind. So they turned the bow into the storm and rode it out as best they could.

Nindemann was put in charge of fashioning a sea anchor. He rather ingeniously constructed something from several oars, a water cask, and spare pieces of lumber, weighing it down with a pickax. The contrivance helped provide stability, but still the water kept pouring into the boat, worrying the bailers all night. One particularly gigantic wave left the cutter "full up to the thwarts," Nindemann said. "Another little sea would have swamped her." It was the most harrowing night they had ever experienced. "Gale increased," jotted Ambler, "we became a wreck, taking in water, wallowing in the trough of the sea the whole night. We got her partially baled out before she caught another . . . Baling, baling all the time."

At dawn, the gale still had not expended its fury. In the muted light, De Long kept a restless eye on the horizon. There was no sign of land; nor was there any sign of Chipp or Melville. The men in De Long's boat spent whatever idle moments they had fretting over the fate of their shipmates. Everyone now seemed resigned to the belief that the sister boats had capsized and that both crews—nineteen men, in all—were dead. One dog and fourteen men were packed into the first cutter: De Long, Ambler, Nindemann, Noros, Erichsen, Kaack, Görtz, Collins, Ah Sam, Alexey, Walter Lee, Dressler, Nelse Iverson, and Boyd. Miserable though they were, they now viewed themselves as the lucky ones.

Throughout the day, all they could do was bob helplessly on the cold gray swells and wait for a break in the weather. At around six in the evening, it seemed to come. With a strange suddenness, the winds abated, and De Long's spirits warmed. But the seas refused to lie down; indeed, they seemed as menacing as ever. So the men were forced to spend yet another night cowering in the boat, rolling on the huge sea, their nerves tensed by the frequent smack of the spray. "Utter misery," Collins wrote. "Hopeless except in the mercy of Almighty God, we sat jammed together."

"No sleep for 36 hours," Ambler wrote. "God knows where we went during the night." At least they had something to turn their gaze heavenward. The clouds had scudded away, and in their place the moon and stars shone crisp and bright. From time to time, auroras billowed across the blue bowl of the sky.

By the next morning, September 14, the seas had moderated enough to allow them to resume the journey. When De Long asked the crewmen if they had anything that could be fashioned into a sail, Nindemann produced a hammock and an old sled cover. Görtz and Kaack pulled out sewing needles and got to work stitching the two articles together into a fair approximation of a mainsail. De Long ordered the sea anchor pulled in and dismantled, while Nindemann repaired the broken mast. Soon they stepped the mast, hoisted the improvised sail, and were on their way again.

This should have been cause for elation, but most of the men—De Long especially—were in no condition to celebrate. The captain's chilblains had returned, and he could no longer take the helm. He complained that he couldn't feel his feet and had what Ambler described as "a nervous chuckle in his throat." De Long propped himself up in his sleeping bag in the stern of the boat, drank some brandy, and tried to write in his journal, but he found that impossible, too—he couldn't feel his hands.

Erichsen, though his feet were also in bad shape, gamely took the helm, and they sailed through the afternoon and all night. At about ten o'clock the following morning, September 15, Nindemann stood up in the stern sheets and spied some low smudges on the horizon that looked to him like land. He reported this to De Long, who was still down in the boat, nursing his hands and feet. The captain seemed doubtful, and when Ambler stood up to look, he couldn't see anything. But a few hours later, the land burst into full view—and it was clear to all that this was not an illusion.

Siberia! The mainland of Asia . . . the delta of the mighty Lena River. How many times over the past three months had they doubted that they would ever reach it? For the first time since they had begun their retreat, they had a visible reason, a reason right in front of them, to believe that they might be saved.

There was a problem, though. Standing at the helm, Erichsen failed to see anything that looked like a true mouth to the river, an artery, a logical inlet into the delta. Not only that, but studying the intervening waters, he could see that a collar of young ice was forming off the coast, building at the place where the outflow of the Lena River found equilibrium with the larger currents of the ocean.

Within a few hours, they began to encounter this new obstacle. It was freshwater ice—recently formed, brittle, fragile, no more than a quarter inch thick. At first they could easily ram through it. But the next morning, September 16, they got stuck, and they had to use their oars to break the ice apart so they could worm their way through the slots and channels.

This technique worked until a new problem abruptly asserted itself: The boat ran aground. Although they were three miles from land, they were stuck fast in the mud. The tidal flats here were less than two feet deep. De Long and his men had come firmly to rest in the long, silty outsurge of one of the greatest rivers on earth.

THE LENA RIVER originates nearly three thousand miles to the south of the Arctic Ocean, in a mountain range near Lake Baikal in the deep interior of Russia, not far from the border with Mongolia. As the river flows through the forested solitudes of Yakutia, it picks up tributary after tributary—the Kirenga, the Vitim, the Olekma, the Aldan, the Vilyui. The Lena is the world's eleventh-longest river, draining the world's ninth-largest watershed, a boggy, mosquitoey swath of tundra and taiga that measures more than 960,000 square miles. The amount of sediment carried by the Lena is extraordinary—and the river's enormous power discharges a plume of silt and debris more than fifty miles out into the Arctic Ocean.

The Lena, like only a few of the world's largest river systems, flows northward, toward a mostly frozen sea. In the fall, it begins to freeze first at its mouth, not at its source, which means that it develops a natural barrier against the force of its own massive current. As winter approaches in the Arctic, the river continues to flow with unchecked power, until it meets the ever-thickening plug of ice at its lower reaches.

The water's only response is to spread out, frantically seeking other paths to the sea. In other words, the ice distorts and magnifies the tendency all rivers have of fanning out at their mouths. The pressures that build behind the Lena's ice dam become so tremendous that the river splays over more than eleven thousand square miles. This riot of swollen currents creates one of the largest and most complicated deltas in the world.

From the air, the Lena delta looks rather like the cross section of an enormous tumor that bulges far out into the Laptev Sea from the Siberian mainland. Inside this protruding mass, 125 miles in width, is a confusing mesh of branched streams twisting and threading across sandy flats pocked by thousands of ponds and lakes and oxbow swamps. The delta has more than fifteen hundred islands—though that number changes all the time. The river, as it pushes through this morass of alluvium, divides into seven main branches, which, in turn, subdivide into scores and scores of lesser ones, an array of channels that redirect themselves from season to season as they course like capillaries toward the Arctic Ocean. The river's assiduous probing continues until early winter, when the weather finally turns so cold that this titanic natural plumbing project backs up entirely—freezing solid all three thousand miles upstream, creating a superhighway of ice.

A report that would come out in 1882 would note, "No chart had been laid down of this desolate region, and indeed it would seem impossible to make any which would not be falsified by the changes which every fresh season brought." Petermann's map was the only one that had been published with any level of detail, but it was largely hypothetical and riddled with major errors. His map showed eight mouths to the delta, when in fact there were more than two hundred—and the few place-names, landmarks, and villages specified on his map were either grossly misplaced or didn't exist at all.

This was the utterly bewildering landscape that De Long and his men approached on the afternoon of September 16, 1881. They were three miles out from the delta, yet they were already stuck, grounded on the river's massive deposits of silt.

When De Long stood up to assess the problem, only one solution came to mind. He had everyone crawl out of the boat to lighten her load, so that she would ride a few inches higher in the water. The men, wading in the riffling currents, gathered around the cutter and began to guide her, sometimes shove her, toward land. Only Snoozer and a few disabled men remained in the boat.

Through the clear, shallow water, the wading men could see that the congealed beds of silt on which they oozed along had been brushed into ornate patterns by the play of the currents. Small fish darted this way and that. The water varied between one and a half and four feet in depth but generally became shallower the closer they drew toward land. The mud sucked at their boots, sometimes pulling them clear off their feet. In frustration, some of the men hurled their mukluks into the cutter and waded barefoot.

Often the boat ran aground, forcing the crew to heel her over and angle the bow toward a more promising channel. It was backbreaking labor, made more unpleasant by the cold of the river, which soon turned their feet and legs numb. While most of the men grunted and strained around the gunwales of the boat, others waded ahead, wielding oars to smash the young ice and scouting the best path toward land.

Throughout the day, they made only halting progress, advancing perhaps a mile. They could move only when the tide was in—at low tide the boat sat stuck in the slough. By late afternoon, said Nindemann, "everyone was pretty well played out." They crawled back into the boat with Snoozer and shared a drab dinner of beef tongue. Afterward, Ambler asked everyone to take off their boots so he could examine their feet. What the doctor saw greatly alarmed him. A day of wading in the frigid water had come at a tremendous cost. The men's feet were badly swollen and had developed a sickening bluish pallor. Ambler feared that frostbite was rampant among the crew. Boyd, Erichsen, Collins, Ah Sam, and Captain De Long were in the worst shape, but everyone's extremities had suffered.

The shallow water had grown quite choppy, "washing in the boat all the time," said Nindemann, "wetting everybody," and rendering their sleeping bags "not fit for use." Hunkered down and shivering on the curved floor of the boat, the men had what De Long called "a most miserable and uncomfortable night." The cutter lay pinned on the Lena's shoals, occasionally nodding in the shifting ebb and flow of current and tide.

EARLY THE NEXT morning, De Long and his men resumed their forward struggle. By midday they had advanced only a half mile across the mazes of water and silt. The situation was diabolical; it seemed as though the land was teasing them. It lay barely a mile and a half off, and yet they could not reach it. De Long feared they would never get ashore—and even if they did, that their feet would surely freeze in the process.

He was thus forced into a Hobson's choice: They would have to abandon the cutter on the shoals and wade to the beach with all their things. De Long had wanted to keep the boat by any means necessary, knowing they would need it to navigate up the river. But he had now come to believe that the boat would kill them before it could play any role in their salvation. They would have to leave it here.

Piling their belongings high in their arms, they tromped toward the shore in a long column, with Snoozer struggling and splashing among them. Nindemann and Noros, who were the strongest of the fourteen men, led the way. They guided a makeshift raft, twined together from oars and odd pieces of lumber, that bore the pemmican and other heavy articles.

De Long, clutching some of the *Jeannette*'s logs and journals, staggered at the back with the worst of the frostbitten. These folio-sized books, though extremely burdensome, had become fetish-like objects for the captain. They were all that was left of the *Jeannette*'s expedition, the only record of their voyage and the only tangible proof of their exploratory and scientific accomplishments. He would hold onto them at all costs—"as long as I have men to carry them."

As they marched across the mud flats, the water came up to their knees, sometimes to their waists, often in a powerful current that swished around their thighs with every straining stride. Even as the water grew shallower, the men could not raise their benumbed legs high enough to break through the veneer of young ice; they simply had to push through it, lacerating their shins until they bled. Snoozer floundered so badly that Alexey picked him up and carried him most of the way on his shoulders.

A little more than an hour later, Nindemann and Noros shoved their raft onto dry land. One by one, the twelve others hobbled in from the tidal flats to join them. Sending up exhausted cheers, they assembled on the beach—dazed, elated, relieved to have crossed this remarkable threshold. They were now standing on the continent of Asia. From the place of the *Jeannette*'s sinking, they had covered nearly a thousand miles—though most of the men, having back-tracked multiple times across the ice cap to haul belongings, actually had trekked a distance in excess of twenty-five hundred miles. Their odyssey had ended one phase and was now beginning an entirely new one. Whatever obstacles might lie ahead, salt water and ocean ice pack would not be among them. Their metamorphosis was complete. Having been creatures of the ice, then of the sea, they were now creatures of the land.

The beach was desolate. A cluttered line of driftwood followed the contour of what looked to be a stagnant river channel. A few seagulls wheeled in the sky. Freezing drizzle slanted sideways in the stiff sea breeze. It was too overcast for De Long to take a positional reading, so he could not determine precisely where they were. He saw no sign of Melville or Chipp, no sign of humans at all—no artifacts, footprints, or dwellings. This place seemed as godforsaken and as lonely as any of the New Siberian Islands.

This surprised De Long. He could only surmise that they had come ashore along some barren back channel of the river, one that Petermann had not mapped. Petermann's charts and notes indicated that there were numerous settlements throughout the delta and that the mouths of the Lena were often busy with small-boat traffic. De Long had been assured that they would meet natives quickly—this was the main reason he had chosen to aim for this point along the Siberian coast.

But Petermann's information was almost entirely wrong. Native Yakuts and other local tribesmen did venture out to the northern reaches of this part of the delta, but only in small groups, and only for a few weeks during the summer. Living out of crude huts, they trapped foxes and hunted reindeer and fished, much as they had for centuries. By mid-September, however, they always returned to their villages far upriver, to escape the dangerous floods that built up behind the seasonal formation of Arctic ice.

De Long, then, had arrived a week too late. "We must look our situation in the face," he gravely wrote, "and prepare to walk to a settlement."

Unbeknownst to De Long, there *was* one large village close to the coast, on the northwestern edge of the delta. It was called North Bulun, a settlement of a hundred people situated on ground high enough to avoid the Lena's seasonal flooding. If De Long had landed only eight miles farther to the west, he would have struck a clear branch of the river that would have led him straight to North Bulun within a day. He and his men would never have had to leave their boat. But he had no way of knowing this. Neither the channel nor the village was on Petermann's map.

THOSE WHO WERE able to walk at all waded back to the grounded cutter for a second load, then a third. As night fell, the men collected a gigantic pile of driftwood and soon had a brilliant bonfire going on the beach. They hung their drenched furs and undergarments out to dry and stood around half-naked, trying to beat and squeeze and knead their insensate limbs back to some approximation of life.

Dr. Ambler was appalled at the condition of the men's feet. In most of them, the signs of frostbite were apparent—purple blisters, waxy skin, nerve damage, the first signs of tissue necrosis. "Everybody was badly frozen," said Nindemann, but the worst were Collins, Boyd, Erichsen, and Ah Sam. The Chinese cook crawled into his sleeping bag and moaned in agony.

Ambler was most worried about Erichsen. The Dane's legs were horribly swollen, his calves had turned rock hard, and his feet were splotched with hideous blisters, which, when Ambler lanced them, spurted a bloody yellow serum. Ambler dressed Erichsen's feet with carbolated petroleum jelly and a bandage of cotton batting and propped him up beside the fire.

While most of the group tried to recuperate around the flames, Nindemann and Noros kept working. In the pitch dark, they waded back to the boat to retrieve a few more articles. An hour later, they returned and dumped the stuff on the beach; then they circled back and did it *again*.

These staunch men seemed almost superhuman—their feet impervious to wet and cold, their circulatory systems robust beyond understanding, an apparently different kind of blood pumping through their veins. No one could keep up with them. "Going out to the boat it was dark," Nindemann said, "and we could not see the fire or the beach; but we felt our way back again through the broken, young ice." De Long was continually amazed by these two men—Nindemann especially. The captain had already made a note to recommend the German for a Congressional Medal of Honor when he had stemmed the flood in the *Jeannette*'s hold; now he seemed worthy of another commendation.

Nindemann and Noros did not get to bed until midnight. But they fell asleep contentedly, seemingly unaffected by their amphibious labors across the freezing tidal flats.

ON SEPTEMBER 19, having reorganized themselves and buried all their inessential belongings—including papers, chronometers, and natural history artifacts—in a cache marked by a tent pole stuck in the sand, De Long and his men prepared to march south over the wastelands of the delta. With only a few days' worth of food left, De Long knew they had to find a way out of this quagmire of mud and sand and water and locate the main channel of the Lena. He read to the men a passage from the Gospel according to Matthew:

> "Therefore take no thought, saying, What shall we eat? Or, What shall we drink? or, Wherewithal shall we be clothed . . . But seek ye first the kingdom of God, and his righteousness; and all these things shall be added unto you. Take therefore no thought for the morrow: for the morrow shall take thought for the things of itself. Sufficient unto the day is the evil thereof."

Dr. Ambler, who'd been overwhelmed with treating so many purpled and frostnipped feet, was pessimistic about their chances of reaching a settlement. "Our outlook at this rate is a poor one," the doctor wrote. "We must move on & get to the river."

De Long, though he could hardly walk, put a more hopeful gloss on their prospects. The captain remained as resolute as ever. In the cache near their campsite, he had left this record in a discarded instrument box:

Monday, 19th of September, 1881.

Lena Delta.
   The following named fourteen persons belonging to the Jeannette landed here on the evening of the 17th inst., and will proceed on foot this afternoon to try to reach a settlement on the Lena River: De Long, Ambler, Collins, Nindemann, Görtz, Ah Sam, Alexey, Erichsen, Kaack, Boyd, Lee, Iverson, Noros, Dressler. A record was left [on] Semenovski

Island buried under a stake. The thirty-three persons composing the offi-cers and crew of the Jeannette *left that island in three boats on the morn-ing of the 12th inst. (one week ago). That same night we were separated in a gale of wind, and I have seen nothing of them since. My boat made the land in the morning of the 16th inst., and I suppose we are at the Lena Delta. After trying for two days to get inshore without grounding, or to reach one of the river mouths, I abandoned my boat, and we waded ashore, carrying our provisions and outfit with us. We must now try with God's help to walk to a settlement. We are all well, have four days' pro-visions, arms and ammunition, and are carrying with us only the ship's books and papers, with blankets, tents, and some medicines; our chances of getting through seem good.*

George W. De Long, Commanding

My darling husband—

I have to keep a brave and hopeful appearance to those around me. I cannot worry them with my troubles. To Sylvie I want to be cheerful. She cannot understand the situation and I do not want her to. I do not think I really knew before how dearly and deeply I love you, and I cannot understand how it is I am willing to make such unladylike declarations now, for you know my characteristic reserve. But I know you are longing for love and affection as much as I am.

It is evening now; I am writing in the library. Little Sylvie is in bed fast asleep, having said her prayers for her father's health and safety. There is a blazing fire in the grate, the two dogs are stretched out on the fur rug in front of it. How would you like to spend the evening with me? Or is it pleasanter where you are? I suppose I mustn't tease you—not until we meet, and I can judge how much teasing you can stand.

Emma

The castaways marched for two days across the soggy labyrinths of the delta, nagged by worries that they might be on the wrong course. They could not move in a straight line. They were forever reaching for some other, drier bank, some more reliable tongue of land, some clearer clue that might lead them out of this malign wilderness. They could never be sure whether the river they were following was *the* river—not some subsidiary stream that might fray or peter out into an impassable bog. On Petermann's chart, this country was labeled SWAMP OVER ETERNALLY FROZEN LAND.

A few hog-backed mountainous forms bulged in the far distance, hovering over intervening patchworks of water of every description: meandering canals, brackish ponds, expansive bays, channels stagnant and channels swift-moving. All of it was turning to ice. The natives and animals knew that it was time to quit this place—in fact, they were already gone. Every instinct had told them that much more ice was coming, and the ice would cause the floods, and the floods would bring smashing restructurings of the existing ice. Such upheaval arrived like clockwork each year. The few dilatory ducks and geese that could be seen from a distance were gathered in flocks as if preparing to migrate. At this point, any animal that was left out here, whether avian or mammalian, was a vagrant, a laggard, as lost and out of place as De Long and his men.

It was a severe country, a land that seemed better suited for mammoths, saber-toothed tigers, and woolly rhinos, a Pleistocene tundra

on a fantastic scale. All along the active channels lay a cluttered fringe
of bleached gray wood that had floated a thousand miles downriver
from where there *were* trees in the green forests of the Russian taiga.
De Long had no choice but to follow the river channels where the
timber was collected—he could not stray far from this abundant
source of heat, any more than a desert traveler could stray from a life-
giving stream.

In some ways, it was the worst time of year to be tromping over
this watery maze. In summer, one could walk over much of it and
raft over the rest. In winter, all the streams and channels would be
frozen solid, creating highways that, despite the killing cold, could
be traversed with relative ease. But this was something in the middle,
an in-between time that stymied movement. The accumulating snow
had begun to obscure the land's clues and patterns, and the ice now
skimming over the river channels was not yet strong enough to sus-
tain a man's weight. It was freezing cold, but with none of the cold's
advantages.

At least there were no mosquitoes. During the peak of summer,
the pests tormented every warm-blooded creature that had the temerity to trespass across the Lena delta. Mosquitoes, swarming clouds of
them, were known to bring down reindeer and drive men to madness.
De Long had missed the insects by no more than two weeks.

As they marched, De Long worried most about the frostbite victims. Boyd and Ah Sam were in bad shape, but they seemed to be
improving. Erichsen's condition, however, was deteriorating. The
last two days of traveling had left him in utter agony. Even though
Nindemann had carved a crutch for him out of driftwood, Erichsen could only hobble along, one awkward shuffle at a time, his eyes
pooling with tears. The men thought it ironic that frostbite would
afflict him the most seriously, he being the only Scandinavian in the
group. Besides, they had come to think of Erichsen as invincible.
"He's as tough as well-tanned leather," Collins had written in one of
his rhymes, "and worth any common three men rolled together." The
Dane was a big, affable man, with a stout constitution and a sunny
disposition, a man so helpful to other people that his comrades were
now slow to recognize how serious his situation was.

During a low moment the previous day, Erichsen had sat down
on the snow-dusted tundra and refused to budge. "I can't go on!" he
cried. *"I can't go on!"* When Nindemann came to his aid, Erichsen
implored him to go away. He would stay there and die; he didn't want

to hold the others up anymore. Nindemann told his friend not to give up. They would make it, he assured the Dane, and soon enough they would all be celebrating in St. Petersburg. But Erichsen roared back, "Go all the way to Petersburg if you want—I can't go any further!"

De Long and Dr. Ambler gathered around Erichsen and eventually coaxed him to stand up and start walking again. But De Long was alarmed, writing, "His condition is serious indeed."

Just how serious became apparent that night after dinner, when Ambler removed the bandage from Erichsen's right foot. The doctor was aghast at what he saw: A large hunk of putrefied flesh from the ball of his foot sloughed off and fell on the ground. Ambler said nothing to Erichsen about this. He discreetly swept it up and then busied himself with dressing the wound. But the doctor had seen a bit of exposed bone. Shaken, he finished wrapping Erichsen's foot, then went off to confer with De Long.

Erichsen had not gotten a good look at his foot, but he knew something was very wrong. He turned to Nindemann in confidence. "Nindemann," he asked, "do you know anything about frostbites?"

Nindemann, who had experienced frostbite in Greenland, tried to answer matter-of-factly. "Yes," he said. "When it first comes on, the flesh turns blue and then black."

Erichsen thought about that for a while, then said, "When the doctor took off the bandage, I saw something dropping from under my foot."

Nindemann could not bear to tell him the truth. "Erichsen, I guess you've been dreaming."

"No," the Dane insisted, worry spreading over his face. "I'm certain of it. I saw something drop from my foot."

ON THE AFTERNOON of September 21, two days after leaving the coast, De Long and his column of men spotted something in the distance that stirred their hearts. Ahead, along a bend of the river, stood two wooden dwellings side by side. One was old and dilapidated, but the other seemed of recent construction. To De Long they appeared more than just crude summer huts, likely "intended for a prolonged residence." Everyone was seized by the same fervent thought: Could they be occupied?

Those marching in the vanguard—Alexey, Nindemann, and Noros—raced ahead. They creaked open the doors but, to their dismay, found both structures empty. There were fresh ashes in the fireplaces, though, and from the condition of the premises, Nindemann concluded that the occupants, whoever they were, had quit the place no more than two weeks earlier. Ambler thought the huts were "in tolerable repair," and inside, the men found a checkerboard, wooden forks, pencil stubs, and "evidences" said De Long, "of the use of tools by somewhat skilled workmen." Nearby was a trap with a fox's head still in it—though the body, said De Long, "had been eaten or cut off close to the neck." Other structures, apparently for hanging and drying meat, could be seen along the river.

Where were the huts' occupants? This was obviously a hunting-and-trapping camp of some kind, but it had the feel of being fairly well established. Could this be the settlement marked on De Long's chart as Tscholbogoje? He shuddered at the thought. What if *all* the places identified on his map as "villages" were nothing more than abandoned hunting lodges? It was "an important question," wrote De Long, "for if this pair of huts make a 'settlement,' our chances of keeping on successfully are very slim indeed."

If this *was* Tscholbogoje, De Long calculated, then he was more than eighty miles away from the next likely settlement on his chart. He did not think his men could go that far. They only had two days' pemmican rations left, he noted, and had "three lame men who cannot make more than five or six miles a day." The disabled trio—Ah Sam, Boyd, and especially Erichsen—left the captain in a quandary. "Of course I cannot leave them," he wrote, "[but] they certainly cannot keep up with the pace necessary."

So De Long formed a plan: They would stay the night in the huts. In the morning, he would send two of his strongest men ahead in hopes of finding a settlement and securing help. All the others would stay here, using the dwellings as a base camp while awaiting rescue. In the relative warmth of the huts, Ah Sam, Boyd, and Erichsen at least stood a chance of healing enough to allow them to walk again should no help arrive within a week.

That afternoon, the men collected driftwood, and soon fires were burning in the huts. Close by, Nindemann found a dead gull that had been caught in a fox trap baited with fish. Ah Sam was promptly handed the bird to make a stew, but when he began to pluck it, he found that it was completely rotten.

De Long sent Alexey out with a Remington to hunt for game while there was still light. He prayed that Alexey would have good fortune—if not, the captain knew, they would soon starve. "Unless Providence sends something in our way," De Long wrote, they would have no choice but to eat Snoozer. After that, they were out of options. De Long punctuated his journal with an unsettling question: "And when the dog is eaten—?"

THAT NIGHT AT about nine o'clock, Alexey returned to the huts. He knocked on the doors and stirred the men, most of whom had drifted off to sleep. He had good news—in fact, he was holding good news in his arms: the haunch of a freshly killed animal. "Captain," Alexey said excitedly. "We got two reindeer. Three miles from here." He had brought in this hindquarter and two deer tongues as proof. "By strategy unsurpassed," De Long wrote, Alexey had "crept upon a herd, and at twenty-five yards' distance dropped two. Well done, Alexey! The darkest hour *is* just before the dawn."

The rest of the meat could be gathered in the morning, but this was cause for immediate celebration. De Long ordered up a meal to be cooked. Roused from their sleep, the joyous men carved up the deer and within an hour were feasting on venison steaks.

The next morning, De Long sent Nindemann, Alexey, and five other men to haul in the two deer carcasses, and they spent the next two days consuming the meat while Ambler did his best to nurse Erichsen, Ah Sam, and Boyd back into marching condition. Having so much fresh meat on hand changed De Long's plans; he decided against sending two men ahead to find a settlement. For now, they would all stay together. "We can remain here a day or two to let our sick people catch up," De Long wrote, "and while living upon deer meat can search for more to cook and carry with us."

Alexey had no more luck finding deer, however, and after two days, De Long decided to resume the march south. He was reluctant to leave the snug warmth of the dwellings—with the fires going, his thermometer had consistently shown a temperature of seventy degrees Fahrenheit inside his hut—but they had to keep moving. Erichsen seemed to be faring better, and Ah Sam and Boyd were nearly healed. De Long left a rickety Winchester rifle in one of the dwellings, as a "surprise for the next visitor." Before departing, De Long wrote a record, translated into six languages, and placed it inside one of the huts, with a request that its finder please forward it to the secretary of the United States Navy.

Arctic Exploring Steamer Jeannette
At a Hut on the Lena Delta
Believed to be near Tcholhogoje

Saturday, 24th of September, 1881

The following-named persons, fourteen of the officers and crew of the Jeannette, reached this place on September 21, on foot, from the Arctic Ocean. We shot two reindeer, which gives us an abundance of food for the present, and we have seen so many more that anxiety for the future is relieved. Our three lame men being now able to walk, we are about to resume our journey, with two day's rations deer meat and two days' rations pemmican and three pounds of tea.

George W. De Long

FOUR DAYS LATER, De Long and his men stumbled upon another hut, this one large enough to hold everyone. To De Long, it seemed like "a palace," though back at home, he guessed, they would deem it a "dirty hovel, unfit for a dog." The hut was built high on a hill above a broad stretch of river, and, like the previous two huts, it seemed to have been recently occupied. Judging by the "fresh embers and meat scraps" found around the place, De Long thought it could have been used as recently as the previous night. Nearby, Alexey spotted moccasin tracks in the snow that he judged to be only a day or two old. A few miles away, he and Nindemann found a tiny hut that contained a fish that was still fresh.

De Long tried to get a fix on their location. By his best guess, they were nearing the end of the delta and drawing close to a place marked on his chart as Sagastyr. Whether Sagastyr was a settlement or just an abandoned hut—perhaps *this* one—he could not know. He was starting to realize how completely sketchy his map was. "It is hard," he wrote, "to make the chart reconcile with the country."

De Long had no idea where he was. But these moccasin tracks—and two more sets of footprints found the next day—fed a hope in all the men that a settlement might be nearby. Who were these people who had left their tracks in the snow? At times, De Long had a strange feeling that he was being followed and watched. This was a ghost country, one whose inhabitants would not reveal themselves. He speculated that survivors from Chipp's boat or from Melville's had already reached a settlement and had initiated a search. "If Chipp or Melville got through," De Long wrote, "they would naturally send back to look for us." This, he thought, might be the explanation behind the fresh footprints: Maybe people were out looking for them, even now.

With this possibility in mind, De Long ordered a signal fire built on the highest part of the promontory and erected a makeshift flag-pole (made from driftwood), with a black blanket serving as a flag. For the next few days, they would stay in the hut and do everything they could to draw attention to themselves. Wrote Ambler: "God grant that our smoke or fire may be seen by some party who can give us assistance."

Ambler thought the hut was "a godsend" as "all of us are more or less used up." Everyone was in dire need of rest. The past four days had been a horrendous trudge. They had camped out each night in temperatures reaching close to zero, with large scraps of tent fabric thrown over them, said De Long, "like tarpaulins over merchandise." They had plunged through ice too many times to recount, and had nearly capsized while crossing a wide, swift river channel in a precari-ous makeshift raft. But for now they were safe again, and at least they had plenty to eat. The day before, Alexey had killed a big buck, just as De Long was noting that their food supply had dwindled to their last rations of pemmican.

"I need hardly say how great the relief was to my overstretched mind," the captain wrote of Alexey's bounty. "Had [Alexey] failed, our provisions would consist of poor Snoozer." De Long had come to see the hand of God behind these timely encounters with game and shelter: "If ever Divine Providence was manifested in behalf of needy and exposed people, we are an instance of it. All that I need to make my present anxiety *nil* is some tidings of the two boats and their occupants."

That was hyperbole, of course. The captain had a long list of other worries—at the top of which remained Erichsen. The past four days had canceled any improvement he had made while recuperating at the previous hut. Now he was in pitiful shape. After consulting with Ambler, De Long wrote in his journal, "The ulcer in Erichsen's foot has sloughed away so much of the skin as to expose the sinews and muscles. The doctor fears that he may have to amputate one half, if not the whole, of both feet."

The smell of the decaying flesh was horrible, and Ambler occupied himself snipping away at it. Erichsen's toes were unrecognizable black stubs. He was also complaining of stiffness in his jaw and what Ambler described as a "loss of power in his right side." The doctor wondered how Erichsen could go any farther. "God knows how long this will continue & the man must finally break down," Ambler wrote. "If we can find a settlement soon I am in hopes of saving his feet, but if not, his feet & possibly his life & that of the whole party would be sacrificed." On this last point, Ambler was adamant; though Erichsen pleaded for it, they would not abandon him. "No man," said Ambler, "will be left alone."

The next day, a gull sailed over their camp, apparently attracted by the black blanket flying on the hill. Alexey promptly shot the hapless bird, and it became a meager soup. Some of the men baited hooks with the gull's entrails and went ice fishing, but they didn't get any bites. Nindemann took off hunting in the surrounding countryside, looking for "anything which would pay." But he, too, was without luck.

Dr. Ambler, meanwhile, spent the day performing a most odious task, which his journal documented in clinical terms. "Removed four toes from Erichsen's right foot & one from left foot, sawing near the tarso-metatarsal junction." The amputation was surprisingly easy for Erichsen, as he had already lost all feeling in his feet. When the pain set in later, Ambler plied him with opiates and tried to reassure him. But the doctor was losing hope for his patient. The other men could not believe the tough, strapping Dane had sunk to this state. Collins lamented how the operation "cripples a big, able man and puts an end to his calling as a seaman." De Long felt personal responsibility for Erichsen's predicament. "A heartrending sight," he wrote, "the cutting away of bones and flesh of a man I hoped to return sound and whole to his friends. May God pity us."

Each night, the men kept the signal fire burning outside the hut, and the black flag snapped in the breeze. But no one came for them. The footprints, whoever they belonged to, disappeared in the mounting snow. De Long could not shake the feeling that he was being watched, yet the spies refused to show themselves. His imagined scenario—that other *Jeannette* survivors were out combing the delta for them—lost force. "I cannot understand how it is," he wrote. "If the others are safe, why do they not come to look for us?"

FOR THE PAST few days, in fact, De Long and his men *had* been followed; he was not imagining it. A week earlier, two Yakut hunters from the village of Zemovialach had crossed the crew's footprints in the snow. Following the tracks for several days, the hunters had stopped at the first pair of huts where the Americans had recuperated. There they saw fresh charcoal from the fires and found the old Winchester De Long had left behind. They took the rifle for themselves and continued to track De Long's party for several more days.

But then they stopped. The two natives, studying the strangers from a safe remove, began to suspect that they were "contrabandists," as they later put it—smugglers, convicts, and thieves. The Yakuts feared that if they showed themselves, these filthy, hairy foreigners would surely kill them. Quietly, they turned back toward their village, which lay nearly a hundred miles toward the southeast on a distant branch of the Lena.

EVEN WHILE LINGERING in the hut, De Long was making plans to move on. After scouting the terrain, he became convinced that the only way they could ever reach the place called Sagastyr—if it existed at all—was by crossing the river on whose high banks their hut was built. But that was much easier said than done: The channel here was more than five hundred yards wide. Either a sturdy raft would have to be constructed now or they would have to wait until more ice built up on the river's surface so they could cross over on foot.

Right now the ice was too precarious to be trusted, so they could not move. Said De Long: "One does not like to feel he is caught in a trap."

The other question was what to do about Erichsen. Could he survive any more traveling? Could Nindemann construct some sort of sled-litter to drag him across the river's ice and the tundra beyond? Ambler, who in a second procedure had amputated a few more of Erichsen's toes, now believed both feet might have to be sawn off entirely. Noting that his patient was suffering from lockjaw, Ambler hypothesized that a massive fever might "intervene and carry him off." Erichsen was often delirious, and he was keeping the men up at night with weird ravings in Danish. "He is weak and tremulous," said

De Long, "and the moment he closes his eyes talks incessantly . . . a horrible accompaniment to the wretchedness of our surroundings." Ambler told De Long that "unless Erichsen can very soon be given the care and medical treatment which only a prolonged stay at a settlement will admit, his life is in danger."

De Long found himself in the midst of a horrible reckoning. Erichsen's survival, it seemed to him, was now pitted against the survival of the whole group. "If we could move on," De Long wrote, "it would probably shorten his life; if I remained here and kept everybody with me, Erichsen's days would be lengthened a little at the risk of our all dying from starvation. This is a crisis in our lives." In the end, De Long went with his better instincts: No man would be left behind. Erichsen would be dragged along, no matter the hardships.

On the morning of October 1—111 days since the sinking of the *Jeannette*—De Long decided that the river channel was sufficiently frozen over to attempt a crossing. A record he left inside the hut noted that while they had "no fear for the future," one of their men was not well, and that his "toes have been amputated in consequence of frost-bite."

As they moved gingerly across the big, icy river, they spread out widely so that their weight was never concentrated in any one place. Even so, the ice tinkled and cracked with each step, sometimes sending out frightening jigsaw patterns. Having strapped Erichsen to a sledge fashioned from two misshapen driftwood logs, they hauled the muttering invalid with several long ropes angled so that the pullers and the pulled stayed safely separated from one another—again, to avoid concentrating their weight.

Eventually, they all made it over safely, and once gathered on the other side, they started out on an excruciatingly difficult march. They covered more than twelve miles over impossible terrain, hauling poor Erichsen every jouncing inch of the way on the "sledge." For two days after that, they continued wandering in the wilderness, making slower progress. At one point, they spotted a man's tracks in the snow and followed them for the better part of a day, until they vanished. De Long began to realize that they were nowhere near Sagastyr, which he had come to believe was "a myth."

His chart was "simply useless," De Long now decided. "I must go on plodding to the southward, trusting in God to guide me to a settlement, for I have long since realized that we are powerless to help ourselves." The topography was unrelenting in its mazelike complexity—he could not find its logic. "I was much bewildered by the frequent narrowing of the river to a small vein of ice," De Long wrote, "and the irregular rambling way in which it ran. Our floundering around was both exhaustive of energy and consumptive of time. There is no use denying it, we are pretty weak."

De Long recognized that given their state, he should probably abandon the heavy journals he was carrying, but he couldn't bring himself to do it—they had become as precious as life itself. "As long as I can get along on my feet," he said, "these records will go with me." He could try to cache them somewhere—and mark the spot with a cairn made of driftwood—but he knew this was all Lena floodplain. Anything he put into the ground would be ruined by the spring floods.

Collins, in particular, took issue with the burden posed by De Long's books. (In his own journal he complained of "logbooks, etc, [that] weighed the men down beyond their strength.") But by this point, the Irishman, smoldering with resentments, had found fault with every aspect of De Long's "general plan of running the machine" and compared the captain to a "horse-leech" that "sucks our chances of escape away." He told several of his confidants that he had been keeping a journal of events—presumably highly critical of De Long— which was tucked away in a pocket of his coat; should something happen to him, he wanted that record sent to the editors of Bennett's *Herald* in New York.

Alexey, who'd been veering off on hunting forays, had enjoyed no luck. De Long had exhausted the last of the pemmican stores; now he and his men were truly starving. This left him no choice. On October 3, he gave the assignment to Iverson, who led Snoozer off behind their open-air encampment and shot him in the head, then butchered and dressed him. "Soon after a kind of stew was made," wrote De Long, "of which everybody except the doctor and myself eagerly partook. To us, it was a nauseating mess." The stew was prepared from the head, heart, kidneys, and liver. "There were some men," said Nindemann, "that did not care much [for] it."

The temperature that night plummeted to near zero, and the men all stayed close to the fire, huddled arm in arm. Alexey and De Long tried to warm each other. Said De Long, "If [he] had not wrapped his sealskin around me and [kept] me warm by the heat of his body, I think I should have frozen to death. As it was, I shivered and shook." For his own protection, Erichsen was kept lashed to the makeshift sled, which was pulled up beside the fire. But his "groans and rambling talk rang out on the night air," De Long wrote, "and such a dreary, wretched night, I hope I shall never see again."

Sometime during the night, Erichsen, in his delirium, tossed his mittens aside. The others failed to notice this until morning, though by then it was too late: Erichsen's hands were frozen nearly solid. Boyd and Iverson rubbed them until some circulation was restored, but Ambler knew that Erichsen's hands would now go the way of his feet. He was unconscious, utterly oblivious to what he had done. At around six in the morning, they strapped him tighter to the sled and resumed their march to the south.

A few hours later, they encountered another hut and immediately took shelter and made a fire. Ambler closely examined Erichsen and found that he'd sunk, said De Long, "very low indeed." His pulse was weak, and he remained unconscious. The line of decay had moved up his ankles to the calves of his legs. De Long led the men in prayers.

TWO DAYS LATER, at eight forty-five in the morning of October 6, Ambler turned to the men still gathered in the hut and shook his head. "It is all over with him," the doctor said, closing Erichsen's eyes. "Peace to his soul."

Hans Erichsen, the thirty-three-year-old career mariner and North Sea fisherman from Ærøskøbing, Denmark, was dead. "Our messmate has departed this life," De Long wrote. "What in God's name is going to become of us?"

They had no tools with which to bury him, and even if they had, it would have been almost impossible in the permafrost. "The seaman's grave is the water," De Long reasoned, and so he decided that they would consign him to the river. They removed and distributed his clothes and sewed up his body in a tent flap, stuffing it with clods of earth to weigh it down. Iverson collected his Bible, and Kaack clipped a lock of his hair. A flag was placed over the corpse, and they dragged him to the riverbank.

After a short solemn ceremony, they hacked a hole in the ice with a hatchet and slipped Erichsen into the cold Lena. Three rifle volleys boomed over the river. Nindemann carved a grave marker out of an old board he found in the hut and hung it up over the door. The inscription read:

IN MEMORY
H. H. ERICHSEN,
OCT. 6, 1881.
U.S.S. *JEANNETTE.*

THE MORNING OF October 9 dawned clear, crisp, and relatively warm after days of freezing mists. De Long called Nindemann over to confer about a plan that had been gestating for several days. He wanted Nindemann to use this break in the weather to push ahead of the group and find help.

Since Erichsen's death, several more cases of frostbite had cropped up among the men. De Long was in especially bad shape, as were Collins and Lee. They had just a few pounds of dog meat left and were subsisting on a kind of grog made from brandy and old tea leaves boiled in river water. As a group, they could not advance more than a few miles a day. "We are all pretty well done up," said De Long, "and seem to be wandering in a labyrinth." Sending Nindemann was, he felt, their last chance.

De Long chose Nindemann because he remained the strongest of the group and the most likely to get through. There was no doubting the German quartermaster's resourcefulness as well as his ferocious competency—and, as his ordeal in Greenland had proved, the man had an uncommon survival instinct. Collins volunteered to accompany Nindemann, but De Long scoffed at the Irishman, saying, "In your condition, Mr. Collins, you would not get five miles away from camp." It was also true that the captain did not trust Collins; some would later speculate, on the basis of no particular evidence, that De Long feared that Collins, if he were to reach safety first, would race to the nearest telegraph station to transmit to the *Herald* a skewed version of the expedition.

Alexey was probably the second-most fit after Nindemann, but De Long wanted the Inuit to stay with the group, as he was the best hunter. With Alexey's shooting prowess and a little divine help, the captain remained optimistic. "I trust in God," he said, "and believe that He who has fed us thus far will not suffer us to die of want now."

Louis Noros was the next-strongest man. He would accompany Nindemann and obey his orders. They would travel light—"just the clothes we stood in," as Nindemann put it, plus a rifle, forty rounds of ammunition, a few blankets, and a little grog to drink. "If you find game," De Long told them, "then return to us."

But if they didn't, the captain wanted them to keep pushing south, aiming for a village called Kumakh-Surt, which he thought might be four days away. "Nindemann, do the best you can," De Long said. "If you find assistance come back as quick as possible, and if you do not, then you are as well off as we are. You see the condition we are in."

De Long gave Ambler the option of going with Nindemann and Noros, but the doctor declined. "I thought," Ambler wrote, "that my duty required me with him & the main body for the present."

The captain said a prayer, and then the men gathered around Nindemann and Noros and shook their hands. They all had tears in their eyes. Collins, his voice trembling with emotion, told Noros, "When you get to New York, remember me."

Then the two men turned and started their march, heading south along the bank. "God give them aid," said Ambler. As they vanished around a bend in the river, De Long's men sent out three cheers.

I would so like to be with you, to see you, to take care of you. I am afraid to think of what condition you may be in. I am trying to wait patiently for news from my own suffering husband, and it is needless to say how very, very anxious I am. I have been brave all through these trying years and I will be so still. I am not a foolish woman and will not lose my head. I will try to banish from my mind all forebodings and melancholy thoughts. How I long to be with you now!

—Emma

By the fall of 1881, Emma De Long had become gravely worried about the *Jeannette*'s fate. The *Corwin* had pulled into San Francisco on October 21, reporting that although it had combed more than eight thousand miles in the Alaskan and Siberian Arctic, its crew had not found a single piece of evidence of the *Jeannette*'s whereabouts, not even a rumor. Furthermore, the *Corwin* party's historic landing on Wrangel, all but proving that it was an island, had dashed one of Emma's last remaining hopes: that her husband and his men had made their way up the hypothetical transpolar landmass toward the North Pole and beyond.

She had become almost laughably absentminded. She broke things, dropped things, wandered out of stores without paying for merchandise. She couldn't think of anything else but the *Jeannette*. Her concerns only deepened on November 11, when the American man-of-war *Alliance* returned from her searches of the waters north of Norway. The *Alliance* had left on June 16 from Norfolk with a crew of nearly two hundred men and had traveled twelve thousand miles. Her captain, Commander George Henry Wadleigh, reported that he had found not a shred of evidence concerning the *Jeannette* or any of her crew members. One of Bennett's best reporters, Harry Macdona, was on board and later published a series of popular *Herald* dispatches recounting the journey.

The *Alliance* had stopped at Reykjavik, becoming the first American Navy vessel to anchor in the Icelandic port. (The Icelanders were captivated by the Americans, especially several black sailors on board, whom they treated, said Macdona, as "escaped curiosities from a museum.") Next, Wadleigh had steered the *Alliance* to Hammerfest, Norway, then on to Spitsbergen, an Arctic island north of Norway. Along the way, the *Alliance* encountered numerous whalers, sealers, and walrus hunters but gleaned no tidings of the *Jeannette*. Wadleigh's men circulated placards printed in multiple languages offering rewards for information leading to the *Jeannette*'s discovery.

The *Alliance* attained a latitude of 80°10' N, some 590 miles south of the North Pole, which was believed to be the highest point ever reached by a man-of-war. But then Wadleigh was halted by the pack. Given the ferocity of the ice barrier he saw, Macdona wondered if mankind would ever reach the North Pole: "No one who has seen this desert of ice, piled upon hummocks and forced into mountainous ridges by a force that the mind cannot comprehend, will venture an opinion as to the years of dreary endeavor yet to be endured before man shall reach that supreme spot."

On returning to the United States, an officer of the *Alliance* echoed Emma De Long's fears succinctly: "We are not so hopeful of the safety of the *Jeannette*'s crew as we were before."

Meanwhile, the third vessel tasked with the search for De Long, the USS *Rodgers,* had scoured many thousands of miles of the Kamchatkan and Siberian coastlines that summer. But her captain, Lieutenant Robert Berry, had exactly the same thing to report: No sign of the *Jeannette.* A party from the *Rodgers* had landed on Wrangel Island a few weeks after John Muir and his colleagues, and they had been able to substantially explore the island, penetrating more than twenty miles inland. They found nothing to suggest that De Long had ever set foot on Wrangel. Now the *Rodgers* was safely harbored for the winter in a cove on the northeastern coast of Siberia and planned to send dog teams along the shore to search for tidings of De Long as far west as the Kolyma River. Among the crew of the *Rodgers* was yet another correspondent for the *New York Herald.*

The failure of all the 1881 summer searches only redoubled the public's desire to learn of De Long's fate. Multiple rescue expeditions were planned for the spring of 1882—and now the search for the *Jeannette* was taking on an international cast. Not since the search for Sir John Franklin had the world shown such intense interest in the fate of a single Arctic exploration party. In Copenhagen, a Lieutenant Howgaard of the Royal Danish Navy was collecting funds to start an ambitious search along the entire coastline of Siberia, retracing the route Nordenskïold had successfully traversed during his recent northeastern passage. In St. Petersburg, Russian authorities sent out alerts to every commandant and tribal representative in northern Siberia. In Canada, Great Britain's Colonial Department wrote letters to all the governors of the Hudson's Bay Company, urging them to inform the trappers and company employees along the Arctic coast of North America to keep a close eye out for the *Jeannette.*

The Royal Geographical Society in London, meanwhile, began to make its own plans for a relief expedition. "The American people may be assured that not only do English geographers feel the deepest sympathy for the gallant explorers on board the *Jeannette,* but that we shall gladly and actively do what lies in our power to make the search complete," the society's Clements R. Markham stated in December.

To an editorial writer in the *New York Herald,* the swell of goodwill surpassed the response seen in the aftermath of Franklin's disappearance. "For a second time in the history of polar research, a great expedition is probably lost in the Arctic," the *Herald* said. "There is to be another Franklin search, with this difference—that was an English and American search of a limited segment of the polar circle; this will be a universal search of the whole border of the 'unknown region,' participated in by nearly all the civilized nations of the earth."

For the past year, Bennett had followed all the talk of rescue operations, but he had been distracted by other things. He had hatched a dream of starting a new newspaper, to be called the *Paris Herald,* that would be targeted primarily at American expatriates like himself. He had bought a beautiful seaside villa on the Côte d'Azur, in a lovely place called Beaulieu. He'd hosted extravagant hunts at his country place near Versailles, and he'd spent much of the year cruising the Mediterranean.

Bennett was further occupied by the opening of his new creation, the Newport Casino, which proved a bigger hit than anyone could have imagined. It was a rambling affair of wood, stone, and fish-scale shingles, with great verandas, open-air bars, and an immaculately manicured tennis lawn set in a courtyard large enough to accommodate thousands of spectators. "There is nothing like it in the old world or new," gushed one newspaper reporter on the occasion of the casino's grand opening. "It is doubtful if a more lively place can be found."

In August, the Newport Casino held the first national championships of the newly formed United States National Lawn Tennis Association. It was the first tennis tournament ever held on American soil. A Harvard man named Richard Dudley Sears dominated it, winning five straight matches. True to Bennett's vision, the Newport Casino became the birthplace of competitive tennis in the United States, and the annual tournament held there would be the forerunner of the U.S. Open. (The Newport Casino hosted the national championships until the summer of 1915, when they were moved to Forest Hills, New York.)

Even with the distractions of his casino, Bennett had kept in regular contact with Emma De Long and had even invited her up to Newport, in the late summer of 1880, to visit his "cottage." The small mansion, called Stone Villa, was conveniently situated right across Bellevue Avenue from the casino. He invited Emma to sail on his new yacht, the *Polynia*, which he'd built at a reported cost of $55,000. Bennett's sister, Jeannette Bell, was also in Newport that summer. She and her husband had recently had a son, but Bennett showed no desire to play the role of a doting uncle. Bennett wrote out an inheritance check for $100,000, set it at the foot of his nephew's crib, and never laid eyes on the boy again.

Bennett promised Emma that he would spare no cost to find her husband. To him, the polar problem was like a rousing match of polo or tennis—a sport that quickened the blood, a bracing challenge, a game. Everything would be all right, he was sure of it. And if it wasn't, that was the risk of playing the game. He could think of no more honorable way to die than in the service of exploration—for the country, for the Navy, for science. And, of course, for the *New York Herald*. "The *Herald* is everything," he once told a reporter. "The man is nothing."

But by the end of 1881, even Bennett was starting to believe that something untoward had happened to the *Jeannette*. He resigned himself to the probability that the ship had been crushed and now slept at the bottom of the sea. As for De Long and his men, James Gordon Bennett remained sanguine. He cabled Emma from Paris:

Have no fears about your husband and his gallant crew. Should the Government be niggardly enough to refuse to send another expedition, I shall do so at my own expense, if it takes my last dollar. I wish I could inspire you with my own confidence in the safety of the Jeannette. Bennett.

As Nindemann and Noros marched over the Lena wastelands, the Siberian winter fell upon them like an untethered weight. Each night grew colder than the last, with temperatures reaching well below zero. It seemed at times that only their constant movement kept them from freezing to death. Sounds became brittle. The fluids in their faces hardened. The snow squeaked underfoot. The cold had become a physical presence, silently snatching the life from the delta in the way that a fire consumes the oxygen in a room. In the coldest hours of the night, their breaths froze in the air and drifted to the ground in glittery clouds, which, according to local tribesmen, made a faint tinkling melody called "the whisper of the stars." (The coldest temperature ever recorded in the Northern Hemisphere, ninety degrees below zero Fahrenheit, would later be captured at a Soviet weather station to the east of the Lena.)

Nindemann and Noros moved steadily and determinedly, but they were too weak to move swiftly. They averaged about thirteen miles a day. Noros spat up blood and began to entertain ideas of shooting himself. In his lowest moments, only thoughts of his family back in Fall River, Massachusetts, kept him from taking his life.

Much of their journey seemed like a dream, a long whiteout of undifferentiated days punctuated by a few moments of haunting clarity: A snowy owl staring at them. A pile of decrepit sleds they smashed up for firewood. The corpse of a native buried in a box on a hill. A crow, circling and circling and circling.

The only landmark that rose above the interminable flats was a rock island, stuck like a plug in the middle of the Lena. The massive crag was known simply as Ostrov Stolb, "Rock Island." In clear weather, it could be seen for a hundred miles. In the refractions of the Arctic atmosphere, Ostrov Stolb assumed various distorted shapes as it hovered over the floodplain; it sometimes looked like a castle fortress, or a whale emerging from the sea, or the back of some enormous prehistoric beast. Whatever form it took, Nindemann and Noros relied on it as their guidepost as they worked their way south.

Lacking tents or any form of shelter, the two men each night became like burrowing animals. They slept in a natural crevice in a riverbank, then in the lee of a bluff, then in the shelter of a decrepit flatboat abandoned in the ice, then in snow caves of their own making.

They lived on residues of nutrition. One day, Nindemann shot a ptarmigan, a species of Arctic grouse. Then he caught a lemming, and they roasted the small rodent, hair and all, on a spit. They boiled tea from the roots of a stunted willow plant. Near the river one day, they found some fish heads to eat. The rest of the time, they were forced to gnaw on their boot soles or to chew swatches of their sealskin pants, which, to make more palatable, they soaked in water and charred in the fire.

A week into their journey, they had grown so weak that they often could not make forward progress against the force of the wind. They had nearly lost all hope when, on the night of October 19, they stumbled upon a collection of huts at a place known to locals as Bulcour. They made a fire inside one of them and collapsed in a heap. All told, they had traveled 129 miles since parting from De Long ten days earlier.

The next day, in one of the neighboring huts, amid a collection of tattered nets, they found a large quantity of dried fish that had the consistency of coarse sawdust. Almost tasteless, it was a kind of fish the natives used not for food but for lamp oil they extracted by heating and pulverizing the flesh. Paying no heed to the blue mold growing all over it, Nindemann and Noros eagerly devoured the fish, shoving handful after handful of the putrid fluff into their mouths. They soon grew violently ill, and by the next day they had developed severe diarrhea, their stools containing a bloody mucus—they were sure they had dysentery. Even so, they kept eating the fish, thinking the sensation of food in their bellies worth the agony.

AROUND MIDDAY ON October 22, they heard a strange whoosh-
ing noise outside their hut. It sounded to them like a large flock of
geese swooping overhead. Their profound hunger had so affected their
hearing that they did not trust their own ears. Nindemann cracked
the door and glimpsed something moving; then, in a blur, he saw the
head and antlers of a reindeer. He grabbed his rifle and was just load-
ing it when the door burst open. There at the threshold stood a native
man in warm furs—and, behind him, a sleigh hitched to a whole
team of reindeer, snorting and stamping in the snow.

The native was shocked to see these two begrimed, half-dead foreigners living in his tribal hut at Bulcour. Nindemann and Noros
were brought to joyful tears at the sight of this visitor, for they had
not laid eyes on a human being, beyond their *Jeannette* shipmates, for
809 days.

Nindemann lurched forward to greet him. Seeing the rifle in
Nindemann's arms, the man recoiled in fear and fell to his knees,
throwing up his hands and pleading with Nindemann not to shoot.
Nindemann tossed the rifle into a corner and beseeched the native to
come inside. The man hesitated, but then took a step forward when
Nindemann offered him a bite of fish. Studying the moldy mush for a
moment, the native, whose name was Ivan, shook his head and indicated by signs and grimaces that it was not fit to eat.

Ivan, noticing the threadbare state of Nindemann's boots, went
out to his sleigh and produced a new pair of deerskin mukluks as
a gift. Nindemann thanked him and then, with Noros, fell into a
frantic pantomime, trying to convey to the native that they were not
alone, that eleven more men were still out in the cold, somewhere to
the north. It was useless—Ivan gave no sign that he understood anything they tried to tell him. Instead, he indicated that he had to leave
and held up four fingers, which Nindemann interpreted to mean that
he would return either in four hours or in four days; Nindemann
could not tell which. Ivan climbed onto his sled and hawed the reindeer into action. He took off toward the west, following the river. A
few minutes later, he was gone.

Nindemann and Noros slumped in silence and looked at each
other, fearing they had made a critical mistake in letting the native
take off without them. They began to despair that they would ever see
their visitor again—that they had lost their last chance at salvation.

Nindemann cursed himself for having brandished his rifle, which he was now sure had frightened Ivan away.

But early in the evening, Ivan returned to Bulcour, accompanied by two stout men on sleighs pulled by dozens of reindeer. The visitors had brought a fresh fish, which they skinned and cut up. Noros and Nindemann promptly devoured every morsel of it, raw. Then Ivan furnished the two wretches with deerskin coats and blankets and guided them out to the sleds, securing them on board like precious cargo.

Soon the whole party took off through the night, over the ice and snow. They rode about fifteen miles toward the west, until they spotted a huddle of deerskin tents pitched in the hills ahead. Perhaps a hundred reindeer were clustered nearby. Through the partly translucent skins of the tents, Nindemann and Noros could see the glow of flickering fires, and the savory smells of cooking food mingled in the air. They could hear laughter and spirited conversations inside the tents, the muffled sounds of women and children.

It was only then that the two castaways became convinced of their good fortune: *They were going to be saved.*

THOUGH THEY DIDN'T know it yet, Nindemann and Noros had fallen in with a group of Yakuts—a large tribe of seminomadic hunter-fishermen who built their world around the reindeer. In their facial features the Yakuts resembled the Mongols, but their language was more closely related to Turkish. Starting in the thirteenth century, the Yakuts had migrated to the high north country of central Siberia from the forests around Lake Baikal. By the 1830s, the Russian state had converted most of the Yakuts—sometimes at gunpoint—to the Eastern Orthodox Church, but they still followed their traditional animist beliefs and relied on the power of their shamans.

The Yakuts were a proud and openhearted people who had long ago figured out the puzzle of the delta and had spent centuries perfecting techniques for thriving in extreme cold; indeed, it seemed to some that they *preferred* the extreme cold, for the solitude it brought and the independence it gave them from the long reach of the czar. Much of their freedom came from their ability to live in a place where no one else much wanted to be. In the land of the Yakuts, the expression went, "God is high up and the czar is far off."

Nindemann and Noros were welcomed into the Yakut camp and

given warm water to clean their filthy hands and faces. But Ninde-mann couldn't wash himself—his hands were crippled from the cold, and his fingernails had become long, jagged claws. A Yakut woman, observing his pitiful condition, kneeled beside him and gently wiped his dirty, frostnipped face. This kind act, this first human touch, overwhelmed him. Nindemann would never forget her.

After a venison feast, Nindemann and Noros lingered by the fire and attempted to explain their predicament to the natives: There were other shipwrecked sailors, starving to the north. Eleven men, trapped in the snow. They tried to convey the situation with stick figures, wild gesticulations, and images drawn in the ashes. But the Yakuts did not seem to have any idea what they were talking about. They just smiled awkwardly and nodded their heads. They were probably still trying to figure out how these two vagabonds had landed in the delta, from what direction they had come, from which nation—or planet—they hailed. The Yakuts likely suspected that Nindemann and Noros were fugitive criminals, political exiles, or pirates. The two Americans, see-ing that they were getting nowhere, gave up for the night and drifted off to sleep.

The next morning the Yakuts broke camp and took off toward the south—exactly the wrong direction if they were going to save De Long. Around midday, the reindeer teams ascended a high hill, from which they could see Ostrov Stolb, the massive rock island Ninde-mann and Noros had used as a guiding landmark. Pointing in the direction of Ostrov Stolb, Nindemann once again tried to tell the story of the *Jeannette* and of their shipmates freezing and starving to the north. He drew diagrams in the snow and pleaded with the group's leader to aim the party in that direction. But the Yakut elder only smiled a sad smile, without registering any further comprehen-sion, giving no indication that he would turn the group around.

The next day the Yakut party reached the small village of Kumakh-Surt—the place De Long had been aiming for when he had dispatched Nindemann and Noros on their errand. It was a feast day in the village, and as Nindemann and Noros were paraded around they became the objects of much curiosity. "Everybody stopped and looked at us," recalled Nindemann. "Everybody wanted to know who we were and where we were from."

Someone handed Nindemann a toy boat, which he used to tell the story of the *Jeannette*. All the villagers gathered around as he related the woeful tale: How the ship had left America and sailed the ocean.

How it had become trapped in the ice and drifted for two years. How it had been crushed and had sunk far to the north. How thirty-three men had traveled for three months over the ice, hauling three boats behind them until they came to open water. And then how the three boats had become separated in a storm.

"I then showed them a chart of the coast line," Nindemann recounted, "and that our boat went in *here,* and we did not know what had become of the other two." He indicated with pencil marks where they had waded ashore and, with vigorous gestures and play-acting, reenacted the way they had marched along the banks of the Lena, and the place where one of their party had died and been buried in the river. "Everybody shook his head," said Nindemann, "as much as to say they felt sorry for it."

Nindemann then showed that he and his present companion had left the captain behind with his men and had wandered the delta for ten days. In pleading tones, he said he now needed the villagers' help to go back and rescue his shipmates before they all died.

When he had finished his tale, Nindemann looked at the Yakuts gathered around him and realized by their vacant expressions that while they might have been dazzled by his performance, they had no idea what he was talking about. "Sometimes it seemed to me as if they understood everything that I wanted," Nindemann said. "Then all at once it seemed that they did not understand a word." Some of them probably thought these were the ravings of a crazy man. Certainly the villagers of Kumakh Surt gave no indication that they would help.

NINDEMANN'S INABILITY TO communicate the dire straits of his shipmates—and his constant awareness that time was draining away—had brought him to the brink of a nervous breakdown. The next day, while still holed up in a hut in Kumakh-Surt, he collapsed in a fit of sorrow and frustration, sobbing uncontrollably. A Yakut woman took pity on him and sat with him long enough to understand his new request: He wanted to be taken to Bulun, the place De Long had mentioned as a larger settlement farther south on the Lena. There, Nindemann hoped to meet someone who might speak English or his native German. Perhaps in Bulun he could find Russian authorities who would understand him—and help him mount a rescue expedition.

As the villagers made arrangements for a reindeer team and a driver, the two Americans composed a written account explaining who they were and what had happened to De Long—a note they planned to give to the authorities in Bulun.

IT WAS THEN that a strapping and somewhat mysterious Russian man named Kuzma arrived in the village and became acquainted with Nindemann and Noros. Though he did not volunteer the information, Kuzma turned out to be an exile, a convicted thief who had been banished to Siberia for his crimes, yet he was educated and apparently well-traveled. It was unclear what Kuzma was doing in Kumakh-Surt, for he lived nearly a hundred miles away, on the far northeastern edge of the delta. Kuzma spoke neither English nor German, but he instantly kindled new hope in Nindemann and Noros. Upon seeing the two bedraggled castaways, the first thing he said was *"Jennetta? Amerikanski?"* Nindemann surmised that Kuzma had read something about the *Jeannette* expedition in a Russian newspaper or had heard about it through conversations with authorities. In any case, he seemed to know something of who they were—and this was a magnificent start.

Kuzma nodded his head vigorously when Nindemann and Noros mentioned that eleven other shipwrecked Americans, including their captain, were still alive but suffering from their travels over the ice. It seemed as though Kuzma suddenly understood everything they were talking about. Upon seeing the note Nindemann and Noros had composed, Kuzma did something strange: He took it from them and slid it into his pocket. Nindemann protested loudly, but Kuzma refused to give it back, and soon he had absconded from the village without any explanation.

The villagers generously gave the two Americans fresh furs and plenty of smoked fish for the journey to Bulun, and the next day, they left by reindeer team, with a competent Yakut driver. They arrived on the evening of October 29. Bulun was a snug settlement of perhaps thirty-five huts and cabins, with a tiny Russian Orthodox church. Nindemann and Noros were received warmly—and were soon met by the village priest and the Russian commandant. They were given a small hut to stay in, and they spent the next few days recovering from their dysentery and resting while awaiting word from the commandant. They were still a sad sight to behold—hobbled, frostnipped, emaciated, their beards wild and tattered. They made a few more feeble attempts to impress upon the villagers the urgent need for mounting a rescue but met with no success.

On the night of November 2, they heard the outer door of their hut creak open. Then the inner door, with its thick insulation of felt and deerskin, cracked a few inches to reveal a stolid man in furs. The light was so dim that the two Americans could scarcely see their visitor, even when he quietly stepped inside. Nindemann was lying on what passed for a bed, while Noros stood beside a table, sawing away at a loaf of black bread with a sheath knife.

Something about this visitor seemed odd. He just stood there by the door and lingered without saying a word. He had a strange grin on his face.

"Hallooo, Noros!" the man said in a booming voice. "How do you do?"

Noros looked up from the bread he was slicing and saw that the stranger was bounding toward him. The man pulled back his hood to reveal a familiar face—and a familiar bald head.

Tears came to Noros's eyes, and he fairly screamed: "My God, *Mr. Melville*—you're alive!"

It had been fifty-one days since the three boats separated in the gale—fifty-one days since the men of De Long's cutter had lost sight of Melville's whaleboat in the storm-tossed Laptev Sea and resigned themselves to the loss of the other two crews. Nindemann and Noros now welcomed Melville into their cabin as a man already mourned. They could scarcely contain their joy at seeing one of their shipmates alive, hearing English spoken again, and learning that they were not alone in this strange land.

"Melville," cried Noros, "we thought we were the only two left! We were sure the whaleboat's crew was all dead, and the second cutter's, too."

Melville removed his furs and embraced his two friends in the wet warmth of the dim cabin. He was scabbed and weather-beaten, his stout face flecked with a few empurpled lesions of frostbite, but he was in far better shape than Nindemann and Noros. Melville's eyes welled with tears at the sight of his comrades—tears of delight and relief but also of sadness, for it pained the engineer to the depths of his soul to contemplate the sorry state to which they had fallen. He could see that these two raccoon-eyed wraiths had tasted the fumes of their own death.

The tale that Melville had to tell bore many resemblances to what had befallen Nindemann and Noros. His, like theirs, was a story of privation and strife and wandering in the wilderness. The ordeal had been, he said, "an incubus of horrors." Yet Melville had had luck on his side.

ON THE AFTERNOON of September 12, the eleven men in the whaleboat—Melville, Danenhower, Newcomb, Leach, Bartlett, Cole, Charles Tong Sing, Henry Wilson, Frank Mansen, Lauterbach, and Aneguin—had pulled away from De Long's cutter "at a spanking rate," as Melville put it. But as the gale grew in fury, part of the rudder was carried away, crippling the vessel. The men in Melville's boat debated whether they could survive the massive swells. Scanning the empty seas, they felt sure they were now the expedition's only survivors. "The general feeling," Melville said, was "that ours was the only boat which outlived the gale."

Melville turned the bow into the wind and, much as De Long had done, constructed an elaborate sea anchor from a mishmash of canvas, oars, and tent poles weighted down with copper kettles attached to a line. The contraption was far from elegant, but it was a bit of genius that worked beautifully, allowing Melville and his crew to ride out the storm.

Still, throughout the night, they were constantly "pumping and bailing with might and main." The waves came in sets of three, and the men timed their bailing so they could brace for the next sequence of incoming sea. The best bailers turned out to be Aneguin and Charles Tong Sing—they crouched together in the bottom of the boat, scooping up water with desperate efficiency. But the lulls between the sets were always too short, and soon "the cruel spray would dash and freeze upon us. . . . It changed to slush the moment it tumbled in." Then the frenzied bailing would begin all over again. Daylight, Melville realized, "did nothing but enhance our misery, since it enabled us to witness each other's wretchedness." Melville was stiff as a mannequin, his hands "swollen, blistered, and split open by the cold and stagnation of my blood." No land was in sight, just an endless roil of pewter-gray sea. The ribbed bottom of the boat, which had been carefully stuffed with clean snow for potable water, was now deluged with ocean spray, so they had nothing fresh to drink.

Lacking instruments, Melville and Danenhower guided the whaleboat toward the delta using nothing more than the sun and stars. Melville had veered off on a very different course from the one

De Long's cutter took. The engineer angled the whaleboat almost due south and was approaching the southeastern fan of the delta, whereas De Long had vectored far to the west, making for the more obscure—and less inhabited—reaches of the delta's northern discharges. As the two parties drew near to land, they had grown several hundred miles apart.

On September 14, the whaleboat came aground on a muddy shoal, yet still Melville could see no land. They backed up from the shallows and worked their way east by southeast, threading through mires of sandbars, until they debouched into an open channel, which proved to be a major arm of the Lena, extending like a brown plume far out into the sea and pulsing with a strong flow. Here they turned due west and alternately rowed and sailed against the current, the brackish water becoming sweeter by the hour. Then, on the morning of September 17, they sighted two spits of land in the distance—marking the true entrance to this mighty branch of the river. At long last, they had reached Siberia.

But as they passed into the Lena and navigated upstream for another day, Melville became more and more puzzled. His chart, which had been copied from Petermann's *Geographische Mitteilungen,* showed numerous places marked WINTER HUTS OF NATIVES. But as the men scanned both banks of the river, they could see no signs of habitation of any kind—just a swift, broad, musky river, more than four miles across, its sandy banks littered with driftwood. Said Melville, "Bitterly we cursed Petermann and all his works which had led us astray."

They had been huddled together in the cramped whaleboat for more than one hundred twenty hours and were in abject condition. "The cold," Melville later wrote, "had robbed us of our vitality, and produced a dullness of mind, movement, and speech." Newcomb complained of aching gums—a telltale sign of scurvy—while others suffered from varying degrees of blindness and a shrill ringing in their ears.

But it was their extremities that plagued them the most. "The cracks in our bleeding hands were in a frightful condition," wrote Melville. "The blisters and sores had run together and our flesh became sodden and spongy to the touch. Our feet, legs, and hands were now entirely bereft of feeling." Leach's feet were especially horrible (almost as bad as Erichsen's had been upon coming ashore); when he pulled off his boots, Leach saw that his toes were turning blue-black, the skin and nails curling backward, said Melville, like feathers singed by a flame.

Not only were the men miserable, some were going insane. Cole could be seen muttering to himself and at times seemed to have lost touch with reality. Danenhower, still incensed by De Long's decision to give Melville command of the whaleboat though the navigator enjoyed higher rank, had fallen into weird ravings and violent outbursts. (It is unclear whether Melville knew that Danenhower had syphilis, but the illness did seem to be manifesting itself in the form of episodic madness.) Once, when Newcomb committed a trivial offense, Danenhower snapped and began to choke the life out of the hapless naturalist, yelling, "If you don't obey me, I'm going to kill you!" The others in the boat had to pull him off Newcomb.

Only one thing held the men together through these nadir moments, enabling them to overlook all transgressions and failings: It was the camaraderie of suffering, the conviction that what they had already been through outweighed everything else. The magnitude of their struggle had forged a forgiving brotherhood. "Our common dangers and miseries had bred a closer fellowship among us," said Melville, "a bond which bound us all."

WHEN IT SEEMED their ordeal had reached its extremity, a blessing came their way: On the morning of September 19, they spotted a collection of huts in what appeared to be a fishing camp. "Our joy," Melville said, "was almost as great as though we had suddenly chanced upon a modern metropolis." They landed and built a roaring driftwood bonfire beside the slatternly, weather-scabbed structures. The welcome warmth of the fire nonetheless put some of the men in agony, as though a million electrified needles were prodding and pricking their extremities.

Although the camp looked to be abandoned for the season, within a few minutes three natives, paddling three dugout canoes, nosed around a sandbar. They were heading off in another direction and appeared to ignore the men and their plaintive cries—or perhaps they were simply shocked and frightened by these eleven wild-looking trespassers now squatting in their fishing camp.

As they retreated across the Lena, Melville ordered a few of the men to jump into the whaleboat with him to give chase. They soon pulled alongside the dugouts, but the natives, "shy of us in evident fear or suspicion," slid away to a safer remove. Melville hailed them in English, then in German, then French, but it was no use. "We all smiled and laughed at my successive fruitless attempts to open up a conversation in every crooked tongue of which I had the slightest smattering," he later recalled.

After much coaxing, one of the natives, younger and less timid than the others, paddled a little closer. Through repetition and gestures, Melville was able to establish that his name was Tomat. He bore himself like a proud warrior and was something of a dandy, with tobacco pouches and a ceremonial pipe dangling from his person, his fur leggings decorated with copper ornaments, and a knife lashed to his thigh. But he was just a teenager—an unlikely savior for a shabby group of shipwrecked sailors from the other side of the planet. Inside his boat were fishing nets made of white horsehair, a recently caught fish, and a goose carcass. Melville told the men to grab hold of Tomat's boat so that he could not get away. The young man seemed momentarily alarmed by this entrapment, but after a bit more gesturing, Melville was able to persuade him and his companions to join the Americans by the bonfire.

Tomat and his companions were members of the Evenk tribe, another group of seminomadic hunter-fishermen widely scattered around north-central Siberia. Of Mongol extraction, and known for their hardy stock of shaggy Arctic horses, the Evenks were at least partly Christianized and spoke a completely different language from that of the Yakuts. Melville and his men sat by the fire with the three natives, who offered up the goose and fish to be cooked.

Over a hastily prepared stew, the Americans tried to communicate with the three Evenks, but they soon gave up and contented themselves with showing each other their belongings. Tomat was especially impressed by the Americans' rifles—and by a small family photograph that Newcomb was carrying. Never having seen a photograph before, Tomat kissed the magical picture over and over again and crossed himself, apparently thinking it was the image of a saint.

Tomat and his companions were friendly enough, but after a time it became clear to Melville that these impoverished natives could not really help his party; they appeared reluctant to lead them to their village, wherever it was. Eleven starving Americans were too many mouths to feed for a people already living on meager Arctic fare. Tomat seemed to think that Melville and his men were supernatural beings who had risen from the ice somewhere far to the north.

Melville began to "discern in their manner a certain fear of us." He suspected from their actions that they "contemplated stealing away and leaving us in the lurch."

Melville now fully realized that although he and his men had made human contact, they were far from being saved. They somehow had to penetrate farther into the Lena delta and reach a settlement substantial enough to accommodate a party as large and needy as theirs. Repeatedly, Melville asked about Bulun, which was clearly marked on his Petermann chart. Tomat, by shutting his eyes and snoring, indicated that Bulun was "many sleeps" from this place and suggested that getting there would be dangerous.

Instead, Tomat led them to his home, a forlorn speck of a place called Little Borkhia that had many more graveyard crosses than living souls. For several nights, the Americans were put up in a yurtlike structure that was "wondrously dirty," as Melville put it, and "pungent [with] the odor of ancient fish and bones; yet we were very glad to be so comfortably housed, for outside a wild snow-storm raged in the night."

From Little Borkhia, Melville and his men worked their way up the "serpentine windings of the river," continually busting through the young ice that was fast forming over the surface. On September 25, they reached a collection of huts known as Arrhu. Four days later, they arrived at the settlement of Zemovialach, which was built on a marshy island in the river. With a population of perhaps thirty Evenks and a few Yakuts, it was the first place they had encountered that might reasonably be called a village.

Melville's intention was to push on quickly for Bulun, but they had arrived in Zemovialach precisely on the cusp of winter—too late for any more boat travel, yet too early for safe ice travel. It was the transition period between navigation and sledding. By grunts and emphatic gestures, the villagers insisted that it was too dangerous to attempt a journey to Bulun until the river thoroughly froze over.

Melville demanded that someone at least take him to Bulun, but he could not find any natives willing to risk the perilous journey. To push on without a guide, Melville believed, would be suicidal—"a game of mock heroics." There weren't enough dogs around Zemovialach to assemble a team; the few Melville saw were "miserable, low curs." Certainly Melville's explorers were in no shape to travel. "I glanced at my men—weak, hungry, and hollow-eyed," Melville wrote. "Looking around at the miserable objects about me, the scant and tattered clothing, crippled feet and legs, I determined the risk too great."

So they dragged the whaleboat from the river and out of the ice's reach and then set up housekeeping on the periphery of the village in a couple of *balagans*—pyramidal wooden structures with earthen roofs, fur-lined floors, and slabs of ice for windows. They would have to wait two or three weeks, maybe longer. This detention was infuriating—"inaction was worse than death by the roadside," said Melville—but they could not avoid it. They were stuck there, on an island in the middle of the Lena as the ice slowly closed in around them. With no prospect of communicating with the outside world, they believed that they were the only survivors of the USS *Jeannette.*

THEIR DE FACTO imprisonment at Zemovialach proved a blessing in disguise, for Melville and his fellow explorers badly needed to rest. The villagers seemed to understand this better than Melville did, and they cared for their frozen guests with extraordinary generosity. The women of the village were especially empathetic, Melville noted— "they examined our frozen limbs, shaking their heads in compassion, and even weeping over our miseries." (Said the half-blind Danenhower: "The native women were always very kind in spite of their ugliness.") The natives had little idea who these foreigners were, what country they were from, or why they had descended on this part of the world. Some seemed to think they had sprung from the ice itself. Yet the people of Zemovialach always showed the whaleboat's crew the seat of honor as they welcomed them into their smoky warm *balagans,* and they shared everything they had.

Which, in truth, wasn't very much. They were a poor people, facing winter—and as it was, their diet was so deficient in vitamins and minerals that blindness was rampant among them. Still, they were able to donate a ration of four good-sized river fish per day, plus what Melville called "a modicum of rancid deer tallow fried in a dirty pan filled with deer hair." From this, they boiled vats of "long soup"—that is, fish and venison stews economically "lengthened" with river water.

Every day the Evenks also shared three or four geese. This latter foodstuff posed a problem for the Americans, for the natives had a peculiar tradition of eating their fowl in an advanced state of fermentation. They liked to kill their geese during the molting season and dry the whole uncleaned carcasses beside their huts for the rest of the summer. By autumn, the birds had become, as some of the men liked to say, "pretty high." Wrote Melville: "The geese were . . . ancient and odiferous, so much so that when we would hang them up their intestines and juices would drop out." Even for explorers who had inured themselves to eat just about anything, it was a bit much.

During this period of "enforced idleness," as Melville referred to their captivity in Zemovialach, the men whiled away the hours singing songs and playing games with tattered assortments of cards. They soaked their swollen limbs in tubs of warm water. They repaired their torn and hole-ridden clothing, sewing new patches onto old patches. They drank cup after cup of bitter tea and smoked cigarettes of a harsh Russian blend of tobacco. They cleaned and groomed their snaggled, hirsute selves, using combs the Evenks made from the fossil ivory of woolly mammoths. They played intense chess matches with gnarled pieces they had carved from driftwood. They wrote letters, which they hoped to mail home as soon as they reached some place of civilization. In the mornings, they wandered down to the ice-encrusted river and helped the Evenks haul in the daily catch.

Aneguin even found time for romance. As a native Inuit, he looked a bit like his Evenk hosts—at least they seemed to think so—and he spoke a few words of Russian, which they could understand. They soon took him in as one of their own. Melville wrote, "Aneguin was visiting around among his copper-colored brethren and sisters, who began to repair his moccasins and clothing; until, finally, it was noised around that Aneguin had found a sweetheart in the village, which he blushingly acknowledged, and in praising her good qualities, said, *'Him plenty good little old woman.'*"

Melville worried about the possibility of scurvy and, given the fetid state of much of their food, recognized the risk that some of his men might contract dysentery or typhoid fever. Even if the local cuisine was dubious, Melville knew that his life, and that of every man in his party, utterly depended on these generous—but traditionally nomadic—Evenks and Yakuts. "What I most feared," said Melville, "was that the natives, being somewhat wandering in their habits, might fold their tents like the Arabs and silently steal away in the night."

Melville was also worried about Cole. His mental state was slipping fast. He seemed to have entered a dream world, and he spent his days talking gibberish. Melville declared him non compos mentis, "not fractious, but jolly and full of all kinds of nonsense. He had lost all trace of time and circumstances." Cole kept saying that he was "tired of the strange, mysterious fellows" who were all around them. He repeatedly insisted that he wanted to see the "old woman." Imagining that he was a professional pugilist, he had started boxing, jabbing at the air or sometimes taking a swing at anyone who got in the way.

Leach was deteriorating, as well—his frostbitten feet were causing him excruciating pain. Parked before the fire, he had become listless, feverish, and despondent, his spirits slowly draining from him. The flesh on his toes had sloughed away, exposing the stubs of his bones. His good friend Bartlett acted as his doctor, attending his every need. "Gangrene had apparently set in," Melville wrote, "and if the toes were neglected for a day the odor was unbearable. Bartlett daily prepared a kettle of hot water in which he bathed and cleaned the sores, and, with a jack-knife in hand, pared away the flesh in a masterly manner."

With Bartlett's constant attention, Leach eventually came around. As his spirit strengthened, his thoughts wandered toward home, and he composed a letter to his mother in Penobscot, Maine:

My dear mother,

We laid in the ice until our ship (our home) was taken from us. Then our hardships began. We encountered a heavy gale, which nearly put an end to our sufferings. My feet were frozen stiff, and my legs were chilled up to my body so badly that I think they could have been taken off without my feeling it. When we got ashore I was in a tight fix. I could not walk, and was in much pain, and my feet had begun to putrefy. Bartlett, one of the men, took a knife and cut out the corrupt places, and cut about half of one of my great toes off, leaving the bone sticking out of the end. It troubles me to walk now, and I think that it will for some time. I make myself as agreeable as possible. The life is not altogether crushed out of me. Oh mother, you can have no idea of what we went through. When I look back it seems more like a strange dream than a reality.

Guess I have written enough about my trials. Gracious! How I want to see the folks at home. Give my love to everybody, in town and out, keep the lion's share for yourself, and believe me, your loving son,

—Herbert

———

THE AMERICANS HAD been in Zemovialach for nearly two weeks when they chanced to meet an interesting visitor. He was a big, full-bearded Russian with the bearing of a soldier who made his living constantly moving about the delta, trading and bartering. It was Kuzma. His home was a half day's dog drive away in a tiny village called Tamoose. There was an air of mystery about Kuzma—he seemed like an operator—but he appeared competent and interested in Melville's plight. "He was a bright, intelligent looking man," wrote Melville, "and I at once hoped far more from him than from any one we had yet met."

Melville had by then learned a bit of pidgin Russian, and Kuzma soon came to understand the outlines of the Americans' story: that Melville and his men were shipwrecked Americans from a vessel called the *Jeannette,* that they had reached Zemovialach by small boat, and that they were holed up here waiting for the ice to harden. Kuzma presented the Americans with some tobacco, five pounds of salt, several bags of rye flour, sugar, and tea, and a reindeer to eat.

Melville struck a deal with Kuzma: If the Russian would go to Bulun and bring back food, clothing, and reindeer teams, Melville would give him the whaleboat plus 500 rubles. Everywhere he went, Kuzma was to broadcast the news that the *Amerikanskis* were offering a reward of 1,000 rubles to anyone who could bring Melville information about the whereabouts of the two other lost parties—even if it was just reports of relics that might have washed up on shore. Kuzma agreed to the deal, but he insisted that it would be another week before he could safely set out on the journey, as the river still wasn't sufficiently frozen over.

Melville was unsure whether he should trust Kuzma—something was slippery about him. In this part of Siberia, Melville said, "I had learned that lying is not considered a sin; on the contrary, if cleverly done, it is rather regarded in the light of an accomplishment." But Melville had no choice but to shake on the deal.

Kuzma wasn't lying, exactly, but he wasn't telling the full truth. What Melville didn't know was that Kuzma, the criminal exile, was under penalty of death should he venture to Bulun by himself. He had to wait until the *starosta*—elder—from his village, a man named Nicolai Chagra, was able to accompany him on the journey. This complication would cause further delays, but on October 16, Kuzma finally did leave for Bulun. If conditions were favorable, he estimated, it would be about a five-day trip.

For nearly two more weeks, the men waited in Zemovialach. "Many and long were our anxious looks from the hut-top," wrote Melville, "but all in vain, for a sight of Kuzma." Finally, on October 29, he did return, and "never was an absent lover welcomed more joyfully."

It was immediately apparent, however, that Kuzma had not fulfilled his end of the bargain. He brought no food, clothing, or reindeer teams—and, as he soon explained, he had not even been to Bulun. However, something interesting had developed during his journey. At a tiny place called Kumakh-Surt, Kuzma had learned something that he felt obligated him to hurry back to Melville. By way of explanation, Kuzma reached into his pocket and handed over a crumpled scrap of paper bearing a message that fairly electrified the Navy engineer. It said, in part:

Arctic steamer Jeannette lost . . . landed on Siberia 25th September or thereabouts; want assistance to go for the Captain and Doctor and (9) other men.
Willliam F. C. Nindemann
Louis P. Noros,
Seamen U.S.N.

Reply in haste: want food and clothing.

Kuzma explained that he had met the two half-dead Americans who'd written the note and that they were now supposed to be recuperating in Bulun. What he didn't realize was that the eleven surviving shipmates Nindemann and Noros had referred to in Kumakh-Surt were *not* the members of Melville's party; Kuzma did not understand that there was yet another party of eleven Americans suffering somewhere out in the delta. The "captain" Nindemann and Noros had mentioned, Kuzma assumed, was Melville.

Melville was immediately spurred into action. He would leave the other men in Zemovialach for now and hasten to Bulun, where, with Nindemann and Noros, he would initiate a search for De Long. Knowing what he now knew, he chided himself for not having forced his way to Bulun sooner. Kuzma helped him put together a dog team from the village of Tamoose, secured two Evenk drivers, and had a new sled constructed.

On the morning of October 31, as the temperature dipped to twenty degrees below zero, Melville and his drivers took off across the frozen tundra, pulled by eleven "mongrels of every hue and build . . . a motley team in full cry, all yelping, snapping, biting, and seizing each other from behind." Now that the river channel was frozen solid, they were able to make surprisingly good time. With the drivers occasionally beating the sled dogs with iron-tipped clubs, they pressed on through a blizzard and reached Bulun in three exhausting days.

It was almost dark when Melville dismounted from his sled and wandered into the heart of the village. Curious Yakuts swarmed around and soon led him to the little cabin where the two *Amerikanskis* were staying. Melville found the latch, and the door creaked open, revealing the countenances of two beloved shipmates he had not seen in fifty-one days.

NINDEMANN AND NOROS were elated to learn that not only Melville but *all* the men in the whaleboat had survived. They stayed up with the engineer, telling him their own doleful tale, including the story of Erichsen's amputations and his burial in the ice. Melville resolved to leave as soon as feasible for the Lena delta. He was shocked and amazed to hear that De Long and his men might still be alive. He would do whatever it took to assemble dog teams, sleds, and provisions for a multiweek search. He had to make haste before the Arctic winter set in for good.

Melville wanted Nindemann and Noros to come with him, but this was, he said, "out of the question." They were "so sick as to be barely able to walk, vomiting and purging violently—the effects of having gorged themselves on decayed fish." Instead, Melville, working off his own Petermann map of the delta, enlisted Nindemann and Noros to make a detailed sketch of their wanderings—showing the location of their landing, the place where they had left De Long, the hut where they had been saved by the Yakut nomads, and various landmarks along the way.

Melville stayed up much of the night composing the text for a telegram to be sent to the London offices of the *New York Herald,* to the U.S. minister in the Russian capital of St. Petersburg, and to William Henry Hunt, the secretary of the Navy in Washington. Melville's urgent message would be relayed south by a succession of dog and reindeer teams to the city of Irkutsk, the location of the nearest telegraph station. Melville knew his telegram would take weeks, if not months, to reach its destination: Irkutsk, located in southern Siberia not far from Lake Baikal, was nearly three thousand miles away.

Melville would leave Nindemann and Noros here in Bulun and arrange for the other men from the whaleboat to convene here. Together, they would head south toward Yakutsk, a small city on the banks of the Lena River, about a thousand miles to the south, that was the closest approximation to "civilization" in this part of Siberia.

Having secured dog teams, a Cossack guide, and several Yakut scouts, Melville departed for the Lena delta on November 5. In Nindemann's hut, he left a message for Danenhower, instructing the navigator to lead the party to Yakutsk. "I have a pretty good chart to search for the missing," Melville said. "If time and weather permit, I will go to the north coast for the ship's papers, chronometer, etc. I may be gone a month. Fear not for my safety. I will see the natives take care of me."

Melville bid his shipmates farewell and prepared to head back into the icy barrens of the Lena. It must have taken every ounce of his resolve, for he, too, was frostbitten, exhausted, and starved, his system ravaged by months of half-rancid food. He was returning to the delta at a deadly time of year—as the Siberian winter was enveloping the land, bringing gale-force blizzards, perpetual darkness, and temperatures that would plunge to more than fifty degrees below zero.

The engineer knew that he was laughably ill-prepared. Though he had a knack for foreign languages, he had no knowledge of the Yakut tongue, and locals, he found, "could not understand my Russian without great torture." He had little experience with dog teams, either, or with surviving on the open tundra. He would be wandering across a mostly uninhabited maze nearly three times larger than the Florida Everglades—but a *frozen* Everglades with only a few discernible landmarks, which were now obscured by ice and snow.

Attempting to find De Long in this white world, he knew, was quixotic—and, in this season, extremely dangerous. Yet there was a chance that the captain and his men were still alive; as long as that remained true, he knew he had to go. He tried to imagine his comrades out there, languishing, gnawing on fish heads or rawhide boot soles as their extremities blackened and their body heat drained away. He could only hope that, like Nindemann and Noros, they'd met sympathetic nomads, or they'd encountered a riverboat on some branch of the Lena, or they'd been picked up by a search party dispatched from an Arctic rescue ship, or they'd lucked upon a herd of migrating reindeer whose meat and fur had kept them alive.

Even if he were to find that De Long and his men had perished, Melville felt, the search would still be significant. Knowing that the delta was home to wolves, foxes, carrion birds, and the occasional polar bear, he wanted, if his shipmates were dead, to "rescue their bodies from the mutilations of wild beasts."

The coming of the spring floods was an even bigger concern. "The face of the country," Melville noted, "clearly showed me that if I delayed until spring, all trace of my comrades would be swept away by the floods, which completely submerge the delta and deposit great driftwood logs forty feet above the river plain."

He also was determined to rescue any cached records or scientific instruments he might be able to find before the spring deluge ruined them. Nindemann had sketched out for Melville the place on the beach where they'd buried the ship's papers, records, chronometers, and natural history artifacts. Finding the cache would be difficult, Melville knew, but these relics were certainly worth saving.

In Bulun, Melville had made the acquaintance of the Russian authority, Commandant Gregory Bieshoff—"a fine specimen of Cossack manhood," as Melville described him, "very large of stature, and a commanding presence." The resourceful Bieshoff had made arrangements for dog teams, provisions, and two native guides. Although Melville had nothing to offer them now, he promised the Cossack that the United States government would ultimately pay the natives day wages and make good on every expense that might be incurred during the search—plus whatever brokerage fees Bieshoff himself might charge.

The two guides, Vasili and Tomat, were young, strong native men who knew the delta and its system of huts and hunting lodges. But they were extremely skeptical of the mission at hand. They thought Melville must be deranged. All their lives, as winter approached, they had headed *away* from the delta, not toward it. This journey violated their every instinct and habit; to Vasili and Tomat, the assignment seemed on the verge of suicidal. But the two men could use the money, and, knowing that human lives were at stake, they said they were willing to try.

On November 5, Vasili, Tomat, and Melville climbed aboard their sleds and headed north. "I set out," Melville later wrote, "full of hopes and fears for the future—hoping for the best, yet fearing the worst."

FOR DAYS AND DAYS, they cut across the white gloom. It was a dreamworld, shrouded in fog, piled in snowdrifts, with few markings of animals or man—"a barren and desolate region," said Melville, "devoid of sustenance." The runners scraped and snagged on the ice. Tomat and Vasili yelled commands in their strange Turkic language. The dogs struggled against their harnesses. The Siberian winds howled.

Melville was aiming for Bulcour, the place where the native named Ivan had first found Nindemann and Noros in the fishing hut. Tomat and Vasili said they knew the place well, and although the land looked featureless to Melville, they seemed sure of the road.

Standing for days on the back of the bouncing sled, Melville could not ignore how much his already-frostbitten feet troubled him. They had become swollen, inflamed, and blistered, and "all feeling," he said, "seemed to have forsaken them." At a tiny collection of huts called Buruloch, a wizened Yakut woman took pity on Melville and rubbed his feet with warm goose grease, a rank-smelling remedy that seemed to work wonders.

When the party got to Bulcour, Melville made a crackling fire and warmed his feet until they throbbed back to life. Looking about the hut, he spied "several little articles that had been left or lost by Nindemann and Noros." Melville also saw the remains of the pulverized fish his shipmates had eaten, but he wisely declined to partake of the putrid stuff. Yet the food he and his guides had to eat was not much better: raw frozen fish, which Vasili and Tomat cut into bite-sized chunks. They also boiled reindeer antlers and hooves and skimmed off the foamy broth. The three men washed it down with a little tea, then drifted off to sleep, with the dogs curled up in a snowbank just outside the door.

The next morning, Melville studied the ground. In places where the winds had blown off the snow, he could faintly trace the old footprints left by Nindemann and Noros in the encrusted ice, where they had "marched out of the jaws of death," as Melville put it. Here and there he could see where Nindemann or Noros had "plunged through the ice while it was yet young." For several days, Melville and his Yakut guides followed the tracks along the river, until they came to a spot Nindemann had marked on his chart as "The Place of the Sleighs." Here, Nindemann and Noros had smashed up some sleds for firewood, and now Melville could see the charred remains of their bonfire. In a hut a few days later, he found a waist belt that had been made in the blacksmith forge on board the *Jeannette*—he recognized the markings on the buckle.

Melville felt like a detective on a scavenger hunt, compiling tiny clues as he traversed an impossibly huge landscape, working off a crude map that was nonetheless surprisingly accurate. So far, Nindemann's chart had made sense; the delta unfolded just as his memory had captured it. Melville drew within just a few miles of the place where Nindemann and Noros had parted company with De Long.

But over the next few days, driving deeper into the icy wastes, Melville became convinced that he had "lost the scent." The footprints faded or became obscured by snow, and the few huts they encountered had clearly not been occupied for many months. Nindemann's chart no longer seemed to fit this bewildering landscape. The entire delta, Melville concluded in disgust, "was nothing but a congregation of islands."

Vasili and Tomat began to question the merits of pushing on with the search. The dogs were half-starved and exhausted now. The temperature had plummeted to forty below zero, and a lashing snowstorm had reduced the visibility to only a few feet. The two guides implored Melville to turn back for Bulun. But the engineer remained, by his own description, "inexorable." Melville goaded them constantly, having picked up on the journey a smattering of Yakut and Russian, which he mingled with a few "choice expletives selected at random from my own rich mother tongue, the import of which they eventually divined from the vehemence of my delivery." Melville sensed that he was drawing close to De Long's location and felt sure they were on the verge of a breakthrough; he could not abandon the hunt now.

But as conditions worsened, Melville began to suspect that his Yakut guides were plotting to desert him. One morning, they tried to do just that: Tomat and Vasili snuck outside the hut where they were staying, loaded up the sleds, and prepared to take off, leaving him stranded—presumably forever. Apprehending this almost too late, the engineer stumbled out the door, grabbed Tomat's iron-shod staff, and, "dealt him a staggering blow." When Tomat and Vasili continued running for their sleds, Melville seized his gun and fired a volley into the air. "The bullet went whistling over their heads," Melville said, "and at the report both natives fell on their faces. Then, turning around on their knees, they began crossing themselves in terror," pleading with Melville not to kill them.

With the crisis momentarily averted, Melville realized that he had to devise a new plan that would regain the Yakuts' confidence. He decided that they would head for the tiny village of North Bulun, a speck of civilization not far from the Arctic coast and one of the only inhabited places in the delta during winter. North Bulun was supposed to be about 120 versts, or eighty miles, to the northwest. There, they would try to procure more provisions and fresh dogs. From North Bulun, they would make an eastward crease along the Arctic coast, in hopes of finding the cache of logbooks and instruments De Long had buried. Using the cache site as a new starting point, they would then try to retrace De Long's trail inland.

Vasili and Tomat seemed to like the new plan—to the extent that they understood it—and in a few days they arrived in North Bulun, where the villagers greeted Melville warmly. He was led to a central yurt and crawled inside to find a dozen souls crowded in the smoky, greasy chamber. "A more motley or odoriferous crowd of mortals I never saw packed within so small a space," Melville wrote.

The Yakuts had heard reports all over this part of the delta about strange footprints seen in the snow. They had also discovered that many of their traps had been torn up and used for firewood. They were "puzzled to know by whom the footprints had been made," said Melville, "fearing at first that some ruffian band of freebooters or fugitive exiles had come their way."

Then several Yakuts approached Melville with relics they had found out in the delta. One native showed him a broken Winchester rifle that someone had left in a hut—Melville recognized it immediately as belonging to the *Jeannette* expedition. Then an old woman came forward and searched "in the inner recesses of her bosom," said Melville, until she pulled out a note De Long had written on September 22. The note, which had been picked up by a hunter, read:

Thursday, 22nd Sept. 1881.

Arctic Exploring Steamer Jeannette
At a Hut on the Lena Delta, believed to be near Tch-ol-booje.
Whoever finds this paper is requested to forward it to the Secretary of the United States Navy. On Monday, Sept. 19, we left a pile of our

effects near the beach, erecting a long pole. There will be found navigating instruments, chronometer, ships' log-books for two years, tents, medicines, &c, which we were absolutely unable to carry. It took us forty-eight hours to make these twelve miles, owing to our disabled men. Last night we shot two reindeer, which gives us abundance of food for the present, and we have seen so many more that anxiety for the future is relieved.

George W. De Long, Lieut. Commanding.

Inspired by these new clues, Melville yearned to get started. The next day, November 13, he left North Bulun with fresh dog teams and several more Yakut guides to accompany Tomat and Vasili. The following day, they reached the coast, where blocks of ice "lay stranded like so many monuments of the Druids." Within a few hours Melville spotted the flagstaff marking the cache, just as De Long had described it. When Melville pointed it out to his dog drivers, they could "scarcely contain themselves in their anxiety to see what was buried there." They dug away the snow and sand and found a miscellany of guns, tents, medical supplies, navigational instruments, a large Bible, and, to Melville's relief, the ship's records, all in good condition. The Yakuts were struck with "wonder and delight . . . [they] had never before seen so much plunder in one heap."

Also in the cache was a large tin box filled with rock specimens, mosses, and other natural bric-a-brac that had been found on Bennett Island. When Melville loaded it carefully, along with the other artifacts, onto the sleds, the Yakuts looked befuddled. They stared disbelievingly into the tin box, then rummaged through its contents. "After some chattering among themselves," said Melville, "they finally burst forth into a loud guffaw at the idiocy of a man who, upon the point of starvation, proposed to encumber himself on a long journey with a load of worthless stones."

Melville searched several hours in vain for the first cutter—the boat De Long had abandoned in the muddy shoals—but concluded that it had been crushed by the ice. He saw no sign of Chipp's boat or his party.

Melville and his dog drivers camped in a hut not far from the coast and made a fire. The Yakuts discovered among the items retrieved from De Long's cache a wicker-covered vessel containing a small quantity of alcohol. "The natives soon learned that I had spirits," wrote Melville, "and all congregated around in the hope of having a spree."

"Just a little! Just a little!" Tomat begged.

Melville refused him, saying that the alcohol was "only good for fire"—it was stove fuel, not for drinking. Then one of the other young Yakuts seized the container and bolted. "I caught him before he reached the door," said Melville, "spilling the alcohol over the floor, whereupon he got down on his stomach and eagerly lapped up the precious fluid." Furious, Melville emptied the remaining contents among the ashes of the hearth, "where it took fire and burned for a long while, greatly to the sorrow of poor Tomat and his friends."

FROM THE ARCTIC coast, Melville turned his search inland, using Nindemann's notes to follow the path De Long had taken. For several days they were clearly on the right course—Melville could see footprints from time to time, and he even traced the track of the makeshift sled on which the cutter's crew had hauled the dying Erichsen across the ice. For several more days, Melville hunted without success for the hut where Erichsen had died and where Nindemann had carved his crude epitaph on an old board.

Melville feared he had lost the trail a second time—and, again, the Yakuts grew apprehensive about continuing the search. But Tomat told Melville something that gave him hope De Long might be alive yet: The Yakuts had what amounted to food depots hidden all over the delta. This was how they survived their wanderings in the harsh and unpredictable climate, how they forestalled disaster on their long forays, a stash of frozen fish here, a trove of goose carcasses there. In fact, just a few miles away, Tomat mentioned, the meat of twenty-three reindeer had been hoisted up on a kind of trestlework platform to keep it clear of the floods and scavenging animals. Melville wondered if by some miracle De Long and his men had found one of these food depots and perhaps were subsisting on its bounty even now. If not, he thought, it was "most pitiful to think how unconsciously near they were to salvation."

By November 20, having made no more discoveries, Melville finally was ready to give up on the search. Even he could see that they were endangering their lives. They were freezing and demoralized, and the dog teams were "completely fagged out," he said. The Siberian winter had proved too formidable a foe.

In the 1860s, the French scientist Louis Figuier had written eloquently about this same country in his book *Earth and Sea,* which was part of the *Jeannette*'s library collection. "The tundra," Figuier said, "is the very grave of nature, the sepulchre of the primeval world . . . Dense grows the atmosphere; the stars wane and flicker; all nature sleeps a sleep that resembles death." In the tundra, he said, "the people, and even the snow, emit a constant smoke, and this evaporation is immediately transformed into millions of icy needles, which make a noise in the air like the crackling of thick silk. The reindeer crowd together for the sake of the warmth derivable from such contiguity, and only the raven, the dark bird of winter, cleaves the somber sky with slow-laboring wing, and marks the track of his solitary flight by a long line of thin vapor."

This was the landscape that had defeated Melville. He would have to return at a different season of the year. For now, he turned south and headed back for Bulun, a week's journey over the same frozen labyrinths. His memory of the trip was a blur of misery. "When night overtook us," Melville said, "I felt as we floundered aimlessly about in the snow that it made little difference to me whether I lived or died. It seemed to me that the terrible journey would have no end. I was awake and aware of all that was transpiring around me, but had lost all feeling and power of speech, and existed like an animated dead man."

Melville began to appreciate more fully why De Long had buried all those relics in the sand: They put a tremendous strain on the dogs. He worried that hauling this burdensome freight could eventually kill not just the dogs but the whole party. "Now and then, I would decide to cache the relics at the first safe place we came to, returning for them when I could; but after a moment's reflection, recalling how persistently we had clung to these treasures—the records and valuable accumulations of our two years of toil and suffering—and setting my teeth against the storm, I would swear a new oath to carry them through, come what might."

MELVILLE ARRIVED IN Bulun on November 27, his face windburned and frostnipped almost beyond recognition. He and his Yakut guides had been gone for twenty-three days and had driven more than fourteen hundred zigzagging miles over the tundra.

Most of the *Jeannette* survivors had headed south with Danenhower for the city of Yakutsk, nearly a thousand miles upriver; only Nindemann, Noros, and a few others were still in Bulun to greet

Melville. The engineer told them how sorry he was to return with no good news—other than having found the cache on the beach. "I regretted my failure to find my lost comrades," he said, but felt "satisfied that I'd done all that was possible for me to do. If De Long and his party were alive and in the hands of natives, they were certainly as well off as myself; if dead, then the natives had been wise in admonishing me that I should die too if I persisted in searching at that season of the year."

Over the course of his search, Melville had at least been able to produce something of value: an accurate chart of the Lena delta, no doubt the most accurate one then in existence—and certainly far better than Petermann's flawed rendering. Had De Long had the benefit of this improved map at the time of his landing, he and his men would have been spared most of their hardships.

After thawing out a few days in Bulun, Melville prepared to go south. The tiny, impoverished town of Bulun could not support them—as it was, the Americans had already overtaxed its meager supplies of food and livestock. Melville, Nindemann, Noros, and the others would push on, via reindeer team, to the provincial capital of Yakutsk, where they would regroup with the other *Jeannette* survivors, heal their wounds, try to communicate with the outside world, and plan a much more thorough search expedition for De Long and Chipp. They would return to the delta in the spring—when the weather was warmer but, hopefully, before the Lena floods came into their full fury.

Melville thanked Commandant Bieshoff for his assistance and urged him to keep the pressure on the sparse native populations of the delta while Melville was away in Yakutsk. "It is my desire and [that] of the government of the United States of America," Melville wrote Bieshoff, "that a diligent and constant search be made for my missing comrades. It is necessary that all—every house and hut, large and small—must be examined for books, papers, or the persons of the party."

On December 1, Melville and the others gathered up the *Jeannette* relics that had been found on the coast and headed south for Yakutsk.

LONDON, DECEMBER 22, 1881

The following telegram was received at the *Herald*'s London office at twenty past two this morning:—

Irkutsk, December 21, 2:05 P.M.

Jeannette was crushed by the ice in latitude 77 degrees 15 min. north, longitude 157 degrees east.

Boats and sleds made a good retreat to fifty miles northwest of the Lena River, where the three boats became separated in a gale.

The whaleboat, in the charge of Chief-Engineer Melville, entered the east mouth of the Lena River on September 17th. It was stopped by ice in the river. We found a native village, and as soon as the river closed I put myself in communication with the commandant.

On October 29th, I heard that the cutter containing Lieutenant De Long, Dr. Ambler, and twelve others, had landed at the north mouth of the Lena. All are in a sad condition and badly frozen. The commandant has sent native scouts to look for them, and will urge vigorous and constant search until they are found.

The second cutter has not yet been heard from. Telegraph money for instant use to Irkutsk.

(Signed), Melville

Navy Department
Washington, DC

December 22d, 1881

To Engineer Melville, U.S.N., Irkutsk:—
Omit no effort, spare no expense, in securing safety of men in second

cutter. *Let the sick and the frozen of those already rescued have every attention, and as soon as practicable have them transported to a milder climate. Department will supply necessary funds.*

Hunt, Secretary

Department of State
Washington, D.C.

A dispatch from Mr. Hoffman, chargé d'affaires of the United States at St. Petersburg, conveying the assurance that the most energetic measures would be taken by the Russian authorities for the discovery and relief of the missing men, was received today by the Secretary of State at Washington.

Immediately upon receipt of the first news about the Jeannette, Mr. James Gordon Bennett, residing in Paris, transferred the sum of 6,000 roubles by telegraph, through Messrs. Rothschilds, to St. Petersburg, with a request to draw on Mr. Bennett for any further sums required for the succor and comfort of Lieutenant De Long and his party.

Dearest George,

I hope to see my own dear husband in a month or two at best, if you are well enough that you can reach St. Petersburg. I want to join you there. I would so like to be with you, to take care of you. I am afraid to think of what condition you may be in. I am not afraid to take the journey. I do not know the possibilities of traveling in Siberia or I would gladly go the whole way to you if you are still ill. I cabled Mr. Bennett asking him if it would be practicable for me to go to you to nurse you. Bennett answered that he had sent a correspondent; even if I could have been there in time to start with him, the extra preparations required to protect a woman against the hardships of Siberian winter travel would have caused serious delay. But I think I could take better care of you than anyone else and make you well and strong.

—Emma

From a distance, the city rose like a vision from the west bank of the frozen Lena: fortress towers, wooden spires, onion domes, a sprawl of weathered homes wreathed in the smoke of a thousand birch fires. Melville could not believe his eyes.

Yakutsk, the capital of an enormous swath of Siberia known as Yakutia, was a settlement of five thousand people, mostly natives, but also with a large population of political exiles and banished criminals. Founded in 1632 as a Cossack *ostrog* (fort), it remained an important outpost of the czar's fur monopoly and the center of a bustling trade in mammoth ivory. Yakutsk was widely considered the coldest city on earth—a designation it still holds today—and the world's largest city built entirely on permafrost. As cold as it was, the first few feet of the soil thawed into miasmal bogs each summer, so that houses had to be built on reinforced pilings to keep the foundations from sagging in the mud.

It had taken Melville nearly a month to reach Yakutsk by reindeer team, traveling over the Verkhoyansk Range, down into the valley of the Yana River. He'd slept in cabins and, occasionally, the horse stables of Yakut families. Along the way, he had crossed south of the Arctic Circle before rejoining the Lena River, which, when frozen solid, functioned as a highway. The thousand-mile journey, while arduous, had brought no calamities.

When he pulled into Yakutsk on December 30, Melville was taken to the home of the highest Russian authority, Governor-General

George Tchernieff. He was a strapping man in full uniform, a bachelor in his early sixties—"straight as a spear-shaft," said Melville, with "flowing white hair and beard, large aquiline nose, handsome face and carriage, and a very soldierly air."

Tchernieff looked Melville over, examining his encrusted face and his filthy furs with such intensity that for a moment Melville did not know what to do; he felt embarrassed by his raggedness. But then Tchernieff embraced the engineer and kissed him on both cheeks. "My son, my son," he moaned in sadness at all that Melville had suffered. Tears rolled down his face as he hugged Melville again and again. "He was a soldier," Melville wrote, "so apologies for my appearance were not necessary."

The governor-general had been expecting Melville's arrival for the past week. Tchernieff invited him inside, and they sat down to a sumptuous lunch: soup, fish, beef, potatoes and other vegetables, a little claret, a little Madeira, a glass of vodka. They finished it off with cigars and a bottle of champagne.

For the past week, Tchernieff had been regularly meeting with Danenhower, who had arrived in Yakutsk with his charge of *Jeannette* survivors on December 17. The governor-general had outfitted the Americans in proper clothes, billeted them in clean apartments with warm bedrooms lit by kerosene lamps, and arranged for them take regular steam baths at the Russian *banya*. He'd also given them spending money and all the food they wanted. He'd arranged for a Cossack to guard and protect Cole—the crazy one, whose dementia had only worsened since leaving the Lena delta. Doctors had attended to Leach's frostbite and Danenhower's eye. Tchernieff had treated the men of the *Jeannette* as though they were prized soldiers from his own garrison.

Now the governor-general wanted to make sure Melville was comfortable. Was there anything else he could do for the Americans?

Yes, there was, Melville replied. He wanted to return to the Lena delta as soon as the weather permitted and renew his search for his lost commander. He wanted dogs, reindeer, and a knowledgeable, multilingual guide. He wanted money and tobacco to serve as gifts along the way. He wanted official letters of support, and provisions enough to prosecute a search that might last two or three months.

"My son, you may have anything you want," Tchernieff assured Melville. "You have the whole Russian nation at your back."

———

WHEN MELVILLE REUNITED with the other *Jeannette* survivors in their warm lodge, he was thrilled to see how good they looked. They were dressed in tight-fitting boots and stylish white shirts with crisp collars. They were given a samovar to make warm tea. "They seemed comfortable and happy," Melville wrote, "and were already on visiting terms with the inhabitants. Many, too, had sweethearts, and had they stayed much longer, some would have had wives."

Danenhower was now completely blind in his left eye, and his right was "suffering by sympathy," as he put it. But he seemed otherwise healthy and in good spirits. "I always hope for the best," Danenhower wrote his mother from Yakutsk, "and I am disposed to look upon the bright side. That philosophy has carried me through very trying experiences during the past three years."

Only one man's condition had deteriorated. Jack Cole was now completely out of his head—his daffiness would have been comical had it not been so sad. He told Melville that he was soon to be wed to Queen Victoria. He had recently come into a fortune, he said, and believed that the Cossack who guarded (and sometimes restrained) him for his own safety was his "body servant." For reasons no one could understand, Cole kept asking his mates for matches, so that he could light a fire.

A photographer in Yakutsk took a group portrait of the thirteen *Jeannette* survivors: Melville, Danenhower, Newcomb, Nindemann, Noros, Wilson, Charley Tong Sing, Aneguin, Lauterbach, Bartlett, Cole, Mansen, and Leach. The photograph was later turned into an engraving that would run in newspapers around the world. The men were gathered tightly together in their thick furs. Danenhower's left eye was covered by a black patch. Collectively, they wore an expression that was neither happy nor sad—simply implacable, determined, and proud.

For the Yakuts, the *Amerikanskis* were a curiosity. As far as anyone knew, no American had visited here since 1787, when a swashbuckling, Connecticut-born explorer named John Ledyard had made his way to this part of Siberia as part of an around-the-globe journey that had been encouraged by Thomas Jefferson, then the ambassador to France. In the broad, snow-covered streets of Yakutsk, the natives swarmed the men of the *Jeannette* and offered them food and

presents. These town-dwelling Yakuts were different from the impoverished natives Melville had met in the delta. They lived in sturdy
wooden homes with doors made of rawhide. Like the Mongols, they
were horse lovers; over the centuries, they had bred a sturdy, shaggy
strain of pony that could withstand the cold. The Yakuts drank great
quantities of mare's milk and preferred horsemeat to beef. The idiom
they spoke was so close to modern Turkish that it was said to be
"intelligible at Constantinople."

They were expert metalworkers and dexterous carvers of ivory. It
was astonishing how much mammoth ivory there was in this part of
the world—the permafrost kept the massive tusks in pristine condition. The Yakuts used the ivory to make jewelry, buttons, utensils,
combs, figurines, and all manner of work implements. According to
their tribal legends, the mammoth was an animal that lived in the
earth and burrowed like a mole, and it died when it came into contact
with fresh air.

WHILE IN YAKUTSK, the *Jeannette* survivors began to glean their
first reports from the outside world. They were still nearly two thousand miles away from the nearest telegraph station, in Irkutsk, but
the settlement did receive occasional rumors and flickerings of international news. Melville learned, for example, that a new American
president, a man named Garfield, had been elected in 1880, while the
Jeannette was stuck in the ice. In July 1881, however, President Garfield had been shot by a delusional assassin. The president had hung
on for weeks but finally had died of his infected wound.

Garfield's assassination resonated particularly strongly with the
Russians Melville met in Yakutsk, for in March of that same year,
Russia had experienced a very similar upheaval: Czar Alexander II
had been slain in St. Petersburg, the victim of a bomb detonated by
anarchists. Alexander II had freed the serfs and had planned other
sweeping reforms, but the succeeding czar, Alexander III, reversed
many of his father's liberal measures. Although St. Petersburg lay
more than five thousand miles from Yakutsk, the impact of the assassination could still be felt.

Already heavily populated with exiles, Yakutsk was seeing an
almost daily influx of new arrivals. They came from all over the Russian Empire, from Moscow, from the Crimea, from Poland. Many
of them were well educated, and most did not know what they had

done to earn their term of banishment—which, often as not, was
for life. Seldom had they even been charged with a crime; they had
simply been issued an "administrative order" and sent east to live out
their lives in a prison without bars. The land itself was harsh and vast
enough to detain them. Their stories were beyond tragic, and they
made Melville realize that the *Jeannette*'s tale of woe was all but swal-
lowed in a land of limitless sorrow.

One of the exiles Melville met was a young nihilist intellectual
named Leon—"a slender, dark, and cadaverous-visaged young man,"
said the engineer, "whose hair was black and long, reaching to his
shoulders." Leon had been arrested in a protest on the streets of Moscow and banished to Siberia for life. While he was en route, a Cossack officer let Leon look at his detention papers, which read: "We
can prove nothing against this man, but he is a student of law and no
doubt a very dangerous man."

Leon introduced Melville to a group of other exiles—young, ide-
alistic intellectuals who for years had been planning to escape from
Siberia by boat. "My coming filled them with the wildest hopes,"
Melville understood, "for heretofore it had been considered as impossible to effect an escape by the ice of the Arctic Ocean as to cross a
living sea of fire. Yet before I left they told me that they intended to
make the attempt." They looked upon the men of the *Jeannette* as a
"most curious phenomenon," said Melville. It was a measure of their
desperation that they could find solace in a shipwreck tale as dark as
the *Jeannette*'s. "We had risen before them," Melville said, "like a pillar of hope."

Leon and his band of exiles had scrounged a few compasses and
other instruments and were attempting to build a sextant. They had
been collecting charts and supplies for the journey. Their plan sounded
deranged, a *Jeannette* voyage in reverse. They intended to construct
a small vessel and float more than a thousand miles down the Yana
River to the Arctic Ocean, and then attempt a voyage of nearly two
thousand miles along the coast of Siberia to the Bering Strait and
Alaska, where they would seek asylum in the free United States. "I
ardently hoped that [they] might be crowned with success," Melville
said. "For here I saw youth, intelligence, and refinement immured for
life in an Arctic desert."

(The following year, Melville learned that Leon, together with
twelve other exiles, did embark on their bold plan of escape. "Eluding
their pursuers," Melville wrote, "they succeeded, after many difficul-

ties, in working their way down the [Yana] River, past a village near its mouth, to within sight of the sea; but the rolling waves paralyzed them with terror." Two of the escapees surrendered themselves to the authorities; the rest were soon captured, and all were sent off to an even more hopeless and squalid exile elsewhere in Siberia.)

TO USHER IN the New Year, Governor-General Tchernieff presided over a party at the public assembly room. There was much drinking, dancing, and gaming, and a large orchestra played through the night. All the elite of Yakutsk were in attendance, as were the men of the *Jeannette*. One high-ranking official turned to Melville and explained with a smile, "On this night, as on no other, every man has his own wife at his side, instead of some other man's."

At the stroke of midnight, Tchernieff announced the start of 1882. He proposed a toast to the life and health of the new czar and to the intrepid men of the USS *Jeannette*. Melville was moved by his warmth, but as the evening wore on and the champagne and vodka flowed without end, he became disgusted. Everyone in Yakutsk, it seemed to him, had been drunk for several weeks and would stay drunk for at least another, as the religious festivals and public holidays continued. "In Russia," Melville wrote, "intoxicating drink is a clog and a curse. I am satisfied that the Russians surpass every nation on the face of the globe in their ingenuity for avoiding work and getting drunk."

The *Jeannette* survivors would stay together in Yakutsk for only another week. Melville finally received the telegram from the Navy Department acknowledging receipt of his earlier transmission and advising him to send most of the survivors south to "a milder climate" so they could recover in preparation for the long journey home, across six time zones to St. Petersburg, then to London, and then by steamer to New York. Danenhower would take nine men—everyone but Bartlett and Nindemann, the two men Melville judged to be the most competent and useful for his coming search in the Lena delta.

On January 9, Danenhower and his charges started by reindeer team toward Irkutsk. Governor-General Tchernieff and half the population of Yakutsk turned out on what Melville described as "a blue frosty day." With tears in their eyes, Melville, Bartlett, and Nindemann bid their countrymen good-bye. Yet many of the citizens of Yakutsk also had tears in their eyes—especially the exiles, who tried to imagine the freedoms the travelers would enjoy on the other end of their journey. The exiles had come, said Melville, "to see the Americans set out for America. They hungrily eyed the travelers and envied them their journey. I pitied the poor exiles, gazing wistfully on our little band of sailors, as though they were so many happy spirits bound for heaven."

In my last letter I had not yet fully realized the situation. I thought you were with Mr. Melville and well cared for. The papers now say you have not as yet been found, that Nindemann and Noros left you all badly frozen and in danger of starvation. All this forms a dreadful picture for me to dwell upon, and I do not know whether I will ever see my own dearest husband again.

The thought of what you have suffered is heartrending. I wish I had listened to no one but had gone right off and tried to get to you whatever the consequences might have been. If I could only be on my way to you, doing something for you! You who are so impatient can well understand the hardship of having to wait supinely day after day, waiting and watching, fearing and hoping. My dearest husband, I am not giving up.

All I can do is put my trust in Providence. I have been struggling day after day between hopes and fears, praying to God every minute. My mind is scarcely in a fit condition to write you even now. Every day, every hour tells. I can only hope you have come across some natives. I suppose your fate is decided one way or the other by this time.

A week later, Melville left Yakutsk, heading in the opposite direction: north, toward the Lena delta. This time he had Nindemann and Bartlett with him, but he was also accompanied by a retinue of soldiers and hired guides. Governor-General Tchernieff had made good on his promise. The Russian nation, it seemed, really *was* at Melville's back. At last, the engineer would have the resources he needed to carry out a thorough search: official letters of support, translators, scouts, laborers, excavation tools, fresh dogs and reindeer, sturdy sleds, a supply train extending all the way north from Yakutsk, and food depots scattered about the delta, stocked with ten thousand dried fish. It was a marshaling of assets that had never been seen in this part of Siberia.

Yet even with all this, the search proved nearly impossible. It took Melville more than a month just to reach the delta, only to find the region buffeted by nonstop gales. The storms blew for more than a month. Most of the time, Melville couldn't budge.

When the weather briefly broke in mid-March, Melville pressed his advantage. Traveling with Nindemann and a team of some of the best hired Yakuts, he made straight for the place where Nindemann and Noros had parted company with De Long. From there, Melville planned to fan out and work south, searching in a systematic fashion, quadrant by quadrant.

For a week, they had no luck at all. But on March 23, while following a broad bend in a frozen back channel of the river, Melville spotted something dark in the snow a few thousand yards ahead. They hurried to it and found that it was a marker of some kind: Four sticks had been propped together and lashed with rope. Hanging from this makeshift construction was a hunting rifle. Melville instantly recognized it as Alexey's Remington. This, Melville reflexively thought, was a bad sign: Alexey was the only real hunter in the group, De Long's mainstay. Melville cleared the barrel and found no note inside. He could not understand why the rifle had been placed there. If it was a marker, what was it meant to mark?

Although everything was buried in deep snow, Melville got a powerful sense that De Long and his men had camped here, along this desolate bend in the river. He asked the Yakuts to scour the flats, while he and a native named La Kentie walked to higher ground to take compass readings and get an overview of the scene. As Melville ascended the bank, he spied an old scrap of clothing, then a pair of mittens, half-buried in the snow. He came to a place where a fire had been built. Huge logs of driftwood, some of them charred, had been hauled up from the river. Nearby was a large cake of river ice that evidently had been intended for drinking water.

Then Melville discerned a familiar object peeking from the snow, not far from the charred logs. It was a copper teakettle, smudged black from innumerable fires. Melville tramped over to pick it up, and as he did he nearly tripped over another object: a human arm and hand, protruding from the snow, frozen solid and cocked at a curious angle. La Kentie dropped his compass and backpedaled in fright, crossing himself.

Around the fire pit, Melville spotted the bodies of two other men. He called for Nindemann, who was off in the distance, searching downriver, along the bank. In this important moment, he wanted Nindemann to be there, to absorb the discovery with him, to be a witness.

While waiting for Nindemann, Melville and La Kentie looked around in the snow. They found a medicine chest, a hatchet, and a tin cylinder, nearly four feet long, in which were stored a large collection of charts and drawings from the *Jeannette*'s voyage.

A few feet from the exposed hand, Melville found a small notebook. He picked it up and immediately recognized the handwriting. It was the "ice journal" Captain De Long had kept since the day the *Jeannette* sank. The leather-bound volume was tattered and water-stained, but the entries were legible. In their descriptions, and in the details Melville was able to tease from the scene before him, a vivid picture of De Long's movements and trials emerged. Melville glanced at the last entry first. The wind rippled the pages as he flipped back through the journal and started to read.

ON OCTOBER 9, the day Nindemann and Noros had left on their separate sojourn to the south, De Long and his men had enjoyed a turn of good luck. That day, Alexey shot three ptarmigans, from which they made a warm soup. Somewhat fortified by this, the eleven men stumbled southward a few miles, following in Nindemann's and Noros's footsteps. By the river's edge, they found a rotten canoe and used it for a shelter that night.

The next day, October 10, Alexey spotted more ptarmigan tracks in the snow, but he could not flush out any game. The men camped in a crevice in a snowbank with nothing to eat but a spoonful each of glycerin, a colorless, flavorless paste from Dr. Ambler's medicine chest. Unsatisfied by this, some of the men began to chew on scraps of their deerskin clothing. "All hands weak and feeble," De Long wrote. "God help us."

For the next two days they could not move; they were too fatigued to walk against the fierce wind. Growing hungrier, they harvested tufts of lichen and Arctic willow from the ground and boiled it into a tea. "Everybody getting weaker and weaker," De Long said. "Hardly strength to get firewood."

On October 13, De Long noted that it was the 123rd day since the *Jeannette* had sunk. He had begun to despair. They had nothing to eat but more willow tea. De Long kept looking toward the south, in the hope that Nindemann would reappear with help from the natives, but no one came. "We cannot move against the wind, and staying here means starvation," he wrote. "No news from Nindemann. We are in the hands of God, and unless He intervenes we are lost."

They managed to drag themselves another mile or two, then realized they were missing Walter Lee. They found him a few hundred yards back, lying in the snow, pleading to be left alone. He said he just wanted to die. He was listless and seemed confused. Everyone gathered around him and recited the Lord's Prayer. They were able to get him on his feet and moving again, then made their camp across a stream in the protection of a snowbank. Soon a gale began to blow, assuring another "horrible night."

The following day brought a little luck once again: Alexey shot a ptarmigan, and that night they had some soup to complement their willow tea. In the morning, October 15, they boiled two old boots for breakfast and gnawed on the leather as best they could. Alexey was not faring well. He was "broken down," wrote De Long, and refused to hunt. Everyone kept looking for signs of Nindemann, and at twilight De Long thought he could see campfire smoke on the southern horizon.

The next morning, Ambler announced that Alexey was dying. The doctor could do nothing for him. His pulse was weak, his pupils dilated. Ambler baptized the Inuit, and De Long read prayers over him.

By sunset, Alexey was gone. Ambler listed the cause of death as "exhaustion from hunger & exposure." De Long draped a Navy ensign flag over him, and the next day they laid him out on the river and covered him with slabs of ice. Thoughts turned to Alexey's wife and little boy, who'd come aboard the *Jeannette* in St. Michael, Alaska.

De Long understood that Alexey wasn't alone—life was ebbing from everyone now. Shivering constantly, they were sloppy and their hands uncoordinated as their circulatory systems shunted blood from their extremities to their vital organs. In the throes of starvation, their bodies had begun to metabolize their own muscles and connective tissues. They were consuming themselves from within.

By October 19, the ten men could not move. They had exhausted their stamina cutting up a tent to improvise footgear—an exercise made necessary by their steady consumption of their own boots and sealskin mukluks.

Now Lee and Kaack began to slip. They were, De Long said, "done up." De Long read the prayers for the sick, which traditionally included this passage from the Book of Psalms: "Out of the depths have I cried unto thee, O Lord . . . Let thine ears be attentive to the voice of my supplications . . . My soul waiteth for the Lord more than they that watch for the morning."

Kaack died around midnight on October 21, and Lee the next day about noon. The men tried to bury their two comrades out on the ice where they had left Alexey, but they could not summon the energy. Collins and Ambler helped the captain drag Kaack and Lee around the corner of their tent so at least the corpses would be out of sight.

Their number had dwindled to eight. By then, everyone surely had the same faraway look that had shone in Kaack's and Lee's eyes. Even if they had spotted game, they had grown too weak to hold a steady aim. Their bellies had drawn up horribly. Those who were dying crawled ever closer to the fire, and some even lay in the smoldering ashes. Their thinking had become foggy, their judgment erratic, their sense of the world shrunken. By now, the heartbeats of some of the weakest probably had lapsed into arrhythmias. Some of the men were likely hallucinating.

De Long wrote:

October 23rd, Sunday.—One hundred thirty third day [since the *Jeannette*'s sinking]. Everybody pretty weak. Slept or rested all day, and then managed to get enough wood in before dark. Read part of divine service. Suffering in our feet. No foot gear.

After that, the journal dropped off into a stark recitation of days passed and deaths noted, as though De Long were a castaway on a desert island, mindful of conserving his strength while marking only the barest of facts.

October 24th, Monday.—One hundred and thirty fourth day. A hard night.

October 25th, Tuesday.—One hundred and thirty fifth day.

October 26th, Wednesday.—One hundred and thirty sixth day.

October 27th, Thursday.—One hundred and thirty seventh day. Iverson broken down.

October 28th, Friday.—One hundred and thirty eighth day. Iverson died during early morning.

October 29th, Saturday.—One hundred and thirty ninth day. Dressler died during night.

October 30th, Sunday.—One hundred and fortieth day. Boyd and Görtz died during night. Mr. Collins dying.

There De Long's journal ended. Melville closed it and looked out over the frozen Lena.

WHEN NINDEMANN ARRIVED, Melville shook his head. "They're here," he said. Three frozen corpses lay at Melville's feet: They were the bodies of Ah Sam, Dr. Ambler, and Captain De Long. On the basis of what Melville had read, he now believed that along the river, not far from the location of Alexey's rifle, they would find eight more.

Melville set two of the Yakuts to digging in the snow down along the river. For hours, they exerted themselves "to their utmost," Melville said. Eventually they excavated the wood and ashes of an old fire pit. They found a tin drinking pot, some scraps of clothing, a woolen mitten, and two tin cases of books and papers. Suddenly the two Yakut men scurried from the pit, "as though the arch-fiend himself was at their heels," Melville said.

They gasped, *"Pomree! Pomree! Dwee pomree!"* (Dead! Dead! Two dead!).

Melville crawled into the hole and glimpsed the partly exposed head of one corpse, then the feet of another. Reluctantly, the Yakuts resumed their work and soon excavated the back and shoulders of a third body.

For two days, the grim work continued. Some of the bodies stuck fast to the ice and had to be pried loose with pieces of timber. Eventually, Melville and his laborers found Kaack, Lee, Iverson, Dressler, Boyd, and Görtz. For a long time they searched for Alexey, to no avail.

They began to lay the bodies out on the snow. Nindemann carefully went through their pockets and put everything he found in separate bags, marked with the men's names. Melville was struck by how "natural" the corpses looked. "The faces of the dead were remarkably well-preserved," he wrote. "They had the appearance of marble, with the blush frozen in their cheeks. Their faces were full, for the process of freezing had slightly puffed them; yet this was not true of their limbs, which were pitifully emaciated, or of their stomachs, which had shrunk into great cavities."

Melville also noted that their shoes had all been eaten. "There was not a whole moccasin left among them, or a piece of hide or skin," he wrote. "The clothing of the dead was badly burnt, [because] they lay so close to the fire; and those who perished first were stripped of their rags. Boyd lay almost in the fire, his clothes scorched through."

Eventually the excavators found Collins. The Irishman's face had been covered with a piece of red flannel cloth. He had a rosary in one of his pockets and a bronze cross around his neck. Also on his person were various papers and a notebook. Nindemann studied Collins for quite a while. Something about him seemed different from the others. For most of the expedition, Collins had been a miserable man, and perhaps he had carried his grievances against De Long to his grave. "He was lying on his back," Nindemann said, "with his fists clenched, and his expression was very bitter. There wasn't a man in the party [who] had such an expression on his face as he had. His teeth were clenched, and his expression was hard, as if he had *died* very hard."

Kaack and Lee had had their clothes picked from their bodies, but otherwise none of the remains had been tampered with. There was no sign of cannibalism—although Melville must have considered that possibility with respect to Alexey, since the Inuit's corpse was never found. Had De Long's men eaten him, the camp surely would have borne the telltale evidence, but Melville's laborers scoured every inch of the area and found nothing to support this hypothesis. Melville and Nindemann reached a far simpler conclusion: Alexey's grave site had collapsed through the ice and his body had been swept away by undercurrents of the Lena.

SAVE FOR ALEXEY, Melville had now accounted for all eleven of the men who were supposed to be in De Long's party. The engineer considered De Long, Ambler, and Ah Sam separately, for their location was nearly a thousand yards from the site where all the other bodies had been found.

Now Melville began to discern the logic of the scene. Since the shipmates had been coming from the north, Alexey had died first, and they had buried him out on the ice not far from the place where they had erected his rifle. Melville reasoned that the marker was meant to be a cairn for any future searchers who might pass this way but it might also have been intended as a memorial to their fallen hunter. After Alexey died, they had camped a hundred yards upriver and built a fire. This is where seven men had died—Kaack, Lee, Iverson, Dressler, Boyd, Görtz, and finally Collins.

At this point, only Ah Sam, Dr. Ambler, and Captain De Long were left. Now Melville thought he understood their logic. De Long had decided to move to higher ground, in part to build a signal fire, in a last-ditch effort to attract the attention of natives. But by then the captain knew that in all likelihood, they would soon follow their comrades in death. He feared that all the bodies, as well as all the *Jeannette*'s records, would wash away in the spring floods, forever expunging all memory of the expedition. So the three men had exhausted their last bit of energy attempting to make a camp on the bluff. They hauled wood up there, and a cake of river ice for drinking water. They brought up the cylinder of nautical charts, Ambler's medicine chest, the teakettle, and a hatchet. Next, they would have gone for the records and books, and perhaps for the bodies, too, but they were too feeble to drag so much stuff uphill through the deep snow.

Wrote Melville: "They must have lost all strength and were not equal to the task, so they sank down from the effort, leaving the records to their fate. They built a fire and brewed some willow tea; the kettle when I found it was one quarter full of ice and willow shoots. The tent-cloth they set up to the southward of them to protect their fire, but the winter winds had blown it down."

Ah Sam was probably the first of the trio to die. When Melville excavated him from the snow, the Chinese cook lay faceup with a serene expression and with his arms folded across his chest, as though they had been carefully placed in that position.

De Long was likely the next one to go. He had not written anything more in his journal after October 30—"Mr. Collins dying"—although Melville did notice that a page had been ripped from the book, and he considered the possibility that De Long had begun a private note to Emma. If so, it was never found.

De Long lay on his right side with his right hand under his cheek, his head pointing north. His feet were drawn up slightly; his left arm was upraised, sharply bent at the elbow, and his hand was bare. By the positioning of things, it seemed to Melville that De Long, in his final act, had raised his left arm and flung his journal behind him in the snow, away from the embers of the fire. His arm had frozen in that odd position—it was the rigid object Melville had almost tripped over when he'd first begun searching the bluff.

Brushing away the snow, Melville found that De Long was wearing a begrimed ulster overcoat on top of his Navy uniform jacket. He had a chronometer around his neck. Nearby was the blue silk flag Emma De Long had sewn for the *Jeannette* expedition, the flag that was to be flown over the North Pole. In the captain's pockets, Melville found a silver watch, five twenty-dollar gold pieces, two pairs of spectacles, and a silk pouch, which appeared to be a keepsake. Inside it, he found a lock of hair and a golden crucifix inlaid with six pearls.

Only Dr. Ambler was left. Melville could not determine for certain that Ambler had died last, but the doctor held De Long's Colt Navy revolver in his right hand. Probably he had removed it from De Long when the captain died.

When he examined Dr. Ambler closely, Melville could see blood on his mouth and beard and in the snow around his head. His first thought was that Ambler had ended his agonies by committing suicide. But Melville could find no wounds, and when he inspected the revolver, there were three loaded cartridges in its chambers: The gun had not been fired.

The engineer looked more closely and soon discovered the source of the blood: Ambler held his left hand close to his lips, and Melville noted a deep bite mark in the flesh between his forefinger and his thumb. The doctor, near the very end, had gnawed at his own hand—perhaps seeking warmth or fluid, or perhaps with no conscious thought at all.

Melville tried to picture Ambler's final moments—one hand holding the revolver, the other hand providing him this strange comfort. "In that desolate scene of death," wrote Melville, Ambler waited, "doubtless in the hope that some bird or beast might come to prey upon the bodies and afford him food. There he kept his lone watch to the last, on duty, on guard, under arms."

Emma De Long, just before she left the *Jeannette* in San Francisco, had pleaded with Dr. Ambler: "Will you be a close companion to my husband? You know how lonely a commanding officer must necessarily be." The surgeon had said he would, and he made good on his vow to the end. De Long and Ambler had died side by side.

Tucked under the waistband of Ambler's trousers, Melville found a journal the doctor had been keeping since the day the *Jeannette* sank. It was mostly a technical log, detailing medicines dispensed, ailments treated, and procedures performed. But near the back, Melville came upon a letter Ambler had penned to his brother in Virginia. He had written it on October 20, the day before Kaack and Lee had died, and two days before Nindemann and Noros were saved by the Yakut natives at Bulcour, 120 miles south of here. Dr. Ambler, already seeing how it would end for him, wanted to wish his family good-bye.

On the Lena

Thursday, Oct. 20, 1881

To Edward Ambler, Esq.,
Markham P.O. Fauquier Co., Va.

My Dear Brother:
    I write these lines in the faint hope that by God's merciful providence they may reach you at home. I have myself very little hope of surviving. We are growing weaker, and for more than a week have had no food. We can barely manage to get wood enough now to keep warm, and in a day or two that will be passed.
    I write to you all, my mother, sister, brother Cary and his wife and family, to assure you of the deep love I now and have always borne you. If it had been God's will for me to have seen you all again, I had hoped to have enjoyed the peace of home living once more. My mother knows how my heart has been bound to hers since my earliest years. God bless her on earth and prolong her life in peace and comfort. May His blessing rest upon you all.
    As for myself, I am resigned, and bow my head in submission to the Divine will. To all my friends and relatives, a long farewell.
        Your loving brother,
        J. M. Ambler

MAY 5, 1882
IRKUTSK
1:20 P.M.

The following dispatch has just reached here by special express from Yakutsk:

I have found Lieutenant De Long and his party; all dead.
All the books and papers have also been found.
I remain to continue the search for the party under Lieutenant Chipp.
Melville

The ten bodies were carefully wrapped in tent canvas and loaded onto sleds. A funeral procession was organized, and Melville led the way south for twelve miles, a dozen dog teams steering across the tundra toward a small mountain, known locally as Kuyel Khaya, that rose four hundred feet above the floodplain. This rocky bluff was as "cold and austere as the Sphinx," said Melville, and it "frowns upon the spot where the party had perished." The Yakuts generally stayed away from this mountain—it was said to be inhabited by witches—but it was the most dominant feature in the northern delta, a place so high it would never wash away.

From lumber scraps they'd found scattered along the river, Melville and his men built a massive coffin—seven feet wide, twenty-two feet long, and twenty-two inches deep—held together by mortise and tenon joints. The bodies were placed inside it, with their faces turned toward the rising sun. Then the top of the coffin was hammered into place.

Next, hundreds of lichen-covered rocks were pried from the permafrost and piled upon the coffin until the monument assumed a pyramidal shape. From driftwood timbers, Bartlett and Nindemann constructed a massive cross, twenty feet high with a twelve-foot crossbeam. They hoisted it with guys fashioned from dog-sled traces, then chocked it into place. With chisel and mallet, they carved out the inscription: IN MEMORY OF THE OFFICERS AND MEN OF THE ARCTIC

STEAMER "JEANNETTE" WHO DIED IN THE LENA DELTA, OCTOBER
1881.

Their somber work was completed on April 7. Melville called
the place Monument Point, but the Yakuts gave it a different name,
one that would stand for more than a century: Amerika Khaya—
"America Mountain." On clear days, the cross would be visible for a
hundred miles, floating in the Arctic atmosphere.

Melville, Bartlett, and Nindemann would spend another month
along the Arctic coast—searching, unsuccessfully, for any sign of
Chipp and his men. But now, with their Yakut friends looking on,
they paid their last respects to George De Long, and to the grand and
terrible voyage of the USS *Jeannette*.

"In the awful silence of that vast waste," Melville wrote, "we tenderly laid our dead comrades to rest. We were overawed by the simplicity of the obsequies, the oppressive stillness, the wonderful wilderness
of white. There, the everlasting snows would be their winding-sheet
and the fierce polar blasts would wail their wild dirge through all
time. Surely heroes never found fitter resting-place."

All this will be forgotten when we meet again; it will seem only as a bad dream—a fearful nightmare that has been successfully passed through. However dangerous your surroundings are at present I can still trust God and hope a little longer. I often dream of you and you seem all right, only sad and not as strong as you used to be. Oh darling! I cannot show you my love, my sympathy, my sorrow for your great sufferings. I pray to God constantly. My own darling husband, struggle, fight, live, come back to me!

Epilogue: As Long as I Have
Ice to Stand On

A little past noon on September 13, 1882, the Cunard liner *Parthia* steamed through the Narrows toward New York Harbor. It was a crisp autumn day, the skies a deep blue, the water catching brilliant disks of sunlight. In the distance, the smoky ramparts of Manhattan stole into view. Melville had not seen his native city in four years. For him, it was the happiest of times, the moment of his long-delayed homecoming, and yet he could not forget the day's gravity: Exactly one year earlier, his whaleboat had become separated from De Long's and Chipp's in the gale.

Most of the *Jeannette* survivors had arrived in New York in May, with Danenhower's party. But Melville was the talk of the country, and his homecoming was viewed as the moment to witness. Thousands of people were gathered at the docks in anticipation of his arrival. In the public eye, the engineer's efforts to find his dead shipmates, pushing against all hope into the Siberian wilds, had become an epic tale of loyal comradeship, captured in songs, poems, and magazine articles, not to mention dozens of articles in the *New York Herald*. If De Long was seen as the martyred hero of the *Jeannette* expedition, then Melville had emerged as its *living* hero. Now all the papers, not just the *Herald,* wanted his time.

James Gordon Bennett was not among the well-wishers gathered along the harbor. The publisher had made good on all his *Jeannette* bills, just as he promised he would. He had certainly gotten his blockbuster: Sending multiple reporters to Siberia, he and his editors had capitalized on the *Jeannette* narrative in ways that may even have eclipsed Stanley's dispatches from Africa. One of his correspondents, William Henry Gilder, had traveled to the Bering Strait to search for the *Jeannette* aboard the relief vessel USS *Rodgers*, but was forced to go inland when a fire completely destroyed the ship. Then a Navy officer from the *Rodgers*, Charles Putnam, became stranded on an ice floe, drifted out to sea, and was never heard from again. By dog-team, Gilder journeyed two thousand miles west across Siberia until he picked up the scent of the *Jeannette* disaster. By intercepting a sealed pouch full of Melville's correspondence and racing his account to the telegraph station in Irkutsk, Gilder was able to break the story of the *Jeannette*'s loss to the world.

Another *Herald* reporter, John P. Jackson, found the grave site of De Long and his men and briefly disinterred the bodies, ostensibly to collect relics and papers, but more likely to search for signs of cannibalism, murder, or other foul play (he found none). When Emma De Long learned about the desecration of her husband's grave, she told Bennett it was "the bitterest potion I have had to swallow in my whole life." Still, Jackson's sensational accounts, like Gilder's, had flown off the newsstands.

ON BOARD THE *Parthia* with Melville that day were two other celebrated survivors of the expedition—Nindemann and Noros—and some very important pieces of freight. In carefully packed crates and boxes were all the logs, charts, papers, and natural history articles from the voyage of the USS *Jeannette*. Melville had De Long's journals, too, and the separate diary the captain had kept during the long march across the ice and through the delta until his death. He also had all the keepsakes that had been found on the bodies of the *Jeannette* dead. For six months, he had kept a close custodial watch over these precious boxes.

To reach New York, Melville, Nindemann, and Noros had journeyed twelve thousand miles around the world: from the Lena delta across the tundra to Yakutsk, then across the taiga to Irkutsk, then across the steppes by horse sleigh to the railhead in Orenburg, then nine hundred dreary miles by train to Moscow.

In St. Petersburg, the czar invited the trio to Peterhof, one of the imperial palaces. Arriving by royal coach, the three Americans were served cognac and cigars and then ushered into one of the palace's great rooms.

Alexander III, a bald, gruff, bearish man with an intense gaze, greeted Melville and the two seamen. The czar was fully aware of the story of the *Jeannette,* and he wanted to commiserate with the Americans on behalf of the entire Russian nation. "I trust," he said, "that it was the rigor of our climate alone, and not the coldness of heart of any of my people, that caused the death of your comrades." Empress Maria Feodorovna tenderly examined Melville's hands and fingers, which still bore the scars of frostbite. "I hope," she said, "that you will not again tempt fortune in the frozen North."

From Russia, Melville and his party passed through Berlin, then made a stop at Nindemann's birthplace, the Baltic Sea island of Rügen. There the German native was hailed at the village gates "by a bevy of rustic maidens," said one newspaper, "bearing flowers and wreaths."

Then it was on to England, where the American explorers caught the *Parthia* from Liverpool and steamed across the Atlantic. As the ship approached New York, she was met by a private yacht, the *Ocean Gem,* filled with city dignitaries, Navy officers, and family members. Transferred to the *Ocean Gem,* the three explorers were swarmed by well-wishers. Melville's brother, two sisters, and a niece were there to embrace him. Nindemann's fiancée, a Miss Newman, quietly waited for him on deck. A *Herald* reporter noted that the couple "spoke only with their eyes, and their faces were so happy that they rained smiles on all around them."

Emma De Long's father, Captain James Wotton, was also on board the *Ocean Gem.* He stepped forward and greeted the survivors as the representative of the De Long family. Approaching Melville, Wotton burst into tears. "My God!" said Melville, who was now crying, too. "You have lost a son, and I a friend!"

Despite his long ordeal, Melville appeared robust. One family member thought he "looked almost the same as ever, except that he had lost a little flesh." His eyes, noted the *Herald* reporter, "beamed with their old, affectionate lustre." Beneath that luster, however, there must have been sadness, for Melville had learned that over the course of the expedition, his wife, Hetty, had all but lost her mind and had nearly killed herself with drink. In Sharon Hill, Pennsylvania, neighbors had seen Hetty walking around town pushing an empty stroller and talking to an imaginary baby. To Melville's relief, Hetty had not come to New York, but he knew he would have to deal with the situation in a few days, once he returned home.

The *Ocean Gem* docked along the pier at Twenty-third Street. Flanked by two long rows of Marines in full regalia, the explorers marched off the dock to their waiting carriages. Melville had a long day ahead of him, with speeches to make and dignitaries to meet. But first, he had to head uptown, with his boxes of papers and relics in tow, to visit Emma De Long.

WHEN SHE FIRST received confirmation that her husband was dead, Emma briefly slipped into a catatonic state. She was in Burlington, Iowa, then, far away from the world, away from the East Coast newspapers and the prying eyes of society. It was almost possible for her to treat the tragic news as though it were an abstraction, a dispatch from another realm. "It was as if the seas had closed over me," she said. "I longed for peace and solitude. I wanted to be let alone, to talk to no one, to feel nothing."

But then she realized it would fall upon her to represent the *Jeannette* expedition, to sift through her husband's papers, to edit and publish his journals, to tend to his legacy and the legacies of the other men, living and dead, of the voyage. As was customary for all lost Navy vessels, there would be an official court of inquiry, which would require her cooperation and testimony. She would need to console the loved ones of those who had died, and to fight for medals, commendations, and pensions. Whether she liked it or not, she was, she realized, the public face of the *Jeannette* expedition. Perhaps for the rest of her life, she would play the role of Explorer's Wife.

Over and over again, she asked herself whether the *Jeannette* expedition was worth it—the suffering, the anguish, the loss of life, for what could only be measured as an incremental advance toward the ultimate attainment of the Arctic grail. "Is it said that too high a price in the lives of men was paid for this knowledge?" she asked. "Not by such calculation is human endeavor measured. Sacrifice is nobler than ease, unselfish life is consummated in lonely death, and the world is richer by the gift of suffering."

Emma moved to her parents' apartment in New York, where, on this fine September day, fresh from the docks, Melville called at her door. He wanted to pay his respects and deliver De Long's papers, journals, and personal effects. But he also came to pledge his loyalty to her, in the spirit, almost, of a medieval knight. He apologized to her for his wife, Hetty—"the unfortunate woman that I married," as he called her—for the strange letters she had written to Emma and for hysterical comments she had made in the press. "I have had a miserable existence for seventeen years," he later wrote Emma, referring to his domestic life. "There seems to be no relief until death clears the obstruction."

Melville told Emma that he remained dedicated to the *Jeannette* expedition. He was immensely proud to have been a part of it. In the years to come, the *Jeannette* voyage would accumulate its critics and doubters, he warned her. Authors would write conflicting histories; grandstanders would try to exploit the story for personal gain. Melville wanted Emma to know that he would fight unrelentingly for the memory of her husband—his beloved captain.

"I will stand by you and De Long," he told her, "as long as I have a piece of ice to stand on."

THAT NIGHT, THE CITY of New York threw Melville, Nindemann, and Noros an honorary banquet at Delmonico's, probably the finest restaurant in Manhattan. More than 150 people, dressed in formal attire, came to toast the three survivors.

Throughout the evening, dignitaries stood up to speak—a federal judge, a U.S. senator, the chief engineer of the Navy, and many others. After a bittersweet toast to the dead, Melville himself was asked to rise and say a few words. He was brief almost to the point of curtness. "Gentlemen," he began in his booming voice, "on behalf of myself and my two comrades, I can only say that we did our whole duty, that we did all that we could do, and that if we had not tried to do that, we would have been no men at all."

The most eloquent tribute of the night was delivered by the mayor of New York, William Russell Grace. Mayor Grace looked over at Nindemann and Noros and recalled the story of their farewell to De Long and his starving men. "At that parting scene," said Grace, "when on the banks of the Lena, standing knee deep in snow, the men gave three cheers to the comrades who were going forth for rescue, the last words from the already closing grave were these: 'When you get to New York, remember me.' Yes, we do remember them. We remember their courage to dare, and still higher courage to endure. Their story is graven on our hearts. This city and this country welcome these three gentlemen home with a joy tempered only with grief for the loss of the brave men who will come home no more."

After the banquet, Melville and his two shipmates were given a carriage tour of the city. When they passed down Broadway, they were dazzled. The thoroughfare was ablaze with light: A newly installed network of brilliant arc lamps had turned the New York night into day.

IN 1883, George De Long's remains, along with those of his comrades, were removed from Amerika Khaya and brought to the United States in a long and elaborate mass funeral procession jointly orchestrated by the U.S. Navy and the Russian government. The secretary of the Navy called De Long and his men "martyrs in the cause of science." After a Manhattan funeral attended by thousands of mourners, De Long was buried, along with five of his fellow explorers, in Woodlawn Cemetery in the Bronx; that same year, his journals from the voyage, edited by Emma De Long, were published to wide acclaim. Although the *Jeannette* expedition became the subject of a naval court of inquiry and a congressional hearing that produced considerable controversy, both tribunals upheld De Long's command and reputation. In 1884, New York City dedicated a prime piece of land along the East River as Jeannette Park (it's now known as Vietnam Veterans Plaza). Six years later, a replica of Melville's Lena monument and cross was erected on the grounds of the Naval Academy in Annapolis, overlooking the Severn River. A mountain range in northwestern Alaska was named in De Long's honor, as were two naval ships. In Russia, the High Arctic islands he discovered—Jeannette, Henrietta, and Bennett—are known as Ostrova De Long.

FOR MORE THAN a century after his death, August Petermann's work continued to be a prominent force in cartography. In 2004, after nearly 150 years of publication, *Petermanns Geographische Mitteilungen* halted its presses in Gotha and closed its doors forever. The geographer's legacy lives on in dozens of place-names scattered about the planet, including the Petermann Ranges of Australia; Petermann Island, off the coast of Antarctica; and the Petermann Glacier of Greenland, one of the world's largest. His name has even been immortalized in space: A feature in the north polar region of the moon is known by astronomers as Petermann Crater. Today, Petermann's rare maps often fetch thousands of dollars at auction and are coveted by fine-art collectors around the world.

THE THEORY OF the Open Polar Sea essentially died with the *Jeannette* voyage, although recent climate projections show that by 2050, significant portions of the polar pack will entirely melt in summertime. After the *Jeannette,* no other Arctic explorer undertook an expedition with a serious intention of meeting an open polar sea. Yet one prominent explorer, Norway's Fridtjof Nansen, did deliberately lock himself in the ice above Siberia in an attempt to re-create the *Jeannette*'s drift. He had read that in 1885, an article of George De Long's sealskin clothing had washed up on the coast of southwest Greenland, having followed the currents of the pack on a slow, deliberate journey of four years and five thousand miles—passing over, or at least very near, the North Pole. Surmising that this relic's drift clearly indicated the prevailing direction of the Arctic ice pack, Nansen, in 1893, attempted to reenact the voyage of the *Jeannette* in a better-designed vessel. Nansen's expedition nearly reached the North Pole, and three years later his stout ship, the *Fram,* popped out of the pack into the North Atlantic, unsuccessful, but unscathed.

GEORGE MELVILLE NEVER quite got the north country out of his system. In 1884, he returned to the Arctic to search for survivors of yet another disastrous American polar effort—the Greely Expedition— and remained a tireless champion of America's push for the North Pole. Melville divorced Hetty and remarried, spending most of his life in Washington. He rose within the ranks to become engineer in chief of the U.S. Navy and, eventually, a rear admiral. Melville presided over an expansive redesign of the fleet, largely completing its conversion from wood to metal, and from wind to steam power. When he retired, in 1903, the U.S. Navy boasted one of the most powerful modernized fleets in the word. Widely sought on the lecture circuit, Melville wrote a popular book on the *Jeannette* expedition, *In the Lena Delta,* and defended De Long to the end. Melville died in Philadelphia in 1912. Two Navy ships—a destroyer tender and an oceanographic research vessel—were named after him. Today, the George W. Melville Award is the Navy's highest honor for accomplishments in nautical engineering.

AFTER RECOVERING FROM his *Jeannette* ordeal, John Danen-hower also enjoyed popularity on the lecture circuit and became a well-known critic of both the De Long expedition and Arctic explora-tion in general. "It is time to call a halt," Danenhower argued, "to fur-ther exploration of the central polar basin. There are better directions for the display of true manhood and heroism." Danenhower married and fathered two children, and for several years, he served success-fully, and seemingly happily, as an officer in the U.S. Navy. But in 1887, his melancholy returned. Alone in his quarters in Annapolis, Danenhower shot himself in the head with a .32-caliber Smith & Wesson revolver.

JOHN MUIR NEVER returned to the High Arctic. After his trip on the *Corwin*, he became gradually embroiled in the conservation battles that led to his co-founding, in 1892, of the Sierra Club. Instru-mental in the creation of Yosemite National Park, Muir is considered one of the fathers of the environmental movement. He died in 1914. *The Cruise of the* Corwin, Muir's posthumously published account of his journey in search of the lost *Jeannette*, is now a classic of Arctic literature.

AFTER WINNING MEDALS and Navy commendations, Charles Tong Sing turned to a life of gambling and crime, resulting in several prison terms. As the head a powerful Chinese criminal syndicate in New York, he was said to be responsible for at least six murders; he became known as Scarface Charley, in reference to a five-inch facial scar from an injury he sustained aboard the *Jeannette*. An 1883 arti-cle in the *New York Times* noted, "Recently he gained an unenviable notoriety in Chinatown through his ferocity and physical prowess, and has been suspected of a number of bold and very adroit robber-ies." Later in life, Charley Tong Sing went clean and reportedly ran a Chinese restaurant in Los Angeles, worked as a court interpreter, and briefly served as a policeman in Portland, Oregon. The circumstances of his death are unknown.

WILLIAM NINDEMANN WAS awarded the Congressional Medal of Honor. He married Miss Newman in New York, as planned, but was soon widowed and left to raise their only son, Billy. Nindemann spent two decades working closely with the Irish-American engineer John Holland, widely regarded as the father of the modern submarine. Serving as a gunner and torpedo operator on Holland's prototypes, Nindemann delivered several of the new undersea vessels to Japan for use in the Russo-Japanese War. In 1913, one year to the day after his son, Billy, drowned in a canoe accident on the Hudson River, Nindemann died in Brooklyn.

JAMES GORDON BENNETT JR. remained the publisher of the *New York Herald* and its sister publication, the *Paris Herald* (forerunner of the *International Herald Tribune*), until his death. He continued to live the high life, in a manner perhaps best exemplified by his construction, in 1901, of his dream yacht. The 314-foot *Lysistrata* boasted, among other amenities, a Turkish bath, a theater, and a padded stall for dairy cows so he could have fresh cream every morning. Bennett's interest in sports only intensified with age. He established cups for yacht racing and automobile racing, and in 1906 he funded an international balloon race, the Coupe Aéronautique Gordon Bennett, which continues today. He remained a bachelor for most of his life, but finally, at the age of seventy-three, married Maud Potter, the widow of George de Reuter of the Reuters news agency family.

Bennett died in 1918 at his seaside villa in Beaulieu, France, surrounded by his beloved dogs. He was buried in Paris, not far from Avenue Gordon Bennett, in a mausoleum decorated with stone owls. In 1924, the *Herald* merged with its archrival, the *New York Tribune*. In addition to Bennett Island, an asteroid—305 Gordonia—was designated in his honor. His name lives on in Great Britain, where the exclamation *"Gordon Bennett!"* is still sometimes used as an expression of absolute incredulity.

THE LAST SURVIVING member of the *Jeannette* expedition was Herbert Leach, the seaman from Melville's party who nearly perished of frostbite in the Lena delta. A native of Penobscot, Maine, Leach worked much of his life in a shoe factory in Massachusetts. In 1928, he joined Emma De Long at the unveiling of an enormous granite statue dedicated to George De Long and the other *Jeannette* dead, at Woodlawn Cemetery. Leach died in 1933.

IN 1909, AMERICAN explorers Robert Peary and Matthew Henson reached the North Pole—though many details of their claim have been disputed. During one of his earlier polar attempts, Peary found a handwritten letter that Emma De Long had penned to her husband in 1881. The letter, still sealed in red wax, had somehow made its way to a remote hut in Greenland, where it lay undisturbed for twenty years. Peary returned the unopened letter to Emma.

IN 1938, Emma De Long, well into her eighties, published her memoir, *Explorer's Wife.* (That same year had seen something of a *Jeannette* revival, with the publication of a best-selling novel, *Hell On Ice,* which was adapted into a nationally broadcast radio drama by Orson Welles.) Emma De Long never remarried, and she lived out her last years alone—happily, she said—on a New Jersey farm she had purchased. "My husband's memory," she said, "is all I have left." Not only was she a widow, but she had lost her only child: Sylvie De Long, after serving in World War I as a Red Cross nurse, marrying, and giving birth to two children, had died in 1925, of a mastoid infection. Emma De Long passed away in 1940 at the age of ninety-one. She was laid to rest beside her husband at Woodlawn Cemetery.

ACKNOWLEDGMENTS

Researching and writing the story of the *Jeannette* expedition has been a peripatetic adventure that ranged over three years and three continents, with so many good souls to thank. First, I must single out Katharine De Long, a distant relation of George De Long's, for bestowing upon me that magical gift all historians fantasize about but rarely get an opportunity to enjoy: an old trunk, rescued from the attic, full of yellowed letters. In this case, the trunk contained the correspondence and personal papers of Emma De Long, which Katharine was kind enough to loan me for the duration of my research.

My work in Paris and Le Havre went off without a hitch, thanks to the tireless and stalwart efforts of Maria Vincenza Aloisi, a veteran Time-Life researcher. I thank also Bernadette Murphy at the *International Herald Tribune* for guiding me down to the basement and opening the paper's musty files on James Gordon Bennett. Elizabeth Alice conducted a valuable reconnaissance of Bennett's villa in Beaulieu-sur-Mer and other old haunts in the south of France. I'm grateful to David Howard and the editors of *Bicycling* for getting me to Paris in the first place, with an assignment to cover the Tour de France.

In Germany, my field researcher, translator, and guide was the ever-resourceful Mieke Hagenah. I thank Horst Richardson and Gunther and Michaela Karsten for their generous hospitality in Erfurt, as well as Dr. Petra Weigel, of the Perthes-Verlag archive in Gotha. Thanks to Andrea and Sven Johns for their warm welcome in Berlin, and to historian and biographer Philipp Felsch for illuminating the life and times of August Petermann.

At Stanford, I thank Mandy MacCalla and the Edwards Media Fellows program for a substantial fellowship that allowed me to inhabit the university's voluminous newspaper archives from the Gilded Age. The staffs at the John Muir National Historic Site in Martinez, California, the Mare Island Museum, and the Vallejo Naval & Historical Museum were most helpful.

Mark Mollan at the National Archives, in Washington, assisted me greatly as I sifted through the mountains of *Jeannette* primary documents housed there. Thanks also to Jim and Penny Conaway, Jessica Goldstein and Peter Braslow, and Ken and Florri DeCell for their generosity during my stays in Washington. James Cheevers, senior curator of the U.S. Naval Academy Museum, in Annapolis, was crucially helpful in the early stages of this project.

A special thanks to journalist and historian Mitchell Zuckoff at Boston University for his collegiality in sharing his trove of *Jeannette* research materials. Archivists at Newport's Redwood Library and Athenaeum generously facilitated my research, as did the curatorial staff at Bennett's Newport Casino, now known as the International Tennis Hall of Fame and Museum.

National Geographic magazine helped support this book in multiple ways, including by sending me to Norway, where I first learned of the *Jeannette* expedition, and then to the Bering Strait and Russia's Wrangel Island. At the magazine, I especially want to thank Jamie Shreeve, Victoria Pope, Oliver Payne, Brad Scriber, Nicholas Mott, and Chris Johns. My work in Russia would not have been possible without the extraordinary efforts of Ludmila Mekertycheva, legendary researcher, translator, and all-around fixer for *National Geographic*. In Moscow, I benefited enormously from the insights of journalists Jim Brooke and Jeffrey Tayler, photographer Sergey Gorshkov, Wrangel Island Reserve director Alexander Gruzdev, and Mikhail Stishov of the World Wildlife Fund. My journey by icebreaker to Wrangel Island and the Arctic coast of Siberia could not have happened without the generosity and hard work of the staff at Heritage Expeditions, especially David Bowen, Rodney Russ, and Leanne Dunhill.

Outside magazine encouraged this book from its inception and helped subsidize my travels—most notably sending me to Russia's Lena delta, one of the most inaccessible places on the planet, to find the *Jeannette* memorial on America Mountain. My heartfelt thanks to Mary Turner, Chris Keyes, Amy Silverman, and the whole team at *Outside*. In Yakutsk, I thank the curatorial staff of the Museum of the Northern Peoples. In helping me reach the remote site of De Long's final wanderings in the Lena delta, I must thank Captain Vitali Zhdanov and his second-in-command, Andrey Krukov, who found a berth for me aboard their working diesel riverboat, *Puteyskiy 405*.

In Santa Fe, I was blessed to have two first-rate research assistants; Devon MacLeod and Alexi Horowitz were creative, dogged, cheerful, thorough, and ultimately indispensable. I'm grateful to my German translator and friend, Dag Dascher, and to William Talbot and Richard Fitch, professional connoisseurs of vintage maps. Thanks also to Dick Stolley, James McGrath Morris, Kevin Fedarko, Molly Leonard, Matthew Hecht, Gene Aker, Elizabeth Hunke, Dr. Renny Levy, and Dr. Robert Reidy. The amazing Revell Carr provided invaluable advice on all things nautical. A big shout-out to the folks at Iconik, my caffeinated writing bunker, and to my good friend and photographic wizard, Gary Oakley.

A warm thanks to George Getschow of the Mayborn Literary Nonfiction Conference, which gave me creative oxygen at a critical moment, and to Steven Hayward and Barry Sarchett at Colorado College, where my time as a visiting professor gave my work a much-needed shot of inspiration. Caroline Alexander, Nat Philbrick, John Bockstoce, David Quammen, Jim Donovan, Ian Frazier, and Bill Broyles provided valuable insights. Special thanks to Dr. Kevin Wood of the Joint Institute for the Study of the Atmosphere and Ocean and to John Hattendorf of the U.S. Naval War College. I was fortunate enough to make useful contact with several descendants of *Jeannette* expedition members, especially Amy Nossum Johnson, Geoffrey Wilson, and Maggie Baker. Ken DeCell's fine eye made my manuscript infinitely better.

For this and all my books, I'm forever grateful to the mighty Sloan Harris and the crew at ICM. I especially want to thank Heather Karpas at ICM New York, as well as Ron Bernstein in Los Angeles. At Doubleday, a big thanks to Todd Doughty, Melissa Danaczko, and, of course, the unstoppable Bill Thomas, who has been my loyal editor and friend for fifteen years now.

Highest praise for last: From London to Le Havre to San Francisco to Siberia, my wife and family saw me through every meandering step of this polar saga—and always showed me what a profound joy it is to be home.

Notes

PROLOGUE: BAPTISM BY ICE

1   On a misty morning: My account of the discovery of Tyson and his party is primarily drawn from Tyson's own account in his book *Arctic Experiences*, originally published in 1874. Other key sources include *Weird and Tragic Shores*, by Chauncey Loomis; *Trial by Ice*, by Richard Parry; and newspaper accounts published in the *New York Herald* in 1873.

2   "God-made raft": Tyson, *Arctic Experiences*, 230.

2   "fools of fortune": Ibid., 310.

2   "like a shuttlecock": Ibid., 322.

3   "Those who have baffled and spoiled": Ibid., 232.

4   "Do it now": Emma Wotton De Long, *Explorer's Wife*, 54.

4   "I never in my life saw such": Ibid., 70.

4   "The 'town,' such as it is": Ibid., 71.

4   "destined always to be separated": Ibid., 58.

5   "I cannot help thinking": Ibid., 85.

6   "narrated with considerable minuteness": *New York Herald*, September 10, 1873.

6   "The officers and crew of the *Polaris*": Ibid.

7   "I shall await with great interest": George Washington De Long, *The Voyage of the* Jeannette, 1:14.

7   "never witnessed a more glorious scene": *New York Herald*, September 10, 1873.

7   "Absolutely hemmed in": Ibid.

7   "Our boat is a beauty": Emma De Long, *Explorer's Wife*, 74.

8   "At every one of the fearful plunges": George De Long, *The Voyage of the* Jeannette, 1:18.

8   "Looking back at it now makes me tremble": Ibid., 1:22.

8   "The waves, lashed to a fury": *New York Herald*, September 10, 1873.

9   "how far the lives of our little party": George De Long, *The Voyage of the* Jeannette, 1:21.

9   "Prosecuting the search for the *Polaris*": Emma De Long, *Explorer's Wife*, 81.

9   "The ship was wild with excitement": George De Long, *The Voyage of the* Jean-
        nette, 1:22.

10   "The adventure had affected him deeply": Emma De Long, *Explorer's Wife,* 89.

10   "the greater became his desire": George De Long, *The Voyage of the* Jeannette,
        1:40.

PART ONE: A GREAT BLANK SPACE

1: A SHOCKING SABBATH CARNIVAL OF DEATH

13   Close to midnight: My description of the Great Animal Hoax is primarily drawn
        from the story itself, originally published in the *New York Herald* on November
        9, 1874, in several different editions. See also Seitz, *The James Gordon Bennetts,*
        304–39, and O'Connor, *The Scandalous Mr. Bennett,* 131.

15   "ability to seize upon dormant situations": Seitz, *The James Gordon Bennetts,*
        271.

15   "gnawing horribly at his head": *New York Herald,* November 9, 1874.

15   "saturating herself in the blood": Ibid.

16   "kept busy dressing the fearful wounds": Ibid.

16   "The hospitals are full of the wounded": Ibid.

16   "groaned" at this remarkable story: Seitz, *The James Gordon Bennetts,* 337.

16   "Of course, the entire story": *New York Herald,* November 9, 1874.

16   "How is New York prepared to meet": Ibid.

17   "No such carefully prepared story": O'Connor, *The Scandalous Mr. Bennett,*
        132.

18   "helped rather than hurt the paper": Seitz, *The James Gordon Bennetts,* 338.

2: NE PLUS ULTRA

19   "a great, sad blot upon the present age": From a letter by Charles Hall, reprinted
        in Loomis, *Weird and Tragic Shores,* 229.

20   "As a family will, of course": Ernst Behm, quoted in T. B. Maury, "The New
        American Polar Expedition and Its Hopes," *Atlantic Monthly,* October 1870.

20   "Man will not be content": Editorial in the *New York Times,* July 26, 1879.

20   "Within the charmed circle of the Arctic": Maury, "New American Polar Expe-
        dition."

21   "immense tract of hitherto unvisited land": C. R. Markham, "Arctic Explora-
        tion," *Nature,* November 30, 1871.

22   "If I do not succeed": Emma De Long, *Explorer's Wife,* 116.

23   "Her famous trip to Cape York": From a series of articles published in the *New
        York Herald* in the fall of 1874, reprinted in Emma De Long, *Explorer's Wife,* 87.

23   "abhorred public acclaim": Emma De Long, *Explorer's Wife,* 88.

24   "Death, in a hundred ghastly shades": *Times* (London), May 24, 1873; also
        quoted in Clements R. Markham, "Arctic Exploration," *Nature,* May 29, 1873.

24   On the night of November 1, 1873: My account of the meeting at Grinnell's
        house is drawn from Emma De Long, *Explorer's Wife,* 89; George De Long *The
        Voyage of the* Jeannette 1:25; and Guttridge, *Icebound,* 21.

3: THE LORD OF CREATION

28   "half a head taller than his competitor": "A Walking Match," *New York Times,*
        May 6, 1874.

28   "pace of both men was terrific": Ibid.

29   "almost pitiable": Ibid.

29   "he walked as much with his arms": Ibid.

29   Whipple "struggled manfully": Ibid.

29   "Oh, I am always walking": Ibid.

30   "The two men were attracted to each other": Emma De Long, *Explorer's Wife*, 91.

31   "Bennett the Terrible": O'Connor, *The Scandalous Mr. Bennett*, 8.

31   "was a ruler over a domain of romance": Crockett, *When James Gordon Bennett*, 19.

31   Bennett had a habit: See Seitz, *The James Gordon Bennetts*, 239.

31   Once, after a musical show in Amsterdam: See Crockett, *When James Gordon Bennett*, 234.

4: FOR YOU I WILL DARE ANYTHING

33   "incessant friction": George De Long, *The Voyage of the* Jeannette, 1:8.

33   "a hungry heart": Emma De Long, *Explorer's Wife*, 41.

33   called his commanding style "monolithic": Hoehling, *The* Jeannette *Expedition*, 62.

33   "a hard thing on the temper": Emma De Long, *Explorer's Wife*, 65.

34   "I never allow any argument": George De Long, *The Voyage of the* Jeannette, 1:24.

34   "a third-rate assemblage": Karsten, *The Naval Aristocracy*, 278–79.

34   a life of "crushing hopelessness": Ibid., 281.

34   "A stagnant navy": Ibid., 282.

35   "morbidly solicitous for him": George De Long, *The Voyage of the* Jeannette, 1:6.

35   "De Long's first encounter with hostile ice": Guttridge, *Icebound*, 8.

35   "found exercise in an intellectual ardor": George De Long, *The Voyage of the* Jeannette, 1:6.

35   "an uneasy desire for larger liberty": Ibid.

36   "in my proper element at last": Emma De Long, *Explorer's Wife*, 9.

36   "I am Midshipman De Long": Ibid., 9.

37   "He got what he wanted": Ibid.

38   "a finished young lady": Ibid., 22.

38   "But we've scarcely met!": Ibid., 26.

38   "I was gradually being drawn": Ibid., 29.

38   "I felt completely lost": Ibid., 33.

38   "As I may not be able to speak to you alone": Ibid., 29.

39   "Your father spoke to me kindly": Ibid., 36.

39   "I am firmly resolved": Ibid., 38.

39   "Poor little silken bag!": Ibid., 35.

40   "For this long, long year I have waited": Ibid., 40.

41   "I melted somewhat": Ibid., 44.

41   "I was falling in love": Ibid., 51.

5: GATEWAYS TO THE POLE

44   a "mischievous" idea: Clements Markham, quoted in John K. Wright, "The Open Polar Sea," *Geographical Review* 43, no. 3 (July 1953).

45   "There is reason to believe": T. B. Maury, "Gateways to the Pole," *Putnam's Magazine* 4, no. 32 (November 1869).

46   "a circulation in the air": Ibid.

46   "Armed in their tropical birthplace": Ibid.

47   "these whales can not travel": Maury, quoted in Wright, "The Open Polar Sea."

48   "There is a river in the ocean": Maury, *The Physical Geography of the Sea,* 25.

48   "they are almost identical": Maury, "Gateways to the Pole."

49   "Santa Claussville, N.P.": For a detailed examination of Thomas Nast's depiction of Santa's polar home, see www.nytimes.com/learning/general/onthisday/harp/1225.html.

49   "free and open Sea": The Dutch tale is quoted at length in Wright, "The Open Polar Sea."

50   large holes at the North and South Poles: Remarkably, Symmes's "holes at the poles" theory lives on in a vibrant and tenacious conspiracy subculture, the Hollow Earthers. See www.hollowplanet.bogspot.com, among other websites.

50   The theory's most indefatigable proponent: See Fleming, *Barrow's Boys.*

51   "Seals were sporting": Maury, *The Physical Geography of the Sea,* 219.

51   "The sea about the North Pole": Hayes, quoted in Mowat, *The Polar Passion,* 117.

52   "are the only practicable avenues": Maury, "Gateways to the Pole."

52   "a great and solid mind": Ibid.

52   "Who shall say": Ibid.

PART TWO: THE NATIONAL GENIUS

6: THE ENGINE OF THE WORLD

55   the city was hosting a world's fair: My description of the Centennial Exhibition is drawn primarily from the *New York Herald*'s copious coverage of the fair throughout the summer of 1876. See also Linda P. Gross and Theresa R. Snyder, *Philadelphia's 1876 Centennial Exhibition,* Charleston, SC: Arcadia Publishing, 2005.

57   "murmuring sound": "Machinery Hall Notes," *Scientific American Supplement,* June 10, 1876.

57   "great pulsating iron heart": "Closing Ceremonies of the Centennial International Exhibition of 1876," *Scientific American Supplement,* December 2, 1876.

57   "an athlete of steel": William Dean Howells, "A Sennight of the Centennial," *Atlantic Monthly,* July 1876.

57   "plunge their pistons downward": Ibid.

58   "The American invents as the Greek sculpted": See the Centennial Exhibition Digital Collection (http://libwww.library.phila.gov/CenCol/overview.htm), offered by the Philadelphia Free Library, under the heading "Machinery Hall."

58   "If we are to be judged": Ibid.

58   "a grand achievement": Petermann's remarks in *The Annual Report of the American Geographical Society for the Year 1876,* 148–56.

59   "the blank spaces of the unknown": J. G. Bartholomew, "The Philosophy of Map-Making and the Evolution of a Great German Atlas," *Scottish Geographical Magazine* 18 (1902): 37.

60   "Without a knowledge of the North Pole": Oswald Dreyer-Eimbcke, "Heinrich Berghaus and August Petermann," *IMCoS Journal* 79 (Fall 1997).

60   "The ice pack as a whole forms a mobile belt": Petermann, quoted in Murphy, *German Exploration of the Polar World,* 18.

60   "very easy, trivial thing": Ibid., 22.
61   "The Americans have eclipsed all other nations": Guttridge, *Icebound,* 17.
61   "high-toned acts of the United States government": Ibid.
61   "I hardly believe that this great work": Murphy, *German Exploration,* 1.
61   "our explorers, one after the other": Ibid., 22.
62   "I was almost killed by the heat": Petermann, quoted in the *New York Herald,*
      July 15, 1878.
62   "I am altogether most happy": Petermann's remarks in *The Annual Report of the
      American Geographical Society for the Year 1876,* 148–56.
62   "All my expectations have been surpassed": Ibid.

7: SATISFACTION
64   "impudent and intrusive": O'Connor, *The Scandalous Mr. Bennett,* 16.
65   "the whip broke at the first blow": Ibid., 23.
65   "You are too ugly a rascal": Seitz, *The James Gordon Bennetts,* 46.
65   "American Society": O'Connor, *The Scandalous Mr. Bennett,* 27.
65   "motherhood is the best cure for the mania": Ibid., 26.
65   "Lofty editorials and public-spirited crusades": Ibid., 30.
66   "figure is most magnificent": Ibid.
66   "the beau ideal of the man of the world": Seitz, *The James Gordon Bennetts,* 266.
66   "it would take an Arabian Night's volume": Ibid., 234.
68   "the tigerish proprietor": Ibid., 224.
68   "a slender, fair-haired girl": O'Connor, *The Scandalous Mr. Bennett,* 136.
68   a woman of "unusual beauty": Seitz, *The James Gordon Bennetts,* 267.
68   "Jimmy Bennett, veteran of fleshpots": O'Connor, *The Scandalous Mr. Bennett,*
      135.
68   "the excuse for much drunkenness": Seitz, *The James Gordon Bennetts,* 267.
69   "had the seat of honor": O'Connor, *The Scandalous Mr. Bennett,* 132.
69   "The match was regarded a brilliant one": *Quebec Saturday Budget,* January 20,
      1877.
69   liable "at any moment": Ibid.
69   "had been some time": Ibid.
70   "pump out the bilge": O'Connor, *The Scandalous Mr. Bennett,* 136.
70   "Bennett forgot where he was": Seitz, *The James Gordon Bennetts,* 268.
70   "fled to Canada": O'Connor, *The Scandalous Mr. Bennett,* 140.
71   "Why don't you kill me": Seitz, *The James Gordon Bennetts,* 268.
71   "blood stained the snow": O'Connor, *The Scandalous Mr. Bennett,* 139.
72   Mr. Bennett "gave full front": *Hartford Weekly Times,* January 13, 1877.
72   "Do you think I did right?": *New York Times,* May 17, 1878.
73   "as to life, limb, or digestion": *New York Times,* January 15, 1918.
73   "did not care to entertain a fellow": O'Connor, *The Scandalous Mr. Bennett,* 142.
74   "a case of Bennett banishing himself": Ibid., 144.
74   "Mr. May declared that": Ibid.

8: THE SAGE OF GOTHA
75   "a tiresome journey": Bennett letter to George De Long, quoted in Emma De
      Long, *Explorer's Wife,* 116.
75   "dreamy drowsy town": "The Unknown Arctic World: Interview with Dr.
      Augustus Petermann," *New York Herald,* July 15, 1878.

76   "He knew how to teach": Ludwig Friedrichsen, quoted in Espenhorst, *Peter-mann's Planet,* 200.

77   "Today Petermann is regarded in all civilized nations": Ibid., 202.

77   viewed as the world's "Polarpapa": Murphy, *German Exploration,* 62.

78   "undeviating affinity for the wrong guess": Ibid., 20–21.

78   "His character combined outstanding virtues": Murphy, *German Explora-tion,* 17.

78   "This Arctic business belongs to the world": *New York Herald,* July 15, 1878.

79   Petermann had a love-hate relationship: German scholar Philipp Felsch con-vincingly develops this theme in his recent biography, *Wie August Petermann: Den Nordpol Erfand.* Felsch further shared his insights during an interview in Berlin, July 2012.

79   "Dr. Petermann has done serious injury": C. R. Markham, "Arctic Exploration," *Nature,* November 30, 1871.

80   "All very easy to write at Gotha": Ibid.

80   "I think it utterly mistaken": Murphy, *German Exploration,* 62.

80   "The world will not fail to recognize": Undated correspondence from the 1870s, Correspondence of August Heinrich Petermann, Perthes Collection, University of Erfurt Gotha Research Library.

80   "the Pole will be found by a navigator": *New York Herald,* July 15, 1878.

82   "It is a well-known fact": Petermann, *The Search for Franklin.*

83   "Perhaps I am wrong": *New York Herald,* July 15, 1878.

83   "A great task must be greatly conceived": Petermann, quoted in Murphy, *Ger-man Exploration.*

83   "from mental overexertion": See Felsch, *Wie August Petermann,* 239.

84   "just returned from a hurried trip to Gotha": Bennett letter to George De Long, reprinted in George De Long, *The Voyage of the* Jeannette, 1:27.

84   "Petermann says it can be done in one summer": Ibid., 1:28.

84   "seriously thinking of getting another vessel": Ibid.

9: PANDORA

85   "He is more than ever disposed": Letter from George De Long to Emma De Long, reprinted in Emma De Long, *Explorer's Wife,* 155.

86   "I have astonished my stomach": Ibid., 110.

86   "The demand for whalebone": Ibid., 113.

86   "fearful day": Ibid., 109.

86   a "tidy" ship: Guttridge, *Icebound,* 28.

87   "answered her helm": Young, *The Two Voyages of the 'Pandora' in 1875 and 1876,* 38.

87   a live polar bear: Ibid., 40.

88   "hopelessly beset": Ibid., 115.

88   "escape was hopeless": Ibid., 116.

88   "severe battle she had endured": Ibid., 137.

88   "A small omission now": George De Long, *The Voyage of the* Jeannette, 1:27.

89   "drawn into the maelstrom": Emma De Long, *Explorer's Wife,* 188.

89   "Where is Papa going?" Ibid.

89   "almost a new vessel": *Times* (London), May 23, 1878.

10: THREE YEARS, OR ETERNITY

92   "kept up a running fire": Emma De Long, *Explorer's Wife*, 123.

93   "See here, De Long": Ibid., 123.

93   "were very much engrossed": Ibid., 124

94   "I would have preferred": Ibid.

94   "we may be gone for eternity": Guttridge, *Icebound*, 28.

94   "impossible to make him come forward": Emma De Long, *Explorer's Wife*, 124.

94   one of Newport's elegant "cottages": One of the nation's best surviving examples of shingle-style architecture, the Isaac Bell House in Newport is now a national historic landmark.

94   Stanley would return to further exploits: See Tim Jeal, *Stanley: The Impossible Life of Africa's Greatest Explorer* (New Haven: Yale University Press, 2007); and Frank McLynn, *Stanley: The Making of an African Explorer* (London: Random House UK, 2004).

95   "Your wife must think a great deal of you": Emma De Long, *Explorer's Wife*, 119.

95   "38 and 5/6 years": Hoehling, *The* Jeannette *Expedition*, 17.

95   "worth his weight in gold": Emma De Long, *Explorer's Wife*, 122.

95   "with all my heart": Guttridge, *Icebound*, 27.

95   "a freezing up in the Arctic": Reference to Bennett's comment is made in De Long to Bennett, May 15, 1879, *Jeannette* correspondence, National Archives.

96   "any lurking effects": Ibid.

96   "They wondered at my daring": Emma De Long, *Explorer's Wife*, 124.

96   "As we were under sail": Ibid., 127.

97   "utterly absorbed in the study": Ibid.

97   "about to part with father and husband": Ibid., 128.

11: A BENEDICTION

98   "the liberal and enthusiastic scholar": *New York Herald*, July 15, 1878.

98   "Tow-headed children": Ibid.

99   "I am very glad": Ibid.

99   "It is not what dogs can do": Ibid.

99   "Mr. Bennett's expedition will find it": Ibid.

100   "Pangs of conscience": Hugo Ewald Weller, *August Petermann: Ein Beitrag zur Geschichte der Geographischen Entdeckungen der Geographie und der Kartographie im 19. Jahrhundert* (Leipzig: Wigand, 1911), 27.

100   hanging from the end of a rope: Several early accounts stated or implied that Petermann died from a self-inflicted gunshot wound, but most Petermann scholars today, including his biographer Philipp Felsch, agree that Petermann hanged himself.

100   "whom he so seriously misjudged": Letter from Clara Petermann to a friend in Gotha, Correspondence of August Heinrich Petermann, Perthes Collection, University of Erfurt Gotha Research Library.

12: SECOND CHANCES

101   "just in time": Emma De Long, *Explorer's Wife*, 130.

101   "clean swift death": Ibid., 129.

102   "its melancholy fate": Ibid., 131.

102   "much to our sorrow": Ibid.

103   "never out of my mind for a moment": De Long to Bennett, May 15, 1879, *Jeannette* correspondence, National Archives.
103   "I believed him": Ibid.
103   "a correct navigator": Ibid.
103   "my desire to touch the soil": Emma De Long, *Explorer's Wife,* 134.
104   "Of how close we had come to eternity": Ibid., 138.
104   "we scarcely dared to breathe": Ibid., 137.

13: THE U.S. ARCTIC EXPEDITION
106   "as much a part of the Mare Island waterfront": Lot, *A Long Line of Ships,* 32.
106   "or they will ruin us": Guttridge, *Icebound,* 41.
107   "laboring to keep down expenses": De Long to Bennett, *Jeannette* correspondence, National Archives.
107   "I do not carry enough guns": Ibid.
107   "Little things run away with the money": Guttridge, *Icebound,* 43.
108   "edit a newspaper": George De Long, *The Voyage of the* Jeannette, 1:38.
108   "refused point blank": Ibid.
109   "unhesitating obedience": Ibid.
109   "He smiles rarely and says very little": Ibid., 43.
110   "The secrets of his home": Guttridge, *Icebound,* 72.
110   "a No. 1 man and a brother": De Long to Danenhower, *Jeannette* correspondence, National Archives.
111   "conspicuously lacking in enthusiasm": Guttridge, *Icebound,* 44.
111   "the durned thing's hollow!": Hamilton, *President McKinley, War and Empire,* 21.
111   "power that is conferred upon admirals": Guttridge, *Icebound,* 5.
112   "prodding them up all the time": De Long to Bennett, *Jeannette* correspondence, National Archives.
112   "I immediately open fire": Ibid.
112   "you are getting your way": Bennett to De Long, *Jeannette* correspondence, National Archives.
112   "if there is a suitable ship": Thompson to De Long, *Jeannette* correspondence, National Archives.
112   "quiet, pleasant gentleman": Emma De Long, *Explorer's Wife,* 147.
113   "He knew nothing about Arctic exploration": Ibid.
113   "but even she did not manage": Ibid.
114   "a strong inclination to jump overboard": Guttridge, *Icebound,* 47.
114   "It is my considered opinion": Ibid., 48.
114   "I cannot replace him": De Long to Bennett, *Jeannette* correspondence, National Archives.
114   "endeavoring to temper justice": Ibid.
114   "bent on going": Ibid.
114   "no steps to imply distrust": Guttridge, *Icebound,* 49.
115   "working like a beaver": De Long to Bennett, *Jeannette* correspondence, National Archives.
115   "everything the *Jeannette* might need": Guttridge, *Icebound,* 52.
116   "attain an increased height": George De Long, *The Voyage of the* Jeannette, 1:29.
116   "I cannot recommend you": Ibid.
116   "men have pined for light": De Long to Bennett, *Jeannette* correspondence, National Archives.

116   "A new sort of urban star": Stross, *The Wizard of Menlo Park,* 77.
117   "I should like to illuminate the ship": De Long to Edison, April 21, 1878, and
       Collins to Edison, May 2, 7, and 9, 1878, Papers of Thomas Alva Edison, Rut-
       gers University.
117   "It will keep them warm": Guttridge, *Icebound,* 51.
117   "have been made to grow by it": De Long to Bennett, *Jeannette* correspondence,
       National Archives.

14: ALL THAT MAN CAN DO
119   "sturdily fortified for ice encounter": Guttridge, *Icebound,* 60.
119   "I am perfectly satisfied": George De Long, *The Voyage of the* Jeannette, 1:34.
119   "He has attended to everything": De Long to Bennett, *Jeannette* correspon-
       dence, National Archives.
120   "great tact in dealing with the frozen foe": *New York Herald,* July 9, 1879.
121   "a student of natural history": Hoehling, *The* Jeannette *Expedition,* 27.
122   "a little bit about everything": Ibid., 30.
122   "and will make a name for himself": George De Long, *The Voyage of the* Jean-
       nette, 1:37.
122   "steal ashore like a phantom": Guttridge, *Icebound,* 53.
123   "head and promoter of the expedition": De Long to Bennett, *Jeannette* corre-
       spondence, National Archives.
123   "I am sure you will agree": Guttridge, *Icebound,* 38.
124   "On reaching Bering Strait": George De Long, *The Voyage of the* Jeannette, 1:39.
124   "tomorrow's sun will shine": De Long to Bennett, *Jeannette* correspondence,
       National Archives.
124   "my resolution increases": Ibid., 64.
125   "I will spare neither money": Ibid., 56.
125   "all that man can do": Nourse, *American Explorations in the Ice Zones,* 372.

15: THE NEW INVADER
126   "taking good care": Emma De Long, *Explorer's Wife,* 159.
127   "his mind had been turning": George De Long, *The Voyage of the* Jeannette,
       1:40.
127   "what a pretty widow": Emma De Long, *Explorer's Wife,* 159.
127   "afraid the sluices would give way": Ibid.
127   "I *shan't* be a widow": Ibid., 160.
127   "engaged in a great undertaking": George De Long, *The Voyage of the* Jeannette,
       1:44.
128   "rigidly in control": Emma De Long, *Explorer's Wife,* 160.
128   "force the Northern Sphinx": *San Francisco Examiner,* July 9, 1879.
128   "the shrine of Arctic discovery": *New York Herald,* July 9, 1879.
128   "Should success crown the efforts": *New-York Commercial Advertiser,* July 8,
       1879.
128   "the verge of a discovery": Hoehling, *The* Jeannette *Expedition,* 32.
128   "Will the new invader": *San Francisco Chronicle,* July 9, 1879.
128   "Regret exceedingly": George De Long, *The Voyage of the* Jeannette, 1:40.
129   "necessary to increase our force": *San Francisco Examiner,* July 9, 1879.
129   "to the protective care": Hoehling, *The* Jeannette *Expedition,* 31.
129   "shaken us adrift": Guttridge, *Icebound,* 6.

129   "Any draft of yours": Emma De Long, *Explorer's Wife,* 157.

129   "Thank God I have a man": George De Long, *The Voyage of the* Jeannette, 1:40.

130   "wolves will all come down": De Long and Newcomb, *Our Lost Explorers,* 39.

130   "picked band of resolute men": Ibid., 22.

130   "see with eyes not material": "Interview with a band of Spirits, interestd in Arctic Explorations," June 30, 1879, Emma De Long Papers.

130   "hollow centre of the earth": George De Long, *The Voyage of the* Jeannette, 1:38.

130   "one of the most difficult things": De Long and Newcomb, *Our Lost Explorers,* 21.

131   "information their experience might afford": Ibid., 29.

131   "How we envy Captain De Long": see www.south-pole.com/aspp005.htm.

132   "ominously silent": De Long and Newcomb, *Our Lost Explorers,* 29.

132   "one of the oldest": Ibid.

132   "Gentlemen, there isn't much": Ibid.

133   "dirty weather": *New York Herald,* July 9, 1879.

133   "She'll have it devilishly thick": Ibid.

133   "Nature relented": Ibid.

133   "bristling back of a huge porcupine": *San Francisco Chronicle,* July 9, 1879.

133   "The taut little bark": *Daily Alta California,* July 9, 1879.

133   "gazing with sorrowful eyes": *San Francisco Call,* July 9, 1879.

134   "I have the honor to inform you": De Long and Newcomb, *Our Lost Explorers,* 19.

134   "quite a mob": George De Long, *The Voyage of the* Jeannette, 1:164.

134   "black with people": Ibid., 1:165.

135   "moved so slowly": *San Francisco Chronicle,* July 9, 1879.

135   "if the wind is favorable": *Vallejo Times,* July 9, 1879.

135   "right royal": Melville, *In the Lena Delta,* 2.

135   "a mortification to me": Guttridge, *Icebound,* 6.

135   "shabby treatment": Emma De Long, *Explorer's Wife,* 164.

135   "fat lumps of white smoke": *New York Herald,* July 9, 1879.

135   "solemn amen to the godspeeds": Melville, *In the Lena Delta,* 2.

135   "brazen throats": *San Francisco Call,* July 9, 1879.

135   "Farewell, brave boys": *New York Herald,* July 9, 1879.

136   "The hour is at hand": Ibid.

136   "Will you be a close companion": Emma De Long, *Explorer's Wife,* 161.

136   "a fortitude that was fairly heroic": *New York Herald,* July 9, 1879.

136   "stand by your captain": Emma De Long, *Explorer's Wife,* 162.

136   "few dry eyes": *San Francisco Call,* July 9, 1879.

136   "The silence was oppressive": William Bradford in the *Boston Herald,* quoted in Emma De Long, *Explorer's Wife,* 162–63.

136   "the full force of my going away": Guttridge, *Icebound,* 7.

136   "devout silent prayer": Emma De Long, *Explorer's Wife,* 163.

137   "I craved only solitude": Ibid.

137   "The ship is now beginning": Guttridge, *Icebound,* 7.

137   "long dark pencil of shadow": *San Francisco Chronicle,* July 9, 1879.

PART THREE: A GLORIOUS COUNTRY TO LEARN PATIENCE IN

16: A CUL-DE-SAC

141 Nordenskiöld had become the first: For the navigator's first-person account of the voyage, see Nordenskiöld, *The Voyage of the* Vega *Round Asia and Europe.*

141 "Somewhere in the fog-wreathed": Guttridge, *Icebound,* 65.

142 "no recognizable branch": *Annual Report of the Superintendant of the United States Coast and Geodetic Survey* 15 (1883), 101–32.

143 "no real gate of entrance": Nourse, *American Explorations in the Ice Zones,* 368.

17: NIPPED

145 "a miserable place": George De Long, *The Voyage of the* Jeannette, 1:48.

145 "as a kind of earthly paradise": Ibid.

145 "wallowed like a pig": Ibid., 1:42.

145 "and some wretchedly poor": Ibid., 1:49.

145 "we let him pun away": Ibid.

146 "almost made me grow gray": Ibid.

146 "Melville would take him ashore": De Long to Emma De Long, August 18, 1879, Emma De Long Papers.

146 "like a corpse resurrected": Ibid., 1:42.

146 "His puns died out for a few days": Ibid., 1:43.

147 "fine animals, young and active": Ibid., 1:48.

148 "I was greatly touched": De Long and Newcomb, *Our Lost Explorers,* 24.

148 "overpowered with emotion": Ibid.

148 "they affectionately parted": Melville, *In the Lena Delta,* 3.

148 "buried by the sea": George De Long, *The Voyage of the* Jeannette, 1:51.

149 "I discharged the Chinese boy": Ibid., 1:52.

149 "trusting in God's protection": De Long and Newcomb, *Our Lost Explorers,* 26.

149 "Stockholm professional beauties": Danenhower, *Narrative of the "Jeannette,"* 3.

150 "all our hearts were thankful": George De Long, *The Voyage of the* Jeannette, 1:57.

150 "our Arctic cruise had actually commenced": Danenhower, *Narrative of the "Jeannette,"* 4.

150 "one mass of snow and frost": George De Long, *The Voyage of the* Jeannette, 1:59.

150 "we distinctly saw land": Ibid.

151 "received in action with the ice": Ibid., 1:60.

151 "our ancient mariner": Melville, *In the Lena Delta,* 16.

152 "ice cut off all chances of retreat": Ibid., 6.

152 "Man proposes but God disposes": George De Long, *The Voyage of the* Jeannette, 1:61.

152 "stood the concussions handsomely": Danenhower, *Narrative of the "Jeannette,"* 5.

153 "We banked fires": Ibid.

153 "It would take an earthquake": George De Long, *The Voyage of the* Jeannette, 1:64.

154 "glorious country to learn patience in": Ibid., 1:60.

154 last sighting anyone ever had: See De Long and Newcomb, *Our Lost Explorers,* 26–27, and Hoehling, *The* Jeannette *Expedition,* 44.

18: AMONG THE SWELLS

155   "give the coach of gaiety a good start": *Newport Mercury,* August 2, 1879.

155   one day in mid-August: My account of Candy's prank at the Reading Room is largely drawn from Newport newspaper accounts from the summer of 1879, and also from John Hanlon, "The Cradle of Tennis Was Meant to Be Rocky," *Sports Illustrated,* September 2, 1968.

156   cradle of American tennis: See International Tennis Hall of Fame & Museum, *Tennis and the Newport Casino* (Charleston, SC: Arcadia, 2011), and C. P. B. Jefferys, *Newport: A Concise History* (Newport: Newport Historical Society, 2008).

19: IF BY ANY MISCHANCE

157   "for a long, long vigil": Emma De Long, *Explorer's Wife,* 171.

157   he had made nine trips to the Arctic: For more on Bradford's biography and art, see Frank Horch, "Photographs and Paintings by William Bradford," *American Art Journal* 5, no. 2 (November 1973), 61–70.

158   "There is no phenomenon": Anne-Marie Amy Kilkenny, "Life and Scenery in the Far North: William Bradford's 1885 Lecture to the American Geographical Society," *American Art Journal* 26, no. 1–2 (1994), 106–8.

158   "began to enjoy myself again": Emma De Long, *Explorer's Wife,* 169.

159   "Half a dozen times a day": Ibid., 177.

160   "lovesick as I was eleven years ago": Ibid.

160   "We are now hoisting": Ibid., 188–89.

20: A DELUSION AND A SNARE

161   "as in a mould": Melville, *In the Lena Delta,* 9.

161   "as if she were in a dry dock": George De Long, *The Voyage of the* Jeannette, 1:77.

162   "no longer tenable": Danenhower, *Narrative of the "Jeannette,"* 13.

162   "the much-boasted continent": Melville, *In the Lena Delta,* 9.

162   "a delusion and a snare": George De Long, *The Voyage of the* Jeannette, 1:180.

162   "until the last trump blows": Ibid., 2:448.

162   "Some of us talked about the polar region": Danenhower, *Narrative of the "Jeannette,"* 18.

164   "Make um more seal": De Long and Newcomb, *Our Lost Explorers,* 280.

164   "quiet dignity": George De Long, *The Voyage of the* Jeannette, 1:133.

164   "contented with each other's society": Ibid., 1:133.

165   "The less I had to do with him": Melville, quoted in Hoehling, *The* Jeannette *Expedition,* 47.

165   "as happy as can be": George De Long, *The Voyage of the* Jeannette, 1:43.

165   "getting up a choir": Ibid., 1:44.

165   "everybody would be coming here": Ibid., 1:99.

165   "more like a man-of-war": Ibid., 1:43.

165   "More and more a treasure": Ibid., 1:48.

166   "bright as a dollar": Ibid., 1:43.

166   "a few barrel hoops": Ibid.

167   "howled dolefully": Ibid., 1:65.

167   "the monarch of the polar regions": Melville, *In the Lena Delta,* 7.

167   "the thing was soon over": George De Long, *The Voyage of the* Jeannette, 1:65.

167   "turned into a holiday": Ibid.

167   "all hands were jubilant": Ibid.

168   "seven beautiful young gulls": De Long and Newcomb, *Our Lost Explorers,* 280.

169   "You give me an earache!": Newcomb, quoted in Hoehling, *The* Jeannette *Expedition,* 59.

169   placed him in "a trap": Guttridge, *Icebound,* 75.

170   "is not worth a damn": George De Long, *The Voyage of the* Jeannette, 1:82.

170   "I begin to fear": Ibid.

171   "gone 'where the woodbine twineth' ": Ibid., 1:77.

21: FOREVER, ALMOST

172   "a bootblack might understand it": Stross, *The Wizard of Menlo Park,* 79.

172   "The electric light is perfected": *New York Times,* October 21, 1879.

173   "only the rich will burn candles": *Thomas Edison: Life of an Electrifying Man,* 14.

173   "Forever, almost": *New York Herald,* October 12, 1879.

22: INVISIBLE HANDS

174   "A rumble, a shriek, a groan": George De Long, *The Voyage of the* Jeannette, 1:85.

174   "a marble yard, adrift": Ibid.

174   "distant artillery": Melville, *In the Lena Delta,* 9.

174   "than an old Turkish graveyard": Danenhower, *Narrative of the "Jeannette,"* 8.

174   "howls most unearthly": De Long and Newcomb, *Our Lost Explorers,* 284.

175   "We live in a weary suspense": Guttridge, *Icebound,* 106.

175   "we watched its terrible progress": Melville, *In the Lena Delta,* 12.

175   "The ship is all right now": De Long and Newcomb, *Our Lost Explorers,* 282.

175   "Her time had not yet come": Melville, *In the Lena Delta,* 13.

176   "The discipline of the ship's company": Ibid., 10.

176   "The pack is no place for a ship": George De Long, *The Voyage of the* Jeannette, 1:94.

176   "I shall undress": Ibid., 1:95.

176   "most awful beauty": George De Long, *The Voyage of the* Jeannette, 2:472.

177   "simply a beautiful spectacle": George De Long, *The Voyage of the* Jeannette, 1:81.

177   "highly prized by all of us": Ibid., 1:105.

178   "books would run away with him": Ibid., 1:94.

178   "One night with Venus": See Flaubert, *The Letters of Gustave Flaubert, 1830–1857,* 1:239.

179   "accept the situation and fight it out": George De Long, *The Voyage of the* Jeannette, 1:105.

179   "dreariest day I have ever experienced": Ibid., 1:102.

179   the sumptuous menu: the bill of fare is reprinted in De Long and Newcomb, *Our Lost Explorers,* 284.

180   "a fine compound": George De Long, *The Voyage of the* Jeannette, 1:101.

181   "Because it supports the house": Ibid., 1:104.

182   "the fingers supple and delicate": Ibid.

182   "we all felt satisfied with the ship": Ibid.

PART FOUR: WE ARE NOT YET DAUNTED

185 "My dearest husband": All excerpts selected here and elsewhere from the letters
     Emma De Long sent to her husband are found in the Personal Papers of Emma
     Wotton De Long, loaned to the author by the De Long family.

23: ON THE LONE ICEBOUND SEA

187 "On the lone icebound sea": De Long and Newcomb, *Our Lost Explorers,* 296.

187 "a very comely young miss": George De Long, *The Voyage of the* Jeannette,
     2:495.

188 "bound by a closer band": Melville, *In the Lena Delta,* 15.

189 "Job was never caught in pack ice": George De Long, *The Voyage of the* Jean-
     nette, 1:196.

189 "as long as she sticks to us": Guttridge, *Icebound,* 133.

190 "hardworking as a horse": George De Long, *The Voyage of the* Jeannette, 1:44.

190 "Not since Adam sinn'd": De Long and Newcomb, *Our Lost Explorers,* 297.

190 "rattled off in fine style": George De Long, *The Voyage of the* Jeannette, 1:156.

191 "where we get all our punishment": Hoehling, *The* Jeannette *Expedition,* 49.

191 "fat as dumplings": George De Long, *The Voyage of the* Jeannette, 1:156.

191 "other dogs him plenty whip": Ibid., 1:81.

192 "possible food for his murderers": Ibid., 1:82.

192 "far from death as ever": Ibid., 1:160.

192 "sinking gradually from view": Ibid., 1:212.

192 "What a life this is": Ibid.

193 "let out a lot of turbid fluid": Guttridge, *Icebound,* 121.

193 "the nerve and endurance of Danenhower": Ibid.

194 "very much use to himself": Ibid., 125.

194 "he can run monotonously, like a clock": George De Long, *The Voyage of the*
     Jeannette, 2:468.

194 "appreciate now his thoughts and feelings": Ibid., 2:480.

194 "a wonderful amount of nonsense": Ibid.

194 "all my labor and zeal": George De Long, *The Voyage of the* Jeannette, 1:185.

195 "We are not yet daunted": *The Voyage of the* Jeannette, 2:500.

195 "a new leaf in our book of luck": Ibid., 2:501.

24: THE DISCOVERED COUNTRY

198 "something, then, besides ice": George De Long, *The Voyage of the* Jeannette,
     2:544.

198 "We have discovered something": Ibid., 2:545.

198 "to let a man realize where he is": Ibid.

198 "a second Goshen": Melville, *In the Lena Delta,* 16.

198 "distinguish the buck from the doe": Ibid., 17.

199 "the treasury without its debts": George De Long, *The Voyage of the* Jeannette,
     2:546.

199 "it has not melted away": Ibid.

200 "a chaos of ice": Melville, *In the Lena Delta,* 19.

201 "It is hard as flint": George De Long, *The Voyage of the* Jeannette, 2:561.

201 "as woebegone as possible": Ibid., 2:562.

202 "the mad pursuit of those behind": Melville, *In the Lena Delta,* 19.

202 "as a basketful of eels": Ibid., 18.

202   "great blast furnace": Ibid., 19.

203   "it grieved him sorely": Ibid., 20.

203   "herculean feats of strength": Ibid., 21.

204   "challenging our strange advent": Ibid., 19.

204   no scrap of terra firma: In 1979, Henrietta Island—"Genriyetty Ostrov," in Russian—would serve as the embarkation point for a famous Soviet skiing expedition to the North Pole.

204   "in the arms of Morpheus": Ibid., 22.

205   "eats of it unsparingly": George De Long, *The Voyage of the* Jeannette, 2:559.

205   "What use is it": Ibid., 2:560.

206   a copper cylinder: This bleak memorial would remain undisturbed for fifty-seven years. In 1938, a team of Russian biologists attached to a Soviet icebreaker climbed Melville's Head and found the case and cylinder lying beside a toppled cairn. The cylinder had been gnawed by polar bears, but inside, De Long's account, written in his elegant spidery hand, was still faintly legible, though the parchment was ruined by water. Nearby, the Russian scientists located the flagstaff that Erichsen had planted, and an assortment of spent shotgun shells—no doubt remnants from Sharvell's guillemot hunting. The artifacts were sent on to St. Petersburg.

206   "flushed with the success of the undertaking": Melville, *In the Lena Delta,* 22.

207   "enduring the agonies of the lost": Ibid., 24.

207   "a delight to us": Ibid.

207   "to make the snow hiss": Ibid.

208   "Away ran Bruin": George De Long, *The Voyage of the* Jeannette, 2:562.

209   "a perilous journey has been accomplished": Ibid., 2:566.

209   "the dogs yelling lustily": Melville, *In the Lena Delta,* 25.

209   "I am glad to see you back": Ibid.

25: TIDINGS

211   "a ground work of truth": Calvin Hooper, *Report of the Cruise of the U.S. Revenue Steamer* Thomas Corwin, *1881,* 9.

211   "a symptom of success": De Long and Newcomb, *Our Lost Explorers,* 38.

211   "I hope the silly prophecies": Emma De Long, *Explorer's Wife,* 192.

212   "as if he sat by her side": Guttridge, *Icebound,* 148.

212   "Arctic exploration is marked": Ibid., 155.

212   "he was in pure white": Ibid., 148.

213   "bring back some tidings": Muir, *Cruise of the* Corwin, xxi.

215   "looking at the biggest picture": Bill McKibben, in his foreword to Muir's *Cruise of the* Corwin, xv.

215   "fine icy time": Muir, *Cruise of the* Corwin, xxxviii.

216   "they go to ruin generally": Ibid., 15.

216   "perfectly nude in the severest weather": Ibid., 33.

216   "generous nature of the natives": Calvin Hooper, *Report of the Cruise of the U.S. Revenue Steamer* Thomas Corwin, *1881,* 18.

217   "women are freely offered": Ibid., 42.

217   "worth coming far to know them": Muir, *Cruise of the* Corwin, 70.

217   "the story had traveled": Ibid., 31.

217   "with many grains of allowance": Ibid.

218   "nearly one quarter slang:": Ibid., 105.

218   "manufactured on the spot": Calvin Hooper, *Report of the Cruise of the U.S. Revenue Steamer* Thomas Corwin, *1881,* 10.

218   "like a perennial mountain spring": Muir, *Cruise of the* Corwin, 57.

218   "one of the worst old rascals": Calvin Hooper, *Report of the Cruise of the U.S. Revenue Steamer* Thomas Corwin, *1881,* 10.

218   "But when pressed": Ibid.

219   "We will seek them": Muir, *Cruise of the* Corwin, 34.

219   "incorrigible white trash": Ibid.

219   "children listened attentively": Ibid., 41.

220   "could still hear his screams": Ibid., 43.

220   "raced about in exuberant sport": Ibid., 49.

221   "faded in the snowy gloom": Ibid.

26: DEATH STROKES

223   "a thing of the past": George De Long, *The Voyage of the* Jeannette, 2:569.

224   "a howling wilderness": Ibid., 2:567.

224   "her cyclopean vise": Danenhower, *Narrative of the "Jeannette,"* 36.

224   "confusion raging about us": Ibid., 30.

224   "like a glass toy": Ibid., 37.

225   "the hideous results of forty dogs": Melville, *In the Lena Delta,* 14.

225   "vegetables grown in the dark": Ibid., 15.

225   "exploded so many theories": George De Long, *The Voyage of the* Jeannette, 2:636.

226   "a grand success": Danenhower, *Narrative of the "Jeannette,"* 37.

226   "crucial moment in our voyage": George De Long, *The Voyage of the* Jeannette, 2:554.

226   "off the launching ways": Danenhower, *Narrative of the "Jeannette,"* 37.

226   "no injury whatever": George De Long, *The Voyage of the* Jeannette, 2:572.

226   "she could bathe her sides": Danenhower, *Narrative of the "Jeannette,"* 38.

227   "strikingly picturesque": Melville, *In the Lena Delta,* 29.

227   "cracking in every part": George De Long, *The Voyage of the* Jeannette, 2:574.

227   "What do you think of it?": Melville, *In the Lena Delta,* 28.

227   "stabbed in her vitals": De Long and Newcomb, *Our Lost Explorers,* 306.

228   "like death strokes": Melville, *In the Lena Delta,* 28.

229   "jumped from their chucks": De Long and Newcomb, *Our Lost Explorers,* 306.

229   "if I had gone down with my ship": George De Long, *The Voyage of the* Jeannette, 2:623.

229   "Goodbye, old ship": Melville, *In the Lena Delta,* 30.

230   "there she goes!": Ibid., 31.

230   "a great, gaunt skeleton": Ibid., 32.

230   "embrace of the Arctic monster": Danenhower, *Narrative of the "Jeannette,"* 43.

231   "any rational hope of aid": Melville, *In the Lena Delta,* 32.

231   "long march to the south": Ibid.

231   "the melancholy howl": De Long and Newcomb, *Our Lost Explorers,* 306.

PART FIVE: THE END OF CREATION

27: ALL MUCKY

235   "If the *Jeannette* is still in existence": *New York Times,* July 21, 1881.
236   "cheerless-looking mass": Muir, *Cruise of the* Corwin, 106.
236   "not a soul was left alive": Ibid., 108.
236   "All *mucky*—all gone": Ibid., 110.
236   "smiled at the ghastly spectacle": Ibid., 86.
236   "picked bare by the crows": Ibid., 109.
237   "it was almost impossible": Calvin Hooper, *Report of the Cruise of the U.S. Revenue Steamer* Thomas Corwin, *1881,* 22.
237   "piled like fire-wood": Muir, *Cruise of the* Corwin, 109.
237   "as long as the rum lasts": Calvin Hooper, *Report of the Cruise of the U.S. Revenue Steamer* Thomas Corwin, *1880,* 11.
238   "most glaring death": Muir, *Cruise of the* Corwin, 109.
239   "every soul of them will have vanished": Ibid., 111.
239   "Had they found the *Jeannette*?": Calvin Hooper, *Report of the Cruise of the U.S. Revenue Steamer* Thomas Corwin, *1881,* 24.
239   Herring and his party: Ibid., 24–29.
242   "a steamer with three masts": Ibid., 31.
242   "accounts would have reached us": Ibid.

28: NIL DESPERANDUM

245   "vagabond insects": Melville, *In the Lena Delta,* 43.
246   "corps of engineers to level": Danenhower, *Narrative of the "Jeannette,"* 48.
246   "terribly confused": George De Long, *The Voyage of the* Jeannette, 2:602.
247   "utterly fagged out": Melville, *In the Lena Delta,* 34.
247   "a more tired and hungry": George De Long, *The Voyage of the* Jeannette, 2:600.
247   "singing is going on all around": Ibid., 2:611.
247   "with such little complaint": Melville, *In the Lena Delta,* 39.
248   "blinks like a drunkard's eye": George De Long, *The Voyage of the* Jeannette, 2:601.
248   "We break camp and start": Ibid., 2:589.
250   "working for our lives": Danenhower, *Narrative of the "Jeannette,"* 50.
250   "very seriously disturbed about him": George De Long, *The Voyage of the* Jeannette, 2:605.
250   "Our outlook": Ibid., 2:638.
250   "I shall get along all right": Ibid., 2:604.
251   "fish, flesh, and fowl to us": Ibid., 2:631.
251   "passed blood freely from bowels": Ambler, "Private Journal," 193.
251   "each to his own taste—*ah!*": Melville, *In the Lena Delta,* 41.
252   "consistency of fresh tripe": Ibid., 38.
252   "draw a breath without pain": Ambler, "Private Journal," 196.
252   "drop me a line": George De Long, *The Voyage of the* Jeannette, 2:605.
253   "uniformly beyond reproach": Ibid., 2:641.
253   "don't do that again!" Ibid.
253   "Consider yourself under arrest": Guttridge, *Icebound,* 181.
254   "enough to make one thoughtful": George De Long, *The Voyage of the* Jeannette, 2:606.

254   "I dodge [them]": Ibid., 2:611.

254   "despondent and suspicious": Melville, *In the Lena Delta,* 41.

255   "we will never get out": Guttridge, *Icebound,* 173.

29: THE PHANTOM CONTINENT

258   "as if still fighting for life": Muir, *Cruise of the* Corwin, 83.

258   "conducting in a dead Indian": Ibid., 115.

259   "idle hours in gambling and quarreling": Ibid., 82.

259   "a rush to the new mines ere long": Ibid., 114.

259   "the rest to be eaten by wolves": Ibid., 128.

260   "curious freaks of refraction": Rosse, *The First Landing,* 2.

260   "smoke from the burning tundra": Muir, *Cruise of the* Corwin, 117.

260   "frost-killed end of creation": Ibid., 202.

260   "as a myth": Rosse, *The First Landing,* 1.

261   "a good deal of bumping": Ibid., 52.

261   "standing on narrow ledges": Muir, *Cruise of the* Corwin, 155.

261   "ocean stretching indefinitely northward": Ibid., 154.

261   "to fix the eye of a mountaineer": Ibid.

261   "waste of ice and sea and granite": Rosse, *The First Landing,* 3.

262   "we could not have failed to see it": Muir, *Cruise of the* Corwin, 178.

262   "learn something of this strange visitor": Calvin Hooper, *Report of the Cruise of the U.S. Revenue Steamer* Thomas Corwin, *1881,* 54.

262   "stained the blue water with his blood": Muir, *Cruise of the* Corwin, 156.

262   "beset by great masses of ice": Rosse, *The First Landing,* 4.

262   "ground in the ice for a winter or two": Muir, *Cruise of the* Corwin, 165.

263   "in case anybody was near to listen": Ibid., 167.

263   "long withdrawing valleys": Ibid., 221.

264   "legible to the dullest observer for years": Ibid., 176.

264   "the Land of the White Bear": Ibid., 177.

265   "The extent of the new territory": Ibid., 169.

265   "in the polar climate": Wrangel would later be claimed by Russia, which controls the uninhabited island today as a highly restricted *zapovednik,* or federal wilderness preserve, which I visited in the summer of 2012 while researching a story for *National Geographic.* Because the *Corwin* party first planted a flag on the island, certain groups in the United States insist Wrangel is rightfully American soil and have lobbied strenuously for the State Department to press its territorial claim in the international courts.

30: A SECOND PROMISED LAND

267   "attend a funeral at any moment": George De Long, *The Voyage of the* Jeannette, 2:601.

267   "limber as a basket": Danenhower, *Narrative of the "Jeannette,"* 55.

267   "The knots and tangles": Ambler, "Private Journal," 199.

267   "Each man had a favorite": Danenhower, *Narrative of the "Jeannette,"* 57.

267   "rags, bags, and old battered boats": Melville, *In the Lena Delta,* 43.

268   "will get himself hurt": Ambler, "Private Journal," 198.

268   "Don't let me see you": Guttridge, *Icebound,* 175.

268   "tackle it again to-morrow": George De Long, *The Voyage of the* Jeannette, 2:668.

269   "The drag, drag, the slips and jerks": Ibid., 2:636.

269   "cheerful and come up smiling": Ambler, "Private Journal," 202.

270   "has been thoroughly exploded": Guttridge, *Icebound,* 124.

271   "our well-wishers at home": George De Long, *The Voyage of the* Jeannette, 2:623.

271   "learn what its application may be": Ibid.

272   "A bright vision arose": Melville, *In the Lena Delta,* 42.

272   "second Land of Promise": Ibid.

272   "straightaway became a Hercules": Ibid., 43.

273   "dined at Delmonico's": George De Long, *The Voyage of the* Jeannette, 2:646.

273   "tasted very well": Ambler, "Private Journal," 200.

273   "The choice parts": George De Long, *The Voyage of the* Jeannette, 2:659.

273   "not as good as seal stew": Ibid., 2:660.

273   "not unlike pig's feet": De Long and Newcomb, *Our Lost Explorers,* 309.

274   "bullets with good results": George De Long, *The Voyage of the* Jeannette, 2:667.

274   "roasted his paws": Melville, *In the Lena Delta,* 42.

274   "a current in our favor": Ibid.

276   "concealed it as long as possible": Ambler, "Private Journal," 197.

276   "a tin cup of tea": Ibid., 200. Some accounts suggest that Dr. Ambler was toast-
      ing the birthday of his sister, not his fiancée.

276   "Island seems to recede": Ibid., 201.

276   "I was fairly staggered": George De Long, *The Voyage of the* Jeannette, 2:654.

276   "we have made another discovery": Ibid., 2:651.

277   "powdered by the hand of time": Melville, *In the Lena Delta,* 43.

277   "crags of indescribable grandeur": De Long and Newcomb, *Our Lost Explorers,*
      310.

277   "enormous swarm of bees": Ibid.

277   "hold a Goliath back": George De Long, *The Voyage of the* Jeannette, 2:661.

277   "the devil to pay": Ambler, "Private Journal," 202.

278   "I take possession of it": George De Long, *The Voyage of the* Jeannette, 2:679.

278   "renewing the electrical connections": Melville, *In the Lena Delta,* 51.

31: EIGHT PRECIOUS DAYS

279   "the roar of distant thunder": Melville, *In the Lena Delta,* 44.

279   "its awful way toward us": Ibid.

279   "lashing it into foam": De Long and Newcomb, *Our Lost Explorers,* 313.

280   "surprised at nothing": George De Long, *The Voyage of the* Jeannette, 2:690.

280   "I added Bennett Island": Ibid., 2:679.

281   "a serious thing for us": Ibid., 2:690.

281   "over-cautious person would avoid it": Melville to Emma De Long, August 27,
      1883, Emma De Long Papers.

281   "dock[s] fallen to decay": George De Long, *The Voyage of the* Jeannette, 2:686.

281   "like that of young veal": Danenhower, *Narrative of the "Jeannette,"* 55.

281   "old ones tough, young tender": Ambler, "Private Journal," 203.

282   "give all hands all the liberty": Ibid.

282   "by what right I dared invade": De Long and Newcomb, *Our Lost Explorers,* 313.

283   "the most extensive breeding ground": Ibid., 312.

283   "a narrow shave": Ibid.

284   "I must think of human life first": George De Long, *The Voyage of the* Jeannette,
      2:691.

284   "The poor brutes": Danenhower, *Narrative of the "Jeannette,"* 57.

285   "clad in their winter garb": Melville, *In the Lena Delta,* 46.

285   "generally a queer day": George De Long, *The Voyage of the* Jeannette, 2:692.

286   "everything over the ice": Ibid., 2:689.

286   "swimming in the clouds": Ibid., 2:694.

286   "the silver glory of the clouds": Melville, *In the Lena Delta,* 47.

32: THE KNOWN WORLD

288   "the maze at Hampton Court": George De Long, *The Voyage of the* Jeannette, 1:205.

288   "skeleton pack": George De Long, *The Voyage of the* Jeannette, 2:706.

288   "Very severe": Danenhower, *Narrative of the "Jeannette,"* 57.

288   "work for a Titan": Melville, *In the Lena Delta,* 47.

289   "very much wasted": George De Long, *The Voyage of the* Jeannette, 2:705.

289   "like a school of whales": Melville, *In the Lena Delta,* 57.

289   "scampered like circus horses": Ibid., 48.

291   "Time was too precious": George De Long, *The Voyage of the* Jeannette, 2:699.

291   "doleful howling": Ibid.

291   "led off to execution": Ibid.

291   "sense enough to remain by us": Danenhower, *Narrative of the "Jeannette,"* 57.

291   "until it becomes perilous": George De Long, *The Voyage of the* Jeannette, 2:699.

292   "angry look": Ambler, "Private Journal," 209.

292   "very peculiar mind": Ibid., 205.

293   "take it as anything you please": See Guttridge, *Icebound,* 186.

293   "it showed plainly enough": George De Long, *The Voyage of the* Jeannette, 2:713.

293   "start on our journey afloat": Ibid., 2:714.

293   "never been afloat at all": Ibid., 2:715.

294   "never get out of the wilderness": Melville, *In the Lena Delta,* 47.

294   "make the best of every misfortune": Ibid., 50.

294   "seem to be against us": Ambler, "Private Journal," 205.

294   "Another lost day": George De Long, *The Voyage of the* Jeannette, 2:717.

294   "a mere question of provisions": Melville, *In the Lena Delta,* 50.

295   "perfectly miserable for want of a smoke": George De Long, *The Voyage of the* Jeannette, 2:719.

295   "Richard is himself again": Ibid.

295   "got considerable comfort": Ibid., 2:721.

296   "in such a hell-gate": Ibid., 2:722.

296   "seriously sought for eatable game": Ibid., 2:723.

297   "waited in wretched discomfort": Ibid., 2:726.

297   "What a cold bath!": Melville, *In the Lena Delta,* 59.

297   "they are doubled in intensity": George De Long, *The Voyage of the* Jeannette, 2:729.

298   "an attack of giddiness": Ambler, "Private Journal," 210.

298   "no one can tell what may occur": George De Long, *The Voyage of the* Jeannette, 2:741.

298   "a good dinner was made of them": Ibid., 2:732.

298   "chilling me to the bone": Ibid., 2:736.

299   "candle-snuffer hills": Ibid., 2:742.

299   "Long windrows of driftwood": Melville, *In the Lena Delta,* 52.

299 "distant scenes and friends": Ibid., 56.

299 "regulation fog": George De Long, *The Voyage of the* Jeannette, 2:741.

299 "padding shyly about": Melville, *In the Lena Delta,* 52.

300 "burrowed his way into the sand": George De Long, *The Voyage of the* Jeannette, 2:737.

300 "very near being smashed up": Danenhower, *Narrative of the "Jeannette,"* 63.

300 "would have been death": De Long and Newcomb, *Our Lost Explorers,* 318.

300 "men performed wonders": Melville, *In the Lena Delta,* 57.

300 "would certainly engulf us": Ibid., 58.

301 "filled her to the thwarts": Danenhower, *Narrative of the "Jeannette,"* 62.

301 "wet and exhausted creatures": George De Long, *The Voyage of the* Jeannette, 2:743.

301 "shivering together in a heap": Melville, *In the Lena Delta,* 59.

301 "all stand it without complaint": Ambler, "Private Journal," 208.

301 "the sleep of the just": Melville, *In the Lena Delta,* 60.

33: SEAS HIGH AND SPITEFUL

302 "on the warpath": George De Long, *The Voyage of the* Jeannette, 2:745.

302 "mere strip of earth": Ambler, "Private Journal," 211.

303 "almost to a knife-edge": George De Long, *The Voyage of the* Jeannette, 2:745.

303 "a royal gorge, indeed": Melville, *In the Lena Delta,* 60.

303 "jolly good soup on the morrow": Ibid.

303 "Our lesser discomforts": George De Long, *The Voyage of the* Jeannette, 2:746.

304 "stood up splendidly to her work": Melville, *In the Lena Delta,* 63.

304 "one of the best fastened boats": Danenhower, *Narrative of the "Jeannette,"* 61.

305 "considered sound and efficient": Melville, *In the Lena Delta,* 49.

305 "not altogether satisfied with the outlook": Danenhower, *Narrative of the "Jeannette,"* 64.

306 "This record of our arrival": George De Long, *The Voyage of the* Jeannette, 2:747.

306 "every one jolly": Melville, *In the Lena Delta,* 61.

307 "plenty of natives there": Ibid.

307 "Don't wait for me": Ibid., 62.

307 "high and spiteful": Danenhower, *Narrative of the "Jeannette,"* 66.

308 "I must run or else I will swamp": Melville, *In the Lena Delta,* 64.

PART SIX: THE WHISPER OF THE STARS

34: LUCKY FOURTEEN

314 "full up to the thwarts": Navy Department, *Loss of the Steamer* Jeannette, 175.

314 "Baling, baling all the time": Ambler, "Private Journal," 211.

315 "No sleep for 36 hours": Ibid.

315 "a nervous chuckle in his throat": Ibid.

317 "No chart had been laid down": George De Long, *The Voyage of the* Jeannette, 2:802. Also see De Long and Newcomb, *Our Lost Explorers,* 102.

318 "pretty well played out": *Loss of the Steamer* Jeannette, 177.

318 "washing in the boat": Ibid., 178.

318 "most miserable and uncomfortable night": George De Long, *The Voyage of the* Jeannette, 2:753.

320 "look our situation in the face": Ibid., 2:754.

321   "Everybody was badly frozen": *Loss of the Steamer* Jeannette, 179.

322   "Our outlook at this rate": Ambler, "Private Journal," 212.

323   "our chances of getting through seem good": George De Long, *The Voyage of the* Jeannette, 2:756.

35: REMEMBER ME IN NEW YORK

326   "tough as well-tanned leather": De Long and Newcomb, *Our Lost Explorers,* 298.

326   "I can't go on!": Nindemann testimony before the Committee on Naval Affairs, *Loss of the Steamer* Jeannette, 180.

327   "His condition is serious indeed": George De Long, *The Voyage of the* Jeannette, 2:761.

327   "do you know anything about frostbites?": *Loss of the Steamer* Jeannette, 181.

327   "I saw something drop from my foot": Ibid.

328   "cut off close to the neck": George De Long, *The Voyage of the* Jeannette, 2:763.

328   "an important question": Ibid.

328   "I cannot leave them": Ibid.

329   "And when the dog is eaten—?": Ibid., 2:758.

329   "By strategy unsurpassed": Ibid., 2:765.

329   "We can remain here a day": Ibid.

329   "surprise for the next visitor": Ibid., 2:767.

330   "fresh embers and meat scraps": Ibid., 2:774.

330   "the chart reconcile with the country": Ibid., 2:769.

331   "If Chipp or Melville got through": Ibid., 2:774.

331   "God grant that our smoke": Ambler, "Private Journal," 214.

331   "more or less used up": Ibid.

331   "like tarpaulins over merchandise": George De Long, *The Voyage of the* Jeannette, 2:762.

331   "some tidings of the two boats": Ibid., 2:772.

331   "he may have to amputate": Ibid., 2:772.

332   "If we can find a settlement": Ambler, "Private Journal," 214.

332   "Removed four toes": Ibid., 214.

332   "May God pity us": George De Long, *The Voyage of the* Jeannette, 2:778.

333   "contrabandists": Hoehling, *The* Jeannette *Expedition,* 125.

333   "caught in a trap": George De Long, *The Voyage of the* Jeannette, 2:775.

333   "intervene and carry him off": Ibid., 2:776.

333   "weak and tremulous": Ibid., 2:784.

334   "his life is in danger": Ibid., 2:776.

334   "simply useless": Ibid., 2:782.

335   "these records will go with me": Guttridge, *Icebound,* 225.

335   "plan of running the machine": Ibid., 210.

335   "a nauseating mess": George De Long, *The Voyage of the* Jeannette, 2:787.

335   "There were some men": *Loss of the Steamer* Jeannette, 190.

336   "such a dreary, wretched night": George De Long, *The Voyage of the* Jeannette, 2:787.

336   "Peace to his soul": Ambler, "Private Journal," 215.

336   "What in God's name": George De Long, *The Voyage of the* Jeannette, 2:790.

337   "wandering in a labyrinth": Ibid., 2:792.

337   "you would not get five miles": Hoehling, *The* Jeannette *Expedition,* 130.

337   "I trust in God": George De Long, *The Voyage of the* Jeannette, 2:791.

337   "just the clothes we stood in": *Loss of the Steamer* Jeannette, 194.

338   "You see the condition we are in": Ibid.

338   "my duty required me": Ambler, "Private Journal," 215.

338   "When you get to New York": De Long and Newcomb, *Our Lost Explorers,* 137.

338   "God give them aid": Ambler, "Private Journal," 215.

36: IF IT TAKES MY LAST DOLLAR

341   "escaped curiosities": De Long and Newcomb, *Our Lost Explorers,* 72.

341   "man shall reach that supreme spot": Ibid., 75.

341   "We are not so hopeful": *Chicago Tribune,* November 12, 1881.

341   Among the crew of the *Rodgers*: For a thorough first-person account of the voyage of the *Rodgers* in search of the *Jeannette,* see Gilder, *Ice-Pack and Tundra.*

342   "The American people may be assured": De Long and Newcomb, *Our Lost Explorers,* 80.

342   "all the civilized nations of the earth": Ibid., 81.

342   "There is nothing like it": *Newport Daily News,* July 29, 1880.

       first tennis tournament ever held: See International Tennis Hall of Fame & Museum, *Tennis and the Newport Casino* (Charleston, SC: Arcadia, 2011), and C. P. B. Jefferys, *Newport: A Concise History* (Newport: Newport Historical Society, 2008). See also Hanlon, "The Cradle of Tennis Was Meant to Be Rocky."

343   invited her up to Newport: See Emma De Long, *Explorer's Wife,* 199.

343   "Have no fears": Ibid.

37: FRANTIC PANTOMIMES

344   marched over the Lena wastelands: My account of the southward march made by Nindemann and Noros is primarily derived from Nindemann's testimony before the Committee on Naval Affairs, found in *Loss of the Steamer* Jeannette, 196–211. See also De Long and Newcomb, *Our Lost Explorers,* 130–38, and George De Long, *The Voyage of the* Jeannette, 2:801–26.

344   "the whisper of the stars": See Middleton, *Going to Extremes,* 50.

344   coldest temperature ever recorded: See Riordan and Bourget, *World Weather Extremes,* 27.

348   "Everybody stopped and looked": *Loss of the Steamer* Jeannette, 206.

349   "they felt sorry for it": Ibid., 207.

349   "did not understand a word": Ibid., 205.

351   "My God, *Mr. Melville*": Melville, *In the Lena Delta,* 164. See also *Loss of the Steamer* Jeannette, 211.

38: INCUBUS OF HORRORS

352   storm-tossed Laptev Sea: My narrative of the Melville party's journey across the Laptev Sea to safety is based on George Melville's lengthy account in *In the Lena Delta,* 65–164, as well as his testimony before the Committee on Naval Affairs, *Loss of the Steamer* Jeannette, 126–34. See also Danenhower, *Narrative of the "Jeannette,"* 65–93, and Newcomb's account in De Long and Newcomb, *Our Lost Explorers,* 318–31.

353   "spanking rate": Melville, *In the Lena Delta,* 65.

353   "nothing but enhance our misery": Ibid., 71.

354   "Bitterly we cursed Petermann": Fleming, *Ninety Degrees North,* 222.

354   "entirely bereft of feeling": Melville, *In the Lena Delta,* 77.
355   "If you don't obey me": Guttridge, *Icebound,* 213.
355   "a bond which bound us all": Melville, *In the Lena Delta,* 78–79.
355   "chanced upon a modern metropolis": Ibid., 81.
356   "We all smiled and laughed": Ibid., 88.
357   "leaving us in the lurch": Ibid., 94.
357   "wondrously dirty": Ibid., 93.
357   "a game of mock heroics": Ibid., 143.
358   "determined the risk too great": Ibid.
358   "weeping over our miseries": Ibid., 113.
358   "in spite of their ugliness": Danenhower, *Narrative of the "Jeannette,"* 87.
358   "a modicum of rancid deer tallow": Melville, *In the Lena Delta,* 111.
359   *"plenty good little old woman"*: Ibid., 129.
359   "What I most feared": Ibid., 128–29.
360   "Gangrene had apparently set in": Ibid., 127.
360   "My dear mother": Leach's letter home is reprinted in De Long and Newcomb, *Our Lost Explorers,* 138–39.
361   "bright, intelligent looking man": Melville, *In the Lena Delta,* 135.
361   "lying is not considered a sin": Ibid., 138.
362   "never was an absent lover": Ibid., 143.
362   "Arctic steamer Jeannette lost": Ibid., 144.
363   "mongrels of every hue": Ibid., 150.
363   "out of the question": Ibid., 165.

39: WHITE GLOOM
365   "without great torture": Melville, *In the Lena Delta,* 279.
366   "mutilations of wild beasts": Ibid., 209.
366   "The face of the country": Ibid.
366   "a fine specimen of Cossack": Ibid., 170.
367   "yet fearing the worst": Ibid., 172.
367   "seemed to have forsaken them": Ibid., 174.
367   "out of the jaws of death": Ibid., 181.
368   "a congregation of islands": Ibid., 216.
368   "vehemence of my delivery": Ibid., 189.
369   "crossing themselves in terror": Ibid., 185.
369   "A more motley or odoriferous": Ibid., 192.
369   "Whoever finds this paper": Ibid., 193.
370   "monuments of the Druids": Ibid., 228.
370   "so much plunder in one heap": Ibid., 202.
370   "a load of worthless stones": Ibid., 206.
371   "where it took fire and burned": Ibid., 207.
371   "most pitiful to think": Ibid., 198.
372   "a long line of thin vapor": Figuier, *Earth and Sea,* 225.
372   "existed like an animated dead man": Melville, *In the Lena Delta,* 220.
372   "come what might": Ibid., 218.
373   "I should die too": Ibid., 221.
373   "It is my desire": De Long and Newcomb, *Our Lost Explorers,* 122.
374   The following telegram was received: Melville's telegram is reprinted in its entirety in De Long and Newcomb, *Our Lost Explorers,* 84–85.

374   "Omit no effort": Ibid., 86.
375   "A dispatch from Mr. Hoffman": Ibid.

40: THE RUSSIAN NATION AT YOUR BACK
378   "straight as a spear-shaft": Melville, *In the Lena Delta,* 273.
378   "He was a soldier": Ibid., 274.
378   "you may have anything you want": Ibid., 276.
379   "They seemed comfortable": Ibid., 272.
379   "I always hope for the best": Danenhower's letter home to his mother was published in the *New York Herald,* December 30, 1881.
379   no American had visited here: For an excellent account of John Ledyard's improbably adventurous life, see Gifford, *Ledyard: In Search of the First American Explorer.*
380   "intelligible at Constantinople": De Long and Newcomb, *Our Lost Explorers,* 145.
380   burrowed like a mole: Ibid., 96.
381   "cadaverous-visaged young man": Melville, *In the Lena Delta,* 247.
381   "a pillar of hope": Ibid., 248.
381   "here I saw youth": Ibid., 250.
381   "Eluding their pursuers": Ibid., 251.
382   "On this night": Ibid., 279.
382   "ingenuity for avoiding work": Ibid., 282.
383   "I pitied the poor exiles": Ibid., 276.

41: THEY THAT WATCH FOR THE MORNING
385   Melville left Yakutsk: The account of Melville's search leading up to the discovery of De Long's final camp is derived primarily from Melville's *In the Lena Delta,* 283–331, as well as Melville's testimony before the Committee on Naval Affairs, *Loss of the* Jeannette, 145–56. See also Nindemann's testimony in *Loss of the* Jeannette, 217–23.
387   "All hands weak and feeble": George De Long, *The Voyage of the* Jeannette, 2:796.
387   "Everybody getting weaker": Ibid.
387   "We cannot move against the wind": Ibid.
388   cause of death as "exhaustion": Ambler, "Private Journal," 215.
389   "One hundred thirty third day": George De Long, *The Voyage of the* Jeannette, 2:797.
389   "Mr. Collins dying": Ibid., 2:800.
390   "as though the arch-fiend himself": Melville, *In the Lena Delta,* 336.
390   "shrunk into great cavities": Ibid., 335.
391   "his clothes scorched through": Ibid., 338.
391   "He was lying on his back": See Hoehling, *The* Jeannette *Expedition,* 163.
392   "winter winds had blown it down": Melville, *In the Lena Delta,* 333.
393   "on duty, on guard, under arms": Ibid., 335.
394   "My Dear Brother": Ambler, "Private Journal," 216.
395   The following dispatch has just reached: Melville's telegram is reprinted in Henry Llewellyn Williams, *History of the Adventurous Voyage,* 70.

42: A WILD DIRGE THROUGH TIME

396   The ten bodies were carefully: My depiction of Melville's monument to his com-
       rades is based in part on my own travels to Amerika Khaya in the summer of
       2012. See also Melville, *In the Lena Delta*, 340–45; Nindemann's testimony in
       Loss of the Steamer Jeannette, 221–22; and De Long and Newcomb, *Our Lost
       Explorers*, 371–73.
396   "In memory of the officers": De Long and Newcomb, *Our Lost Explorers*, 372.
397   "In the awful silence": Melville, *In the Lena Delta*, 344.

       When I visited the site of Amerika Khaya in the summer of 2012, Melville's
       memorial was still there. A group of Russian scientists had recently spruced up
       the site and repaired the large cross, which, on clear days, is visible all the way to
       the Arctic Ocean.

EPILOGUE: AS LONG AS I HAVE ICE TO STAND ON

401   a crisp autumn day: My description of Melville's arrival in New York is primarily
       based on accounts in the *New York Herald*, September 14, 1882.
403   "the rigor of our climate": Melville, *In the Lena Delta*, 412.
403   "you will not again tempt fortune": Ibid.
403   "bevy of rustic maidens": De Long and Newcomb, *Our Lost Explorers*, 398.
403   "spoke only with their eyes": *New York Herald*, September 14, 1882.
403   "You have lost a son": Ibid.
403   "he had lost a little flesh": Ibid.
403   all but lost her mind: See Guttridge, *Icebound*, 264–65.
404   "as if the seas had closed over me": Emma De Long, *Explorer's Wife*, 220.
404   "the gift of suffering": George De Long, *The Voyage of the* Jeannette, 2:869.
405   "the unfortunate woman": Melville to Emma De Long, August 24, 1882, Emma
       De Long Papers.
405   "I will stand by you": Emma De Long, *Explorer's Wife*, 225.
405   "we did our whole duty": De Long and Newcomb, *Our Lost Explorers*, 476.
406   "brave men who will come home no more": Ibid., 476–77.

SELECTED BIBLIOGRAPHY

JEANNETTE EXPEDITION JOURNALS, DIARIES, AND OFFICIAL GOVERNMENT PUBLICATIONS

Ambler, James Markham. "The Private Journal of James Markham Ambler, M.D., Passed Assistant Surgeon, United States Navy, and the Medical Officer of the Arctic Exploring Steamer *Jeannette*." Published in the *United States Naval Medical Bulletin*, Navy Dept. Bureau of Medicine and Surgery (Volume 11). Washington: Government Printing Office, January 1917.

Danenhower, John Wilson. *Lieutenant Danenhower's Narrative of the "Jeannette."* Boston: James R. Osgood and Company, 1882.

De Long, George Washington. *The Voyage of the* Jeannette: *The Ship and Ice Journals of George W. De Long, Lieutenant-Commander U.S.N. and Commander of the Polar Expedition.* Edited by Emma De Long. 2 vols. Boston: Houghton, Mifflin, 1883–84.

Harber, Giles. *Report of Lieut. Giles B. Harber, U.S.N., of His Search for the Missing People of the* Jeannette *Expedition, etc.* Washington, DC: Government Printing Office, 1884.

Jeannette *Inquiry. Before the Committee on Naval Affairs of the United States House of Representatives, Forty-eighth Congress.* Washington, DC: Government Printing Office, 1884.

Loss of the Steamer Jeannette: *Record of the Proceedings of a Court of Inquiry Convened at the Navy Department, 1882.* Washington, DC: Government Printing Office, 1882.

ARCHIVES, MUSEUMS, AND PERSONAL PAPERS

Dartmouth College Library, Hanover, NH. George Wallace Melville Papers, 1881–82, including his Arctic journal.

National Archives, Washington, DC. Official U.S. Navy papers of the USS *Jeannette* Arctic Exploring Expedition, Naval Records Collection, records groups 24, 43, and 45.

National Archives at San Francisco, San Bruno, CA. Letters sent to the Bureau of Steam Engineering on the outfitting of the USS *Jeannette*.

Personal Papers of Emma Wotton De Long. Includes photographs, correspondence, and manuscripts. Loaned to the author by De Long descendant Katharine De Long.

Rutgers University, New Brunswick, NJ, Papers of Thomas Alva Edison.

Thomas Edison National Historic Park, West Orange, NJ.

United States Naval Academy Museum, Annapolis, Maryland. The De Long Family Papers and the *Jeannette* Expedition Artifacts Collection.

University of Erfurt Gotha Research Library, Gotha, Germany. The Correspondence of August Heinrich Petermann, Perthes Collection.

Vallejo Naval and Historical Museum, Vallejo, CA. Collected papers on the reconstruction and launch of the USS *Jeannette*.

PAMPHLETS AND MONOGRAPHS

Annual Report of the Superintendant of the United States Coast and Geodetic Survey. Vol. 15, 1883.

Bent, Silas. *An Address Delivered Before the St. Louis Mercantile Library Association, January 6th, 1872, upon the Thermal Paths to the Pole, the Currents of the Ocean, and the Influences of the Latter upon the Climates of the World*. St. Louis: R. P. Studley Co., 1872.

Geographical Society of the Pacific. *An Examination into the Genuineness of the "Jeannette" Relics: Some Evidence of Currents in the Polar Regions*. San Francisco: John Partridge, Printer and Publisher, 1896.

Hooper, Calvin. *Report of the Cruise of the U.S. Revenue Steamer* Thomas Corwin, *in the Arctic Ocean, 1880*. Washington, DC: Government Printing Office, 1881.

———. *Report of the Cruise of the U.S. Revenue Steamer* Thomas Corwin, *in the Arctic Ocean, 1881*. Washington, DC: Government Printing Office, 1884.

Hooper, Samuel L. *Occasional Papers of the California Academy of Sciences: The Discovery of Wrangel Island*. San Francisco: Academy, 1956.

Knorr, E. R. *Papers on the Eastern and Northern Extensions of the Gulf Stream*. Washington, DC: Government Printing Office, 1871.

Melville, George. "Remarks on Polar Expedition." *Proceedings of the American Philosophical Society* 36 (October 29, 1897): 454–61.

Nelson, Edward W. *Report upon Natural History Collections Made in Alaska Between the Years 1877 and 1881*. Washington, DC: Government Printing Office, 1887.

Petermann, August H. *The Search for Franklin: A Suggestion Submitted to the British Public*. London: Longman, Brown, Green, and Longmans, 1852.

Rosse, Irving C. *The First Landing on Wrangel Island—with Some Remarks on the Northern Inhabitants*. New York: 1883. Reprint, Lexington, KY: Filiquarian Publishing, 2012.

NEWSPAPER ARCHIVES CONSULTED

Chicago Tribune

Daily Alta California

Newport Daily News

Newport Mercury

New-York Commercial Advertiser

The New York Herald

The New York Times

The Philadelphia Inquirer

The Philadelphia Public Ledger

The San Francisco Call

San Francisco Chronicle

The Times (London)

The Vallejo Evening Chronicle

SELECTED ARTICLES

Hanlon, John. "The Cradle of Tennis Was Meant to Be Rocky." *Sports Illustrated*, September 2, 1968.

Horch, Frank. "Photographs and Paintings by William Bradford." *American Art Journal* 5, no. 2 (November 1973): 61–70.

Houston, Robert B., Jr. "If It Had Been God's Will: Dr. James M. M. Ambler and the *Jeannette* Expedition." *Virginia Cavalcade*, Summer 1986, 16–29.

Kilkenny, Anne-Marie Amy. "Life and Scenery in the Far North: William Bradford's 1885 Lecture to the American Geographical Society." *American Art Journal* 26, no. 1–2 (1994): 106–08.

Lamb, Julia. " 'The Commodore' Enjoyed Life—but N.Y. Society Winced." *Smithsonian*, September 1978, 132–40.

Maury, T. B. "The Gateway to the Pole." *Putnam's Monthly Magazine*, November 1869.

Tammiksaar, E., N. G. Sukhova, and I. R. Stone. "Hypothesis Versus Fact: August Petermann and Polar Research." *Arctic* 52, no. 3 (September 1999): 237–44.

BOOKS

Albanov, Valerian. *In the Land of White Death: An Epic Story of Survival in the Siberian Arctic*. New York: Modern Library, 2000.

Anderson, Alun. *After the Ice: Life, Death, and Geopolitics in the New Arctic*. New York: HarperCollins, 2009.

Baldwin, Hanson. *Admiral Death: Twelve Adventures of Men Against the Sea*. New York: Simon and Schuster, 1939.

Bancroft, Hubert Howe. *The Works of Hubert Howe Bancroft*. Vol. 33, *History of Alaska, 1730–1885*. San Francisco: A. L. Bancroft & Company, 1886.

Berens, S. L., and John E. Read. *Nansen in the Frozen World.* Chicago: National Publishing Co., 1897.

Berton, Pierre. *Prisoners of the North.* New York: Carroll & Graf, 2004.

Bockstoce, John R. *Whales, Ice, and Men: The History of Whaling in the Western Arctic.* Seattle: University of Washington Press, 1986.

Borneman, Walter R. *Alaska: Saga of a Bold Land.* New York: HarperCollins, 2003.

Brandt, Anthony. *The Man Who Ate His Boots: The Tragic History of the Search for the Northwest Passage.* New York: Alfred A. Knopf, 2010.

Cane, André. *Hôtes James Gordon Bennett: Hôte Prestigieux et Fantasque de la Côte d'Azur.* Saint-Paul-de-Vence: Bernard de Gourcez, 1981.

———. *James Gordon Bennett.* Saint-Paul-de-Vence: Bernard de Gourcez, 1937.

Carlson, Oliver. *The Man Who Made News: James Gordon Bennett.* New York: Duell, Sloan and Pearce, 1942.

Caswell, John Edwards. *Arctic Frontiers: United States Explorations in the Far North.* Norman, OK: University of Oklahoma Press, 1956.

Cherry-Garrard, Apsley. *The Worst Journey in the World.* New York: Penguin Classics, 2005.

Clarke, Arthur C. *Voice Across the Sea.* New York: Harper & Row, 1959.

Crockett, Albert Stevens. *When James Gordon Bennett Was Caliph of Bagdad.* New York: Funk & Wagnalls, 1926.

De Long, Emma Wotton. *Explorer's Wife.* New York: Dodd, Mead, 1938.

De Long, George W., and Raymond Lee Newcomb. *Our Lost Explorers: The Narrative of the* Jeannette *Arctic Expedition as Related by the Survivors.* Hartford: American Publishing Company, 1882.

De Long, Thomas A. *The De Longs of New York and Brooklyn.* Connecticut: Sasco Associates, 1972.

Di Duca, Marc. *Lake Baikal: Siberia's Great Lake.* Chalfont St. Peter: Bradt Travel Guides, 2010.

Di Robilant, Andrea. *Irresistible North: From Venice to Greenland on the Trail of the Zen Brothers.* New York: Alfred A. Knopf, 2011.

Dolin, Eric Jay. *Leviathan: The History of Whaling in America.* New York: Norton, 2007.

Dowdeswell, Julian, and Michael Hambrey. *Islands of the Arctic.* Cambridge: Cambridge University Press, 2002.

Ellsberg, Edward. *Hell on Ice: The Saga of the* Jeannette. Connecticut: Flat Hammock, 1938.

Emerson, Charles. *The Future History of the Arctic.* New York: PublicAffairs, 2010.

Espenhorst, Jurgen. *Petermann's Planet: A Guide to German Hand-atlases and Their Siblings Throughout the World, 1800–1950.* Schwerte: Pangaea Verlag, 2003.

Felsch, Philipp. *Wie August Petermann: Den Nordpol Erfand.* Schweden: Sammlung Luchterhand, 2010.

Figuier, Louis. *Earth and Sea,* London: T. Nelson and Sons, 1870.

Fiske, Stephen. *Off-Hand Portraits of Prominent New Yorkers.* New York: Arno Press, 1884.

Flaubert, Gustave. *The Letters of Gustave Flaubert, 1830–1857.* Vol. 1. Cambridge, MA: Harvard University Press, 1980.

Fleming, Fergus. *Barrow's Boys: A Stirring Story of Daring, Fortitude, and Outright Lunacy.* New York: Grove, 2001.

———. *Ninety Degrees North: The Quest for the North Pole.* New York: Grove, 2001.

Frazier, Ian. *Travels in Siberia.* New York: Farrar, Straus and Giroux, 2010.

Frost, Orcutt. *Bering: The Russian Discovery of America.* New Haven: Yale University Press, 2003.

Gifford, Bill. *Ledyard: In Search of the First American Explorer.* New York: Harcourt, 2007.

Gilder, William Henry. *Ice-Pack and Tundra: An Account of the Search for the* Jeannette *and a Sledge Journey Through Siberia.* New York: Charles Scribner's Sons, 1888.

Gordon, John Steele. *A Thread Across the Ocean: The Heroic Story of the Transatlantic Cable.* New York: Perennial, 2002.

Gray, Edward G. *The Making of John Ledyard: Empire and Ambition in the Life of an Early American Traveler.* New Haven: Yale University Press, 2007.

Gusewelle, C. W. *A Great Current Running: The U.S.-Russian Lena River Expedition.* Kansas City: Lowell Press, 1994.

Guttridge, Leonard F. *Ghosts of Cape Sabine: The Harrowing True Story of the Greely Expedition.* New York: G. P. Putnam's Sons, 2000.

———. *Icebound: The* Jeannette *Expedition's Quest for the North Pole.* Annapolis: Naval Institute Press, 1986.

Hamilton, Richard F. *President McKinley, War and Empire.* New Brunswick, NJ: Transaction Publishers, 2007.

Harvey, Miles. *The Island of Lost Maps: A True Story of Cartographic Crime.* New York: Random House, 2000.

Hearn, Chester G. *Navy: An Illustrated History.* London: Zenith, 2007.

———. *Tracks in the Sea: Matthew Fontaine Maury and the Mapping of the Oceans.* New York: International Marine/McGraw-Hill, 2002.

Heuglin, M. Theodor von, and August Heinrich Petermann. *Reisen Nach dem Nordpolarmeer in den Jahren 1870 und 1871. In (drei) Theilen und Einem Wisenschaftlichen Anhang.* With a foreword by August Petermann. Braunfdjweig: Drud un Berlag von George Wejtermann, 1872.

Hoehling, A. A. *The* Jeannette *Expedition: An Ill-Fated Journey to the Arctic.* New York: Abelard-Schuman, 1967.

Holland, Clive. *Farthest North: Endurance and Adventure in the Quest for the North Pole.* London: Robinson, 1994.

Hudson, Frederic. *Journalism in the United States: From 1690 to 1872.* New York: Harper & Brothers, 1873.

Jefferys, C. P. B. *Newport: A Concise History.* Newport: Newport Historical Society, 2008.

Kalman, Bobbie, and Ken Faris. *Arctic Whales and Whaling.* New York: Crabtree, 1988.

Karsten, Peter. *The Naval Aristocracy: The Golden Age of Annapolis and the Emergence of Modern American Navalism.* Annapolis: Naval Institute Press, 2008.

Kennan, George. *Siberia and the Exile System.* 2 vols. New York: Century Co., 1891.

———. *Tent Life in Siberia: An Incredible Account of Siberian Adventure, Travel, and Survival.* New York: Skyhorse, 2007.

Kish, George. *North-east passage: Adolf Erik Nordenskiold—His Life and Times.* Amsterdam: Nico Israel, 1973.

Kolbert, Elizabeth, ed. *The Arctic: An Anthology.* London: Granta, 2008.

———, ed. *The Ends of the Earth: An Anthology of the Finest Writing on the Arctic.* New York: Bloomsbury, 2007.

———. *Field Notes from a Catastrophe: Man, Nature, and Climate Change.* New York: Bloomsbury, 2006.

Laney, Al. *Paris Herald: The Incredible Newspaper.* New York: D. Appleton-Century, 1947.

Lansing, Alfred. *Endurance: Shackleton's Incredible Voyage.* New York: Carroll & Graf, 1959.

Larson, Edward J. *An Empire of Ice.* New Haven: Yale University Press, 2011.

Lecanu, Gérald. *Mémoire en Images: Le Havre.* Saint-Cyr-sur-Loire: Alan-Sutton, 1995.

Lessard, Suzannah. *The Architect of Desire: Beauty and Danger in the Stanford White Family.* New York: Dial, 1996.

Linder, Chris. *Science on Ice: Four Polar Expeditions.* Chicago: University of Chicago Press, 2011.

Littlepage, Dean. *Steller's Island: Adventures of a Pioneer Naturalist in Alaska.* Seattle: Mountaineers, 2006.

Loomis, Chauncey C. *Weird and Tragic Shores: The Story of Charles Francis Hall, Explorer.* New York: Alfred A. Knopf, 1971.

Lopez, Barry. *Arctic Dreams: Imagination and Desire in a Northern Landscape.* New York: Bantam, 1986.

Lot, Arnold S. *A Long Line of Ships: Mare Island's Century of Naval Activity in California.* Annapolis: United States Naval Institute, 1954.

Lourie, Peter. *Whaling Season: A Year in the Life of an Arctic Whale Scientist.* New York: Houghton Mifflin Books for Children, 2009.

Markham, Albert Hastings. *The Life of Sir Clements R. Markham.* London: Murray, 1917.

Matthiessen, Peter. *Baikal: Sacred Sea of Siberia.* San Francisco: Sierra Club Books, 1992.

Maury, Matthew Fontaine. *The Physical Geography of the Sea.* New York: Harper & Brothers, 1856.

McGhee, Robert. *The Last Imaginary Place: A Human History of the Arctic World.* New York: Oxford University Press, 2005.

McGinniss, Joe. *Going to Extremes.* New York: Alfred A. Knopf, 1980.

McGoogan, Ken. *Fatal Passage.* New York: Carroll & Graf, 2001.

———. *Race to the Polar Sea: The Heroic Adventures of Elisha Kent Kane.* Berkeley: Counterpoint, 2008.

Melville, George. *In the Lena Delta.* London: Longmans, Green and Co., 1885.

Middleton, Nick. *Going to Extremes,* London: Channel 4 Books, 2001.

Millard, Candice. *The Destiny of the Republic: A Tale of Medicine, Madness and the Murder of a President.* New York: Doubleday, 2011.

Morris, James McGrath. *Pulitzer: A Life in Politics, Print, and Power.* New York: HarperCollins, 2010.

Mowat, Farley. *The Polar Passion.* Salt Lake City: Peregrine Smith Books, 1973.

———. *The Siberians.* New York: Bantam Books, 1970.

Muir, John. *The Cruise of the* Corwin. New York: Houghton Mifflin, 2000.

Murphy, David Thomas. *German Exploration of the Polar World: A History, 1870–1940.* Lincoln: University of Nebraska Press, 2002.

Nansen, Fridtjof. *Farthest North: The Incredible Three-Year Voyage to the Frozen Latitudes of the North.* New York: Modern Library, 1999.

———. *The First Crossing of Greenland.* London: Birlinn, 1902.

Nichols, Peter. *Final Voyage.* New York: G. P. Putnam's Sons, 2009.

Niven, Jennifer. *Ada Blackjack: A True Story of Survival in the Arctic.* New York: Hyperion, 2003.

———. *The Ice Master: The Doomed 1913 Voyage of the* Karluk. New York: Hyperion, 2000.

Noble, Dennis L., and Truman R. Strobridge. *Captain "Hell Roaring" Mike Healy: From American Slave to Arctic Hero.* Tallahassee: University Press of Florida, 2009.

Nordenskiöld, Adolf Erik. *The Voyage of the* Vega *Round Asia and Europe.* New York: Macmillan and Co., 1882.

Nourse, J. E. *American Explorations in the Ice Zones.* Boston: D. Lothrop Company, 1884.

O'Connor, Richard. *The Scandalous Mr. Bennett.* New York: Doubleday, 1962.

Ovsyanikov, Nikita. *Polar Bears: Living with the White Bear.* Hong Kong: Voyageur, 1996.

Parry, Richard. *Trial by Ice: The True Story of Murder and Survival on the 1871* Polaris *Expedition.* New York: Ballantine, 2001.

Perry, Richard. *The* Jeannette, *and a Complete and Authentic Narrative Encyclopedia of All Voyages and Expeditions to the North Polar Regions.* San Francisco: A. Roman, 1883.

Petermann, August Heinrich, and Thomas Milner. *The Atlas of Physical Geography.* London: Wm. S. Orr and Co., 1850.

Philbrick, Nathaniel. *In the Heart of the Sea: The Tragedy of the Whaleship Essex*. New York: Penguin, 2000.

———. *Sea of Glory: America's Voyage of Discovery; The U.S. Exploring Expedition*. New York: Penguin, 2003.

Poe, Edgar Allan. *The Narrative of Arthur Gordon Pym and Related Tales*. New York: Oxford University Press, 1994.

Potter, Russell A. *Arctic Spectacles: The Frozen North in Visual Culture, 1818–1875*. Seattle: University of Washington Press, 2007.

Rawicz, Slavomir. *The Long Walk*. Guilford, CT: Lyons Press, 2010.

Riffenburgh, Beau. *The Myth of the Explorer*. Oxford: Oxford University Press, 1994.

Riordan, Pauline, and Paul Bourget. *World Weather Extremes*. Fort Belvoir, VA: U.S. Corps of Army Engineers, Engineer Topographic Laboratories, 1985.

Robertson, Charles L. *The "International Herald Tribune": The First Hundred Years*. New York: Columbia University Press, 1987.

Robinson, Michael F. *The Coldest Crucible: Arctic Exploration and American Culture*. Chicago: University of Chicago Press, 2006.

Sachs, Aaron. *The Humboldt Current: Nineteenth-Century Exploration and the Roots of American Environmentalism*. New York: Penguin, 2006.

Sale, Richard. *The Scramble for the Arctic: Ownership, Exploitation and Conflict in the Far North*. London: Frances Lincoln, 2009.

Sante, Luc. *Low Life: Lures and Snares of Old New York*. New York: Farrar, Straus and Giroux, 1991.

Seitz, Don C. *The James Gordon Bennetts: Father and Son*. New York: Bobbs-Merrill, 1928.

Smits, Jan. *Petermann's Maps: Carto-bibliography of the Maps in "Petermanns Geographische Mitteilungen," 1855–1945*. Goy-Houten: Hes & De Graaf, 2004.

Smyth, W. H. *The Sailor's Word-Book*. London: Conway Maritime, 1991.

Steele, Peter. *The Man Who Mapped the Arctic*. Vancouver, BC: Raincoast, 2003.

Stefansson, Vilhjalmur. *The Adventure of Wrangel Island*. New York: Macmillan, 1925.

Still, William N., Jr. *American Sea Power in the Old World: The United States Navy in European and Near Eastern Waters, 1865–1917*. Westport, CT: Greenwood, 1980.

Stross, Randall. *The Wizard of Menlo Park: How Thomas Alva Edison Invented the Modern World*. New York: Three Rivers, 2007.

Tayler, Jeffrey. *River of No Reprieve: Descending Siberia's Waterway of Exile, Death, and Destiny*. New York: Mariner Books/Houghton Mifflin, 2006.

Thomas Edison: Life of an Electrifying Man. Minneapolis: Filiquarian Publishing, 2008.

Thubron, Colin. *In Siberia*. New York: HarperCollins, 1999.

Toll, Ian W. *Six Frigates: The Epic History of the Founding of the U.S. Navy*. New York: Norton, 2006.

Tyson, George E. *Arctic Experiences: Aboard the Doomed* Polaris *Expedition and Six Months Adrift on an Ice-Floe.* New York: Harper Brothers, 1874. Reprint, New York: Cooper Square Press, 2002.

Vidal, Gore. *1876: A Novel.* New York: Random House, 1876.

Wheeler, Sara. *The Magnetic North: Notes from the Arctic Circle.* New York: Farrar, Straus and Giroux, 2011.

Williams, Glyn. *Arctic Labyrinth: The Quest for the Northwest Passage.* New York: Allen Lane, 2009.

Williams, Henry Llewellyn. *History of the Adventurous Voyage and Terrible Shipwreck of the U.S. Steamer "Jeannette," in the Polar Seas.* New York: A. T. B. De Witt, 1882.

Worster, Donald. *A Passion for Nature: The Life of John Muir.* New York: Oxford University Press, 2008.

Young, Allen. *Cruise of the 'Pandora.' Extracts from the Private Journal Kept by Allen Young, Commander of the Expedition.* London: Wm. Clowes & Sons, 1876.

Young, Allen William. *The Two Voyages of the 'Pandora' in 1875 and 1876.* London: Edward Stanford, 1879.

Photo Credits

Center: The *Jeannette*, then known as the *Pandora*. U.S. Naval Academy Museum
Bottom left: William Nindemann. U.S. Naval Historical Center
Bottom right: William Dunbar. Emma De Long Papers

PAGE 6

Top: The *Jeannette* in Le Havre. U.S. Naval Historical Center
Bottom: The *Jeannette*'s sinking, by George Louis Poilleux-Saint-Ange. Alexandre Antique Prints

PAGE 7

Top: Ice retreat engraving. U.S. Naval Historical Center
Middle: Rowboat engraving. U.S. Naval Historical Center
Bottom: Lena River delta. United States Geological Survey

PAGE 8

Top right: Some of the crew in Yakutsk, Siberia. U.S. Naval Institute
Middle left: Rear Admiral George Melville. Wikimedia Commons
Bottom right: The *Jeannette* monument. U.S. Naval Historical Center

ABOUT THE AUTHOR

Hampton Sides is the author of the best-selling histories *Hellhound on His Trail, Blood and Thunder,* and *Ghost Soldiers.* He lives in New Mexico with his wife, Anne, and their three sons.